John Searle

From his groundbreaking book *Speech Acts* to his most recent studies of consciousness, freedom, and rationality, John Searle has been a dominant and highly influential figure among contemporary philosophers. This systematic introduction to the full range of Searle's work begins with the theory of speech acts and proceeds with expositions of Searle's writings on intentionality, consciousness, and perception, as well as a careful presentation of the so-called Chinese Room Argument. The volume considers Searle's recent work on social ontology and his views on the nature of law and obligation. It concludes with an appraisal of Searle's spirited defense of truth and scientific method in the face of the criticisms of Derrida and other postmodernists.

This is the only comprehensive introduction to Searle's work. As such, it will be of particular value to advanced undergraduates, graduates, and professionals in philosophy, psychology, linguistics, cognitive and computer science, and literary theory.

Barry Smith is Julian Park Professor of Philosophy at the State University of New York at Buffalo and director of the Institute for Formal Ontology and Medical Information Science at the University of Leipzig.

Contemporary Philosophy in Focus

Contemporary Philosophy in Focus offers a series of introductory volumes to many of the dominant philosophical thinkers of the current age. Each volume consists of newly commissioned essays that cover major contributions of a preeminent philosopher in a systematic and accessible manner. Comparable in scope and rationale to the highly successful series **Cambridge Companions to Philosophy**, the volumes do not presuppose that readers are already intimately familiar with the details of each philosopher's work. They thus combine exposition and critical analysis in a manner that will appeal both to students of philosophy and to professionals as well as to students across the humanities and social sciences.

FORTHCOMING VOLUMES:

Paul Churchland edited by Brian Keeley
Ronald Dworkin edited by Arthur Ripstein
Jerry Fodor edited by Tim Crane
David Lewis edited by Theodore Side and Dean Zimmerman
Hilary Putnam edited by Yemima Ben-Menahem
Charles Taylor edited by Ruth Abbey
Bernard Williams edited by Alan Thomas

PUBLISHED VOLUMES:

Stanley Cavell edited by Richard Eldridge
Donald Davidson edited by Kirk Ludwig
Daniel Dennett edited by Andrew Brook and Don Ross
Thomas Kuhn edited by Thomas Nickles
Alasdair MacIntyre edited by Mark Murphy
Robert Nozick edited by David Schmidtz
Richard Rorty edited by Charles Guignon and David Hiley

John Searle

Edited by

BARRY SMITH
*State University of New York at Buffalo
and University of Leipzig*

CAMBRIDGE
UNIVERSITY PRESS

PUBLISHED BY THE PRESS SYNDICATE OF THE UNIVERSITY OF CAMBRIDGE
The Pitt Building, Trumpington Street, Cambridge, United Kingdom

CAMBRIDGE UNIVERSITY PRESS
The Edinburgh Building, Cambridge CB2 2RU, UK
40 West 20th Street, New York, NY 10011-4211, USA
477 Williamstown Road, Port Melbourne, VIC 3207, Australia
Ruiz de Alarcón 13, 28014 Madrid, Spain
Dock House, The Waterfront, Cape Town 8001, South Africa

http://www.cambridge.org

First published 2003

Printed in the United States of America

Typefaces Janson Text Roman 10/13 pt. and ITC Officina Sans   *System* LaTeX 2$_\varepsilon$ [TB]

A catalog record for this book is available from the British Library.

Library of Congress Cataloging in Publication data
John Searle / edited by Barry Smith.
    p.   cm. – (Contemporary philosophy in focus)
Includes bibliographical references and index.
ISBN 0-521-79288-6 (hb) – ISBN 0-521-79704-7 (pbk.)
1. Searle, John R.   I. Smith, Barry, Ph. D.   II. Series.
B1649.S264 J63   2003
191 – dc21   2002038846

ISBN 0 521 79288 6 hardback
ISBN 0 521 79704 7 paperback

Contents

Contributors

FRED DRETSKE has taught at the University of Wisconsin and Stanford University. He is currently a research Fellow at Duke University. His research has been concentrated in the areas of epistemology and the philosophy of mind. His books include *Seeing and Knowing* (1969), *Knowledge and the Flow of Information* (1981), *Explaining Behavior* (1988), *Naturalizing the Mind* (1995) and, most recently, a collection of essays, *Perception, Knowledge, and Belief* (2000).

GEORGE P. FLETCHER is Cardozo Professor of Jurisprudence at Columbia University Law School in New York. He is the author of eight books, including *Rethinking Criminal Law* (1978), *Loyalty: An Essay on the Morality of Relationships* (1993), *With Justice for Some: Victims' Rights in Criminal Trials* (1995), *Basic Concepts of Legal Thought* (1996), *Basic Concepts of Criminal Law* (1998), and *Romantics at War: Glory and Guilt in the Age of Terrorism* (2002). His current fields of interest include biblical jurisprudence, nationalism, and collective guilt, as well as the basic conepts of comparative law and criminal law.

NICK FOTION is Professor of Philosophy at Emory University. He has authored several books, including *John Searle* (2000) and *Toleration* (with Gerard Elfstrom, 1992). He has also coedited several books, including *Moral Constraints on War* (2002) and *Hare and Critics* (1988). He is the author of scores of articles, mainly in the areas of the philosophy of language, ethical theory, military ethics, and medical ethics.

NEIL C. MANSON has studied and taught philosophy in London and Oxford and has been a junior research Fellow in philosophy at King's College, Cambridge, lecturing in both philosophy and history and the philosophy of science. His main areas of interest are the philosophy of mind, the philosophy of psychology, epistemology, and the philosophical views of Nietzsche, Freud, and Wittgenstein. He is currently engaged in a bioethics research project at King's College, Cambridge, focusing on informed consent and genetic information.

JOSEF MOURAL is an assistant professor of philosophy at Charles University, Prague, who works and publishes mainly on ancient philosophy (Socrates, Plato, skepticism), modernphilosophy (Hume, the reception of skepticism), classical phenomenology (the later Husserl, the early Heidegger, Patočka), and Searle's theory of institutions.

KEVIN MULLIGAN is Professor of Analytic Philosophy at the University of Geneva. He is the editor of *La Philosophie autrichienne: De Bolzano à Musil* (with Jean-Pierre Cometti, 2001) and the author of numerous articles on ontology, the philosophy of mind, and Austrian philosophy from Bolzano to Wittgenstein and Musil. He has contributed chapters to *The Cambridge Companion to Husserl* and *The Cambridge Companion to Brentano*.

BRIAN O'SHAUGHNESSY has degrees from Melbourne and Oxford and teaches at King's College, London. He is the author of many articles in the philosophy of mind, of a two-volume work on physical action entitled *The Will* (1980), and of a large-scale study of consciousness and perception entitled *Consciousness and the World* (2000).

JOËLLE PROUST works in the field of the philosophy of mind as a director of research at the Institut Jean-Nicod (CNRS, Paris). Her books and articles are devoted to the philosophical history of logic (*Questions of Form*, 1989), to intentionality (*Comment l'Esprit vient aux Bêtes*, 1997), to consciousness of agency (both normal and psychopathological), and to animal cognition.

FRANÇOIS RECANATI is a research director at the Centre National de la Recherche Scientifique (CNRS), Paris. He has published many papers and several books on the philosophy of language and mind, including *Meaning and Force* (1988), *Direct Reference* (1993), and *Oratio Obliqua, Oratio Recta* (2000). He is a cofounder and past president of the European Society for Analytic Philosophy.

BARRY SMITH is Julian Park Professor of Philosophy at the State University of New York at Buffalo and director of the Institute for Formal Ontology and Medical Information Science ⟨http://ifomis.de⟩ at the University of Leipzig. He is the author of *Austrian Philosophy* (1994) and of some 300 articles on ontology and other topics in philosophy and neighboring disciplines. He is the editor of *The Monist: An International Quarterly Journal of General Philosophical Inquiry*.

LEO ZAIBERT teaches philosophy at the University of Wisconsin at Parkside. He works in the philosophy of law, social and political philosophy, and the philosophy of mind and is the author of *Intentionality and Blame* (forthcoming). He has also published articles on the philosophical analysis of the criminal law, on legal ontology, and on the history of the common law.

1 | John Searle: From Speech Acts to Social Reality

BARRY SMITH

It was in the Oxford of Austin, Ryle, and Strawson that John Searle was shaped as a philosopher. It was in Oxford, not least through Austin's influence and example, that the seeds of the book *Speech Acts*, Searle's inaugural magnum opus, were planted.[1] And it was in Oxford that Searle acquired many of the characteristic traits that have marked his thinking ever since. These are traits shared by many analytic philosophers of his generation: the idea of the centrality of language to philosophy; the adoption of a philosophical method centred on (in Searle's case, a mainly informal type of) logical analysis; the respect for common sense and for the results of modern science as constraints on philosophical theorizing; and the reverence for Frege, and for the sort of stylistic clarity that marked Frege's writings.

In subsequent decades, however, Searle has distinguished himself in a number of important ways from other, more typical analytic philosophers. While still conceiving language as central to philosophical concerns, he has come to see language itself against the background of those neurobiological and psychological capacities of human beings that underpin our competencies as language-using organisms. He has embraced a radically negative stand as concerns the role of epistemology in contemporary philosophy. And he has braved territory not otherwise explored by analytic philosophers in engaging in the attempt to build what can only be referred to as a Grand Philosophical Theory. Finally, he has taken the respect for common sense and for the results of modern science as a license to speak out against various sorts of intellectual nonsense, both inside and outside philosophy.

Searle was never a subscriber to the view that major philosophical problems could be solved – or made to evaporate – merely by attending to the use of words. Rather, his study of the realm of language in *Speech Acts* constitutes just one initial step in a long and still unfinished journey embracing not only language but also the realms of consciousness and the mental, of social and institutional reality, and, most recently, of rationality, the self, and free will. From the very start, Searle has been animated, as he would

1

phrase it, by a sheer respect for the facts – of science, or of mathematics, or of human behaviour and cognition. In *Speech Acts*, he attempts to come to grips with the facts of language – with utterances, with referrings and predicatings, and with acts of stating, questioning, commanding, and promising.

At the same time, Searle has defended all along a *basic* realism, resting not only on respect for the facts of how the world is and how it works, but also on a view to the effect that realism and the *correspondence theory* of truth 'are essential presuppositions of any sane philosophy, not to mention any sane science'.[2] The thesis of basic realism is not, in Searle's eyes, a theoretical proposition in its own right. Rather – and in this, he echoes Thomas Reid – it sanctions the very possibility of our making theoretical assertions in science, just as it sanctions the attempt to build a comprehensive theory in philosophy. This is because the theories that we develop are intelligible only as representations of how things are in *mind-independent* reality. Without the belief that the world exists, and that this world is rich in sources of evidence independent of ourselves – evidence that can help to confirm or disconfirm our theories – the very project of science and of building theories has the ground cut from beneath its feet.

Searle holds that the picture of the world presented to us by science is, with a very high degree of certainty, in order as it stands. He correspondingly rejects in its entirety the conception of philosophy accepted by many since Descartes, according to which the very existence of knowledge itself is somehow problematic. The central intellectual fact about the contemporary world, Searle insists, is that we already have tremendous amounts of knowledge about all aspects of reality, and that this stock of knowledge is growing by the hour. It is this that makes it possible for a philosopher to conceive the project of building unified theories of ambitious scope – in Searle's case, a unified theory of mind, language, and society – from out of the different sorts of knowledge that the separate disciplines of science have to offer. We thus breathe a different air, when reading Searle's writings, from that to which we are accustomed when engaging with, for example, Wittgenstein, for whom the indefinite variety of language-games must forever transcend robust classification.

As concerns the willingness to speak out, John Wayne–style, against intellectual nonsense, Searle himself puts it this way:

> If somebody tells you that we can never really know how things are in the real world, or that consciousness doesn't exist, or that we really can't communicate with each other, or that you can't mean 'rabbit' when you say 'rabbit,' I know that's false.[3]

Philosophical doctrines that yield consequences that we know to be false can themselves, by Searle's method of simple reductio, be rejected.

Searle uses this method against a variety of targets. He uses it against those philosophers of mind who hold that consciousness, or beliefs, or other denizens of the mental realm do not exist. He directs it against the doctrine of linguistic behaviourism that underlies Quine's famous 'gavagai' argument in *Word and Object*[4] for the indeterminacy of translation. As Searle puts it: 'if all there were to meaning were patterns of stimulus and response, then it would be impossible to *discriminate* meanings, *which are in fact discriminable*'.[5] Searle insists that he, like Quine and everyone else, knows perfectly well that when he says 'rabbit' he means 'rabbit' and not, say, 'temporal slice of rabbithood'. Quine, he argues, can arrive at the conclusion of indeterminacy only by assuming from the start that meanings as we normally conceive them do not exist.

When Searle turns his nonsense-detecting weapons against the likes of Derrida, then the outcome is more straightforward, being of the form: 'He has no clothes!' Searle points out what is after all visible to anyone who cares to look, namely, that Derrida's writings consist, to the extent that they are not simple gibberish, in evidently false (though admittedly sometimes exciting-sounding) claims based (to the extent that they are based on reasoning at all) on simple errors of logic.

SPEECH ACT THEORY: FROM ARISTOTLE TO REINACH

Aristotle noted that there are uses of language, for example prayers, that are not of the statement-making sort.[6] Unfortunately, he confined the study of such uses of language to the peripheral realms of rhetoric and poetry, and this had fateful consequences for subsequent attempts to develop a general theory of the uses of language along the lines with which, as a result of the work of Austin and Searle, we are now familiar.

Two philosophers can, however, be credited with having made early efforts to advance a theory of the needed sort. The first, significantly, is Thomas Reid, who recognized that the principles of the art of language are

> to be found in a just analysis of the various species of sentences. Aristotle and the logicians have analyzed one species – to wit, the *proposition*. To enumerate and analyze the other species must, I think, be the foundation of a just theory of language.[7]

Reid's technical term for uses of language such as promisings, warnings, forgivings, and so on is 'social operations'. Sometimes he also calls them 'social acts', opposing them to 'solitary acts', such as judgings, intendings, deliberatings, and desirings. The latter are characterized by the fact that their performance does not presuppose any 'intelligent being in the universe' other than the person who performs them. A social act, by contrast, must be directed to some other person, and for this reason it constitutes a miniature 'civil society', a special kind of structured whole, embracing both the one who initiates it and the one to whom it is directed.[8]

The second is Adolf Reinach, a member of a group of followers of Husserl based in Munich during the early years of the last century who distinguished themselves from later phenomenologists by their adherence to philosophical realism. Husserl had developed in his *Logical Investigations*[9] a remarkably rich and subtle theory of linguistic meaning, which the group to which Reinach belonged took as the starting point for its own philosophical reflections on language, meaning, and intentionality. Husserl was interested in providing a general theory of how thought and language and perception hook onto extra-mental reality. His conception of meaning anticipates that of Searle in treating language as essentially representational. Husserl's theory of meaning is, however, internalistic in the following special sense: it starts from an analysis of the individual mental act of meaning something by a linguistic expression as this occurs in silent monologue. The meaning of an expression is the same (the very same entity), Husserl insists, independently of whether or not it is uttered in public discourse.

But how are we to analyze, within such a framework, the meanings of those special kinds of uses of language that are involved in promises or questions or commands? It was in the effort to resolve this puzzle that Reinach developed the first systematic theory of the performative uses of language, not only in promising and commanding but also in warning, entreating, accusing, flattering, declaring, baptizing, and so forth – phenomena that Reinach, like Reid before him, called 'social acts'.[10]

Reinach presented his ideas on social acts in a monograph published in 1913 (four years before his death on the Western Front) under the title *The A Priori Foundations of the Civil Law*. He concentrated especially on the act of promising, applying his method also to the analysis of legal phenomena such as contract and legislation and describing the theory that results as a 'contribution to the general ontology of social interaction'. His work comprehends many of the elements that we find in the writings of Austin and Searle, and even incorporates additional perspectives deriving from

Reinach's background as a student of law. Unfortunately, however, Reinach's theory of social acts was doomed, like Reid's theory of social operations before it, to remain almost entirely without influence.

SPEECH ACT THEORY: FROM AUSTIN TO SEARLE

Anglo-American philosophy during the first half of the twentieth century was shaped above all by the new Frege-inspired logic. One side-effect of the successes of this new logic was to consolidate still further the predominance of the Aristotelian conception of language as consisting essentially of statements or propositions in the business of being either true or false. All the more remarkable, therefore, is the break with these conceptions that is represented by the work of Austin and Searle. The beginnings of this break are documented in Austin's 1946 paper "Other Minds,"[11] in a discussion of the way we use phrases such as 'I am sure that' and 'I know that' in ordinary language. Saying 'I know that S is P', Austin tells us, 'is *not* saying "I have performed a specially striking feat of cognition...".' Rather, 'When I say "I know" I give others my word: I give others my authority for saying that "S is P"' (*Philosophical Papers*, p. 99).

And similarly, Austin notes, 'promising is not something superior, in the same scale as hoping and intending'. Promising does indeed presuppose an intention to act, but it is not itself a feat of cognition at all. Rather, when I say 'I promise',

> I have not merely announced my intention, but, by using this formula (performing this ritual), I have bound myself to others, and staked my reputation, in a new way. (p. 99)

Austin's ideas on what he called *performative utterances* were expressed in lectures he delivered in Harvard in 1955, lectures that were published posthumously under the title *How to Do Things with Words*.[12]

Performative utterances are those uses of language, often involving some ritual aspect, that are themselves a kind of action and whose very utterance brings about some result. Of an utterance such as 'I promise to mow your lawn', we ask not whether it is true, but whether it is successful. The conditions of success for performatives Austin called *felicity conditions*, and he saw them as ranging from the highly formal (such as, for example, those governing a judge when pronouncing sentence) to the informal conventions governing expressions of gratitude or sympathy in the circumstances of everyday life. Austin pointed also to the existence of a further set of conditions, which have to do primarily with the mental side of performatives – conditions to the effect that participants must have the thoughts, feelings, and intentions appropriate to the performance of each given type of act.

RULES, MEANINGS, FACTS

By the end of *How to Do Things with Words*, however, Austin has given up on the idea of a theory of performatives as such. This is because he has reached the conclusion that all utterances are in any case performative in nature, and thus he replaces his failed theory of performatives with the goal of a theory of speech acts in general. Austin himself focused primarily on the preliminaries for such a theory, and above all on the gathering of examples. In "A Plea for Excuses,"[13] he recommended as systematic aids to his investigations three 'source-books': the dictionary, the law, and psychology. With these as his tools, he sought to arrive at 'the meanings of large numbers of expressions and at the understanding and classification of large numbers of "actions"' (*Philosophical Papers*, p. 189).

Searle's achievement, now, was to give substance to Austin's idea of a general theory of speech acts by moving beyond this cataloguing stage and providing a theoretical framework within which the three dimensions of utterance, meaning, and action involved in speech acts could be seen as being unified together.

It is the three closing sections of Chapter 2 of *Speech Acts* that prepare the ground for the full-dress analysis of speech acts themselves, which is given by Searle in the chapter that follows. These three sections contain Searle's general theories of, respectively, rules, meanings, and facts. All three components are fated to play a significant role in the subsequent development of Searle's thinking.

He starts with a now-familiar distinction between what he calls *regulative* and *constitutive* rules. The former, as he puts it, merely regulate antecedently existing forms of behaviour. For example, the rules of polite table behaviour regulate eating, but eating itself exists independent of these rules. Some rules, on the other hand, do not merely regulate; they also create or define new forms of behaviour. The rules of chess create the very possibility of our engaging in the type of activity that we call playing chess. The latter is just: acting in accordance with the given rules.

Constitutive rules, Searle tells us, have the basic form: X counts as Y in context C.[14] Consider what we call *signaling to turn left*. This is a product of those constitutive rules that bring it about that behaving inside moving vehicles in certain predetermined ways and in certain predetermined contexts *counts as* signaling to turn left. The action of lifting your finger in an auction house *counts as* making a bid. An utterance of the form 'I promise to mow the lawn' in English *counts as* putting oneself under a corresponding obligation. And as we see from these cases, the Y term in a constitutive rule characteristically marks something that has consequences in the form of rewards, penalties, or actions that one is obliged to perform in the future. The constitutive rules themselves rarely occur alone, so it may be that when applying the *X counts as Y* formula we have to take into account whole systems of such rules. Thus we may have to say: acting in accordance with all or a sufficiently large subset of these and those rules by individuals of these and those sorts *counts as* playing basketball.

The central hypothesis of Searle's book can now be formulated as follows: speech acts are acts characteristically performed by uttering expressions in accordance with certain constitutive rules. In order to give a full analysis of what this involves, Searle must give an account of the difference between merely uttering sounds and performing speech acts, and this means that he must supply an analysis, in terms of the *counts as* formula, of what it is to *mean something* by an utterance. His analysis stands in contrast to that of Husserl (or of Aristotle) in the sense that it starts not with uses of language as they occur in silent monologue but rather with acts of speech, acts involving both a speaker and a hearer. More precisely still, Searle starts with the utterance of sentences, since he follows Frege in conceiving word meanings as derivative of sentence meanings. Searle is inspired, too, by the notion of non-natural meaning advanced by Grice in 1957.[15] His analysis, then, reads as follows:

To say that a speaker utters a sentence T and means what he says is to say that the following three conditions are satisfied:

(*a*) the speaker has an intention I that his utterance produce in the hearer the awareness that the state of affairs corresponding to T obtains,
(*b*) the speaker intends to produce this awareness by means of the recognition of the intention I,
(*c*) the speaker intends that this intention I will be recognized in virtue of the rules governing the elements of the sentence T. (*Speech Acts*, pp. 49 f., parentheses removed)

The *X counts as Y* formula is here applied as follows: a certain audio-acoustic event *counts as* the meaningful utterance of a sentence to the extent that these three conditions are satisfied.

On the very next page of *Speech Acts*, Searle then introduces the concept of 'institutional fact', defined as a fact whose existence presupposes the existence of certain *systems of constitutive rules* called 'institutions'. He refers in this connection to a short paper entitled "On Brute Facts," in which Elisabeth Anscombe addresses the issue of what it is that makes behaving in such and such a way a *transaction* from which obligations flow.

'A set of events is the ordering and supplying of potatoes, and something is a bill,' she tells us, 'only in the context of our institutions':

> As compared with supplying me with a quarter of potatoes we might call carting a quarter of potatoes to my house and leaving them there a 'brute fact'. But as compared with the fact that I owe the grocer such-and-such a sum of money, that he supplied me with a quarter of potatoes is itself a brute fact.[16]

Brute facts are, for Anscombe, themselves such as to form a hierarchy. The brute facts, in cases such as those just described, are

> the facts which held, and in virtue of which, in a proper context, such and such a description is true or false, and which are more 'brute' than the alleged fact answering to that description....I will not ask here whether there are any facts that are, so to speak, 'brute' in comparison with leaving a quarter of potatoes at my house. (p. 24)

For Searle, by contrast, there is one single level of brute facts – constituted effectively by the facts *of natural science* – out of which there arises a hierarchy of institutional facts at successively higher levels. Brute facts are distinguished precisely by their being independent of all human institutions, including the institution of language.

It is of course necessary to use language in order to state brute facts, but the latter nonetheless obtain independently of the language that we use to represent them. Just as the Moon did not come into existence with the coming into existence of the linguistic resources needed to name and describe it, so the fact that the Earth is a certain distance from the Sun did not become a fact because the linguistic resources needed to express this distance became available at a certain point in history.

When you perform a speech act, you create certain institutional facts (you create what Reid referred to as a miniature 'civil society'). Institutional facts exist only because we are here to treat the world and each other in certain, very special (cognitive) ways within certain special (institutional) contexts. In his later writings, Searle will speak of a contrast between observer-independent features of the world – such as force, mass, and gravitational attraction – and observer-relative features of the world – which include, in particular, money, property, marriage, and government. The latter are examples of institutions in Searle's sense, which means that they are systems of constitutive rules. Every institutional fact – for example, the fact that John promised to mow the lawn – is thus 'underlain by a (system of) rule(s) of the form "X counts as Y in context C"' (*Speech Acts*, pp. 51 f.).

Searle goes further than Austin in providing not only the needed general framework for a theory of speech acts but also a richer specification of the detailed structures of speech acts themselves. Thus he distinguishes between two kinds of felicity conditions: conditions on the *performance* of a speech act and conditions on its *satisfaction*. (You need to fulfil the first in order to issue a promise, the second in order to keep your promise.) Conditions on performance are divided still further into preparatory, propositional, sincerity, and essential conditions (*Speech Acts*, pp. 60 ff.). When I promise to mow your lawn, the preparatory conditions are that you want me to mow your lawn, and that I believe that this is the case, and that neither of us believes that I would in any case mow your lawn as part of the normal course of events; the propositional conditions are that my utterance 'I promise to mow your lawn' predicates the right sort of act on my part; the sincerity condition is that I truly do intend to mow your lawn; and the essential condition is that my utterance *counts as* an undertaking on my part to perform this action.

In "A Taxonomy of Illocutionary Acts,"[17] Searle offers an improved classification resting on a distinction between two 'directions of fit' between language and reality – from word to world, on the one hand, and from world to word, on the other. The shopping list you give to your brother before sending him off to the shops has a world-to-word direction of fit. The copy of the list that you use for checking on his return has a direction of fit in the opposite direction. *Assertives* (statements, averrings) have a word-to-world direction of fit; *directives* (commands, requests, entreaties) have a world-to-word direction of fit, as do *commisives* (*promises*), which bind the speaker to perform a certain action in the future. *Expressives* (congratulations, apologies, condolences) have no direction of fit; they simply presuppose the truth of the expressed proposition. *Declaratives* (appointings, baptizings, marryings), by contrast, bring about the fit between word and world by the very fact of their successful performance.

PROMISE AND OBLIGATION

On more traditional accounts, a promise is the expression of an act of will or of an intention to act. The problem with this account is that it throws no light on how an utterance of the given sort can give rise to an obligation on the part of the one who makes the promise. A mere act of will has, after all, no quasi-legal consequences of this sort. Searle explains how these consequences arise by means of his theory of constitutive rules. The latter affect our behaviour in the following way: where such rules obtain, we can perform certain special types of activities (analogous to playing chess), and in virtue of this our behaviour can be interpreted by ourselves and by others in terms of certain very special types of institutional concepts. Promisings are utterances that count as falling under the institutional concept *act of promise*, a concept that is logically tied to further concepts, such as obligation, in such a way that wherever the one is exemplified, so too is the other. When I engage in the activity of promising, I thereby subject myself in a quite specific way to the corresponding system of constitutive rules. In virtue of this, I count as standing under an obligation.

Such systems of constitutive rules are the very warp and woof of our behaviour as language-using animals. As Searle puts it, we could not throw all institutions overboard and 'still engage in those forms of behaviour we consider characteristically human' (*Speech Acts*, p. 186).

It is against this background that Searle gives his famous derivation of 'ought' from 'is'. This consists in the move, in four logical steps, from a statement about a certain utterance to a conclusion asserting the existence of a certain obligation, as follows:

(1) Jones uttered the words 'I hereby promise to pay you, Smith, five dollars.'
(2) Jones promised to pay Smith five dollars.
(3) Jones placed himself under an obligation to pay Smith five dollars.
(4) Jones is under an obligation to pay Smith five dollars.
(5) Jones ought to pay Smith five dollars. (*Speech Acts*, p. 177)

The move from (1) to (2) is sanctioned, Searle holds, by an empirical fact about English usage to the effect that anyone who utters the given words makes a corresponding promise (provided only that, as can here be assumed to be the case, the conditions on successful and nondefective performance of the act of promising are as a matter of fact satisfied). The move from (2) to (3) follows from what Searle sees as an analytic truth about the corresponding institutional concepts – namely, that a promise *is* an act of placing oneself under a corresponding obligation. Similarly, we go from (3) to (4) and from (4) to (5) in virtue of what Searle takes to be analytic truths – namely, that if one has placed oneself under an obligation then one is under an obligation, and that if one is under an obligation then (as regards this obligation) one ought to perform the corresponding action.

All but the first clause in Searle's argument states an institutional fact. The argument is designed to capture the way in which language enables us to bootstrap ourselves beyond the realm of brute facts in such a way that we can perform actions that we could not otherwise perform, actions whose performance belongs precisely to the realm of institutional facts. Language, above all, enables us to bind ourselves in the future, not only in acts of promising but also in a range of other ways.

Note that Searle's argument, as formulated here, has a certain individualistic character. This can be seen by contrasting it with that of Reinach, for whom there is an additional feature of the social act of promising – namely, that the promise may not merely be heard but also be accepted by the one to whom it is addressed.[18] Reinach hereby stresses, to a greater degree than Searle at this stage, the relational character of the promise: claim and obligation stand in a relation of mutual dependence, which reflects the reciprocity of promiser and promisee. Promising, for Reinach, manifests one of a series of basic forms of what we might call *collective intentionality.*

SPEECH ACTS AND SOCIAL REALITY

Increasingly in the course of his career Searle is not content to study mere uses of language. He is perfectly clear that, even when we have classified and fully understood the uses of verbs or adverbs of given types, there will still remain genuine philosophical problems to be solved: the nature of obligation, for example, or of power or of responsibility, or – a subject addressed in Searle's most recent writings – the issue of what it is to perform an act freely or voluntarily or rationally. In order to solve these problems we need, as he slowly comes to recognize, to study not only language but also brains, minds, the laws of physics, the forms of social organization.

After a series of works in the philosophy of language applying and expanding the new speech act theory, Searle thus ventures into new territory, with influential books on intentionality, on mind and consciousness, and on the so-called Chinese Room Argument, contributions discussed in detail in the remaining chapters of this volume. In *Intentionality*,[19] Searle generalizes the ideas underlying his speech act theory to a theory of intentionality.

In each speech act, we can abstractly distinguish two components: the *type* or *quality* of the act (sometimes called its illocutionary force) and the (normally propositional) *content* of the act. Each can vary while the other remains constant, as we can command or request or express our desire that John should mow the lawn. In *Intentionality*, now, this distinction is generalized to the sphere of cognitive acts in general, in such a way as to yield an opposition between *propositional modes*, on the one hand, and *intentional contents*, on the other (a distinction that echoes Husserl's distinction in the *Logical Investigations* between the *quality* and *matter* of a mental act).

The notion of a direction of fit is generalized in a similar manner: beliefs are now seen as having a mind-to-world direction of fit, desires a world-to-mind direction of fit, and so forth, for each of the different types of mental act.

The notion of conditions of satisfaction, too, is generalized:

> My belief will be satisfied if and only if things are as I believe them to be, my desires will be satisfied if and only if they are fulfilled, my Intentions will be satisfied if and only if they are carried out. (*Intentionality*, p. 10)

From here, Searle develops an entirely new theory of intentional causation, turning on the fact that an intention is satisfied only if the intention itself causes the satisfaction of the rest of its conditions of satisfaction. Thus for my intention to raise my arm to be satisfied, it is not enough for me to raise my arm; my raising my arm must itself be caused by this intention.

In *Intentionality*, Searle makes a fateful move by allying himself with those, such as Aristotle, Brentano, Husserl, and Chisholm, who see our linguistic behaviour as reflecting more fundamental activities and capacities on the deeper level of the mental – above all, the capacity of the mind to represent states of affairs. Thus he accepts what has been called the 'primacy of the mental', acknowledging that language 'is derived from Intentionality and not conversely' (*Intentionality*, p. 5). Indeed, language is now seen as being only one domain in which we transfer intentionality onto things that are intrinsically not intentional (another illustration of this phenomenon – of what Searle now calls 'derived intentionality' – is provided by the domain of computer processing).

In *The Rediscovery of Mind*,[20] Searle's theory of intentionality is set within a naturalistic ontological framework of what he calls 'causal supervenience'. Consciousness

> is a causally emergent property of systems. It is an emergent feature of certain systems of neurons in the same way that solidity and liquidity are emergent features of systems of molecules. (*Rediscovery*, p. 112)

In *The Construction of Social Reality* – hereinafter *Construction* – this same ontological framework of naturalistic emergentism is applied to the analysis of social reality. The publication of the latter work thus represents a return to the project of a general ontology of social interaction that had been adumbrated by Searle a quarter-century earlier.

A HUGE INVISIBLE ONTOLOGY

Searle begins *Construction* with the following simple scene:

> I go into a café in Paris and sit in a chair at a table. The waiter comes and I utter a fragment of a French sentence. I say, '*un demi, Munich, à pression, s'il vous plaît.*' The waiter brings the beer and I drink it. I leave some money on the table and leave. (p. 3)

He then points out that the scene described is more complex than it appears to be at first:

> [T]he waiter did not actually *own* the beer he gave me, but he is *employed by* the restaurant which owned it. The restaurant is *required to post* a list of the *prices* of all the *boissons*, and even if I never see such a list, I am *required to pay* only the listed price. The *owner* of the restaurant is *licensed by* the French *government* to *operate* it. As such, he is *subject to* a thousand *rules* and *regulations* I know nothing about. I am *entitled* to be there in the first place only because I am a *citizen* of the *United States*, the *bearer of* a *valid passport*, and I have *entered France legally*. (p. 3)

The task Searle then sets for himself is to describe this 'huge invisible ontology', which is to say, to give an analysis of those special objects, powers, functions, acts, events, states, properties, and relations – picked out in italics in the passage just quoted – that do not belong to the realm of brute physical reality but rather to the realm of institutions. This task is to be realized in terms of the machinery of constitutive rules and institutional facts set forth by Searle in his earlier work, but here supplemented by new conceptual tools. In addition, there will be a new emphasis upon the way in which, in acting in accordance with constitutive rules, we are able to impose certain special rights, duties, obligations, and various other sorts of what Searle now calls 'deontic powers' on our fellow human beings and on the reality around us. We are thereby able to bring into existence a great wealth of novel forms of social reality in a way that involves a kind of magic. Searle's task is to dispel the sense of magic by means of a new type of ontology of social reality.

In *Intentionality*, Searle presents a new foundation for the theory of speech acts in terms of the contrast between intrinsic and derived intentionality. Meaning is just one of the phenomena that arise when we transfer intentionality onto things that are intrinsically not intentional. Searle's original theory of these matters has, as we have seen, a certain individualistic bias. Now, however, he must squarely face the problem of how to account for the *social* characteristics of speech acts and of other, related phenomena within the framework of his earlier theory of derived intentionality.

The crucial turning point here is the article "Collective Intentions and Actions," published in 1990.[21] Recall that Searle's philosophy is intended to be entirely naturalistic. Human beings are biological beasts. Searle now recognizes that, like other higher mammals, human beings enjoy a certain sui generis – which means: irreducible – capacity for what he calls 'collective intentionality'. This means that they are able to engage with others in cooperative behaviour in such a way as to share the special types of beliefs, desires, and intentions involved in such behaviour. The capacity for collective intentionality is a capacity that individuals have to enjoy intentional states of a certain quite specific sort. Nonhuman animals manifest this capacity, at best, in very rudimentary forms – for example, in hunting or signaling behaviour. The history of the human species, by contrast, has shown that we are able to engage in ever more complex forms of collective intentionality of seemingly inexhaustible variety, effectively by using language and other symbolizing devices to perform collaborative actions such as promising and legislating and regulating air traffic flow (and arguing about the nature of constitutive rules). Language is now conceived by Searle as the basic social institution, because it is language – or language-like systems of symbolization – that enables these new forms of collective intentionality to exist at ever higher levels of complexity.

THE ONTOLOGY OF SOCIAL REALITY

The doctrine of collective intentionality allows a refinement of the ontology of brute and institutional facts, as this was sketched by Searle at the beginning of his career. Now we should more properly distinguish between brute facts on the one hand, which are those facts that can exist independent of human intentionality, and *dependent* facts of different sorts. Above all, we must distinguish between what we might call subjective dependent facts, facts that depend on *individual* intentionality – for example, the fact that I am feeling angry – and social facts, which depend on *collective* intentionality.

Institutional facts, now, are those special kinds of social facts that arise when human beings collectively award what Searle calls *status functions* to parts of reality. This means functions – such as those of customs officials (with their rubber stamps) – that the human beings involved could not perform exclusively in virtue of their physical properties.

Consider the way in which a line of yellow paint can perform the function of a barrier because it has been collectively assigned the status of a boundary marker by human beings. The yellow paint is unable to perform this function by virtue of its physical properties. It performs the function only because we collectively accept it as having a certain status. Money, too, does not perform its function by virtue of the physical properties of paper, ink or metal, but rather by virtue of the fact that we, collectively, grant the latter a certain status and therewith also certain functions and powers.

Sometimes a status function can be imposed simply by declaring it to be so, as in the case of promising. Here, I impose upon myself, by declaration, the status function of being obliged. Sometimes special rituals or ceremonies are involved, which is to say complexes of actions, which also serve to broadcast to the world the new status functions that have been set in place together with their concomitant deontic powers. By exchanging vows before witnesses, a man and a woman bring a husband and a wife into being (out of X terms are created Y terms, with new status and powers).

The structure of institutional reality is accordingly a structure of power. Powers can be positive, as when John is awarded a license to practice medicine, or negative, as when Mary has her license to drive taken away for bad behaviour, or when Sally is obliged to pay her taxes. Powers can be substantive, as when Margaret is elected prime minister, or attenuated, as when Elton is granted the honorary title of Knight Bachelor, Commander of the British Empire. Chess is war in attenuated form, and it seems that very many of the accoutrements of culture have the character of attenuated powers along the lines described by Searle. Kasher and Sadka propose to account for the entirety of cultural evolution by applying Searle's distinction between regulative and constitutive rules.[22]

THE *X COUNTS AS Y* THEORY OF INSTITUTIONAL REALITY

Searle's theory of collective intentionality, of status functions and of deontic powers, is a brilliant contribution to the ontology of social reality. As he puts it:

> [There is a] continuous line that goes from molecules and mountains to screwdrivers, levers, and beautiful sunsets, and then to legislatures, money, and nation-states. The central span on the bridge from physics to society is

collective intentionality, and the decisive movement on that bridge in the creation of social reality is the collective intentional imposition of function on entities that cannot perform these functions without that imposition. (*Construction*, p. 41)

Searle's account of the way in which so much of what we value in civilization requires the creation and the constant monitoring and adjusting of the institutional power relations that arise through collectively imposed status functions is certainly the most impressive theory of the ontology of social reality that we have. His account of how the higher levels of institutional reality are created via iteration of the *counts as* formula, and also of how whole systems of such iterated structures (for example, the systems of *marriage* and *property*) can interact in multifariously spreading networks, opens the way for a new type of philosophical understanding of human social organization.

The account presented in *Construction* is not without its problems, however – problems that, as we shall see, have led Searle to modify his views in more recent writings. It will nonetheless be of value to map out the account as originally presented, in order both to understand how the problems arise and to throw light on the challenge that Searle faces in attempting to reconcile realism in the domain of social reality with the naturalistic standpoint that is so central to his philosophy.

A realist ontology of social reality I take to be an ontology that holds prices, debts, trials, suffragette rallies, and so forth, to exist; our reference to these entities is not a *façon de parler*, to be cashed out in terms of reference to entities of other, somehow less problematic, sorts. Nothing is more certain than death, and taxes. Naturalism we can then provisionally take to consist in the thesis that prices, trials, monastic orders, and so forth exist *in the very same reality* as that which is described by physics and biology. For Searle, as we have seen, is interested in the philosophical problems that arise precisely in the world that is presented to us by natural science, a world that contains not only language-using organisms but also brains and positron emission tomographs.

Searle formulates his views in *Construction* in terms of the notion of constitutive rules, and thus in terms of the *X counts as Y* formula with which we are by now so familiar. Naturalism I take to imply that both the X and the Y terms in the applications of this formula must range in every case over token physical entities, be they objects or events or entities of some other category. This is in keeping with statements such as the following:

I start with what we know about the world: the world consists of entities described by physics and chemistry. I start with the fact that we're products of evolutionary biology, we're biological beasts. Then I ask, how is it possible *in a world consisting entirely of brute facts*, of physical particles and fields of force, how is it possible to have consciousness, intentionality, money, property, marriage, and so on?[23]

The X and Y terms are thus parts of physical reality.

We get the full power of Searle's theory, however, only when we recognize that a Y term can itself play the role of a new X term in iterations of the *counts as* formula. Status functions can be imposed not only upon brute physical reality in its original, unadorned state but also upon this physical reality as it has been shaped by earlier impositions of function: a human being can count as a citizen; a citizen can count as a judge; a judge can count as a Supreme Court justice, and so forth, with new status functions being acquired at each step and presupposing those that went before. But the imposition of function gives us thereby nothing (physically) new: Bill Clinton is still Bill Clinton even when he *counts as* President; he is still a part of physical reality, albeit with new and special powers. Mrs. Geach was still, even after her marriage, Miss Anscombe; and Miss Anscombe was throughout her life just as much a part of physical reality as you and me.

There are, therefore, on this reading of Searle's views, no special classes of social or institutional entities, in addition to the physical entities with which we have to deal:

> [I]f you suppose that there are two classes of objects, social and non-social, you immediately get contradictions of the following sort: In my hand I hold an object. This one and the same object is both a piece of paper and a dollar bill. As a piece of paper it is a non-social object, as a dollar bill it is a social object. So which is it? The answer, of course, is that it is both. But to say that is to say that we do not have a separate class of objects that we can identify with the notion of social object. Rather, what we have to say is that something is a social object only under certain descriptions and not others, and then we are forced to ask the crucial question, what is it that these descriptions describe?[24]

What the description describes is an X term, a part of physical reality. And again:

> when I am alone in my room, that room contains at least the following 'social objects'. A citizen of the United States, an employee of the state of California, a licensed driver, and a tax payer. So how many objects are in the room? There is exactly one: me. ("Reply to Smith")

Thanks to certain cognitive acts on the part of human beings – cognitive acts that are themselves to be understood, naturalistically, in terms of the physics and biology of the human brain – a certain X term begins at a certain point in time to fall under certain descriptions under which it did not fall before, and a Y term thereby emerges.

The latter begins to exist because an X term, a part of physical reality, has acquired certain special sorts of status functions and therewith also certain special sorts of deontic powers. But while the Y term is in a sense a new entity – after all, President Clinton did not exist before his inauguration on January 17, 1997 – this new entity is from the physical perspective *the same old entity as before*. What has changed is the way the entity is treated in given contexts and the descriptions under which it falls.

To say that X counts as Y is to say that X provides Y's physical realization because X is identical to Y. Note that a much weaker relation is involved where one entity merely *presupposes* the existence of another, so that the first is existentially dependent on the second. A symphony performance, for example, is in the given sense merely dependent for its existence on the members of an orchestra. An election is merely dependent on the existence of certain polling places: it is not also identical to these polling places. When X *counts as* Y, however, X and Y are physically speaking one and the same.

All of this goes hand in hand with Searle's insistence that whenever a status function is imposed there has to be something that it is imposed upon. Sometimes this is itself the product of the imposition of another status function. Eventually, however, just as Archimedes had to have a place to stand, so the hierarchy must bottom out in some portion of physical reality whose existence is not a matter of human agreement. As Searle argues so convincingly in the second half of *Construction*, and against what is propounded by sundry postmodernists and social constructionists, it could not be that the world consists of institutional facts all the way down, with no brute reality to serve as their foundation.

OBJECTS AND REPRESENTATIONS

Note that the range of X and Y terms, even on the simple version of the theory set forth here, includes not only objects (individual substances such as you and me) but also entities of other sorts – for example, *events*, as when an act of uttering such and such a sequence of words counts as the utterance of a sentence of English.

> Often, the brute facts will not be manifested as physical objects but as sounds coming out of peoples' mouths or as marks on paper – or even thoughts in their heads. (*Construction*, p. 35)

Naturalism should now imply that when a given event counts as an utterance, or as the making of a promise, the event itself does not physically change; no new event comes into being, but rather the event with which we start is treated in a special way. This is Searle's account of how, by being apprehended in a certain way, an utterance (X) counts as a meaningful use of language (Y), which in turn counts as an act of promising (Z). Here again, the Y and Z terms exist simultaneously with the corresponding X term; they are both of them, after all, physically identical therewith. The Z term serves additionally as a trigger for the coming into existence of additional deontic powers on the part of the human being who has made the promise: the latter becomes *obliged* to realize its content, and the new Y term thus created – the obligation – continues to exist until it is waived or fulfilled.

As Searle himself puts it:

> I promise something on Tuesday, and the act of uttering ceases on Tuesday, but the obligation of the promise continues to exist over Wednesday, Thursday, Friday, etc. ("Reply to Smith")

Now, however, he goes on to make what, against the background of Searle's naturalism, is a fateful admission:

> And that is not just an odd feature of speech acts, it is characteristic of the deontic structure of institutional reality. So, think for example, of creating a corporation. Once the act of creation of the corporation is completed, the corporation exists. It need have no physical realization, *it may be just a set of status functions*. ("Reply to Smith," italics added)

Searle hereby reveals that his social ontology is committed to the existence of what we might call 'free-standing Y terms', or, in other words, to entities that (unlike President Clinton or Canterbury Cathedral or the money in my pocket) do not coincide ontologically with any part of physical reality. One important class of such entities is illustrated by what we loosely think of as the money in our bank accounts, as this is recorded in the bank's computers. In *Construction* we find the following passage:

> [A]ll sorts of things can be money, but there has to be some physical realization, some brute fact – even if it is only a bit of paper or a blip

> on a computer disk – on which we can impose our institutional form of status function. Thus there are no institutional facts without brute facts. (*Construction*, p. 56)

Unfortunately, however, as Searle now acknowledges, blips in computers do not really count as money, nor can we use such blips as a medium of exchange:

> On at least one point it seems to me ... the account I gave in [*The Construction of Social Reality*] is mistaken. I say that one form that money takes is magnetic traces on computer disks, and another form is credit cards. Strictly speaking neither of these is money, rather, both are different representations of money. The credit card can be used in a way that is in many respects functionally equivalent to money, but even so it is not itself money. It is a fascinating project to work out the role of these different sorts of representations of institutional facts, and I hope at some point to do it. ("Reply to Smith")

In reformulating his views on this matter, Searle is thus led to recognize a new dimension in the scaffolding of institutional reality, the dimension of representations. The blips in the bank's computers merely *represent* money, just as the deed to your property merely *records* or *registers* the existence of your property right. The deed is not identical to your property right, nor does it *count as* your property right. An IOU note, similarly, records the existence of a debt; it does not *count as* the debt. It is an error to run together records pertaining to the existence of freestanding Y terms with those freestanding Y terms themselves, just as it would be an error to regard as the X terms underlying obligations, responsibilities, duties, and other deontic phenomena the current mental acts or neurological states of the parties involved. As Searle himself writes:

> You do not need the X term once you have created the Y status function *for such abstract entities as obligations, responsibilities, rights, duties, and other deontic phenomena*, and these are, or so I maintain, the heart of the ontology of institutional reality. ("Reply to Smith," italics added)

The very hub and nucleus of institutional reality, on Searle's account, is thus itself constituted by free-standing Y terms, entities that do not coincide with any part of physical reality.

As the case of money shows, some social objects have an *intermittent* realization in physical reality. Others, such as corporations and universities, have a physical realization that is *partial* and also *scattered* (and also such as to involve a certain turnover of parts). Yet others, such as debts, may have no physical realization at all; they exist only because they are reflected in records or representations (including mental representations). A full-dress ontology of social reality must address all of the different types of cases mentioned, from Y terms that are fully identical to determinate parts and moments of physical reality, to Y terms that coincide with no determinate part or moment of physical reality at all, together with a range of intermediate cases.

THE MYSTERY OF CAPITAL

Free-standing Y terms, as might have been predicted, are especially prominent in the higher reaches of institutional reality, and especially in the domain of economic phenomena, where we often take advantage of the abstract status of free-standing Y terms in order to manipulate them in quasi-mathematical ways. Thus we pool and securitize loans, we depreciate and collateralize and ammortize assets, we consolidate and apportion debts, we annuitize savings – and these examples, along with the already-mentioned example of the money existing (somehow) in our banks' computers, make it clear that the realm of free-standing Y terms must be of great consequence for any theory of institutional reality.

That this is so is made abundantly clear in Hernando De Soto's work *The Mystery of Capital*,[25] a work inspired by *The Construction of Social Reality* that also goes some way toward realizing Searle's 'fascinating project' of working out the role of the different sorts of representations of institutional facts. As De Soto shows, it is the 'invisible infrastructure of asset management' upon which the astonishing fecundity of Western capitalism rests, and this invisible infrastructure consists precisely of *representations* – for example, of the property records and titles that capture what is economically meaningful about the corresponding assets – representations that in some cases serve to determine the nature and extent of the assets themselves.[26]

Capital itself, in De Soto's eyes, belongs precisely to the family of those free-standing Y terms that exist in virtue of our representations:

Capital is born by representing in writing – in a title, a security, a contract, and other such records – the most economically and socially useful qualities [associated with a given asset]. The moment you focus your attention on the title of a house, for example, and not on the house itself, you have automatically stepped from the material world into the conceptual universe where capital lives. (*The Mystery of Capital*, pp. 49 f.)

As those who live in underdeveloped regions of the world well know, it is not physical dwellings that serve as security in credit transactions, but rather the *equity* that is associated therewith. The latter certainly depends for its existence upon the underlying physical object; but there is no part of physical reality that *counts as* the equity in your house. Rather, as De Soto emphasizes, this equity is something abstract that is *represented* in a legal record or title in such a way that it can be used to provide security to lenders in the form of liens, mortgages, easements, or other covenants in ways that give rise to new types of institutions, such as title and property insurance, mortgage securitization, bankruptcy liquidation, and so forth.

SOLUTIONS TO THE PROBLEM OF FREE-STANDING Y TERMS

A number of alternative responses to the problem of free-standing Y terms are advanced by Searle. The first is to propose that the *X counts as Y* formula is not to be taken literally at all; it is intended, rather, as a 'useful mnemonic'. Its role is

> to remind us that institutional facts only exist because people are prepared to regard things or treat them as having a certain status and with that status a function that they cannot perform solely in virtue of their physical structure. ("Reply to Smith")

People are, in a variety of sometimes highly complex ways, 'able to *count something* as something more than its physical structure indicates' ("Reply to Smith"). Unfortunately, however, this replacement formula is itself in-applicable to the problematic cases. For what is it that people are able to count as 'something . . . more than its physical structure indicates' in the case of, for example, a collateralized bond obligation or a statute on court enforcement? Surely something that *has* a physical structure – but there is nothing in physical reality that *counts as* an entity of the given type.[27]

Recall that the virtue of the *counts as* formula was that it promised to provide us with a clear and simple analytic path through the 'huge invisible ontology' of social reality. There are no special 'social objects', but only parts of physical reality that are subjected, in ever more interesting and sophisticated ways, to special treatment in our thinking and acting:

> [M]oney, language, property, marriage, government, universities, cocktail parties, lawyers, presidents of the United States are all partly – but not entirely – constituted under these descriptions by the fact that we regard them as such.[28]

If something is a social object only under certain descriptions and not others, however, then the admission of free-standing Y terms means that we are no longer able to give an answer to what Searle refers to as the 'crucial question', namely: 'what is it that these descriptions describe?'[29] For in the case of free-standing Y terms, there is no object to *be* constituted under a description.

In accepting the existence of free-standing Y terms – in accepting, for example, that a corporation need have no physical realization – Searle accepts that a theory formulated exclusively in terms of the *counts as* formula can provide only a partial ontology of social reality. Such a theory is analogous to an ontology of works of art that is able to yield an account of, for example, *paintings* and *sculptures* (the lump of bronze *counts as* a statue) but not *symphonies* or *poems*. For a symphony (as contrasted with the performance of a symphony) is not a token physical entity at all; rather – like a debt, or a corporation – it is a special type of abstract formation (an abstract formation with a beginning, and perhaps an ending, in time).[30]

A careful reading of *The Construction of Social Reality* does, however, yield some of the resources which are required for the construction of the needed more complete ontology. Consider, first of all, passages such as the following, in which Searle refers to the 'primacy of acts over objects' in the social realm. In the case of social objects, he tells us,

> the grammar of the noun phrase conceals from us the fact that, in such cases, process is prior to product. Social objects are always . . . constituted by social acts; and, in a sense, *the object is just the continuous possibility of the activity*. A twenty dollar bill, for example, is a standing possibility of paying for something. (*Construction*, p. 36)

> What we think of as social *objects*, such as governments, money, and universities, are in fact just placeholders for patterns of activities. I hope it is clear that the whole operation of agentive functions and collective intentionality is a matter of ongoing activities and the creation of the possibility of more ongoing activities. (p. 57)

Certainly there are patterns of activities associated with, say, the government of the United States. But we cannot identify the one with the other. Governments, after all, can enter into treaty obligations; they can incur debts, raise taxes; they can be despised or deposed. (Patterns of activity cannot do or suffer any of these things.) A theory that was forced to regard all such statements as *façons de parler*, in need of being cashed out in terms of statements about patterns of activity, would fall short of the standards that need to be met by Searle's realist ontology of the social world. (This is not least because, if a social ontologist tells you that there are really no such things as debts, prices, taxes, loans, governments, or corporations, then the argument of simple reductio comes into play once more.)

Patterns of activity are, rather, indispensable accompaniments to all Y terms, whether or not the latter coincide with parts of physical reality that lie beneath them. In doing justice to this fact, as in recognizing the importance of records and representations, Searle brings us closer to the needed complete ontology.

HIGHER STILL, AND HIGHER

Free-standing Y terms, too, will in each case be associated with a specific repertoire of physical presuppositions. While a corporation is not a physical entity, if a corporation is to exist, many physical things must exist, many physical actions must occur, and many physical patterns of activity must be exemplified. Thus there must be notarized articles of incorporation (a physical document), which have been properly filled out and filed. There must be officers (human beings) and an address (a certain physical place), and many of the associated actions (such as, for example, the payment of a filing fee) are themselves such as to involve the results of the imposition of status functions upon physical phenomena at lower levels. Records and representations themselves are entities that belong to that domain of institutional reality that is subject to the *X counts as Y* formula.

When once this entire panoply of institutional facts is in place, raised up above the level of the brute facts of moving and thinking and speaking, then a corporation exists. Yet the corporation is still no part of physical reality.

All of this suggests the following as an explicit statement of a modified Searlean strategy for unfolding the huge invisible ontology underlying social reality. This will consist, first of all, in the description of the properties of those social entities (lawyers, doctors, cathedrals, traffic signs; speeches, coronations, driving licenses, weddings, football matches) that do indeed coincide with physical objects or events. These provide, as it were, the solid scaffolding that holds together the successive levels of institutional reality as it rises up, through the imposition of ever new complexes of status functions, to reach ever new heights. At the same time, the description will explain how these social entities form a web – the web of institutional facts – within which, however, there are also to be found, as it were in the interstices of the web, additional social entities – what we have here been calling free-standing Y terms – sustained in being by records and representations and by associated patterns of activities. The latter are thereby anchored by their physical presuppositions, but they do not exist in such a way that they themselves would coincide directly with anything in physical reality. These free-standing Y terms can then themselves give rise to new, elevated pillars in this great institutional edifice – in the way in which, for instance, the securities markets have given rise to derivative instruments that are increasingly remote from the physical reality that lies beneath.

The view in question is then perfectly consistent with Searle's naturalism; then, however, the latter must be interpreted not as a view to the effect that all of the parts of institutional reality are parts of physical reality, but rather as the thesis that all of the *facts* that belong to institutional reality should supervene (in some sense) on facts that belong to physical reality – so that nothing should be true in institutional reality except in virtue of some underlying features of physical reality, including the physical reality of human brains. Naturalism can be saved, because the status functions and deontic powers with which our social world is pervaded do, after all, depend in every case on quite specific attitudes of the participants in given institutions, and indeed in such a way that on any examination of such phenomena we will be brought back to the *counts as* phenomenon.

THE PRIMACY OF REALITY

The question that Searle is trying to answer in his ontology of society is: 'How can there be objective facts that are facts only because we think they are facts? How can there be facts where, so to speak, thinking that it is so makes it so?' Searle has shown that in order for such facts to exist, it is essential that people have certain attitudes, and he has also shown that those attitudes are in large part constitutive of the given facts. It could not turn out that, unbeknownst to the members of a social club, the club itself did not in fact exist.

In his most recent book, however, entitled *Rationality in Action*,[31] Searle puts a new gloss on this doctrine, which suggests the need for at least a terminological revision of his theory. In the case of institutional facts, Searle points out,

the normal relationship between intentionality and ontology is reversed. In the normal case, what is the case is logically prior to what seems to be the case. So, we understand that the object seems to be heavy, because we understand what it is for an object to be heavy. But in the case of institutional reality, the ontology derives from the intentionality. In order for something to be money, people have to think that it is money. But if enough of them think it is money and have other appropriate attitudes, and act appropriately, then it is money. *If we all think that a certain sort of thing is money and we cooperate in using it, regarding it, treating it as money, then it is money.* (*Rationality in Action*, pp. 206 f., italics added)

For Searle, therefore, institutional reality is marked by the fact that what *seems* to be the case determines what *is* the case. That this thesis cannot be accepted in general is shown by considering examples of institutional facts that pertain to the past. As Searle himself puts it in another context:

[T]he New York Yankees won the 1998 World Series. In order for their movements to count as winning it, those movements had to take place in a certain context. But once they have won it, then they are the victors of the 1998 World Series for all time and for all contexts. ("Reply to Smith")

If tomorrow, and for all time thereafter, we all think that the Buffalo Bills won the 1998 World Series, will that mean that this was in fact the case? Surely not, for once institutional facts have been laid down historically as the facts that they are, then they become like other facts – like the facts that one can look up in an encyclopedia – and this means that they enjoy the same sort of priority over mere beliefs as is enjoyed by the facts of natural science.

What the present example tells us is that, for some institutional facts at least, there can occur a transformation, so that what had begun as an institutional fact in Searle's technical sense – and is thus, by definition, a product of our imposition of status functions – is transformed into a fact of another category, which is not itself an institutional fact in spite of the fact that it pertains to the realm of institutional reality. Already every fact of the form 'F is an institutional fact' may qualify for membership in this latter category.

This being recognized, then it becomes clear that there are many other sorts of facts that similarly pertain to the institutional realm but that are yet not subject to Searle's seems-is-prior-to-is dispensation. Inspection reveals that such facts may obtain even simultaneously with the associated impositions of function – for example, where there is a conflict of the contexts within which institutional facts arise or some other defect in the process of status function imposition.[32]

Consider an area of territory X in, say, Kashmir, an area that India claims as part of India and that Pakistan claims as part of Pakistan. X *counts as* Indian territory in India-friendly contexts, and as Pakistani territory in Pakistan-friendly contexts. What is the correct account of the ontology of this piece of territory and of the institutional facts in which it participates? An expert might examine all of the underlying legal, geographic, historical, and psychological facts of the matter, adopting a neutral, scientific perspective, and conclude that neither side has a legitimate claim to the territory in question. This expert view may well (let us suppose for the sake of argument) be correct, yet it is a view that is embraced by none of the participants involved on the ground in Kashmir. The facts of the matter on the level of institutions are in the given case accordingly entirely analogous to brute facts: only the external context-free description can do them justice. But these, then, are facts about institutions for which *is* is prior to *seems*. It now goes without saying that there are many, many institutional facts of this sort in the realm of economic activity. There, too, thinking does not (or does not forever) make it so.

CONCLUSION: FREEDOM AND THE SELF

Rationality in Action is in other respects, however, a worthy continuation of the bold project of a grand theory initiated in Searle's earlier writings. In particular, it extends his theory of institutional reality by drawing attention to the way in which the machinery of constitutive rules enables human beings to create what he calls 'desire-independent reasons for action'. We have already seen that it is possible to use the power of collective acceptance to impose a function on an entity in cases where the entity cannot perform that function in virtue of its physical properties. This is what happens when we make a promise: we bind ourselves to performing certain actions in the future by using the power of collective acceptance to impose the corresponding function on our utterance and thus the status function of obligation upon ourselves.

In this way, we make commitments that constitute reasons for acting in the future that are independent of our future and perhaps even our present desires. All uses of language, according to Searle, involve the making of commitments of the mentioned kind, commitments that create desire-independent reasons for action. Constraints of rationality, such as consistency and coherence, are in this way *already built into language*. For if you make an assertion, you are thereby committed to its being true and to your being able to provide the corresponding evidence.

Rationality in Action contains at the same time a further radical departure from Searle's earlier views. For like so many analytic philosophers, Searle had earlier fallen victim to Hume's scepticism as concerns the notion of the self, taking Hume's 'when I turn my attention inward, I find particular thoughts and feelings but nothing in addition by way of the self' to overwhelm our commonsense recognition that selves exist. But it is only for a self, as Searle now shows, that something can be a reason for action, and only the self can serve as the locus of responsibility. In order for rational action to be possible at all,

> [o]ne and the same entity must be capable of operating with cognitive reasons as well as deciding and acting on the basis of those reasons. In order that we can assign responsibility, there must be an entity capable of assuming, exercising and accepting responsibility. (p. 89)

The self, too, it follows from this, is the locus of freedom; and indeed, as Searle conceives matters, the self's exercise of rationality and its acting under the presupposition of freedom are coextensive.[33]

This move away from Hume is still marked by a certain hesitation, however, so that there is a peculiar two-sidedness to Searle's treatment of self and freedom in this new work. For on the one hand, he writes of them in terms reminiscent of his treatment, in his earlier writings, of obligations and other deontic powers, as if they were abstract entities, the reflections of the logic of our language. This is manifested in statements such as, 'It is a formal requirement on rational action that there must be a self who acts' (p. 93), and indeed in Searle's many references to our acting 'under the presupposition of freedom'. On the other hand, he is happy to affirm that the self is conscious, that it is an entity that is capable of deciding, initiating, and carrying out actions (p. 95), and he is happy also that 'we have the *experience of freedom* . . . whenever we make decisions and perform actions' (p. 95, italics added).

The tension here is at least analogous to that noted earlier between Searle's realism – which means here the acknowledgement of the fact that the self and freedom do indeed exist – and his naturalism, which implies a conception of the phenomena in question as supervening on some determinate parts or moments of physical reality. But now our earlier resolution of this tension might help us again. For it suggests a conception of the self – and of mental reality in general – as being, like governments and economies, such as to fall somewhere between those concrete Y terms that are fully coincident with some determinate parts and moments of an underlying physical reality, and those abstract Y terms that, at the opposite extreme, coincide with no determinate parts or moments of physical reality at all.[34]

This does not, to be sure, tell us what the self, and freedom, are. Nor does it tell us how their existence can be compatible with the universal applicability of the laws of physics. It does, however, relieve us of the obligation to find some determinate part of physical reality (the brain? the body? some part of the central nervous system?) to which the self would correspond, and thus opens up a broader range of alternative conceptions of the relationship between the self and that which underlies it physically.

In *Rationality in Action* and in his earlier works, Searle has set himself the task of describing in naturalistic fashion the way in which human beings and the societies they form actually work. Searle has come closer to fulfilling this task than any other philosopher. Indeed, it can be said that his work represents a new way of doing philosophy. He has shown how we can move toward a philosophical understanding of culture, society, law, the state, of freedom and responsibility, of reason and decision, in a framework that takes naturalism seriously and yet is realistic about the social and cultural and institutional levels of reality by which our lives are so pervasively shaped. His contributions will surely have important implications for the development of moral, legal, and political philosophy in the future.[35]

Notes

1. Searle was born in Denver in 1932. He spent some seven years in Oxford, beginning as an undergraduate in the autumn of 1952 with a Rhodes Scholarship and concluding as a lecturer in philosophy at Christ Church. He has spent almost all of his subsequent life as professor of philosophy in Berkeley. Searle's Oxford dissertation on the theory of descriptions and proper names contains an incipient treatment of the topic of speech acts, but the latter grew in importance only after he left Oxford, making itself felt in the article "What Is a Speech Act?," in Max Black (ed.), *Philosophy in America* (Ithaca, N.Y.: Cornell University Press, 1965), pp. 221–39, and in the book *Speech Acts* itself (Cambridge: Cambridge University Press, 1969), which was completed in 1964.
2. See p. iii of John Searle, *The Construction of Social Reality* (New York: Free Press, 1995).
3. Gustavo Faigenbaum, *Conversations with John Searle* (Montevideo: Libros En Red, 2001), p. 29.
4. W. V. O. Quine, *Word and Object* (Cambridge, Mass.: MIT Press, 1960).
5. "Indeterminacy, Empiricism, and the First Person," *The Journal of Philosophy* 84: 3 (1987): 123–146, 125, italics added.
6. *De Interpretatione* (17 a 1-5).
7. Thomas Reid, *The Works of Thomas Reid*, ed. Sir William Hamilton (Edinburgh: James Thin; London: Longmans, Green, 1895), p. 72.

8. See Karl Schuhmann and Barry Smith, "Elements of Speech Act Theory in the Work of Thomas Reid," *History of Philosophy Quarterly* 7 (1990): 47–66, for further details.

9. *Logische Untersuchungen* (Halle: Niemeyer, 1900–01); English translation by J. N. Findlay, *Logical Investigations* (London: Routledge and Kegan Paul, 1970).

10. See Kevin Mulligan, "Promisings and Other Social Acts: Their Constituents and Structure," in Kevin Mulligan (ed.), *Speech Act and Sachverhalt: Reinach and the Foundations of Realist Phenomenology* (The Hague: Nijhoff, 1987), pp. 29–90; Brigitte Nerlich and David D. Clarke, *Language, Action and Context: The Early History of Pragmatics in Europe and America, 1780-1930* (Amsterdam and Philadelphia: John Benjamins, 1996); and Barry Smith, "Towards a History of Speech Act Theory," in A. Burkhardt (ed.), *Speech Acts, Meanings and Intentions: Critical Approaches to the Philosophy of John R. Searle* (Berlin and New York: de Gruyter, 1990), pp. 29–61.

11. *Proceedings of the Aristotelian Society* 20 (supp.) (1946), reprinted in Austin's *Philosophical Papers* (Oxford: Clarendon Press, 1961), pp. 44–84; hereinafter: *Philosophical Papers*.

12. J. L. Austin, *How to Do Things with Words* (Oxford: Oxford University Press, 1962).

13. "A Plea for Excuses: The Presidential Address," *Proceedings of the Aristotelian Society* 57 (1956–57): 1–30, reprinted in *Philosophical Papers*, pp. 123–52.

14. In *Mind, Language and Society* (New York: Basic Books, 1999), Searle writes: 'Constitutive rules always have the same logical form. . . . They are always of the logical form such-and-such counts as having the status so-and-so' (pp. 123 f).

15. H. P. Grice, "Meaning," *The Philosophical Review* 64 (1957): 377–88.

16. G. E. M. Anscombe, "On Brute Facts," *Analysis* 18: 3 (1958): 24.

17. First published in K. Gunderson (ed.), *Language, Mind and Knowledge: Minnesota Studies in the Philosophy of Science*, vol. 7 (Minneapolis: University of Minnesota Press, 1975), pp. 344–69; reprinted in Searle, *Expression and Meaning: Studies in the Theory of Speech Acts* (Cambridge: Cambridge University Press, 1975), pp. 1–29.

18. Adolf Reinach, "Die apriorischen Grundlagen des bürgerlichen Rechts," *Jahrbuch für Philosophie und phänomenologische Forschung* 1/2 (1913), as reprinted in Adolf Reinach, *Sämtliche Werke: Kritische Ausgabe mit Kommentar* (Munich and Vienna: Philosophia, 1988), p. 204. English translation by J. F. Crosby as "The Apriori Foundations of the Civil Law," *Aletheia*: 3 (1983): 1–142. Compare also the discussion in Anthonie Meijers, *Speech Acts, Communication and Collective Intentionality: Beyond Searle's Individualism* (Leiden: Rijksuniversiteit, 1994).

19. John Searle, *Intentionality: An Essay in the Philosophy of Mind* (New York: Cambridge University Press, 1983).

20. John Searle, *The Rediscovery of Mind* (Cambridge, Mass: MIT Press, 1992).

21. In P. Cohen, J. Morgan, and M. Pollack (eds.), *Intentions in Communication* (Cambrige, Mass.: MIT Press, 1990), pp. 401–15.

22. Asa Kasher and Ronen Sadka, "Constitutive Rule Systems and Cultural Epidemiology," *The Monist* 84: 3 (2001): 437–48.

23. Faigenbaum, *Conversations*, p. 273, italics added.

24. "Reply to Barry Smith," *American Journal of Economics and Sociology*, forthcoming (2003). Hereinafter "Reply to Smith."

25. Hernando De Soto, *The Mystery of Capital: Why Capitalism Triumphs in the West and Fails Everywhere Else* (New York: Basic Books, 2000).

26. See Barry Smith and Leo Zaibert, "The Metaphysics of Real Estate," *Topoi* 20: 2 (2001): 161–72.

27. A further problem turns on the fact that the concept of institutional fact is itself defined by Searle as: a fact that can exist only within human institutions. But the latter are themselves defined as systems of constitutive rules, which are themselves defined in terms of the *counts as* formula (*Construction*, pp. 27, 43 f). Thus, even if it would be possible to restate the whole thesis of *Construction* without using the formula, since this thesis is itself about 'how institutional facts are created and sustained' we would be left in the dark as to precisely what the thesis amounts to.

28. *Mind, Language and Society: Philosophy in the Real World* (New York: Basic Books, 1999), p. 113.

29. "Reply to Smith."

30. The theory of such historically rooted abstract formations was first set forth by Reinach in "The A Priori Foundations of the Civil Law" and applied to the ontology of literature and other art forms by Reinach's student Roman Ingarden, above all in his *The Literary Work of Art: An Investigation on the Borderlines of Ontology, Logic, and Theory of Language* (Evanston, Ill.: Northwestern University Press, 1974). See also the discussion of abstract artifacts in Amie Thomasson, *Fiction and Metaphysics* (Cambridge: Cambridge University Press, 1999).

31. John Searle, *Rationality in Action* (Cambridge, Mass.: MIT Press, 2001).

32. See Barry Smith, "The Chinese Rune Argument," *Philosophical Explorations* 4: 2 (2001): 70–7 (with response by Searle).

33. This thesis is criticized in Leo Zaibert, "On Gaps and Rationality," *Philosophical Explorations* 4: 2 (2001): 78–86 (with response by Searle).

34. Suppose you believe that p and you believe that q, and that both of these beliefs are realized in corresponding physical states of your brain. The doctrine of freestanding Y terms then gives us the possibility of accounting for the fact that you believe also, in the given circumstances, that p *and* q, that p *or* q, and so forth, even where no beliefs of just these forms are similarly physically realized in your brain.

35. With thanks to Michael Gorman, Nicholas Fotion, Ingvar Johansson, Anthonie Meijers, and Leo Zaibert for helpful comments.

Literature

Anscombe, G. E. M. 1958. "On Brute Facts." *Analysis*, 18:3, 22–5.

Austin, J. L. 1946. "Other Minds." *Proceedings of the Aristotelian Society*, 20, 148–87. Reprinted in Austin 1961, 44–84.

Austin, J. L. 1956–57. "A Plea for Excuses: The Presidential Address." *Proceedings of the Aristotelian Society*, 57, 1–30. Reprinted in Austin 1961, 123–52.

Austin, J. L. 1961. *Philosophical Papers*. Oxford: Clarendon Press.

Austin, J. L. 1962. *How to Do Things with Words*. Oxford: Oxford University Press.

De Soto, H. 2000. *The Mystery of Capital: Why Capitalism Triumphs in the West and Fails Everywhere Else*. New York: Basic Books.

Faigenbaum, Gustavo. 2001. *Conversations with John Searle*. Montevideo: Libros En Red.

Grice, H. P. 1957. "Meaning." *The Philosophical Review*, 64, 377–88.

Husserl, Edmund. 1900–01. *Logische Untersuchungen*. Halle: Niemeyer. English translation by J. N. Findlay as *Logical Investigations*. London: Routledge and Kegan Paul, 1970.

Kasher, Asa, and Sadka, Ronen. 2001. "Constitutive Rule Systems and Cultural Epidemiology." *The Monist*, 84:3, 437–48.

Meijers, Anthonie. 1994. *Speech Acts, Communication and Collective Intentionality: Beyond Searle's Individualism:* Leiden: Rijksuniversiteit.

Meijers, Anthonie. 2003. "Can Collective Intentionality Be Individualized?" *The American Journal for Economics and Sociology*, 62, 167–84.

Mulligan, K. 1987. "Promisings and Other Social Acts: Their Constituents and Structure." In Mulligan (ed.), *Speech Act and Sachverhalt: Reinach and the Foundations of Realist Phenomenology*. The Hague: Nijhoff, 29–90.

Nerlich, Brigitte, and Clarke, David D. 1996. *Language, Action and Context: The Early History of Pragmatics in Europe and America, 1780–1930*. Amsterdam and Philadelphia: John Benjamins.

Quine, W. V. O. 1960. *Word and Object*. Cambridge, MA: MIT Press.

Reid, T. 1895. *The Works of Thomas Reid*, edited by Sir William Hamilton. Edinburgh: James Thin; London: Longmans Green.

Reinach, Adolf. 1913. "Die apriorischen Grundlagen des bürgerlichen Rechts." *Jahrbuch für Philosophie und phänomenologische Forschung*, 1/2, 685–847. Reprinted in Reinach, *Sämtliche Werke. Kritische Ausgabe mit Kommentar*. Munich and Vienna: Philosophia, 1988. English translation by J. F. Crosby as "The Apriori Foundations of the Civil Law." *Aletheia*, 3 (1983), 1–142.

Schuhmann Karl, and Smith, Barry. 1990. "Elements of Speech Act Theory in the Work of Thomas Reid." *History of Philosophy Quarterly*, 7, 47–66.

Searle, John R. 1965. "What Is a Speech Act?" In Max Black (ed.), *Philosophy in America*. Ithaca, NY: Cornell University Press; London: Allen and Unwin.

Searle, John R. 1969. *Speech Acts: An Essay in the Philosophy of Language*. Cambridge: Cambridge University Press.

Searle, John R. 1975. "A Taxonomy of Illocutionary Acts." In K. Gunderson (ed.), *Language, Mind and Knowledge: Minnesota Studies in the Philosophy of Science*, vol 7. Minneapolis: University of Minnesota Press, 344–69. Reprinted in Searle, *Experience and Meaning: Studies in the Theory of Speech Acts*. Cambridge: Cambridge University Press, 1975, 1–29.

Searle, John R. 1983. *Intentionality: An Essay in the Philosophy of Mind.* New York: Cambridge University Press.

Searle, John R. 1987. "Indeterminacy, Empiricism, and the First Person." *The Journal of Philosophy*, 84:3, 123–46.

Searle, J. 1990. "Collective Intentions and Actions." In P. Cohen, J. Morgan, and M. Pollack (eds.), *Intentions in Communication.* Cambridge, MA: MIT Press, 401–15.

Searle, John R. 1992. *The Rediscovery of the Mind.* Cambridge, MA: MIT Press.

Searle, John R. 1995. *The Construction of Social Reality.* New York: Free Press.

Searle, John R. 1999. *Mind, Language and Society: Philosophy in the Real World.* New York: Basic Books.

Searle, John R. 2001. *Rationality in Action.* Cambridge, MA: MIT Press.

Searle, John R. 2003. "Reply to Barry Smith." *American Journal of Economics and Sociology*, 62, 299–309.

Smith, Barry. 1990. "Towards a History of Speech Act Theory." In A. Burkhardt (ed.), *Speech Acts, Meanings and Intentions: Critical Approaches to the Philosophy of John R. Searle.* Berlin and New York: de Gruyter, 29–61.

Smith, Barry. 2001. "The Chinese Rune Argument" (with response by Searle). *Philosophical Explorations*, 4:2, 70–7.

Smith, Barry. 2003. "The Construction of Social Reality." *American Journal of Economics and Sociology*, 62, 285–99.

Smith, Barry, and Zaibert, Leo. 2001. "The Metaphysics of Real Estate." *Topoi*, 20:2, 161–72.

Zaibert, Leo. 2001. "On Gaps and Rationality" (with response by Searle). *Philosophical Explorations*, 4:2, 78–86.

2 From Speech Acts to Speech Activity

NICK FOTION

I. SPEECH ACT THEORY

Speech act theory developed during the middle of the twentieth century out of a sense of dissatisfaction on the part of writers such as J. L. Austin[1] and John Searle[2] about how language was viewed by the logical positivists and others. It is fair to say that at that time, the positivists (e.g., A. J. Ayer, G. Bergmann, R. Carnap, H. Feigl, V. Kraft, M. Schlick, and F. Waismann) dominated philosophy.[3] Their interest in language, which was great, focused on how language works in scientific settings. It also focused on the meaning that language has on the sentential level. For the positivists, sentences have meaning seemingly in relative isolation from the settings in which they are used. Further, sentences have meaning if and only if their truth conditions can be established. Thus if someone wants to assert the sentence "The cat is on the mat," he would have to know how to determine its truth or falsity. If, as in the claim "The Spirit of Good is in everyone's heart," the speaker cannot tell us, even in principle, how she knows that it is true (or false), the sentence is meaningless.

In one sense, Austin and Searle looked at language in the same way. They too focused their attention on the sentential level. But they viewed sentences not as artifacts that carry meaning on their own shoulders, but as *issuances* by speakers for the benefit of their hearers. Beyond that, sentences are issuances, performances, or actions that carry meaning only when the role of the speakers, the hearers, and the rest of the context of the issuance are taken into account. Whole speech acts, not sentences as such, are the units of language in need of analysis. In this connection, Searle has labeled speech acts "the basic or minimal units of linguistic communication."[4]

Given that, it is not surprising that when engaged in study of the philosophy of language, Searle found himself attending to the nuances of various kinds of speech acts. It seemed to him that his job was to identify the rules that constitute the different things that we want to say (do) when we use language. If I am keen on making a promise, I will, when I actually make it, oblige myself to do some action and commit myself to do something that I am capable of doing. In promising, I will also express my intention to do what I promised. Further, I will do what I promised in the future (i.e., it makes no sense to promise to do something yesterday, or even now), and I will do it because my hearer wants me to. If, by contrast, I issue an order, I will want the order carried out, and I will issue an order that the hearer is capable of carrying out. Also if I issue an order, I will possess some sort of social status advantage over my hearer. Even assertions, the kind of sentences beloved by all positivists, fall into the speech act mold. If, now, I assert that that cat is indeed on the mat, I do so insofar as I present some new information to my hearer and express myself as believing what I say. I also indicate that I know what I am talking about (i.e., that I am in position to know whether the cat is or is not on the mat). As it turns out, then, each kind of speech act has its own set of rules that identify it for what it is.

II. NOT GOING FROM SPEECH ACTS TO SPEECH ACTIVITY

In contrast to the extensive work that Searle did with speech acts, he worked only sporadically with speech activity (discourse). One major exception is his article "The Logical Status of Fictional Discourse."[5] Here he talks extensively about how speech acts, strung together, form speech activity of a very special kind. There are some other exceptions, minor ones, as well. Here and there he tells us how expressions such as 'therefore' cue us that an argument (i.e., a series of speech acts) has taken place, and also that a bet is not really a speech act but a series of speech acts that represents speech activity.

In this chapter, I want to show that the relatively small amount of work that Searle has done on speech activity is not an indication that he cannot deal with the subject. Rather, he simply didn't make the move from speech acts to speech activity. Put differently, I want to show that the instruments found in Searle's theory are as fully capable of answering important questions pertaining to speech activity as they are of dealing with speech acts.

I will begin with his fiction paper. But I will not limit myself to this paper, since it addresses only one form, albeit an interesting one, of speech activity. My concern is to answer Searlian-type questions about speech activity in general and, in so doing, to exhibit the power of the sort of language analysis that Searle likes to engage in.

III. FICTION

The main question Searle poses in his article on fictive discourse is:

> [H]ow can it be both the case that words and other elements in a fictional story have their ordinary meanings and yet the rules that attach to those words and other elements and determine their meanings are not complied with: how can it be the case in "Little Red Riding Hood" both that "red" means red and yet that the rules correlating "red" with red are not in force?[6]

In other words, how are we able to understand a work of fiction even though the writer seemingly violates some important rules of language use? Among others that could be listed, he lists four such speech act rules.

1. The essential rule: the maker of an assertion commits himself to the truth of the expressed proposition.
2. The preparatory rule: the speaker must be in a position to provide evidence or reasons for the truth of the expressed proposition.
3. The expressed proposition must not be obviously true to both the speaker and hearer in the context of the utterance.
4. The sincerity rule: the speaker commits himself to a belief in the truth of the expressed proposition.[7]

To be sure, a novel is such a complex work that it often contains speech acts, and pieces of discourse, that violate none of these rules. This happens, for example, in Leo Tolstoy's *Anna Karenina*[8] when we are told truly things about Moscow and St. Petersburg. Similarly when, in *Three Lives*,[9] Gertrude Stein describes how people lived in the American South in the late nineteenth and early twentieth centuries, she violates none of the four rules. But for the most part, these works contain speech acts strung together that are not truthful. People such as Anna herself; her lover, Count Vronsky; Levin and Kitty in *Anna Karenina*; and the Anna in *Three Lives*, as well as Melanctha, are all imaginary. In a novel, even real characters such as Napoleon might be made to say and do things that they did not say or do in real life. So clearly, writers such as Tolstoy and Stein violate the essential and the sincerity rules. Neither commits to the "truth of the expressed proposition" and neither "commits himself to a belief in the truth of the expressed proposition." As to rules 2 and 3, they do not seem to have application to novels, so in that sense they too are violated.

But in a novel, a short story, a comic book story, or a play on television or on stage, are the authors, in fact, violating the rules of everyday speech?

Searle says, not really. They are certainly not violating them in the way that someone who is trying to deceive us is. Rather, here is what is happening. Searle says that the four speech act rules just listed should be thought of as vertical rules.[10] They are semantic and pragmatic in nature. They help us to connect to the world. Fiction writers don't so much violate these rules as put them in the deep freeze. They suspend them via horizontal conventions that, he says, are extralinguistic and nonsemantic in nature. Putting it differently, they are conventions on the level of speech activity rather than on the level of speech act. When these conventions are invoked, it is as if fiction writers rather openly tell their readers, "I am going to pretend, why don't you pretend along with me."

Searle doesn't make it clear how exactly these conventions are supposed to be expressed; perhaps they are expressed in more than one way. But one plausible way is as follows. When writing fiction it is permitted to suspend

1. the axiom of existence that says that successful reference requires the existence of what is referred to;

2. the rule that commits the speaker to the truth of the expressed proposition;

3. [in a play] the commitments the actors make (so the marriage ceremony on stage doesn't really marry the actors);

4. [in a play] the declarations made (so that wars are not started and people are not excommunicated);

5. the rule about writing in accordance with the laws of nature (so that, e.g., people can fly around on their own, as they do in the movie *Crouching Tiger, Hidden Dragon*);

6. and so on.

These suspension conventions do not exhaust the conventions for fiction. Additionally, one obvious convention is that fiction must tell a story – and not, for example, simply tell us about a series of related or unrelated events. Another is that the story needs to be told in a minimally consistent way.

One other convention needs special mention. Searle notes in his fiction article that

> [t]here is no textual property, syntactical or semantic, that will identify a text as a work of fiction. What makes it a work of fiction is, so to speak, the illocutionary stance that the author takes toward it, and that stance is a matter of the complex illocutionary intentions that the author has when he writes or otherwise composes it.[11]

Now surely Searle is right in telling us that the body of a fictive text is most often indistinguishable from a nonfictive one. Authors who are good at their craft pretend so well that they could fool us completely if they wished to do so. Searle is also right in telling us that writing fiction is an intentional activity. However, he can't be right in suggesting that we need to fathom the author's private intentions in order to differentiate fiction from nonfiction. Why? Simply because we have linguistic conventions that tell us about authorial intentions. Actually, these are conventions about conventions. One such is to put the label "Fiction" on the cover of the book. Or, at the beginning of the text, one can say "Once upon a time. . . . " In the former case, the author and/or the publisher are issuing a *master speech act*.[12] In the latter case, the author is issuing such an act. In either case, these master speech acts are commissives of a special kind. They announce to readers that the author (and/or publisher) intends to do what he says he will do. Or a novel can start with fantastic events: "Jim decided not to go to work in his car. Instead, he stepped outside, took a mighty leap and moments later found himself outside his office ten miles away." Where else but in fiction could such powers of leaping be found? There are, then, a cluster of conventions that tell us about the author's intentions. As a group, these conventions identify fiction as a language-game on the level of speech activity, not on the level of the speech act. I'll have more to say about authorial intentions and purposes shortly.

IV.   HISTORICAL FICTION (DOCU-DRAMAS), BIOGRAPHIES, AND AUTOBIOGRAPHIES

So far, we have identified a Searlian model for analyzing speech activity. This model involves identifying a cluster of horizontal conventions that constitute whatever speech activity is under analysis. These conventions must be seen as distinct from the rules that govern speech acts themselves. For Searle, it is a mistake to talk of, for example, a form of speech activity as if it were some special illocutionary act.[13] But, so far, the conventions found on the speech activity level have been those of a very unusual form of speech activity. Searle claims that fiction is a parasitic form. We understand fiction by contrasting it with more conventional truth-telling practices. Because we do, many of the key conventions for fiction have to do with suspending the rules governing what we can think of as more normal uses of language.

But now as we move away from fiction, we should not expect that the conventions would be as unusual as they are for fiction. One major exception, however, concerns historical fiction (docu-dramas). Because historical fiction is still fiction, the suspended conventions that make "pure" fiction possible will still apply. But because historical fiction is also history, the suspended conventions will themselves be suspended. Part of a work of historical fiction will be expected to adhere to the rules or conventions of ordinary truth-telling speech activity. That is, that part of the work will be made up mainly of strings of ordinary assertive speech acts. For readers, the conflicting conventions that the author follows pose a problem. Since the conventions tell the author that she should follow the "normal" rules (conventions) for asserting at certain times, but not at other times, the poor readers (viewers) are left in a quandary. This is especially so if the author is so skilled that she makes it almost impossible for her readers to tell whether certain textual claims are true or not.

There is no such problem with a work of nonfiction such as a biography. Now the conventions stipulate that the main reference of the work is, and the predicating in the work is about, some person other than the author, and that the "truth telling" rules apply. So biographical authors commit themselves to what they say, have evidence for what they say, provide new information, and believe what they say. When an author does not in fact tell the truth, we think that an error has been made in reporting, or that he is lying. The conventions for autobiographies are obviously the same, except that now the author and the main reference of the text are the same, and the predicating in the text is mainly about the author. The conventions for general nonfiction allow writers to refer across the board to any and all objects, and to choose to talk about any aspect of (to predicate about) those things or creatures to which they have chosen to refer. Thus authors can write about the great plague of London, Alexander the Great, the status of women in nineteenth-century America, ocean temperatures over the years, and so on. They can also write about how the plague affected religious beliefs, about Alexander's injuries, and so on – they can write about whatever they wish.

In addition to conventions for truth telling, reference, and predication, there are conventions pertaining to the structure of any form of speech activity. Works of fiction, biographies, and autobiographies are likely to possess a time-line structure. They tell stories, and these stories naturally unfold over time. The structure of a scientific article is, of course, different. Time now is less important. Conventions now dictate that a section in a scientific article be reserved for stating the problem, another for describing the design of the experiment and the equipment used, another for presenting the data, and finally, a summary and conclusions section.

So far, I've been focusing on identifying the conventions for speech activity where assertives and pretend-assertives are the dominant speech act within the activity. But if that's what I'm up to, there are variations on this theme to consider. Think here of a conversation with a neighbor whom one has not seen for several weeks, or a news report about a flood in the newspaper, on television, or on the radio. Or think about the weather report (accompanied by a prediction), testimony given in court, the log of a ship or an airplane, a patient's chart in the hospital, a sales (and/or annual) report of a corporation, the minutes of a department meeting, a lecture on Kant and his categorical imperative.

Each kind of assertive-based speech activity has some of its own conventions, but even when the conventions are apparently the same, the strictness with which they are applied can vary. Take the case of the conventions pertaining to being a witness in court. One convention for this form of speech activity is that the witness is not to issue directive speech acts ("He should be hanged") or even to express his own views on the matter ("I think he's guilty"). And the truth-telling conditions are held to the highest standards. Speculation is discouraged. Only what is known, in the strictest sense, is allowed as testimony. By contrast, truth telling is adhered to in a conversation with a neighbor, but not to such a high degree. Speculation is allowed, even encouraged. Reports from the mass media seem to fall somewhere between courtroom testimony and over-the-back-fence conversations. Some other forms of speech activity differ in other ways. The events of department meetings are reported in the minutes of the meeting chronologically, but news items on the radio usually are not. Instead, they are reported in terms of their perceived importance to the audience.

At least one other consideration needs to be taken into account if we are to characterize more fully, in Searlian-like terms, the sort of speech activities we are considering. One needs to ask: what is the purpose of this speech activity? That is, what does the speaker intend to accomplish? The right answer is: any one of several things. Novelists, engaged as they are in "pseudo" referring and predicating, might wish, for example, to entertain, cheer, frighten, or enlighten, their readers. Any one novelist might intend to bring about more than one of these effects. After all, a novel, as a long string of speech acts, is not necessarily restricted to satisfying just one purpose. The author's intent can be to entertain her readers but also to enlighten in a certain way. Consider how this might be done. Her intent to entertain emerges from the excitement inherent in her storytelling. We read her intent from the text, as it were, by how we are taken up into the story. Her intent to enlighten also comes from the text. Let us suppose that her intent is to write an antiwar novel. Wisely, she does not do this by preaching, and in so doing, issuing a long and boring series of directive speech acts (à la Tolstoy). Instead, her text is dominated by assertive speech acts. She describes in detail what war is like – its pain, its horror, the destruction that it brings forth. She then leaves it up to the reader to decipher her message.

Other forms of speech activity can and often are more explicit in telling us about the speaker's purpose. Scientific essays quite commonly tell us about authorial purpose in the statement of the problem. The statement not only tells us that the intent is to describe, but also tells us what specifically is to be described. The intent of engaging even in ordinary conversation is often revealed through the issuance of master speech acts, as in "Let me tell you what happened on our vacation" or "What direction do you think the stock market will take next year?"

In characterizing those forms of speech activity dominated by assertive speech acts, we have so far identified several types of conventions. One type deals with truth conditions. A related convention, or set of conventions, deals with how strictly the truth conditions are to be applied. A third type deals with reference, and a fourth with predicating related to the reference. A fifth deals with the structure of the speech activity (discourse), such as writing or speaking along a time line. And a sixth deals with purpose. These conventions, like most of the others, give speakers (writers) wide latitude in their use of language, thus enabling them to engage in an almost infinite number of language-games (on the speech activity level).

V. MIXED TYPES

As we have seen, types of speech activity dominated by assertions are common enough. However, perhaps even more common are those types of speech activity in which several kinds of speech acts are found. An example is when a decision needs to be made. Should the family buy that house? Well, facts need to be cited so that, in one form or other, the truth-telling conventions will be in place. Those deciding to buy the house won't necessarily look at the facts carefully, but the conventions for making such decisions are in place that would permit them to do so. It is part of the "logic" of this sort of decision making that reasons (based on facts) can always be cited. Moral decisions are the same in this respect. Decisions about ethics and about personal matters such as buying a house differ, however, when it comes to reference. With personal decisions, facts related to what certain individuals like or prefer are the norm, while with ethics, everyone's likes (and/or preferences) need to be taken into account objectively. But in both cases, with both personal and ethical decisions, the kind of speech acts cited are mixed. Assertions are issued in abundance, but so are other kinds of speech acts such as directives, commissives, expressives, and perhaps even declarations.

This mixture of speech acts is seen in a variety of other speech activities. Here is a sample of what surely is an almost endless list:

brief friendly meeting in the morning while going to work

a debate (as against an argument)

a departmental meeting (business or academic)

a discussion of a dramatic news event (e.g., what happened on September 11, 2001)

editorial writing (for newspaper or magazine)

gossiping

an interview of a politician (on television)

praying

preaching

a sales phone conversation

It is interesting to note how the conventions vary within each type, and thus help to identify the activity as the type that it is. As a starter, take the case of the brief friendly meeting in the morning while going to work. As with most other speech activities, there is considerable latitude as to what can be said. But typically, the conversation will begin with a pair of expressive speech acts (e.g., "Good morning"), followed perhaps by directives inquiring about the health of the conversationalists, and then followed by some assertions ("I am well"). The conversation then typically ends with more expressives ("Have a good day"). There is probably some restriction as to subject matter, so that one is not likely to engage in a brief theological discussion at one of these meetings. But nothing is forbidden by the conventions. Recently, in a brief friendly meeting in the morning while leaving the grocery store, a lady greeted me, handed me some religious literature, and then talked about how, by being "born again," we could all achieve a perfect society. She ended the conversation by sweetly saying "Have a good morning."

Contrast such meetings with a piece of editorial writing. What one refers to, and what one says about what is referred to, are open-ended. One can editorialize on almost any subject. But there is some structure. Certainly at or near the end of the editorial there is likely to be a recommendation (one or more directives issued), and before that there will be at least one supporting argument. The argument can contain other directives, assertions about people's needs, and other assertions describing some situation. Because of these assertions, the truth-telling rules (conventions) will be in place. It may be that editorial writers, being partisan by nature, can't always be trusted to tell the truth, the whole truth, and nothing but. But the editorial genre demands that the truth-telling rules (conventions) be followed and, if they are not, that the writer be subject to criticism. And, for sure, editorials have a purpose – perhaps more than one. More often than not, the purpose is concerned with turning the reader into a fellow partisan.

Now contrast editorial writing with praying. Praying introduces a new dimension into the mix of conventions. With editorial writing, there need be no restrictions on whom the listeners are. In his communicative activity, the writer can reach some subgroup of the whole society, or everybody. But with praying, only certain deities are the listeners. God, Jesus, Mary, Moses, St. Nicholas, and/or Buddha can be prayed to, but one's wife, friend, or enemy cannot. Many other speech-activity forms place similar restrictions on who can listen in, or on who can speak. A legislative decision made in a closed session is an example. Only members of the legislature can engage in the discussion of the issues vexing the government, and only they, in the end, can vote. Other examples of limited participation are discussions in committee, a court, an academic department, and even the family.

But prayer has some other distinctive features. It normally has a certain structure. Prayer activity might begin with a master speech act, "Let us pray." Then it would be normal to begin the prayer proper by praising the deity. At this point, assertives would be the dominant speech act. "You are the mighty one who created everything, who is all powerful and all good." Phase two of the main part of the prayer might begin by singing the praises of the deity for things the deity has done for the speaker. "Thank you for this food, the good harvest, the bonus money we received. . . . " Now expressives are dominant. Then, no doubt, it is time to ask for favors. Strangely enough, it appears that the deity needs to be directed to do right. "Oh Lord, give us this and give us that." Finally, the stopper "Amen" signals the end of the prayer. This structure is certainly not mandatory. In sheer desperation, the prayer could start with a special pleading – "Oh Lord keep this boat afloat until help arrives" – and dispense with the soft-soaping process.

VI. SOMEWHAT MIXED SPEECH ACTIVITY – GETTING ALONG WITHOUT ASSERTIVES

In the mixed types, as described in section V, there was always a place for assertive speech acts. Assertives were always part of the mixture. Even when the main purpose of the speech activity was to issue directives of one sort or another, it seemed necessary to issue assertives to help back those directives. But though engaging in directive-type speech activity invites assertives, assertive-type speech activity does not necessarily invite directives, commissives, and the other types of speech acts. Assertive speech activity can go on by itself, even at great length, as we have seen – for instance, in a novel or a scientific essay.

Even so, it is possible to find some types of speech activity that do without assertives. To be sure, they are typically quite brief, as if to suggest that we find it quite difficult to use our language at great length without asserting. Betting is an example. As a speech activity, making a bet can be done at a moment's notice. Sam says, "I'll bet you $10 that the home team will win tonight," and Sonny replies, "You're on." No assertives here. Just a directive/conditional commissive to get things going, and a commissive to tie the bet together. As we have seen, some prayers can get along without assertives as well. When there is urgency, we can dispense with the preliminaries of praising the deity and get down to the business of asking for new favors. Speech activity involving certain kinds of decisions can also get along without assertives. "Where shall we meet?" "Well, how about at Dusty's? Is that OK?" "Yes, I'll be there at noon promptly." This brief conversation gets along quite well with directives and commissives alone. Of course, facts that underlie even this simple decision could be cited. "Where shall we meet? I need to talk to you about the money that you owe me, and that I need urgently." But if the participants understand the facts, there is no necessity to cite them in the conversation.

VII. PURPOSE

I ordered the various speech activity types into the categories of "assertive dominated," "mixed," and "somewhat mixed" (i.e., doing without assertives) more for the sake of convenience than for theoretical reasons. Having done so, and having sampled various types of speech activity, it is time to see if any order emerges. Is there, for example, a taxonomy of speech activity, much as Searle found that there is for speech acts? On the speech act level, he identified twelve dimensions that allow speech acts (illocutionary acts) to differ from one another.[14] He focused on three of these dimensions, and then went on to identify five basic kinds of speech acts. The three key dimensions are:

1. *Differences in the point (or purpose) of the (type of) act.* [Where the point or purpose of some description is to represent something as true or false, while the purpose of a promise is to commit the speaker.]

2. *Differences in the direction of fit between words and the world.* [Where a description fits or matches our words to the world, while an order fits or matches the world to the words.]

3. *Differences in the expressed psychological states.* [Where the expressed psychological state of a description is that the speaker believes what is said, whereas the expressed psychological state of an order is that the speaker wants done what is ordered.]

The other dimensions are secondary, in the sense that they allow speakers to vary the basic speech acts without changing them. Thus the dimension registering *differences in the force or strength with which the illocutionary point is presented* allows General Smith to *order* Private Jones to do as he says, but does not allow Adams, who has no rank over anybody, to order Baker around. All Adams can do is to *ask* or *plead* that Baker do as he says. But in both cases, in spite of the variation in the strength of what each speaker says, the speech acts are attempts to direct the behavior of the hearer.

So when Searle's task is to decide whether a speech act is an assertive rather than a commissive, he does not look at the dimension of strength, or at any of the other eight dimensions, but at the three dimensions of purpose, fit, and psychological state. It turns out, then, that a speech act is an assertive if its purpose is to represent some truth, if it has a word-to-world direction of fit (the word matches the world), and if the speaker believes what he says. If, instead, the speech act uttered is a commissive, then the purpose of the speech act is to commit the speaker, and the direction of fit is world to word (the world is to be made to match the word). Also, the expressed psychological state is that the speaker has every intention of doing what he promises.

Searle is able to develop a taxonomy in spite of the seeming chaos of the variety of speech acts found in our natural language. Similarly, to find order on the speech activity level one must also deal with the variety of types of speech activity. But one must also deal with the extended nature of speech activity. Speech activity runs all the way from a bet that might take two speech acts to pull off, to a long Tolstoy-like novel where the string of speech acts goes on for hundreds of pages. Given the variety and the often extended length of speech activity, one might wonder whether uncovering or devising a taxonomy of speech activity is even possible.

If there is any hope for a taxonomy, it might be thought best to start by identifying the point or purpose of a segment of speech activity. After all, for Searle, the point or purpose of a speech act is the most important of the three main dimensions.

Consider, then, finding the point or purpose of betting. Assume that you are wondering what Sam and Sonny are talking about together. You listen in and pick up their conversation. Sam says, "I'll bet you $10 the home team wins," and Sonny replies by saying "You're on." Sam's speech act tells us not only that he wants to make this particular bet of $10, but also that he wants to engage in the activity of betting. The purpose or point of the speech activity is revealed within the speech activity, much as it is revealed when Jeff utters the speech act "I promise to marry you." Jeff's purpose is to make a commitment. In a similar fashion, a creature from another planet, who just happens to knows English, might wonder about some unusual activity going on in a church. He sees two young people – the boy dressed in black, the girl in white – standing before an alter, and in the process, he hears lots of talk. The creature can identify the purpose of the activity by listening to some of the talk. When one or the other of the participants says certain things, such as "I do take thee as my lawfully wedded wife" or "I thee wed," the purpose of what is going on is revealed. It is true that our creature could get other clues about what is happening. He could simply be told that the gathering is a marriage ceremony. The minister himself could do the telling, by saying something like "We are gathered here together to join in matrimony ...," or one of the witnesses might explain to the strange-looking creature that he is attending a wedding ceremony.

So, at least some of the time, uncovering the purpose of the speech activity seems to be a useful move in identifying stretches of speech activity. It even seems like a useful move in dealing with prayer. The purpose of this speech activity is revealed when someone in the group issues the master speech act "Let us pray," even though this speech act, like the minister's "We are gathered here together to join in matrimony ...," does not count as a prayer performative. One has not prayed by saying "Let us pray." Rather, an announcement has been made that praying will begin immediately.

The same point applies to a newspaper editorial. The purpose of an editorial becomes known when we locate some writing on the editorial page. Then we know what sort of speech activity is to be expected. To be sure, we do not know yet what the specific (political) purpose of the editorial is. For that, it might be useful to read the title of the editorial. But our concern is not with identifying the specific purpose of the writer (e.g., her desire to argue that women are still being discriminated against in the workplace). Rather, it is to look for criteria that help in identifying the nature of a stretch of discourse. In order to do that, it appears, once again, that uncovering the purpose of the discourse is a useful move.

It should be noted that some of the ways of uncovering that purpose identified so far may not be as certain as they seem. Again, take the case of the editorial. The writing may appear on the editorial page, and the author may even claim that she is writing an editorial. But the piece may be just a whimsical essay that meets none of the of the standards or conventions of editorial writing. No facts are cited, no reasons are given for the views expressed, and no argument at all is presented. Something more seems to be needed to make an editorial an editorial than the claim that it is an editorial.

There are even more complications involved in using purpose for identifying a kind of speech activity when, as in a novel, we consider long stretches of discourse. As we have seen already, a novel's purpose may be to amuse, to entertain, to take the readers imaginatively away from their miseries, to help them achieve catharsis, to enlighten and bring about a change in their attitudes and behavior. More than likely there is no one purpose but some combination of purposes here. But, in and of themselves, these purposes do not make the speech activity a novel. These same purposes could be present in the writer of a short story, a biography, an autobiography, or some similar work of nonfiction. The needed additional element seems to be an appeal to the conventions favored by Searle that cancel the truth-telling rules, and those concerned with storytelling and the length of the work in question.

Some of these points about purpose can be stated differently. An author can say that the purpose of the writing he is engaged in is to write a novel. His goal is to write a novel, as well as to entertain, (etc.) his readers. That purpose might be made manifest on the title page by means of a master speech act saying "A Novel." And we can be fairly sure that if the author says it is a novel, then indeed it is. But in the end, it is a novel not because he says it is, but because it meets certain criteria (i.e., conventions) of novelhood. So as useful as determining what the purpose of a novel is, it is necessary to look beyond the writer's purpose to determine what is actually taking place on the speech activity level.

VIII. SOME CONCLUSIONS

I have been working in a Searlian world to see what he might say about speech activity (discourse) analysis. The work has been preliminary in nature. The subject is too complex to allow for anything more than a sketch of how things might go. They seem to be going in the following direction – expressed here as a series of steps.

1. *When listeners approach a stretch of speech activity they should look for clues left by the speaker about the speaker's purpose.* The clues can be found at times in, but more often outside, the text proper. Inside, the clues are no different from those found at the speech act level (e.g., "I bet you" is no different from "I promise you"). The outside clues are master speech acts. These acts indicate that the speech activity to follow will be of a certain sort. In some settings, these master speech acts are commissives, as when the mother tells the child, "I will tell you a story." In others they are directives, as when the child says to her mother, "Tell me a story." Either way, the listeners to these linguistic goings-on are given an idea of what to expect. But two points about this first step. First, it does not guarantee that what follows is in accordance with the master speech act. Although our language contains conventions that encourage the use of such acts to help us understand what speakers are saying, employing these acts is not the same as employing a convention *in* the speech activity (the text). Master speech acts cannot guarantee that the promise to speak in a certain way will be kept, or guarantee that the directive to speak in a certain way will be followed. So to be sure that we are hearing what we've been told we will hear, more needs to be done than merely finding out what the purpose of the speaker is. Second, although taking this first step is very important in coming to understand what others are saying to us, it is not necessary. The speaker may leave no clues at all about what he is saying. So again, there is a need to move on to step 2.

2. *Observe carefully what kind of speech acts are being employed and, in a pre-liminary way, classify what is being said as falling under one of three headings: assertive-dominated speech activity, mixed speech activity, or partially mixed speech activity (that excludes or tends to exclude assertives).* These are the

same headings that I used earlier, for the sake of convenience. But now I am staying with them, since they seem to be useful in giving us a proper speech activity taxonomy. It is as if, at least to some extent, a speech activity taxonomy reflects the taxonomy of speech acts. Assertives on the speech act level have their own heading in the taxonomy of speech activity. The other speech act types do not have their own taxonomic heading, but they still help, in combination, to form the other two headings. These three headings tell us in the most general way what is happening in a stretch of speech activity. One needs, of course, to be wary while ruminating within this step. A stretch of speech activity might be 100 percent assertive and yet, through the use of indirect speech, the author may be issuing directive speech acts. This can happen in a story that describes the death of a drug addict in gruesome detail. On the surface, the author is merely describing; but deep down, he may be trying to teach us a lesson (i.e., issuing directives).[15]

3. *If the speech activity in question is assertive-dominated, determine what species of such activity is being exhibited.* At this point, there is no set way to make this determination. One just has to know what the conventions are for the various assertive speech activities and stay alert. Are the conventions canceling the truth-telling rules being invoked? If so, then we are probably dealing with some kind of fiction. Is there a story line here? If there is, the speech activity could be fiction, or it could be biographical or autobiographical. But it certainly isn't scientific discourse. Does the speech activity report that the author followed strict procedures of observation, testing, and so forth? Then we suspect that the discourse falls under some scientific heading.

4. *If the speech activity in question is "mixed," determine what species of such activity is being exhibited.* Again, there is no calculus to tell us what to look for. However, in most cases we know the conventions well enough that it is relatively easy to identify which species of "mixed" speech activity one is listening to. Even if no master speech act announces the beginning of a prayer, for example, the conventions pertaining to talking to and about the deity give it away as a prayer. Also, the subject matter (i.e., the predicating) often makes it clear what sort of "mixed" discourse the speaker is engaging in. It may be said explicitly in the text itself that a moral issue is being discussed. In a departmental meeting, there are a variety of clues – formal motions, who the participants are, and so on – to tell an observer what is going on. Speakers leave clues all over the place that tell listeners what is going on at the speech activity level.

5. *If the speech activity in question is "partially mixed," again, determine what species of such activity is being exhibited.* Doing this is even easier than in step 4, since these speech activities are briefer, and there are fewer conventions that control them.

In sum, adopting a Searlian-like approach to speech activity brings order to chaos. It is true that this order does not match that found at the speech act level. This is so because our language is a many-splendored creature. Using the five kinds of speech acts and their variations as building blocks, we are able to create an almost unlimited number of different kinds of speech activities (or language-games). Still, we can find order in what otherwise would seem to be chaos because conventions that control the variety of speech activity tend to fall under one of three headings, and because these conventions, although numerous, are not difficult to recognize.

Notes

1. J. L. Austin, *How to Do Things with Words* (New York: Oxford University Press, 1962).
2. John R. Searle, *Speech Acts: An Essay in the Philosophy of Language* (Cambridge: Cambridge University Press, 1969).
3. Richard Rorty (ed.), *The Linguistic Turn: Recent Essays in Philosophical Method* (Chicago: University of Chicago Press, 1967). See especially Rorty's "Introduction," pp. 1–53.
4. Searle, *Speech Acts*, p. 16.
5. John R. Searle, "The Logical Status of Fictional Discourse," in his *Expression and Meaning: Studies in the Theory of Speech Acts* (Cambridge: Cambridge University Press, 1979), pp. 58–75.
6. Ibid., p. 58.
7. Ibid., p. 62.
8. Leo Tolstoy, *Anna Karenina* (New York: Modern Library, 1950).
9. Gertrude Stein, *Three Lives* (Norfolk, Conn.: Modern Library, 1933).
10. Searle, "Logical Status," p. 66.
11. Ibid., p. 65–6.
12. Nick Fotion, "Master Speech Acts," *The Philosophical Quarterly* 21: 84 (1971): 232–43. See also "Speech Activity and Language Use," *Philosophia* 8: 4 (1979): 615–38. These articles explain how master speech acts announce and control the speech activity that follows. Thus when one says "Describe exactly what happened," this master speech act signals the intent of the speaker to engage in a certain kind of speech activity rather than another kind.
13. Searle, "Logical Status," p. 63.

14. John R. Searle, "A Taxonomy of Illocutionary Acts," in his *Expression and Meaning*, p. 2.

15. In figuring out what a stretch of speech activity is all about, we rarely take this step consciously. Rather, we intuitively move to one of the next three steps. Even those steps are not consciously taken most of the time. Rather, we simply sense what conventions are at work in that setting. The steps, then, are ones that we would take were we not so well tuned to understanding what others are saying.

3 | Intentions, Promises, and Obligations

LEO ZAIBERT

In a long and fruitful career, John Searle has, in a courageous but at the same time somewhat maverick fashion, campaigned against fashionable and unfashionable views alike. An exhaustive list of the battles Searle has fought would be far too long for my purposes here, but its more prominent items would have to include his campaigns against functionalism and physicalism in the philosophy of mind, against classical formulations of the mind/body problem, against the very idea of artificial intelligence, against the supposed gap between 'is' and 'ought', against understanding language as merely the manipulation of signs, against the classical model of rationality, and against the standard conceptions of social philosophy as a wholly owned subsidiary of political philosophy. Searle has, famously, devised clever thought experiments and hard-hitting arguments that seem, on first approximation, to suggest a somewhat piecemeal, playful approach. Under more careful consideration, however, it becomes clear that Searle's academic endeavors are integrated into a coherent whole, adding up to a comprehensive philosophical *programme*. Most recently, Searle himself has stated that his main preoccupation in philosophy is to answer the questions: "how do the various parts of the world relate to each other–how does it all hang together?"[1]

Here I wish to investigate precisely the alleged comprehensiveness of Searle's philosophy, with special emphasis on his general *social* ontology, focusing on the three topics of intentions, promises, and obligations. Though Searle's treatment of each of these topics would be worthy of a separate study, analyzing them together will help to make explicit some connections between different aspects of Searle's philosophical system, bringing forth its organic nature. For of all the intentional phenomena that Searle investigates, intentions figure most prominently in his theory of promises. Moreover, of all the speech acts that Searle investigates, promises are the most important. Human beings create social reality by engaging in speech

With thanks to Rafael Tomás Caldera, John Longeway, Fabio Morales, Barry Smith, Aaron Snyder, and Elizabeth Millán-Zaibert.

acts that give rise to obligations, and, according to Searle, promising is conspicuously present in "almost all" speech acts.

While Searle's philosophical system is one of the most comprehensive in the contemporary tradition of analytic philosophy, nonetheless his system neglects the realm of morality. This neglect is significant for several reasons. First and foremost, it is significant because morality is surely "part of the world." Second, it is puzzling that a philosophical system that is intimately concerned with obligations would ignore specifically moral obligations; after all, these are important kinds of obligations. Finally, the neglect of morality is important in light of the fact that one of Searle's earliest and most influential pieces – and indeed, the one that has been most frequently reprinted – has been assumed to deal with a major ethical problem.[2] The title of the article in question has become part of our philosophical household lore: "How to Derive 'Ought' from 'Is'."[3]

Much needs to be done before I can tackle this neglect. First, I will present Searle's system and explain how it hangs together in terms of the three concepts around which my investigation revolves.

I. THE BELIEF/DESIRE ANALYSIS OF INTENTIONAL STATES

Searle's philosophical system is far-reaching and sophisticated. In just the couple of introductory paragraphs here, I have already referred to some concepts that might not be entirely familiar (intentional states, speech acts), and to some others that, though perhaps familiar, have a technical meaning within Searle's philosophy (promises, obligations). If we are to understand Searle's philosophy, brief definitions of some of these concepts are needed. I will begin with the concept of an intentional state:

> Intentionality is that property of many mental states and events by which they are directed at or about or of objects and states of affairs in the world. If, for example, I have a belief, it must be a belief that such and such is the case; if I have a fear, it must be a fear of something or that something will occur; if I have a desire, it must be a desire to do something or that something should happen or be the case; if I have an intention, it must be an intention to do something.[4]

Since beliefs, desires, and intentions (together with fears, likings, feelings, perceptions, and countless other mental states) have the property of intentionality, they are called intentional states. As can be seen, the variety of intentional states is staggering. A popular and elegant approach to the analysis of intentional states is to attempt to explain many of them in terms of two very basic, primitive intentional states: beliefs and desires. Searle, in tune with the prescriptions of this approach, understands beliefs and desires very broadly: 'belief' includes "feeling certain, having a hunch, supposing and many other degrees of conviction," and 'desire' includes "wanting, wishing, lusting and hankering after, and many other degrees of desire."[5] Availing himself of these two concepts and of basic modal logic, Searle investigates the results of applying the belief/desire model to the analysis of several intentional states. For example, the analysis of 'fearing that p' should look roughly like this:

(1)   Fear (p) $\rightarrow$ Bel ($\diamond$p) and Des ($\sim$p)
        (If one fears that p, then one believes that p is possible, and one
        desires not p.)

The analysis of 'expecting that p' goes like this:

(2)   Expect (p) $\leftrightarrow$ Bel (Fut p)
        (If one expects that p, then one believes that p will happen, and to
        believe that p will happen is to expect that p.)

The analysis of 'being sorry that p' would be:

(3)   Sorry (p) $\rightarrow$ Bel (p) and Des ($\sim$p)
        (If one is sorry that p, then one believes that p, though one desires
        that not p.)[6]

In spite of the belief/desire model's charm, Searle is keenly interested in investigating its shortcomings. The system seems too coarse to be capable of distinguishing between similar (yet different) intentional states. Searle points out that "being annoyed that p, being sad that p, and being sorry that p are all cases of:

(4)   Bel (p) and Des ($\sim$p)

but they are clearly not the same states."[7]

Nuances of many other intentional states elude the model as well. Consider, for example, being terrified that p. This is not captured by what would at first glance seem like the obvious analysis,

(5)   Terror (p) $\leftrightarrow$ Bel ($\diamond$p) and Strong Des ($\sim$p),

for, as Searle points out, one could believe that an atomic war could occur, very much hope that it will not occur, and yet not be terrified at all.[8]

Being terrified includes a certain raw feeling that is not captured by any combination of belief and desires, whatever their contents.

The main problem that Searle sees with the belief/desire model is not its general coarseness but, specifically, its inability to yield a plausible account of intentions. He tells us that "perhaps the hardest case of all is intention," and regarding the plausible candidate for an analysis of intention,

(6)   Intend (I do A) → Bel (◊I do A) and Des (I do A),

he admits that it constitutes "only a very partial analysis." The crucial missing element is "the special causal role of intentions in producing our behavior."[9] In spite of the fact that Searle warns that "intendings and intentions are just one form of Intentionality among others, they have no special status" (Searle 1983, p. 3), intentions are nevertheless special.[10] The event that includes the conditions of satisfaction of my intention "has to come about 'in the right way'."[11] So here we get the first glimpse of the uniqueness of intentions. They are unlike other intentional states because their conditions of satisfaction are somehow special. In order to grasp what exactly is so special about intentions, we need first to define two concepts: (1) conditions of satisfaction and (2) "coming about in the right way" (which, for our purposes, can be equated with the expressions "intentional causation" and "causal self-referentiality").

"Conditions of satisfaction are those conditions which . . . must obtain if the [intentional] state is to be satisfied."[12] The condition of satisfaction of Susan's belief that it is raining is that it is indeed raining. The condition of satisfaction of Robert's desiring that the weather improve is that the weather improves. The condition of satisfaction of Mary's intention to become rich, however, is not that she indeed becomes rich. For her intention to be satisfied, she must become rich in a special way. Thus, while we might easily grasp the meaning of conditions of satisfaction in general, in order to understand the specific case of the conditions of satisfaction of intentions, we need to understand intentional causation.

In the case of human action, intentional causation is a form of self-reference. In Searle's own words, "it is part of the content of the intentional state . . . [of intending] that its conditions of satisfaction . . . require that it cause the rest of its conditions of satisfaction."[13] Thus, "if I raise my arm, then my intention in action has as its conditions of satisfaction that that very intention must cause my arm to go up."[14] And thus, in order for Mary's intention to become rich to be satisfied – to be carried out – she must become rich in a special way. She must become rich as a result of *her intending to become rich*. One difference between mere desires and intentions should then be clear. If Mary merely desires to become rich, then, from the perspective of the satisfaction of her desire, it does not matter at all how she becomes rich. This special way in which the conditions of satisfaction of intentions must be brought about cannot be captured by the belief/desire analysis of intentional states, and that is why Searle rejects it.

II. INTENTIONS AND ACTION

The intimate connection between intentions and actions thus begins to emerge. Even if Mary does not engage in any action whatsoever, her *desire* to become rich will, *eo ipso*, be satisfied when she becomes rich. But the conditions of satisfaction of intentions require that the agent *act*. Searle points out that there is something odd about the fact that while we have "no special names for the conditions of satisfaction of beliefs and desires," "we have a special name such as 'action' and 'act' for the conditions of satisfaction of intentions."[15] (I shall follow Searle in equating 'acts' and 'actions'.)

Searle begins a chapter of *Intentionality* entitled "Intention in Action" by examining syntactic similarities between the deep structures of sentences reporting intentional states in the following ways:

> I believe + I vote for Jones
> I want + I vote for Jones
> I intend + I vote for Jones

These structures are all very similar. Searle points out that the last two can be rewritten as follows:

> I want to vote for Jones.
> I intend to vote for Jones.[16]

While Searle is obviously right, it is puzzling that he would put these syntactical remarks to use as a way to distinguish between two groups of intentional states: (a) beliefs and (b) desires and intentions gathered together. After all, Searle's main goal is to show the uniqueness of intentions, not of beliefs, and this discussion actually groups intentions together with desires. Thus, Searle does not decisively utilize the syntactic analysis of propositions expressing intentional states in showing how unique intentions really are. What his syntactic analysis shows is that beliefs are unique – hardly what he is interested in showing.

What, then, is the syntactic difference between a desire and an intention? In order to answer this question, it is worthwhile to tinker with the modal emphasis of Searle's approach. Granted, the deep structures of propositions expressing intentions and propositions expressing desires *could* both be transformed along the lines sketched earlier. But only propositions expressing intentions *must* be transformed in such a way. What I have in mind follows from the fact that, as even Searle's incomplete analysis mentioned earlier in (6) shows, one can only intend one's own future actions. It is impossible to intend anything other than one's own actions; that is, one cannot intend that the sun rise, or that one's friend recover from her ailment, and so on.

Unlike sentences expressing desires, which permit a connection both through the infinitive and through any other particle, such as 'that', sentences expressing intentions *must* include the infinitive. "I desire to vote for Jones" and "I desire that you vote for Jones" are equally sensible. But "I intend that you vote for Jones" is not sensible, and "I intend that I vote for Jones" is just a clumsy way of saying "I intend to vote for Jones." We could desire (hope, wish, etc.) any conceivable thing; but the scope of those things that we can intend is limited by rational considerations that are stricter than those for desires (which are rather lax). The fact that I can intend only something I believe it is possible for me to do is a way of expressing the causal self-referentiality of intentions. (It should be kept in mind that to point out that someone actually says "I intend that the sun rise tomorrow" or "I intend that you become a lawyer" is not to present valid counterexamples to this thesis.)

The interest here does not lie in mere words. A particularly valuable and ubiquitous characteristic of Searle's philosophy, including his views on intentionality, is his concern with the facts of the world, rather than merely with the notation used to describe those facts. My goal in further developing Searle's inquiry into the linguistic analysis of propositions expressing intentional states is to reveal an independent underlying ontological fact about intentions that its linguistic rendering helps to make explicit. I can intend or try to do only things that I believe are up to me. This is a fact that derives from the causal self-referentiality of intentions, from that very special feature of intentions to which Searle has devoted so much attention.

This fact is captured nicely, I think, by my suggestion that we can only intend *to*, try *to* (and further promise *to*, as shall be made clear later), and that we cannot intend *that* or try *that* (or promise *that*). And when I criticize the use of 'intending that', it should be remembered that this is not a mere terminological discussion. A person can hardly try that someone else does this or that – unless, of course, this is just shorthand for saying something along the lines of "I will try to make sure that John does this or that." I cannot intend that my wife is happy, but I of course could intend to make her happy. Moreover, though I can intend to make my wife, Elizabeth, happy, it is hard to see how I could possibly intend to make, say, Queen Elizabeth II happy. For it is necessary that the person intending to do such and such believe that it is up to him to accomplish such and such. I have no relationship whatsoever with Queen Elizabeth II, and thus I am aware that I am in no position to intend to make her happy. Since the connection between desires and actions is loose, and since I could wish for many things that I do not believe are up to me, I could, without any problem, wish to make Queen Elizabeth II happy.

III.   CAUSALITY AND ITS DISCONTENTS

The intimate connection between intentions and actions explains why intentions are so important for Searle's social ontology. We create social reality by engaging in speech acts, and speech acts are, after all, actions, and actions are but the conditions of satisfaction of intentions.[17] To perform a speech act, to echo the famous title of J. L. Austin's book,[18] is to do something with words. Speaking is acting. Questioning, requesting, ordering, asserting, apologizing, criticizing, promising, and many other familiar forms of behavior are speech acts, and, clearly, they are instances of acting. The importance of speech acts in Searle's overall philosophical system is that it is through speech acts that we create social institutions. It is by engaging in the speech act of saying *I hereby declare you husband and wife* or *I hereby sell my car*, or by enacting a law that states that everyone born in French territory is French, or that anyone with German parents is German, and so on, that social reality is created. Yet, the relationship between intentions and actions is fraught with difficulties. One of these difficulties is known as the problem of deviant causal chains. Given intentional causation, there is always a limited number of causal chains that would render the bringing about of a certain result a genuine condition of satisfaction of an intention. All other causal chains are deviant.

For example, let us suppose that Jack intends to kill his neighbor Jill. He has been planning to kill her for a while. One day he goes to a store to buy a weapon. While he is driving to the store, a careless pedestrian walks right in front of Jack's car, and he tries in vain to avoid the collision. The pedestrian dies instantly. Suppose that the pedestrian happened to be Jill.

Examples of this kind abound in the literature. The point of the example, of course, is that Jack intends to kill Jill, he brings about Jill's death, and yet he does not kill Jill intentionally. Running over an unknown pedestrian who happened to be Jill is not the condition of satisfaction of Jack's intention to kill Jill. Had Jack merely desired to kill Jill, running over her accidentally would have been a condition of satisfaction of that desire. Strictly speaking, there are deviant causal chains only in the case of intentions, not in the case of desires. Intentions are, after all, special.

Searle, along with many contemporary authors, worries about the problem of deviant causal chains. He thinks, moreover, that his solution to this problem is "not entirely satisfactory" and that "something may still be eluding us."[19] Though I am not interested here in attempting to find a solution to the problem of deviant causal chains, I do wish to specify the scope of the problem, and to explore why it is less relevant to the analysis of the intentional state of intending than Searle thinks.

Though I have been trying to make explicit the way in which, within Searle's philosophy, intentions are more closely linked to actions than any other intentional state, I have tried to explain intentions proper, that is, the intentional state of intending. I have not tried to explain actions. I could intend to become a millionaire, and I might never actually get around to engaging in any behavior whatsoever in pursuit of that goal. Whether or not I try to satisfy (carry out) my intention, whether the content of my intention comes about through a deviant causal chain or in some other way, or does not come about at all, my intention can nonetheless exist. And the logical structure of an intention is that it could be satisfied only by a future action of the person having the intention. To worry too much about the problem of deviant causal chains is to conflate the analysis of the intentional state of intending with the analysis of actions.

To be sure, this is a subtle point. Intentions and actions are intimately linked; intentions do constitute a special intentional state in virtue of the way in which they are linked to actions. But the connection is not so intimate as to render the result that there are no token intentions without there being token intentional actions. Intentions can exist without their conditions of satisfaction ever materializing. Moreover, the existence of an intentional action X does not even require the existence of an intention to do X, though it might require the existence of some intention to do something (different from X) on the part of the agent.[20] Many contemporary authors have argued – convincingly, in my opinion – against the view that holds that an intention to do X is a necessary condition for X-ing being an intentional action.[21]

What complicates the connection between intentions and actions in Searle's case is that though he speaks generally about 'intentions' *simpliciter*, he in fact distinguishes between two types of intentions: (1) prior intentions and (2) intentions-in-action. Prior intentions are "external" to the action, and intentions-in-action are "internal" to the action. 'Internal' here means being "part of" the action. There is a sense, then, in which the connection between intentions-in-actions and actions is much more intimate than the connection between prior intentions and actions. And thus, the discussion of deviant causal chains can be separated much more easily from the discussion of prior intentions than from the discussion of intentions-in-action.

I have doubts about the cogency and usefulness of this distinction; many of my doubts stem from my reading of Brian O'Shaughnessy's "Searle's Theory of Action."[22] Like O'Shaughnessy, I have difficulty accepting that there is anything beyond a mere temporal difference between, as Searle would have it, "intentions which are formed prior to action and those that are not."[23] Furthermore, I think that Searle has tacitly admitted that for some purposes the distinction is immaterial. In responding to O'Shaughnessy's objections to the distinction between prior intentions and intentions-in-action, Searle posed the following question: "why should we call this interior Intentional content [an intention-in-action] an 'intention'?"[24] His answer deserves to be quoted fully:

> At one level, it does not matter. The notion 'intention-in-action' is just a technical term. As long as you recognize the nature of the component, and in particular its causally self-referential conditions of satisfaction, it is not of very great interest what we choose to call it.[25]

I think that without risking oversimplification, we could here ignore the distinction between prior intentions and intentions-in-action.[26] Prior intentions and intentions-in-action are, in any event, equally causally self-referential intentional states; they both require intentional causation if they are to be effectively satisfied. What I have to say here, and most of what Searle has to say in connection with the way in which intentions are fundamental to the construction of social reality, applies equally to both types of intentions.

IV. COLLECTIVE INTENTIONALITY

Searle is interested in explaining how those bits of reality such as marriages, nationalities, central banks, and other man-made institutions are created.

He refers to the realm to which all of these bits belong as social reality, and it is undeniable that the interest in social reality expands the scope of his philosophical system. In order to understand Searle's social ontology we need to understand a special form of intentionality, what Searle calls "collective" intentionality.

Accounting "for our social reality within our overall scientific ontology," Searle tells us, "requires exactly three elements. The assignment of function, collective intentionality, and constitutive rules."[27] And since Searle states that the assignment of function is a "feature of intentionality"[28] and that constitutive rules are, in some cases, the result of intentionality,[29] we can focus just on collective intentionality. Moreover, among all the necessary conditions for the existence of social reality, collective intentionality plays the leading role, for Searle also tells us that "the central span on the bridge from physics to society is collective intentionality."[30]

Collective intentionality gives rise to institutional facts. The best way to understand what these are is to examine the distinction between brute facts and institutional facts.[31] Brute facts exist independent of human cognition, and they are the paradigmatic component of nature; whereas institutional facts depend on human cognition for their existence, and they are the paradigmatic component of social reality. 'The heart pumps blood' states a brute fact; 'The function of the heart is to pump bood' states an institutional fact. Searle deems this distinction crucial to his aims. Indeed, this distinction informs the formula that Searle uses to explain social reality: "X counts as Y in context C."[32] This rectangular sheet of green paper (brute fact X) counts as money (institutional fact Y) in the United States (context C). By contrast, that Mount Everest has such and such height, that the Earth occupies the third innermost orbit around the Sun, would still be facts even if there were no human to observe them.

Institutional facts – for example, that Bob is married, that Jane holds a Ph.D., that Charles is British – require collective intentionality. This intentionality is collective in the sense that one person's belief that, say, wrapping paper is money would not be enough to turn wrapping paper into money. Beliefs of this sort, if they are to have any efficacy whatsoever, need to be held by collectives. How large must these collectives be? Though this question concerns only the implications of Searle's theory, not its logical structure, it is a difficult and important question that Searle does not address.

If my circle of friends and I collectively believe that the sheets of paper on my desk are money, are they money? This problem is not at all trivial, as more poignant examples make clear. Think of the Basques, or the Palestinians (or the Israelis under British mandate), or the Republican

Irish (and so on). These are groups that collectively believe that such and such territory, currently a part of another nation, should count as their nation. In cases like these, however, collective intentionality is rather ineffective in creating the sought-after institutional facts. Age-old conflicts over sovereignty, as well as intricate landed property disputes, have scarcely been, and probably will never be, solved by merely appealing to collective intentionality.

A problem that concerns the core of Searle's philosophical system, however, is that the talk of collective intentionality is surrounded by a dangerous halo; the expression might suggest something akin to "the idea that there exists some Hegelian world spirit, a collective consciousness, or something equally implausible."[33] Searle sensibly rejects such hypotheses. He believes that "the capacity for collective intentionality is biologically innate"[34] and that it can be explained without appealing to collective souls and the like. Humans can, perhaps, collectively fear, or collectively believe, or collectively hope, but given what we know about Searle's theory of intentions, it is hard to see how they could collectively intend. After all, we have seen how different intentions are from other intentional states. It seems as if Searle now lumps together all intentional states under the heading "collective intentionality," and thus as if he would be ignoring the difference between intentions and other intentional states that we have analyzed here.

Yet, the lumping together is a problem with the label "collective intentionality" alone – Searle is emphatic about the importance of collective intentions (or we-intentions, as he also calls them) for social ontology.[35] One reason for this should by now be obvious: intentions are closely connected to actions, and collective intentions are closely connected to collective actions.

The very idea of a collective intention, however, is difficult to fathom. For if intentions need to be causally self-referential, if the actions that constitute their conditions of satisfaction need to be caused by the very mental state of intending, how could they be collective (if there exists no "collective mind")? The exact contours of many mental states are known only to the person having the mental state. In many cases, only the agent having a given intention can know exactly the extent of that intention. There are obvious epistemological limitations upon our knowledge of the contents of other minds. Thus, and to repeat, while perhaps we could collectively wish, fear, believe, and so on, it seems that to intend collectively has to be different. In order for Colette to intend X, she must believe that X is up to her. But if X is a collective action – an action requiring contributions from other people, other minds – the degree to which Colette can fully intend

X is debatable. At any rate, how Colette can intend such a thing is not at all obvious.

Moreover, we know that only intentions can give rise to deviant causal chains. But how would deviant causal chains operate in the case of collective intentions? Let us imagine that Bob, a member of a soccer team, "intends" to win the match he is playing, and let us suppose that he believes that all the other members of the team also "intend" to win the match. Bob believes that they collectively intend to win the match. Bob is wrong; his ten teammates have been bribed, and they are trying to lose the match. Yet, Bob's team wins the match, in spite of ten of the eleven players' intentions. There is no way in which Bob can be certain that this collective intention was brought about through a deviant causal chain, because he cannot be certain about the contents of his teammates' minds. Yet, in the case of singular intentions it is always self-evident to the person having the singular intention whether or not the conditions of satisfaction of the intention are met.

I am skeptical about the possibility of collective intentions, and elsewhere I have written about the problems Searle faces in this regard. I shall not reproduce these arguments here.[36] But the nature of my criticism is such that I can succinctly summarize my case. For all the importance Searle attaches to we-intentions, he does not present any account of them whatsoever. In *The Construction of Social Reality*, Searle says very little about the structure of collective intentions; he merely refers the reader to his article "Collective Intentions and Actions."[37] Stunningly, however, this article does not contain any account of we-intentions, either. In the end, then, nowhere has Searle ever analyzed we-intentions. And given his views on individual intentions, the missing explanations are in order, since there are obvious and good reasons why we-intentions, if they exist at all, must be problematic entities.

V. PROMISES AND OTHER SPEECH ACTS

Another way in which intentions are important in Searle's philosophy derives from the prominent role that they play in another element of Searle's general social ontology: promises. There exists a smooth symmetry between the role that intentions play in Searle's theory of intentionality and the role that promises play in his speech act theory: intentions are a unique intentional state (in the sense already analyzed), and promises are a unique speech act (in a sense to be analyzed immediately). Searle has always used

promises as his favorite example of a speech act. Moreover, Searle has
recently claimed that "every speech act contains a promise."[38]

Searle has put forth a set of necessary and sufficient conditions for
something to be a genuine promise. "A speaker S utter[ing] a sentence
T in a presence of a hearer H"[39] is a promise only if the speaker has the
following five intentions:

(1) S intends to do A,

(2) S intends that the utterance of T will place him under an obligation to
do A,

(3) S intends to produce in H the knowledge (K) that the utterance of T is
to count as placing S under an obligation to do A,

(4) S intends to produce K by means of the recognition of his intention,
and,

(5) [The speaker] intends to make his intention recognized in virtue of (by
means of) H's knowledge of the meaning of T.[40]

In addition, Searle suggests the additional necessary conditions:[41]

(6) Normal input and output conditions obtain,

(7) S expresses the proposition that p in the utterance of T,

(8) In expressing that p, S predicates a future act A of S,

(9) H would prefer S's doing A to his not doing A, and S believes H would
prefer his doing A to his not doing A,

(10) It is not obvious to both S and H that S will do A in the normal course
of events,

(11) The semantical rules of the dialect spoken by S and H are such that
T is correctly and sincerely uttered if and only if [the previous] conditions
obtain.[42]

Now, given what we already know about Searle's theory of intentions, it
is plainly visible that conditions (1) and (8) are redundant. If an intention
has to be causally self-referential, and if its condition of satisfaction has to
be a future action of the agent having the intention, then it follows that a
speaker cannot intend anything other than a future action of his own. If
we keep in mind Searle's concept of an intention, together with some of its
natural implications, other revisions to his analysis of promises are in order.

Let us analyze condition (2) above. Why must the speaker *intend* that
uttering some words place him under an obligation? Why could he not just
desire to place himself under an obligation? If we can only *intend to*, and
never *intend that*, this condition needs reformulation. Moreover, placing
myself under an obligation is something that does not depend entirely on

me, as it requires the existence of a set of institutions that might not be either created or known by me. I might happen to find myself in a society whose institutions are not familiar to me. I might in this case promise to do X, hoping that this will place me under an obligation, and that my utterance will produce, in my audience, the awareness that I wish to place myself under an obligation, and so on. But in this case it is difficult for me to intend to place myself under an obligation, since whether or not I effectively so place myself is not entirely up to me.[43]

Searle is aware that in some cases it is hard to intend certain things, and that in those cases it is easier to desire those very things. Searle once presented this famous example:

> Suppose that I am an American soldier in the Second World War and that I am captured by Italian troops. And suppose that I wish [sic] to get these troops to believe that I am a German soldier [and in order to get them to release me, I try to fool them by] address[ing] my Italian captors with the following sentence: *Kennst du das Land wo die Zitronen blühen?*[44]

Searle preempts possible objections along the lines that the American soldier could not possibly intend to produce the desired effects, given that it would be irrational for him to believe that those effects were sufficiently up to him. He tells us:

> If it seems implausible that one could intend to produce the desired effects with such an utterance in these circumstances, a few imaginative additions to the example should make the case more plausible, e.g., I know that my captors know there are German soldiers in the area wearing American uniforms. I know that they have been instructed to be on the lookout for these Germans. . . . I know that they have lied to their commander by telling him that they can speak German when in fact they cannot, etc.[45]

This example occurs in the context of Searle's criticism of Paul Grice's theory of meaning.[46] I am not interested in that discussion here. What is of interest to me is that Searle explicitly recognizes that it is easier to desire X than it is to intend X. Yet, Searle's analysis of the speech act of promising requires five intentions and no desires. Can any of these intentions be replaced by desires?

In order to answer this question, it is worthwhile to contrast Searle's analysis of promises with that of another contemporary philosopher. John Rawls tells us that "promising is an act done with the public intention of deliberately incurring an obligation."[47] Rawls, like Searle, suggests that the promisor needs to intend to place himself under an obligation. Unlike

Searle, however, Rawls does not require that intentions have as conditions of satisfaction future actions carried out by the agent having those very intentions. Moreover, Searle requires four other intentions in addition to this one, and it is regarding these other intentions that Rawls's account of promising is quite different from Searle's.

Let us take a look at the three intentions (3), (4), and (5) (which Searle presents as one single requirement). Let us begin with (3). How could I intend to produce knowledge in someone else? According to Searle, in order for a given state of affairs to be the condition of satisfaction of an intention, it is necessary that whether or not the state of affairs obtains be entirely up to the agent having the intention (the state of affairs is a future *action* of the agent). Further, "intending to produce knowledge in someone else" sounds a lot like *intending that someone else knows*, and this is problematic in light of what I have already suggested regarding the problems of "intending that." Of course, at this point obvious questions suggest themselves. Why is Searle so tenacious regarding an intention in (3)? Why does he not simply demand that the promisor *wish* to produce knowledge in the hearer (while, perhaps, adding that the promisor wishes that the knowledge he wishes to produce be the result of his making a promise)? It seems sensible to restrict the object of a promise to future actions of the agent. (Otherwise, people could promise things that are not up to them.) But it does not seem sensible to require that the agent intend to produce knowledge, since this is, in view of Searle's own thesis, a difficult thing to intend.

If we go back to Rawls's treatment of these conditions, we find that he suggests that when we make a promise, "we *want* [the] obligation to exist and to be known to exist, and we *want* others to know that we recognize this tie [created by the promise] and intend to abide to it."[48] Naturally, we could intend to abide by what we have promised, but I do not think (and neither does Rawls) that we could intend that our intention in promising be known to exist, or intend that others recognize details of our internal mental activities, and so on. Rawls requires only one intention in promising, whereas Searle requires five. Yet, it is Searle's own theory of intentions that better explains why there should not be so many intentions involved in making a promise.

Similar concerns, perhaps even more pressing ones, can be voiced regarding Searle's conditions (4) and (5). It might be doubtful whether a person can really intend to produce knowledge in someone else; but I think that the possibility of an agent's intending that a certain proposition that another agent knows be known as a result of a given specific process is more doubtful. Not only, then, is the person hearing the promise gaining certain knowledge as a result of someone else's intentions, but someone else's intentions also specify exactly how such knowledge is acquired.

These concerns could be addressed very easily. All Searle would need to do is to specify that the only required intention in the institution of promising is the intention to perform the promised act, and that the conditions expressed in (2), (3), (4), and (5) merely express desires, along lines similar to those that Rawls follows. Perhaps Searle has reasons to insist that the conditions expressed in (2), (3), (4), and (5) be intentions and not mere desires; if so, Searle would do us a great service were he to explain these reasons. And understanding promises well is crucial to understanding Searle's overall philosophy. For the institution of promising, as I shall show next, plays a prominent role in Searle's social ontology. So, having addressed a certain tension between Searle's account of intentions in *Intentionality* and the way in which he uses "intentions" when dealing with two foundational aspects of his social ontology – that is, in his discussion of we-intentions and promises – we are ready now to examine the important role that promises play in Searle's philosophy.

VI. PROMISES, OBLIGATIONS, AND THE IS/OUGHT GAP

Whatever the peculiarities of their logical structure, it should be quite unproblematic to see that promises are intimately linked to obligations (or "commitments," – Searle uses the two expressions interchangeably).[49] There is an obvious connection between saying *I promise to pay you five dollars* and having some sort of obligation to pay you five dollars. Clearly, one way in which we obligate ourselves is by making promises. This is hardly a problematic claim. But Searle focuses so much on this way of committing ourselves that it seems, at times, as if this were the only way in which human beings can generate obligations. Clearly, it is not. Neglecting the study of other forms of obligation undermines the alleged comprehensiveness of Searle's philosophy.

Furthermore, the intimate connection between promises and obligations explains why this speech act was the one that allowed Searle to derive an 'ought' from an 'is', and thus to cast doubt upon a well-respected and long-enduring philosophical thesis. I shall ignore the issue of whether this derivation is correct; instead, I shall argue that even if correct, it has far fewer implications, and far less significance for moral philosophy, than Searle and his commentators have assumed.

One of the central problems in moral philosophy, sometimes even called *the* central problem in moral philosophy,[50] is the problem of the derivability of a moral statement from a (set of) nonmoral statement(s). Other names for this problem are "the naturalistic fallacy" and the "is/ought question." In 1964, Searle wrote a famous and influential article in which he allegedly derived an 'ought' from an 'is' – that is, an evaluative statement from purely descriptive statements. The provocatively titled article "How to Derive 'Ought' from 'Is'" (Searle 1964), while not straightforwardly claiming to solve this thorny and important problem, was by and large interpreted as if it did.[51] It does not. Searle does not address the classical problem in moral philosophy. I will spare the reader a repetitious discussion of the logic of Searle's analysis, and just focus on the scope of Searle's thesis. From purely descriptive statements, Searle derived an evaluative statement all right, but not a *moral* statement.

The best place to begin this discussion is with Searle's view on "The Naturalistic Fallacy Fallacy."[52] Searle claims that this "is the fallacy of supposing that it is logically impossible for any set of statements of the kind usually called descriptive to entail a statement of the kind usually called evaluative."[53] Searle's discussion of the naturalistic fallacy, then, should be understood in light of his view on the naturalistic fallacy fallacy. In Searle's own words,

> the view that descriptive statements cannot entail evaluative statements, though relevant to ethics, is not a specifically ethical theory; it is a general theory about the illocutionary force of utterances of which ethical utterances are only a special case.[54]

Here is Searle's gambit in embryo. He treats the traditional problem of the naturalistic fallacy as a peculiar form of a more general problem of speech act theory. He wishes to solve a general problem of the normativity of speech acts, but many authors have assumed that Searle has solved the specific problem of moral normativity. Searle, however, is emphatic about the fact that whatever relevance his views have vis-à-vis morality is a mere side-effect of his concern with a logical problem about the illocutionary force of certain expressions. As a propaedeutic warning, Searle tells us: "we must avoid . . . lapsing into talk about ethics or morals. We are concerned with 'ought' not 'morally ought'."[55] Searle presents another warning: "Let us remind ourselves at the outset that 'ought' is a humble English auxiliary, 'is' an English copula; and the question whether 'ought' can be derived from 'is' is as humble as the words themselves."[56] The humble sense of 'ought' with which Searle is concerned is the same sense in which, in a chess game, you ought to move your king when under attack; the sense in which, when driving in the United States, you ought to drive on the right side of the street, and so on. This sense of 'ought', interesting as it might be, is of little and, at best, indirect significance for moral philosophy.

This humble, nonmoral sense of 'ought' in which Searle is interested is reminiscent of another derivation of 'ought' from 'is'. A. N. Prior presented the following example. From the premise that "Tea drinking is common in England," one could validly derive that "either tea drinking is common in England or all New Zealanders ought to be shot"[57] (Brink 1989, p. 150). Of course, this derivation constitutes no solution whatsoever to the metaethical problem regarding the nature of moral propositions (and Prior was aware of this). From any given proposition, any other proposition could be derived via addition. As David Brink and Charles Pigden have pointed out in their discussions of the naturalistic fallacy, a defender of the view that there is a gap between nonmoral and moral statements might overcome this sort of maneuver simply by adding to the general thesis that the gap exists between descriptive and nonvacuously evaluative statements.[58]

To be sure, Searle's derivation of an 'ought' from an 'is' is not as vacuous as Prior's provocative ploy. But it is similarly irrelevant to ethics. Searle's derivation merely tells us something about the meaning of 'promise'. Promising *means* undertaking an obligation, and undertaking an obligation *means* that one ought to do whatever one is obliged to do. But this sense of obligation has little to do with morality. As Searle admits, "whether the entire institution of promising is good or evil, and whether the obligations undertaken in promising are overridden by other outside considerations are questions which are external to the institution itself."[59] Yet these external considerations are, precisely, *moral* considerations. And there is something odd, then, about Searle's attempt to examine the *general* problem of the naturalistic fallacy, for the classical interest in the naturalistic fallacy has always been focused narrowly on the ethical dimension. So it has been for Hume,[60] for Moore,[61] for Popper,[62] and for Brink.[63] These authors leave no doubt that they are dealing with an ethical problem. But Searle does not address the ethical dimension of the problem.

Searle's treatment of the is/ought problem is reminiscent, too, of D. D. Raphael's interpretation of the connections between a famous Shakespearean exchange and the justification of political obligations. Raphael wonders how to answer the question, "Why does the citizen have a duty to obey the laws of the State?" He then points out a possible answer to this question, which is "simple and obvious," and which has a lot to do with the logical structure of the relationship between state and citizen. "It follows logically that if the State is authoritative, i.e. has the right to issue orders to its citizens and the right to receive obedience from them, the citizens are obliged to obey those orders."[64] Raphael emphasizes the downright platitudinous character of this sort of answer further: "the citizen is legally obliged to obey the law because the law *is* that which imposes legal obligations."[65] And then Raphael compares this sort of answer to the passage in which Hamlet is asked by Polonius, "What do you read my lord?" and Hamlet replies, "Words, words, words." The answer evades the point of the question. Though these answers are "formally correct," they tell us "virtually nothing."[66] Something similar happens with Searle's derivation of an 'ought' from an 'is' in the case of promises. The very meaning of promising is that one ought to do what one has promised to do. But this sense of 'ought' is indeed humble, and it is dramatically different from the sense of 'ought' that has preoccupied moral philosophers for ages.

Toward the end of his derivation of 'ought' from 'is', Searle asks, "what bearing does all this have on moral philosophy?" Searle's answer deserves to be quoted in full:

> At least this much: It is often claimed that no ethical statement can ever follow from a set of statements of fact. The reason for this, it is alleged, is that ethical statements are a sub-class of evaluative statements, and no evaluative statements can ever follow from a set of statements of fact. The naturalistic fallacy as applied to ethics is just a special case of the general naturalistic fallacy. I have argued that the general claim that one cannot derive evaluative from descriptive statements is false. I have not argued, or even considered, that specifically ethical or moral statements cannot be derived from statements of fact.[67]

Clever as Searle's gambit is, it nonetheless misrepresents the case that has traditionally been made by those who believe that there is an is/ought gap. Classical moral philosophers have not subsumed the ethical problem under the general speech act problem, in order then to show that since there is a gap concerning the general problem, the gap must extend to the particularly ethical aspect of the problem. It has been enough to point out that there is no way to bridge the gap in the particular case of morality. Searle is rather alone in his interest in the *general* naturalistic fallacy.

Though it is still debated whether Searle succeeded in his derivation of an 'ought' from an 'is', the overwhelmingly typical view continues to be that his treatment of this problem is very important for moral philosophy. A small number of authors have taken issue with the moral import of Searle's derivation – a list of such authors would include Witkowski,[68]

Genova,[69] and Cameron.[70] My arguments regarding the relative moral insignificance of Searle's derivation of an 'ought' from an 'is' are substantially different from those found in the literature. But there is a compelling reason for taking a fresh look at Searle's views on the naturalistic fallacy. This reason is best seen if we pay attention to the chronology of Searle's writings.

"How to Derive 'Ought' from an 'Is'" appeared first in 1964; it was later reprinted with some modifications in *Speech Acts*.[71] The publication of *Speech Acts* provided a background and context that helped to dispel some misunderstandings concerning the ways in which Searle's seminal article had been interpreted. In the first version of the article, Searle stated that he was going to show that the venerable view that claimed that 'ought' cannot be derived from 'is' was flawed. He was going to present a lone counterexample to that view. Then he said:

> It is not of course to be supposed that a single counter-example can refute a philosophical thesis, but in the present instance if we can present a plausible counter-example and can in addition give some account or explanation of how and why it is a counter-example, and if we can further offer a theory to back up our counter example – a theory which will generate an indefinite number of counter-examples – we may at least cast considerable light on the original thesis.[72]

The full-blown theory to back up this counterexample has been long in coming. *Speech Acts* was indeed the first step, but the full-blown generalization of the counterexample takes place only in two recent, major works: *The Construction of Social Reality* (1995) and *Rationality in Action* (2001). Searle's philosophy has indeed gained in depth and comprehensiveness with these recent works; but at the same time the neglect that morality suffers within his system becomes ever more obvious, and worthy of attention. In the next section, I wish to show how pervasive Searle believes promises to be, and how, in spite of the fact that the world Searle investigates includes "the world of Supreme Court decisions and of the collapse of communism,"[73] in spite of the fact that Searle now cares about marriages, money, and property rights, he has yet to say much about morality.[74]

VII. THE UBIQUITY OF PROMISES AND MORALITY

Searle's most recent book, *Rationality in Action*, appeared in Spanish first, then in English in 2001. The English and Spanish versions are virtually identical.[75] For my purposes here there is one interesting difference, which I will discuss in due course.

> [T]he single most remarkable capacity of human rationality, and the single way in which it differs most from ape rationality, is the human capacity to create and to act on desire-independent reasons for action. The creation of such reasons is always a matter of an agent *committing* himself in various ways.[76]

At first sight, it might look as if the mechanism through which we obligate ourselves had little necessary connection to promising, but on further analysis it becomes clear that the institution of promising is crucially linked to the remarkable human capacity to create desire-independent reasons. When we obligate ourselves, we impose conditions of satisfaction upon conditions of satisfaction. Searle's own example eloquently explains what he means by imposing conditions of satisfaction upon conditions of satisfaction:

> Suppose a speaker utters a sentence, for example, 'It is raining', and suppose he intends to make the assertion that it is raining. His intention in action is, in part, to produce the utterance 'it is raining'. That utterance is one of the conditions of satisfaction of his intention. But if he is not just uttering the sentence, but actually *saying that* it is raining, if he actually *means* that it is raining, then he must intend that the utterance have satisfied truth conditions. . . . that is, his meaning intention is to impose conditions of satisfaction (i.e. truth conditions) on conditions of satisfaction (the utterance).[77]

Searle claims that to impose conditions of satisfaction on conditions of satisfaction is, *eo ipso*, a commitment. The speaker is committed to the truth of the claim that it is raining; she is committed to not saying things that contradict the view that it is raining, and so on. (Notice, however, that Searle continues to appeal to intentions in ways that are at odds with his own theory of intentions. For it is hard to see how one could *intend* that the truth conditions of the utterance be satisfied – that is, that it is actually raining – though, once more, it is quite natural for someone to *hope* that it is raining.) This commitment constitutes a desire-independent reason for action. And there is nothing moral about it: "'You ought to tell the truth', 'You ought not to lie', and 'You ought to be consistent in your assertions' are *internal* to the notion of assertion."[78]

Searle's account of the way in which we create desire-independent reasons for action is confessedly naturalistic: "there must not be any appeal to anything transcendental, non-biological, noumenal, or supernatural. . . . there is no need for any help from general principles, moral rules, etc." We should be able to explain all this "without the assistance of substantive moral principles."[79] Something similar happens with Searle's notion of being obligated. Searle is interested only in the nonmoral senses of this term. The preceding remarks make it abundantly clear that Searle's agenda is to avoid moral principles (together with anything noumenal, transcendental, etc.). The obligations that concern him are those that arise from the very meaning and the very logical structure of speech acts.

While so far we have dealt exclusively with the example of making an assertion and the commitments that arise from it, Searle further tells us that "all of the standard forms of speech acts with whole propositional contents involve the creation of desire-independent reasons for action."[80] So his example could be extended to cover requests and orders – that is, if I request X from you, or if I order you to do X, I am, among other things, committed to not preventing you from doing X, and so on. Searle admits that there are ways in which we could commit ourselves without the help of any speech act. For example, "one may commit oneself to a policy just by adopting a firm intention to continue with that policy."[81] While this private decision might be a genuine commitment, its enforcement is so impractical that we might as well follow Searle in ignoring it. But there are other commitments that Searle does not mention that are important and ought not be ignored. These are the commitments that we have that are not the result of voluntary exchanges. For example, I have never promised that I will not intentionally and unjustifiably injure a fellow human being, yet I am wholeheartedly committed to not doing this. This is an enforceable commitment, both legally and morally. And it is such a deep commitment that if I were ever to promise to hurt someone, the commitment that might arise from the act of promising would be overridden by this nonpromissory commitment.

The tight connection between promises and the imposition of conditions of satisfaction on conditions of satisfaction is now surfacing. Promises constitute the most obvious and ubiquitous case of a speech act by which we impose conditions of satisfaction upon conditions of satisfaction, thus committing ourselves. The same commitment that a promise generates is generated by an assertion, though the case of promising is perhaps more explicit. That is why Searle tells us in *Razones Para Actuar* that "all speech acts have an element of promising."[82] This seems exaggerated. It is hard to see where in the speech act of asking, say, *What time is it?* the element of promising is to be found. Yet, many – perhaps most – though not "all" or "almost all" speech acts, do include the element of promising. Asserting, requesting, ordering, and so on, are all forms of committing ourselves, because all of these speech acts contain elements of promising. Searle is explicit about this: "For a long time philosophers tried to treat promises as a kind of assertion. It would be more accurate to think of assertions as a kind of promise that something is the case."[83]

Promises are the germ of all of the obligations and commitments with which Searle is concerned. We have seen that in spite of the frequent inclusion of his "How to Derive 'Ought' from 'Is'" in volumes devoted to moral philosophy, Searle's article, as a token of Searle's whole philosophy, has little to do with morality. The commitments and obligations that arise from promises face another difficulty. Even if Searle is right about the structure of promises and about how this structure pervades most other speech acts, it is not at all clear why these speech acts should obligate us. This difficulty casts doubt on the value of talking about obligations that can nevertheless be overridden without addressing at all what the overriding criteria might be. To the examination of this problem I shall devote the remainder of this chapter.

VIII.   RATIONALITY AND THE BINDING FORCE OF OBLIGATIONS

Why should the obligations I undertake be binding on me? Why should I keep my promises? These questions, when asked from the perspective of moral philosophy, are of utmost importance. Yet, from within Searle's proud, confessedly nonmoral stance, they lose a lot of their bite. Moreover, Searle's answer to these questions contains precious little about morality. The gist of Searle's answer is extraordinarily simple. Why are someone's commitments binding on him? "Because they are *his* commitments."[84] There is more to it than this, but not *much* more. That is, commitments are binding when agents freely and intentionally make assertions and thus commit themselves to their truth. It is not rationally open to agents to say that they are indifferent to truth, sincerity, consistency, evidence, or entailment.[85] The elements that might afford a substantial answer to our question are (1) the conjunction of voluntariness and intentionality in the undertaking of the commitment and (2) recognitional rationality.[86] Both fail, however.

The conjunction of voluntariness and intentionality is a nonstarter; it just pushes the question one level up. Instead of asking 'Why should the commitments I undertake be binding on me?', we would now ask 'Why should the commitments that I voluntarily and intentionally undertake be binding on me?' And to this reformulated question, the only answer Searle gives is: recognitional rationality. What is, then, recognitional rationality?

In *Rationality in Action*, Searle presents a sophisticated account of the logical structure of reasons. Only a brief sketch of certain aspects of this account is necessary for my purposes here. There are internal reasons and external reasons for human action. Internal reasons are recognized by the agent, and external reasons are not so recognized:

> A reason for an action is only a reason if it is, or is part of, a total reason.... A total reason, in principle, might be entirely external.... Yet, in order for ... an external reason to function in actual deliberation, it must be represented by some internal intentional state of the agent.[87]

There are many reasons, say, for me to shave my beard, though I ignore them. But, of course, in order for any of those reasons to function in deliberation, they must be part of the contents of some of my intentional states. Searle is aware, however, of the obvious problem:

> [T]his makes it look as if what really matters is not the fact itself [the reason], but the belief [the intentionally apprehended reason]. But that is wrong. The belief is answerable to the facts. Indeed in some cases rationality can require one belief rather than another.[88]

And then Searle admits: "it might look as if an infinite regress threatened: rationality requires the belief, but the acquisition of the belief itself requires rationality."[89] (Rationality requires the belief, but the belief itself must be rational, so then the belief requires another belief in order to be rational, and this one another and so on, ad infinitum.)

The stage is set for recognitional rationality's entrance; deus ex machina, it is supposed to solve Searle's problems, both the infinite regress that worries him and, more important for our purposes here, the explanation of the binding force of our commitments. Yet, for all the confidence that Searle has in it, recognitional rationality utterly fails to solve these problems. Searle describes recognitional rationality in the following way:

> Rationality may require that an agent under certain epistemic conditions simply recognize a fact in the world such as *the fact that he has undertaken an obligation* or that he has a certain need, or that he is in a certain kind of danger, etc., even though there are no rational processes, no activity of deliberation, leading to the rational result. The acquisition of a rational intentional state does not always require a rational process of deliberation, or indeed any process at all.... [R]ational recognition of the facts does not necessarily require deliberation.[90]

Recognitional rationality does prevent the infinite regress, but it exacts too high a price. The notion of rationality that Searle defends in *Rationality in Action* is coextensive with the central notion of that book: the gap, that is, the notion of freedom of the will. Searle presents many formulations that indicate how important the gap is for rationality: "rationality requires the gap"; "rationality is impossible without a gap," and so on.[91] That is, in order for a given action to be rational, there must exist a certain gap, where deliberation is possible. Yet, recognitional rationality operates in the absence of such a gap. But if the intentional states that are the basis for rational decision making need to be rational themselves, and if their rationality does not derive from their having been formed in the context of any gap(s), the notion of rationality becomes unintelligible. 'Rational' when referring to recognitional rationality is dramatically different from 'rational' when referring to any of the other cases Searle discusses. Thus, at the very least, a clarification of these different senses of rationality is in order, particularly if we keep in mind that it is precisely this type of rationality that is supposed to account for the binding force of our commitments.

Consider one of the examples of recognitional rationality that Searle presents in *Rationality in Action*. A person sees that a truck is bearing down on her. According to Searle, perceiving the truck gives her – without deliberation – reasons for action. Yet, the question as to what makes the action of moving out of the truck's path rational remains unanswered – as unanswered as the question about the binding force of the obligations that arise from promises. If recognitional rationality is what explains the binding force of our commitments and obligations, it turns out that "seeing" that I have a commitment is just like seeing that a truck is bearing down on me. Knowing what my obligations are would be as simple, and as devoid of deliberation, as the act of seeing a truck bearing down on me. Would that more philosophical problems were so easy!

Searle, in any case, is concerned only with the nonmoral aspects of commitments, and this renders his treatment of commitments and obligations extremely narrow. It is valuable, once again, to contrast Searle's view of the binding force of promises with Rawls's views, as Rawls is a representative case of a philosopher interested in moral philosophy. Regarding the lack of binding force of coerced or involuntary promises, Rawls suggests that "it would be wildly irrational in the original position to agree to be bound by words uttered while asleep, or extorted by force."[92] And while this "wild irrationality" might resonate with Searle's talk of the failures of recognitional rationality, the two theories are quite different in this respect. Rawls thinks that it is wildly irrational to set up the institution of promising, from the perspective of agents in the original position (i.e., from the perspective of agents who ignore the details of their place in an ideal society whose institutional foundations they are creating), without setting up certain minimal conditions. But for Rawls, it is not necessarily wildly irrational to fail to see that one is under an obligation arising from a promise one has made (though this might not relieve one of the obligation).

Searle believes that all of the obligations that arise from the act of promising are "internal" to the promise itself. And it would be a failure of recognitional rationality if one were to fail to see any of them. There is no need to appeal to external moral principles or to anything noumenal, transcendental, and so on. Searle in effect equates, as we have seen, making assertions with making promises. And just as saying "It is raining" commits me to upholding the truth of such a proposition, saying "I hereby promise to call you" commits me to calling you. Searle's discussion of commitments is a rather sterile treatment of a very fertile theme.

Unlike Searle, Rawls, a good representative of the orthodoxy that Searle has fought, believes that the obligation to keep a promise arises from an independent, *moral* principle. Rawls claims that

> it is essential . . . to distinguish between the rule of promising and the principle of fidelity. The rule is simply a constitutive convention, whereas the principle of fidelity is a moral principle, a consequence of the principle of fairness.[93]

For Rawls, then, the binding force of promises derives ultimately from the principle of fairness, a moral principle that would be chosen in the original position. By contrast, the binding force with which Searle is concerned is completely internal to the institution of promising, and it arises in absolute independence from any moral principle whatsoever.

The way to resolve the impasse between Searle and classical conceptions of the binding force of our promises, exemplified here by Rawls's account, is to remember that the sorts of obligations with which Searle is concerned are nonmoral. Searle is just concerned with those commitments and obligations that stem from the constitutive conventions that give rise to promises. I do not think that Rawls would disagree with the claim that promising inherently creates certain obligations whose binding force derives simply from the constitutive rules of the speech act of promising. But Rawls and others would insist that the binding force of the moral obligations that a given promise might engender has to derive from a source external to the constitutive conventions that gave rise to the promise in the first place.

Searle's suggestion that all speech acts involve a bit of promising leads him to underestimate the importance of obligations that do not arise from the very meaning of a certain speech act. He states:

> To think that the obligation of promising derives [externally] from the institution of promising is as mistaken as to think that the obligations I undertake when I speak English must derive from the institution of English: Unless I think English is somehow a good thing, I am under no obligations when I speak it.[94]

Yet, there are different types of obligations that arise from promises. Certainly, the obligations that arise from the very meaning of the act of making a promise ought to be internal to that very act. But there are moral consequences of making promises that do not arise from the very act of making those promises. Those other obligations derive from external principles – such as, in Rawls's case, the principle of fidelity. If I use the English language to gratuitously insult someone, the obligation to apologize that might ensue is not internal to the act of insulting, and it is not part of the constitutive rules of any speech act. This type of obligation is one among many other obligations that have been central to moral philosophy and that Searle does not discuss, or even acknowledge.

Of course, if the very logic of the act of promising is said to generate all types of obligations that might relate to a given promise, then someone promising, say, to be a slave would be, *eo ipso*, obligated, in all its senses, to be a slave. Searle analyzes this case and says that the reason why a slave has no reason to obey the slave owner is that a slave does not typically exercise any freedom when he promises to be a slave.[95] But what if she did? That is, what if someone intentionally and freely were to promise to give herself over in slavery? Searle would presumably claim that the person who freely and intentionally promises to be a slave has an obligation to be a slave. Yet, Searle also admits that any obligation that arises from a genuine promise could be overridden by external considerations. But he does not at all investigate when and which external considerations have overriding force. We could sensibly insist on the fact that the promisor's only obligation, assuming that she acts intentionally and freely, is the constitutive obligation arising from the meaning of the act of promising. She has no moral obligation to be a slave, and the lack of sufficient binding force of this obligation (the fact that it would be overridden by external considerations) can be explained only by appealing to an external moral principle. Given that Searle separates the binding force of promissory obligations from moral principles, he would have to maintain deafening silence as to why someone who has intentionally and freely given herself up into slavery, or to be the victim of torture, does not have an obligation to be a slave or to be tortured.

CONCLUSION

I have tried to canvass Searle's philosophy through an analysis of the interconnections of his theory of action, his theory of speech acts, and his general social ontology. I have argued that Searle's account of intentions is so rigorous that even he himself at times betrays it. I have also shown how Searle uses promises in the deployment of his social ontology. And I have suggested that, for all the many different topics that Searle has touched upon, and against preponderant opinions, Searle has not discussed ethics. Of course, this need not be a devastating objection. It is at least in part because Searle has been interpreted as dealing with ethics, and because Searle himself claims that he aims at some sort of comprehensive philosophical system, that the neglect of ethics within his philosophy deserves special attention.

Searle's forays into the derivation of evaluative statements from purely descriptive statements might still raise an important issue for philosophy in general and even perhaps, indirectly and in ways that need elaboration, for morality. There are different types of normativity. Searle is right when he asserts that "normativity is pretty much everywhere"[96] – in assertions and requests just as much as in promises and commands. But it is not *moral* normativity or aesthetic normativity that is pretty much everywhere. And generally, when philosophers argue about the nature of normativity, or its sources, they are concerned at least in part precisely with that type of normativity with which Searle is unconcerned.[97] Surely it would be an interesting enterprise to study the different types of normativity, and this enterprise might contain lessons valuable for moral philosophy. There might be commonalities between different types of normativity, and thus Searle's analysis of the general normativity of meaning might contain lessons applicable to the specifics of moral normativity.

My suggestion that Searle's sophisticated philosophical system is not as comprehensive as he thinks it is, or as it should be, must be read above all as an exhortation. It would be valuable to see where ethics fit within his scheme. Given that Searle has claimed that "realism and a correspondence conception [of truth] are essential presuppositions of any sane philosophy,"[98] given that he is so interested in the ontology of aspects of the world that are not studied by physics, it would be interesting to discover what his views are regarding, say, *moral* realism and other metaethical issues. Are there any moral facts? If so, are they brute facts or social facts? If not, how would his views of the status of morality be consistent with his ontology of social reality? In spite of the fact that Searle has charged the classical tradition in philosophy with suffering from "an unhealthy obsession with something called 'ethics' and 'morality',"[99] one still hopes that someday Searle will deal with these questions.

Notes

1. John R. Searle, *The Construction of Social Reality* (New York: Free Press, 1995), p. xi.
2. See the references in Ernest Lepore and Robert Van Gulick (eds.), *John Searle and His Critics* (Oxford: Blackwell, 1991), p. 394. Over ten years ago, Lepore and Van Gulick counted fifteen reprints (in different languages) of the article in volumes devoted to ethics.
3. John R. Searle, "How to Derive 'Ought' from 'Is'," *Philosophical Review* 73 (1964): 43–58.
4. John R. Searle, *Intentionality: An Essay in the Philosophy of Mind* (Cambridge: Cambridge University Press, 1983), p. 1.
5. Ibid., p. 29.
6. Ibid., pp. 31–2.
7. Ibid., p. 36.
8. Ibid., p. 31.
9. Ibid., p. 34.
10. Searle, moreover, avoids potential ambiguity regarding the term 'intentional' by distinguishing between uppercase 'Intentionality' as a property of mental states and events and lowercase 'intentionality' as a property of human actions. I shall generally ignore the uppercase/lowercase distinction here, since the ways in which I use 'intentional' leave no room for ambiguity.
11. *Intentionality*, p. 82.
12. Ibid., pp. 12–13.
13. Ibid., p. 122.
14. Ibid.
15. Ibid., p. 81.
16. Ibid., p. 80.
17. Ibid., p. 122 and passim.
18. J. L. Austin, *How to Do Things with Words* (Oxford: Oxford University Press, 1962).
19. *Intentionality*, p. 139.

20. See Donald Davidson, *Essays on Actions and Events* (Oxford: Oxford University Press, 1980).

21. I have argued against this view as well; see Leo Zaibert, "Collective Intentions and Collective Intentionality," *American Journal of Economics and Sociology* 62 (2002): 209–232. This view has come to be called, a bit acrimoniously, the "simple view"; see also Michael Bratman, *Intentions, Plans, and Practical Reason* (Cambridge, Mass.: Harvard University Press, 1980).

22. Brian O'Shaughnessy, "Searle's Theory of Action," in Ernest LePore (ed.), *John Searle and His Critics* (Oxford: Blackwell, 1991), especially pp. 271–9.

23. Ibid., p. 263.

24. Ibid., p. 297.

25. Ibid.

26. For more on the nature of this distinction, and for analyses of dimensions of the distinction between prior intentions and intentions-in-action that are relevant and interesting, see Joelle Proust's chapter in this volume.

27. *The Construction of Social Reality*, p. 13.

28. Ibid., p. 14.

29. Ibid., pp. 43ff.

30. Ibid., p. 41.

31. Institutional facts are a subset of social facts. There is an uneasy relationship between the distinction between brute and institutional facts, on the one hand, and the title of Searle's book *The Construction of Social Reality*, on the other. Searle is much more concerned with institutional facts than with social facts; perhaps the book should have been more accurately titled *The Construction of Institutional Reality*. Both social and institutional facts, in any event, require collective intentionality (*The Construction of Social Reality*, p. 26).

32. Ibid., p. 28 and passim.

33. Ibid., p. 25.

34. Ibid., p. 37.

35. Ibid., pp. 26ff.

36. See Zaibert, "Collective Intentions and Collective Intentionality." Skepticism regarding collective intentions need not extend to skepticism regarding collective actions. Winning a soccer match, for example, is something that cannot be done other than by a collective. But this does not entail that there exists any collective intention at play here. The eleven players of a soccer team might collectively wish to win, and, in addition, they might have complicated sets of interrelated individual intentions.

37. John R. Searle, "Collective Intentions and Actions," in P. Cohen *et al.* (eds.), *Intentions in Communication* (Cambridge, Mass.: Bradford Books, 1990).

38. John R. Searle, *Rationality in Action* (Cambridge, Mass: MIT Press, 2001), p. 208.

39. John R. Searle, *Speech Acts: An Essay in the Philosophy of Language* (Cambridge: Cambridge University Press, 1969), p. 59.

40. Ibid., p. 60.

41. The reason I alter Searle's own numbering and ordering of the conditions is that I want to group together those conditions that directly involve promissory intentions.

42. *Speech Acts*, pp. 57–61.

43. Other, less constructivist accounts of promises, most notably Adolf Reinach's – Adolf Reinach, "Die apriorischen Grundlagen des bürgerlichen Rechts," *Jahrbuch für Philosophie und phänomenologische Forschung* 1:2 (1989): 685–847; Eng. trans. by J. F. Crosby as "The Apriori Foundations of the Civil Law," *Aletheia* 3 (1983): 1–142 – might avoid making the obligatoriness of a promise depend on social institutions by suggesting that promises are obligatory a priori. As Barry Smith points out, "for Reinach promise and obligation are elements in a complex natural hierarchy of universally instantiable categories.... Reinach holds... that there is a family of uninventable and intrinsically intelligible categories which serve as the necessary basis for rule-formation in the institutional sphere. Thus there could not, according to Reinach, arise institutions which did not reflect the basic categories of, for example, utterance-phenomena, claims, obligations, and their interrelations." Barry Smith, "An Essay on Material Necessity," in P. Hanson and B. Hunter (eds.), *Return of the A Priori* (*Canadian Journal of Philosophy*, supplementary volume 18, 1992).

44. John R. Searle, *Speech Acts: An Essay in the Philosophy of Language* (Cambridge: Cambridge University Press, 1969), p. 44.

45. Ibid.

46. Paul Grice, *Studies in the Way of Words* (Cambridge, Mass.: Harvard University Press, 1989), pp. 86ff., 213ff.

47. John Rawls, *A Theory of Justice*, rev. ed. (Cambridge, Mass.: Harvard University Press, 1999), p. 305.

48. Ibid., emphasis added.

49. Luis M. Valdés Villanueva, the translator of *Rationality in Action* into Spanish, translates (correctly, I think) 'commitment' as '*compromiso*'. The etymological connection between 'promise' and 'compromise' is much weaker in English than it is in Spanish. In English, 'compromise' has multifarious meanings, and the most popular ones have little connection with being obligated and much to do with reaching diplomatic solutions to impasses. In Spanish, unlike English, the connection between promises (*promesas*) and the generation of obligations (*compromisos*) is evident in the very words used to express that connection.

50. See W. D. Hudson (ed.)., *The Is/Ought Problem* (London: Macmillan/St. Martin's Press, 1969).

51. See, for example, the articles by R. M. Hare, by J. E. McClellan and B. P. Komisar, and by James and Judith Thomson in Hudson (ed.), *The Is/Ought Problem*.

52. *Speech Acts*, pp. 132ff.

53. Ibid., p. 132.

54. Ibid.

55. Ibid., p. 176.

56. Ibid.

57. A. N. Prior, *Logic and the Basis of Ethics* (Oxford: Oxford University Press, 1949). See also David Brink, *Moral Realism and the Foundations of Ethics* (Cambridge: Cambridge University Press, 1989), p. 150.

58. Brink, *Moral Realism*, pp. 149ff.; Charles R. Pigden, "Naturalism," in Peter Singer (ed.), *A Companion to Ethics* (Oxford: Blackwell, 1991), pp. 421ff.

59. *Speech Acts*, p. 189.

60. David Hume, *A Treatise Concerning Human Understanding*, ed. L. A. Selby-Bigge (Oxford: Clarendon Press, 1888), pp. 469–70.

61. G. E. Moore, *Principia Ethica* (Cambridge: Cambridge University Press, 1959), pp. 12–13 and passim.

62. Karl Popper, *The Open Society and Its Enemies*, rev. ed. (Princeton, N.J.: Princeton University Press, 1966), vol. 1, pp. 62–79.

63. Brink, *Moral Realism*, pp. 144–70.

64. D. D. Raphael, *Problems of Political Philosophy*, 2nd ed. (Atlantic Highlands, N.J.: Humanities Press, 1990), p. 175.

65. Ibid.

66. Ibid.

67. *Speech Acts*, p. 187.

68. Ken Witkoski, "The 'Is-Ought' Gap: Deduction or Justification," *Philosophy and Phenomenological Research* 39 (1979): 233–45.

69. A. C. Genova, "Institutional Facts and Brute Values," *Ethics* 81 (1970): 36–54.

70. J. R. Cameron, "'Ought' and Institutional Obligation," *Philosophy* 46 (1971): 309–22.

71. *Speech Acts*, pp. 175–98.

72. "How to Derive 'Ought' from 'Is'," p. 43.

73. *The Construction of Social Reality*, p. 120.

74. Of course, Searle has made some *remarks* on ethics. In *Rationality in Action* (pp. 149 ff.), for example, there is an interesting (though brief) section entitled "Egotism and Altruism in the Beast." Nonetheless, Searle's scant remarks on ethics are peripheral to his philosophy and smack of marginalia.

75. John R. Searle, *Razones Para Actuar: Una Teoría del libre Albedrío* (Oviedo: Nobel, 2000); John R. Searle, *Rationality in Action* (Cambridge, Mass.: MIT Press, 2001).

76. Ibid., p. 167.

77. Ibid., p. 173.

78. Ibid., p. 173ff. and passim.

79. Ibid., p. 171.

80. Ibid., p. 174.

81. Ibid., p. 175.

82. *Razones Para Actuar*, p. 208. In *Rationality in Action*, whose text is virtually identical to that found in *Razones Para Actuar*, Searle nevertheless qualifies this claim by adding one word: in English, he says "almost all speech acts have an element of promising" (*Rationality in Action*, p. 181).

83. Ibid.

84. Ibid., p. 176.

85. Ibid., p. 175ff.

86. For all Searle has done by way of analysis of intentional actions, he has yet to define voluntary actions. It is likely that if an action is done intentionally, then it is, by default, also done voluntarily; see L. A. Zaibert, "Intentionality, Voluntariness and Criminal Liability," *Buffalo Criminal Law Review* 1(2) (1998): 340–382.

87. *Rationality in Action*, pp. 115, 116, 116.

88. Ibid., p. 117.

89. Ibid.

90. Ibid., pp. 117–18, emphasis added.

91. Ibid., p. 61ff. and passim.

92. *A Theory of Justice*, p. 304.

93. Ibid.

94. *Rationality in Action*, p. 199.

95. Ibid., pp. 198–9.

96. Ibid., p. 182.

97. See, e.g., Christine Korsgaard, *The Sources of Normativity* (Cambridge: Cambridge University Press, 1996).

98. *The Construction of Social Reality*, p. xiii.

99. *Rationality in Action*, p. 182.

4 Law

GEORGE P. FLETCHER

1. LAW IN SEARLE

The law is a system of verbal interactions. It is the arena of speech acts par excellence. What we do in the law is to make claims, justify violations, argue precedents, assert interpretations of statutory language, and seek social stability by convincing others that a certain rule is indeed "the law." All of these interactions require language. The idea of law without language is about as plausible as the idea of baseball without balls and bats.

Legal examples play a prominent part in John Searle's thinking about language. The examples that appeal to him are precisely those that illustrate verbal interaction in reliance on legal rules. Thus the law provides some of the best examples of performatives. Saying "I do" in a marriage ceremony effects the marriage. Saying "I divorce you" three times in certain Muslim countries terminates the marriage. Saying "This is yours" effectively transfers title under certain conditions.

These verbal expressions are performatives in the sense that the very act of reciting the words brings about a change in legal relationships. There are also performatives in areas outside the law. Games provide sterling examples. When the referee calls "Strike three," he declares the batter out. Games are like legal systems in the sense that they rest on accepted rules that express a common understanding about the practical consequences of reciting words under certain circumstances.

These performatives provide the foundation for Searle's theory of constitutive rules. Constitutive rules stand in contrast to regulative rules. The two are defined in the following passage from *Speech Acts* (Searle 1969, p. 33):

> I want to clarify a distinction between two different sorts of rules, which I shall call *regulative* and *constitutive* rules. . . . As a start we might say that regulative rules regulate antecedently or independently existing forms of behavior, for example, many rules of etiquette regulate interpersonal

relationships which exist independently of the rules. But constitutive rules do not merely regulate, they create or define new forms of behavior. The rules of football or chess, for example, do not merely regulate playing football or chess, but as it were they create the very possibility of playing such games.

Regulative rules attach consequences to phenomena that exist independently of the rules. Many rules of the legal system are of this sort: "If you kill another person, you go to jail for life." The form of the proposition is *if X, then Y*, where Y is a sanction imposed for engaging in conduct X. "The whole point of the criminal law," Searle claims, "is regulative, not constitutive" (Searle 1995, p. 50).

But, as Searle would concede, the regulative sanction Y can be restated as a consequence of a change in legal status that is defined by engaging in conduct X. Thus the proposition translates into the following constitutive rule: "If you intentionally kill another human being, you are guilty of murder. If you are found guilty of murder you are subject to life imprisonment." This proposition illustrates Searle's basic formula for constitutive rules:

X counts as Y in C.

In this formula, X stands for a fact about the world (killing), an event that can be described as a brute fact; Y is the legal status (being guilty of murder) that X acquires as a result of application of the constitutive rule; and C stands for the context in which X occurs.

The sharp distinction between brute facts (X) and institutional facts (Y) is essential to Searle's scheme. Institutional facts derive from brute facts by the application of a constitutive rule within some context C. Let us say a few words by way of clarification about each of these four terms in the formula: X, "counts as," Y, and C.

The X Term

In the easiest case, the X term consists in an event in the world that would be ontologically the same whether people perceived the event or not. These brute facts – for example, facts pertaining to the behavior of molecules – supposedly exist independently of language and interpretation. This is Searle's realism about the world. At one point, Searle contrasts "brute physical facts" with "mental facts" (Searle 1995, p. 121). The example of the brute fact is "There is snow on top of Mt. Everest." For Searle, there is "snow" on top of "Mount Everest" regardless of human perceptions and understanding.

Let us take a closer look at Searle's example from the law, namely, that killing under certain circumstances makes one guilty of murder. The fact of killing is hardly as straightforward as the facts of snow and of Mt. Everest, which are relatively free of interpretation. The term "killing" is used in the law only when one person causes the death of another person. Each of these terms – "person," "causes," "death," "another" – entails difficult questions and generates new formulas of the form "X counts as Y in C." For example, the concept of the person requires its own constitutive rule. It might read like this: "A fetus that has reached viability is a person." But now we have a problem with the concept of viability, which entails another proposition of the form "X counts as Y in C." Searle recognizes the possibility of these iterative functions, but he assumes that we eventually hit bedrock – a point where no further constitutive rules are necessary. Whether legal discourse rests on a bedrock of brute facts is by no means clear.

Significantly, Searle argues that the very articulation of words can satisfy the X term in his formula. This is the structure of performatives. The words are spoken and the requirements of X are satisfied. Then, a certain event – a speech act – is thought to occur as Y. The use of performative language X makes Y happen.

The Relationship "Counts As"

Searle claims that the transition from X to Y relies ineluctably on language. "The move from X to Y is eo ipso a linguistic move." His example is scoring points in a game of, say, football. Prelinguistic beings and animals cannot score points. They can kick the ball over the goal, thus satisfying the X term. But, Searle holds, without language they cannot be said to be kicking the ball *in order* to score a point. They can accidentally act according to the rule, but, without language, they cannot act because of the rule. They cannot think to themselves: I am doing this because if I do, a certain result will follow. There might be some debate, however, about whether conditioned behavior by dogs (whining to be fed) is equivalent to ringing a bell in order to summon the waiter.

Searle is probably right that the relationship "counts as" presupposes the use of language, but it does not follow from this indispensability of language that brute facts exist prior to their description in a language. The world – external reality, as Searle puts it – might exist. But the view according to which the mass of objects in a world without language would have no boundaries, no differentiation, cannot be ignored. More important for our purposes, however, is Searle's stress on the role of language in converting "brute facts" into institutional facts.

It is not so clear how X, the brute fact, becomes Y, the institutional fact. What does "counting as" actually amount to? Searle's technique is to assume a rule, a constitutive rule, which applies to X and converts X to Y. But what makes this rule binding? When I say the words "I promise," how do I and others conclude that a rule applies such that whenever someone says "I promise," he or she promises? In his earlier work, Searle referred to a practice that made the constitutive rule applicable. The rule was somehow implicit in a customary way of doings that was a called a "practice." In his more recent work, the word "practice" seems to have passed into disuse; the more common term is "acceptance." If the constitutive rule is accepted, then it applies to the event X and converts it to Y.

Both the terms "practice" and "acceptance" enjoy an illusion of immediacy and unanimity. Searle himself offers the ambiguous event of the American patriots' declaring independence from George III on July 4, 1776. In retrospect, we say that they issued a Declaration of Independence that took effect immediately. At the time, however, no one knew whether it was realistic to speak of independence. The same is true of the Constitution. It supposedly went into force in 1789, but many observers, particularly in Europe, hardly expected George Washington to surrender power when the "Constitution" required him to do so in 1797. The Declaration of Independence and the Constitution both have a force that they are accorded, as lawyers say, *nunc pro tunc* – now for then. We read the effect of these documents back into history only because we now accept them as binding.

Lawyers and philosophers might well think differently about the homogeneity of the acceptance that supposedly enables constitutive rules to work. In Searle's sense, constitutive rules are a matter of logical necessity. If you move your knight in any way that isn't allowed by the rules of chess, you simply are not playing chess. This sense of "logical necessity" depends on a strong consensus about the rules that apply in playing chess. For lawyers, however, dissensus and conflict are the basic rule of life, and therefore it is hard for lawyers to believe that any acceptance of any rule applies across the board. The problem would be in determining how much acceptance should be necessary to say that the constitutive rule holds. In New York City, for example, "traffic signals" at street corners display alternating green, yellow, and red lights. For many pedestrians, the red light stands for a command: do not cross the street. For others, the red light means: cross the street only if you are careful. In other words, the command not to cross is partially but not fully accepted. It is difficult to know, then, whether the brute fact of a red light in this context generates the institutional command not to cross even if there are no cars coming. Another example is the posted speed limit in the United States. When the number 65 appears as a posted limit, drivers naturally ask themselves, "What do you really mean? At what speed will the police issue tickets?" The brute fact is the number 65. The institutional fact of the speed limit, as effectively understood, varies from driver to driver. Some understand the institutional fact as a limit of 65 mph, others as 70 mph, and still others as 75 mph.

Philosophers are inclined to think of language as their paradigm of acceptance. Educated native speakers speak alike in 99.99% of all linguistic situations (they might differ on niceties such as "different than" and "different from"), and therefore they feel authorized to correct others who are still aspiring to master the language. If language is the model "practice" or the standard of "acceptance," then the phenomenon is relatively uncontroversial. "X counts as Y in C" works when it ascribes meaning (Y) to words spoken in the language (X).

But, it is worth noting, understanding the meaning of the number 65 on the speed limit sign differs from judgments about the speed at which the police will enforce the speed limit. If someone said that the sign reads 75 mph, when she meant that the police would enforce the speed limit at 75 mph, the error would be obvious to all.

The Y Term

The key to the Y term is the distinction between institutional and brute facts. The point of constitutive rules is that they generate institutional facts, such as money. Institutional facts have the following six properties (Searle 1995, p. 121). First, they are mental as opposed to brute facts. Second, they are intentional as opposed to nonintentional. Intentionality is "the capacity of the organism to represent objects and states of affairs in the world to itself" (Searle 1995, p. 7). The example given of a nonintentional mental state is "I am in pain." This is nonintentional, one surmises, because first-person pain statements are not representations about the world beyond the organism.

Third, the important examples of institutional facts are collective rather than singular. The institutions of money, marriage, and property require a collective understanding. An individual standing alone could not plausibly think of an object as "his" unless there were good reason to think that others would concur in the claim of ownership. This is an uncontroversial point.

More difficult is the apparatus that Searle develops to support his idea of collective intentionality. He claims that individuals can use a collective "we" in formulating their understandings of the world. There will be more about this claim later.

Fourth, institutional facts – at least facts such as money – require the collective assignment of a function to a process. There has to be a point to exchanging pieces of paper called dollar bills. The fact that people engage in this ritual is not enough to account for the phenomenon. Nonintentional phenomena can have collectively assigned functions. Searle's favorite example is the assignment of the function of "pumping blood" to the heart.

While the function or purpose of exchanging dollars is part of the idea of money, the functions of marriage and property are not so clear. Some people think that the function of property is to protect the privacy of the owner; others make the instrumental claim that property serves the goal of efficient economic exchanges. It is not necessary to resolve that dispute in order to acknowledge that property exists as a collective intentional phenomenon.

To summarize, in Searle's scheme, those facts that are (1) mental, (2) intentional, (3) collective, and (4) receive an assigned function must satisfy additional requirements in order to be institutional facts. They must (5) have agentive functions and (6) be status functions. Agentive functions are those that we assign to things that serve our purposes. We might say that the heart has the function of pumping blood without thereby thinking of anything that we gain by this function. Of course, the very fact that we say that the function of the heart is to pump blood – rather than, say, to make a thumping noise – says something about us and our system of values. This kind of "interest" is not enough for Searle to think of the function as agentive. Money clearly has an agentive function, because the purposes we assign to those bits of green paper have a direct bearing on our economic lives.

The final distinction is between agentive functions that are causal and those that assign statuses. The concept of money assigns a status, as do the institutions of property and marriage. The contrary example is "This is a screwdriver," which highlights the instrumental understanding of this particular agentive function assigned to objects shaped like screwdrivers. This distinction is a bit mysterious and not worthy of too much attention. The conclusion, however, is important. The existence of money is an institutional fact, but the existence of screwdrivers is not.

Searle introduces one further distinction that raises some problems. He claims that money is a nonlinguistic fact but that promises are (merely!) linguistic facts. It is not clear what he means by this, except to suggest that money presupposes a real object (the bits of green paper) and that promises to pay do not count as money. If this is the argument, it is surely mistaken. Credit cards create a form of money. As economists understand the phenomenon, debt increases M1, the money supply. The credit received in these transactions can be resold in secondary markets. Is this debt something more than the linguistic fact of a promise to pay? But, of course, if promises to pay are money that can be used to purchase goods and services, then we should have problems with the entire scheme of inferring institutional facts from brute facts such as pieces of green paper. It might be possible to save Searle's system with a complicated series of iterative transactions beginning with the linguistic fact "I promise to pay," but the resultant scheme will face difficulties when people persist in inventing new forms of payment that are equivalent to traditional forms of money.

The mistake of associating money with things resembles the mistake of assuming that property rights must be connected to things. Although transactions in physical objects may lie at the origin of property, the notion has grown beyond the realm of the tangible. Consider copyright, the common law property right in creative writings. It is not the thing that is owned but rather the right to control reproduction of the thing. This right remains in the hands of the copyright holder even if the concrete writing that gives rise to the claim belongs to another. Letters are a good example. The letter as physical object belongs to the recipient, but the writer retains the copyright. Whether this kind of institutional fact falls into the category of the linguistic or the nonlinguistic may not be subject to clear resolution.

The Context C

The context consists in the circumstances required for application of the constitutive rule. Saying "I do" concludes a marriage only if the background conditions are specified. It has to be wedding ceremony, not a play or a rehearsal for a wedding. The person officiating must be authorized by law to perform the ceremony. The requisite number of witnesses must be present; the parties must be of age; they cannot be related to each other in any prohibited way – the conditions are almost endless.

There is an interesting problem in deciding whether particular facts are constitutive of the X term or fall into the C category. Let us return to the example of killing (X), which becomes murder (Y) in the context C. The problem is: what belongs to X and what defines the background conditions C? Is the fact that the intended object of the killing is a "person" rather than a fetus at an early stage of gestation part of the background circumstances, or is it constitutive of the X term? One could describe the X term as "killing a living thing." Whether the thing killed is understood as a person might be part of the context C. The more one drives the X term back toward "brute facts," the more one will be inclined to pack factors like "personhood of the being killed" into the context C. But at a certain point, the X term can suffer no further abstraction. "Killing" has a natural meaning in the language, and this accepted meaning includes many of the factors that might technically be regarded as circumstances – for example, the personhood of the victim, the intention of the "killer," the causal relationship between the "killer's" actions and the death.

There is some disagreement about whether the conditions for C can be specified in advance as a set of necessary and sufficient conditions. H. L. A. Hart once argued that the conditions for a successful performative should be understood as defeasible. The result Y follows in the normal case; but in an abnormal case, the apparent killing would not qualify as a murder. It is not possible to specify all of these circumstances in advance. For example, in warfare, killing is not murder. Nor is killing murder when committed in self-defense. Whether the necessity of saving lives can justify a killing is disputed in the law. And there is still disagreement about whether excuses, such as insanity, affect the operation of the rule that converts homicide into murder. It could be said, in ethics as well as in law, that an insane assailant does commit murder, but the murder is excused. But in my view, Hart's original insight is correct: there is no way to specify all of the circumstances bearing on justified homicide in advance. There will also be debate about the possibility of adding previously unrecognized grounds of justification.

Hart's original position finds resonance in Searle's approach to deriving 'is' from 'ought' (Searle 1969a). The logical transition from the fact "I promise X" to the conclusion "I ought to do X" follows in the normal case. But there might be a whole array of conflicting factors that render the situation abnormal and therefore block the inference from 'is' to 'ought.' Searle captured this requirement of normalcy by adding a ceteris paribus clause to every stage of his derivation of the 'ought' statement from the 'is' statement. This possibility of unforseen changes in the circumstances is quite familiar to international lawyers. The basic rule of international treaty making is *pacta sunt servanda* (treaties are binding), with the escape clause added: *rebus sic stantibus* (unless the circumstances change). In the normal case, the fact of making the treaty entails a duty to perform.

In conclusion, there seem to be two distinct paths for reaching the conclusion that certain bits of green paper count as money. One path is to apply the formula "X counts as Y in C," where X refers to the green paper and Y is the same piece of paper with the status of money. The other path is to apply the series of six ordered distinctions, set forth earlier, in order to establish that money is an institutional fact. The fact of understanding a piece of paper as money must be (1) mental, (2) intentional, and (3) collective; and it must (4) represent an assigned function, (5) stand for an agentive function, and (6) have a status function. It is not at all clear that these two paths always converge. There might be many institutional facts derived by the first formula for constitutive rules that do not satisfy the requirements of the six ordered distinctions in Searle's decision tree (Searle 1995, p. 121). I have mentioned the example of marriage, which is undoubtedly an institutional fact, but about which there might well be disagreement on whether the institution has a function and what that function is.

The aspect of the law that appeals to Searle, it is worth noting, is not the sanctions, a feature that some positivists, such as the nineteenth-century philosopher John Austin, thought to be essential to a legal system. It is rather the language by which sanctions are demanded, justified, and rationalized that informs Searle's theory. This is the internal, as opposed to the external, aspect of the legal culture. The linguistic, internal aspect of law is replete with institutional facts and constitutive rules. The problems of greatest concern to legal philosophers lie elsewhere. A survey of five of these disputed areas reveals the fecundity of Searle's intellectual apparatus.

2. SEARLE IN LAW

The Law and the Facts

The distinction between the law and the facts is fundamental to the way lawyers approach the world. In the classic syllogism of legal reasoning, the law is expressed in the major premise and the facts are stated in the minor premise. The judge determines the law and instructs the jury accordingly; the jury finds the facts and is supposed to apply the law, as stated in the instructions, to the facts so determined. This simple model of judicial reasoning conforms to Searle's formula for constitutive rules. The judge determines the constitutive rule, "X counts as Y in C," the jury finds X and C, applies the rule, and concludes Y.

In practice, however, this sharp cleavage between facts and law breaks down. There are many mixed questions of fact and law, which are left to the jury's determination. The most common is the question of reasonable behavior. In a negligence case, the jury decides whether the plaintiff and the defendant behaved as a reasonable person would have under the circumstances.

The discussion of negligence in the law brings to the fore the distinction between objective and subjective criteria, a distinction that concerns Searle in various contexts. This distinction intersects with another, namely, that between the ontological and the epistemic. The fact that there is snow on the mountain is objective in both senses. There is indeed snow on the mountain (if the claim is true), and the fact obtains regardless of subjective perception. When the element of human purpose is introduced, then facts become ontologically subjective – a screwdriver, for example, is used to turn screws. Epistemic subjectivity seems to require some personal input in making an evaluative decision. Searle's example is the judgment "The moon is beautiful tonight."

Artifacts of the law such as contracts, corporations, and property rights serve human purposes, and therefore they are ontologically subjective. Admittedly, there is some disagreement about whether the perception of these institutional facts is epistemically subjective or objective. Those who think that you can read the law off the words printed on the page of a statute would be inclined to think that the existence of contracts, corporations, and property rights is objective; but the inclination in legal thought today is to recognize the input of personal judgment in asserting and affirming legal rights and duties.

Searle's categories provide a useful lens for understanding and interpreting a wide range of jurisprudential positions. The classic view of legal norms held that they are objectively epistemic. There is some sense in which positivists today – including leading figures such as H. L. A. Hart and Jules Coleman – hold to this position of epistemic objectivity. They believe that it is possible to determine whether a particular rule is or is not a rule of law by determining whether it derives from a "rule of recognition" – a practice in the society of recognizing certain sources as authoritative sources of law. Ronald Dworkin, by contrast, has repeatedly asserted that the rule of recognition is inherently incomplete; it cannot provide a foundation for all of the "principles" and other values applied in the course of legal debate. As I read Dworkin, his view should be understood as endorsing the role of personal input in asserting principles and their weight in resolving legal disputes. Contemporary positivists, following Hart, hold to a narrower view of law, tied to a rule of recognition; and yet they have no objection to the use of extralegal moral norms in resolving disputes.

The so-called legal realists, led by figures such as Jerome Frank and Karl Lewellyn, adopted another version of epistemic subjectivity. Their highly influential view is that judges always bring to bear personal and subjective values in deciding cases. Justice Oliver Wendell Holmes, Jr. captured the realist position in one line when he wrote: "Abstract principles do not decide concrete cases." The realists would, of course, be highly skeptical of anything like Searle's formula "X counts as Y in context C" as an account of legal reasoning. Bruce Ackerman interpreted the realist movement of the 1930s and 1940s as a necessary step in the restructuring of American law from a reactive system designed to protect private rights to an activist and interventionist system designed to promote the welfare of society. According to this view, the guiding motives of legal reform stood for a coherent "subjectivist" view of what the law should be.

The "realists" went further than attacking the epistemic objectivity of the law. Under the rubric of "fact-skepticism," some also argued that the finding of facts was always, or at least typically, subjective. This critique of the objectivity of the legal system is expressed in the claim that all decision makers exercise "discretion" in finding either the law or the facts. We will return to this topic later.

The critical legal studies movement went one step further and argued, at least in its dominant form, that the political purposes behind legal argument were themselves torn by contradiction and radical uncertainty. The system did not even rise to the level of being epistemically subjective, to the extent that Searle's concept implies a coherent and consistent effort to determine what the law is.

Law as Fact

Let us recall Searle's proposition that the criminal law is basically about regulating behavior but that some constitutive rules are necessary to express legal propositions of status and liability. Significantly, many jurisprudential efforts have sought to maximize the extent to which legal phenomena are subject to reformulation as purely regulative rules about factual events. Thus the punishment of murderers can be restated without using the concept of murder, or arguably any legal concept at all. The argument is that this can be done by recasting legal rules in hypothetical form: "If A, B, . . . and M are all satisfied, then the defendant shall be locked up in a penitentiary." A through M cover all of the factual and procedural events that must occur before the defendant is punished. This view is sometimes attributed to Hans Kelsen, who was the first major positivist thinker of the twentieth century.

Hart responded to this view by distinguishing between primary and secondary rules. Primary rules attach sanctions to behavior. They are of the form, "If you injure another person, you must pay damages." Secondary rules are prescriptions for bringing about institutional facts. They are of the form, "If A offers to do X if B does Y, and B agrees, then A and B have made a contract." These prescriptions are like recipes, except that the outcome is not a cake but a contract. They are classic examples of constitutive rules of the form "X counts as Y in C." The failure to follow the rules does not result in a sanction but merely in a failed performance: no Y is produced. The distinction between primary and secondary rules has much in common with Searle's distinction between regulative and constitutive rules.

The debate between Kelsen and Hart centered on whether the failure of the attempted transaction should be treated as a sanction. In Searle's terms, this would be equivalent to asking whether the failure to realize a constitutive rule constituted a penalty for breaching a regulative rule. If you move your knight in the wrong way, you are "penalized" by having your move disqualified. Hart held that reducing "failed performances" to "sanctions for violations" misconstrued the phenomena at work. Hart's distinction between primary and secondary rules conforms more closely to the way lawyers actually think about what they are doing, and part of that thought process consists in applying constitutive rules for creating institutional facts such as contracts, corporations, marriages, and copyrights. The significant feature of these facts is that they may come into being without anyone ever suffering any sanctions.

Discretion

The "realist" thrust during the 1930s and 1940s led to the view that judges always make a "choice" when they decide disputes. The same is true of juries – they are always exercising discretion in applying the law to the facts. If this were correct, it would represent a serious challenge to a view such as Searle's, according to which linguistically formulated constitutive rules operate in the law to create institutional facts. These facts would not come into being by the operation of rules, but by virtue of the choice or discretion exercised by the decision maker. Searle's formula would have to be reformulated as "X counts as Y in C if the decision maker thinks so." This view about discretion in judging is well entrenched in American legal thought.

Dworkin responded to the orthodox "realists" by developing an argument about why their use of discretion should be understood in various weak senses that would not undermine the application of constitutive rules. It is not clear whether Dworkin's argument won many adherents, as the responses to his classic article "The Model of Rules" (1969) went off in several different directions.

The precise difference between discretion in the strong and weak senses is not so clear, but there is one restriction on discretion implicit in the meaning of the word. If the object of the decision is either true or false, then the decision maker does *not* have discretion in deciding whether it is true or false. The paradigm cases of discretion in the law are those where there is no issue of truth. They are administrative decisions – to allocate funds efficiently, to manage trials, to grant or not grant additional broadcasting licenses. The standard for discretion is not truth but good management. Within the realm of his discretion, a decision maker cannot be mistaken. Thus if we believe, with Searle, that external reality exists and that it is structured more or less as we suppose it to be in our scientific world picture, then there is a truth to be discovered about the facts underlying legal disputes. The task of juries is to find this truth, and if they get it wrong then they are mistaken. If there is a fact of the matter, then there is no room for choice or personal preference in deciding what the facts are.

The difficult question is whether there is truth in law in the same way that there is truth about the external world. Does the law permit an inquiry that resembles the nondiscretionary effort to determine the facts of a case? There is a truth about the perennial question of whether the defendant "did it." Is there a corresponding truth about whether what he did should be classified as murder, manslaughter, or justifiable self-defense? If there is, then judges and juries do not have discretion in determining and applying the law. Hart thought that this was true about the core cases that fell under legal rules. Yet he was willing to recognize discretion in the penumbra of the rule's application. Dworkin tried to go further than Hart on this point. To make his case, he needed an argument about why legal propositions should be true or false in the same way that factual claims are true or false. He found this argument in the claim that for every legal dispute, there might be a "right answer." As long as there might be a right answer, then judges are obligated to try to find it. They may not fall back on their preferences or discretion as a way of resolving the dispute.

Intelligibility

Yet there is no way of proving that there is a right answer. The problem is similar to the one that Searle eventually concedes about efforts to establish external reality. At the end of *The Construction of Social Reality*, Searle insists (1) that attempts to show that external reality does not exist fail, quite grotesquely, and (2) that the existence of the external world is presupposed by our most basic behavior. Yet at the same time, he acknowledges that all proofs of reality's existence fail, and therefore he falls back on the assumption that we presuppose external reality in order to make sense of the vast body of discourse that proceeds as though the world did exist. This is "the argument of intelligibility," and it appealed to Dworkin as well. The argument for the existence of right answers in legal disputes is that the participants in these disputes proceed on the assumption that there is a right answer. Lawyers come into court making arguments about rights and what the Constitution requires. If there were no truth possible in these arguments, we could not intelligibly grasp the claims they were making.

Arguments from intelligibility seem to work only for those who intuitively share the beliefs of those they are trying to render intelligible. The argument goes something like this. "I believe that other people are making sense. Therefore, I assume what I need to assume in order to account for my belief." Others are intelligible, and I am intelligible to myself; therefore, I must be making assumptions about the grid of beliefs in which this conversation occurs.

For this argument to work, the speaker must assume the intelligibility of his own first-person statements. If we were simply observing others as they talk – say, about astrology or their cult gods – we could find them intelligible even if we posited that they were talking about imaginary entities. But if we sincerely make statements about the facts of the world or about rights and duties embedded in legal discourse, then we must be making assumptions about the existence of those things that we are talking about.

This argument does not prove as much as one might wish. All it establishes, so far as I can tell, is a set of beliefs about the world. Whether these beliefs are warranted is not self-evident.

Acceptance and Authority

The operation of constitutive rules presupposes acceptance of these rules. For a brute fact to become an institutional fact, the transformation must find support in the attitudes of those for whom the institutional fact resonates as true. If no one accepts that "X counts as Y in C," it would be difficult to assert the existence of the rule.

This way of thinking about institutional facts runs afoul of one of the basic premises of modern legal culture. We can state this premise as the evolution of validity as a substitute for acceptance as a criterion for a law's having force. In customary legal systems, all laws must be directly accepted.

They arise by interaction within the society and come to be accepted as binding. Habit becomes binding. Customs become law. That is, in Hart's felicitous phrase, people eventually start behaving in conformity to rules not just "as" a rule but "because of" the rules.

When modern legislatures start enacting new laws, these laws become binding – at least according to the conventional view – not because they are accepted but because they are validly enacted. All that needs to be accepted by the society, according to Hart, is the rule of recognition that establishes the constitutional order, which in turn confers legislative authority on certain bodies.

The question, then, is whether legislative authority can establish constitutive rules that are not accepted but that are operative solely on the basis of legislative authority. This is not a simple question. Searle gives the example of knighthood, the meaning of which evolved as kings started knighting persons who did not display the abilities possessed by medieval knights. Over time, the title became honorific, and no one was surprised if a newly knighted politician had no retinue and no fencing skills. In this case, the authoritative practice changed the meaning of the concept, but this might not always happen.

Consider the case of marriage. Suppose that legislatures recognize homosexual marriages, but that the society fails to accept the idea. People begin to distinguish between real marriages and technical marriages, in the way that some people in religious cultures distinguish between real marriages (in the church) and civil marriages. That is, the constitutive rule, "X counts as Y in C," does not necessarily expand just because the legislature redefines it to accommodate new cases of X. There might be cases in which the constitutive rule changes over time and other cases in which it does not. If this is true, then there is some residual force to Searle's argument that constitutive rules always require acceptance. Authority is not sufficient to change the rule if the people who apply the rule in their daily lives are not convinced that they should make the shift.

Collective Intentions

Recall the stage in Searle's argument at which he introduces collective intentions in order to express the idea that an entire group of people assign a function to a particular object. Legal theory has long struggled with the problem of collective intentions, and it may be that Searle's views here could fill an important gap in the way that lawyers think about the problem.

The most significant arena of collective intention is the enactment of legislation. Parliamentary bodies act as a group in voting on bills. Their intentions in passing the bill then seem, to subsequent interpreters, to provide an important guide for construing their words. After all, if a single officer gave a command to a soldier, "Go up the hill," the soldier would surely want to know which hill the officer had in mind. If a group of people give the command "Go up the hill," the recipient of the command should also want to know which hill the commanders have in mind.

The problem, of course, is that when a group of people give the command, they may have several different hills in mind. And this is frequently the case with legislation. Those who vote on the bill may have several different objectives for agreeing on the same language. In what sense, then, do legislators act with a collective intention? Perhaps there is no collective intention at all but merely a collection of individual parallel intentions.

Searle claims that a collective intention exists when each of the actors conceives of himself as participating in a coordinated action. 'Coordinated' means that each actor is aware of the others' acts and sees her action as an aspect of the entire effort. Each violinist plays her part, but together the orchestra plays the symphony. No individual could play the symphony alone, as no single player could execute a pass play in football. These coordinated actions require a common consciousness that "we" are doing this thing together. Searle's recognition of "we-intentions" strikes me as more convincing than the competing theory, which reduces all collective activity to individuals having the individualized intention to play their musical parts in anticipation that others will act with harmonious intentions. A "we-intention" comes into being if people think to themselves as they are doing it, "we intend."

In the case of a legislature, the minimal collective intention we can attribute to the majority is the collective intention to pass the bill as written. Different people may have different ulterior motives for coming to an agreement on the language of the law, but that is their business. Under this analysis, the ulterior purposes of the individual legislators should not bear on the interpretation of the collective decision. The only "we-intention" expressed in the collective command "Go up the hill" is the intention to use those words in expressing the command.

Of course, when there are two hills that might be referred to, there might be a way of fathoming that the collective commanders meant to refer to hill A rather than hill B. This would require ascribing to the collective actor an additional intention to refer to hill A. This is where we enter the thicket of contemporary debates about statutory interpretation. The notion of legislative purpose – to solve a particular problem or to address a particular evil – may be the consequence of a collective purpose, but the "purpose" may simply be the best construction that can be assigned to the language of the statute in the time and place of its enactment. This is the approach that Dworkin called interpreting the statute by placing it in its best light.

The interpretation of legislative language often passes itself off as the discovery of a collective intention, but in fact the interpretation represents the collective assignment of a new meaning to the old words. The history of the equal protection clause of the Fourteenth Amendment illustrates this phenomenon. We do not know what the collective intention of those who adopted this amendment was, and certainly we do not know their purposes with regard to school integration. For the first half of the twentieth century, the court and most of the legal profession collectively read the amendment to mean that segregated schools could be "separate but equal." Then, in 1954, the Court unanimously assigned a new meaning to the words, and this soon came to be accepted by the legal profession and by most Americans – namely, that segregated schools were inherently unequal.

Our easy reliance on the phrases "collective intention," "collective assignment," and "acceptance" illustrates how useful Searle's conceptual framework can be in formulating views in legal philosophy.

5 | Action

JOËLLE PROUST

Among the many important new views developed in Searle's *Intentionality* is an innovative theory of action. This theory involves two kinds of claims. First, it suggests that action itself (rather than the beliefs and desires that might contribute to causing it) has a general structure common to all of the Intentional[1] states, and a specific causal-reflexive structure that it shares with perception and memory. Second, it explores the way in which actions performed without a prior intention are still intentional, and share in part the same structure as planned actions. The combination of these two features allows one and the same theory to account for embodied action, for dependence of content on context, and for metacognition, in an impressively economic way. The goal of this chapter will be to explore the several facets of this theory of action. We will also suggest some possible extensions.

John Searle's project in *Intentionality* is to accommodate action within this general approach. The mental state of intending to act, too, he wants to understand within the framework of a theory of Intentionality, that is, a theory of the central features that constitute representations as conditions of satisfaction. There is indeed a promising analogy between intending and other mental states such as desire and belief. Just as a perception is *veridical*, a belief is *true*, a desire is *fulfilled*, if and only if the states of affairs they represent obtain, so, similarly, an intention is *carried out* if a change in the world occurs as required by its conditions of satisfaction. The notion of a direction of fit, which had been successfully applied to speech acts,[2] applies across all of the Intentional states, including intention and action. Perceptions and beliefs have a mind-to-world direction of fit: their conditions of satisfaction are essentially determined by the way the world is, independent of the thinking subject. Desires, wishes, and intentions, by contrast, have a world-to-mind direction of fit: their conditions of satisfaction require some specific change in the world.[3] It is intrinsic to the representational nature of the Intentional states that the latter *might* in one way or another fail to fit. This possibility is conceptually dependent on the very idea that a representation is *directed at* a state of affairs, *constituted by its conditions of satisfaction*. The two kinds of directions of fit therefore correspond to two ways in which an Intentional state can fail: either because the mind fails to register correctly a state of affairs or a property, or because the world fails to match the mental representation in regard to some relevant state of affairs or property.

Two obstacles need to be overcome, however, in order for this assimilation of intending to Intentional states to be really convincing.[4] First, there is a series of asymmetries between the conceptual analysis of action, on the one hand, and that of belief and desire, on the other, that needs an explanation:

1. Intentions have "actions" as conditions of satisfaction, whereas there is no special name for the conditions of satisfaction of beliefs and desires.
2. There are many states of affairs that are not objects of belief, and many states of affairs that are not desired, but there are no actions without corresponding intentions (even though the latter may be poorly reflected in the eventual outcome of our acting).

The second obstacle that an adequate theory has to overcome is that of accounting for actions whose prior intentions are satisfied in terms of their general goal, but in a deviant, unanticipated way. Such actions are normally taken to be unintentional. I may do something that I intend to do, and nevertheless fail to satisfy my intention.[5] In Davidson's famous example,[6] a climber may want to loosen his hold on a rope in order to be safe at the expense of another climber's life, and become so unnerved by his intending to do so that he does in fact loosen his hold. Why can't he be said to have loosened it intentionally, given that he was forming the very intention to loosen it?

The analysis of action that Searle provides seeks to solve such puzzles, first by completing the traditional view of prior intention by giving an intentional account of impulsive and subsidiary action, through what he calls "intention-in-action"; and second, by introducing a factor of causal reflexivity into the conditions of satisfaction of an action. Let us examine these two features of his analysis in turn.

1. INTENTION-IN-ACTION

An intention, like a perception or a memory, is a mental event. It has a representational content and a psychological mode, and its direction of fit is world to mind. Every action must minimally include an intentional movement, that is, a movement caused by a concomitant intention. In Searle's terms, "An action ... is any composite event or state that contains the occurrence of an intention-in-action" (*Intentionality*, p. 108).

Acting does not involve simply performing a goal-directed movement; it involves the movement's being caused by a corresponding intention. In the case of an unplanned simple physical action, such as extending one's arm while talking, there must be at least the following components in the conditions of satisfaction of the action, conditions that constitute the Intentional content of the corresponding "intention-in-action":

(1)   that there be an event of extending my arm,

and

(2)   that this intention-in-action causes that event.[7]

Condition (1) states that the action is satisfied in part if some specific bodily movement is performed. But of course not *any* movement will allow us to perform successfully a given action. It has to be specified independently of the event of moving. This is what an intention-in-action does: it presents the kind of movement that is to be performed, and in virtue of this presenting, *causes* the bodily movement. Condition (2), accordingly, states that the bodily movement is caused by the intention-in-action that presents it as part of its conditions of satisfaction. The reason an intention-in-action is said to *present* rather than to *represent* the bodily movement that it causes is that it gives us "direct access to it" in a distinctive experience (*Intentionality*, p. 46). Perception and memory, similarly, offer direct access to the states of affairs they represent, and therefore also involve presentations, in contrast to other representational states, such as belief.

The following formula represents the structure of a simple physical action.[8] The action in this simple case consists in the intention-in-action (with the content expressed in parenthesis) causing a bodily movement. Causal reflexivity is one of the conditions of satisfaction of the intention-in-action, the other being its causal role in producing a bodily movement [i.e., (1) and (2) above, shown in the left-hand part of the formula]. The right-hand part expresses (in capital letters) the causal effect of this intention-in-action upon the bodily movement in the actual world.

(3)   **ia** (this **ia** causes **bm**) CAUSES BM

In other words, an intention-in-action's having as a condition of satisfaction that it causes a specific bodily movement (the mental component of the action) normally causes a performance of that bodily movement (the physical component of the action).

We will come back later to the causal reflexivity [expressed in (2) and (3) by the demonstrative *this*] that constitutes part of the conditions of satisfaction of every intention. For now, let us concentrate on the very idea of an intention-in-action. In the text quoted at the beginning of this section, Searle claims that a bodily movement may be part of an action even when not caused by a prior intention. Searle is thus breaking with a whole tradition according to which whatever mental content there is to action resides in the deliberative process that occurs prior to action. He finds himself on the side of those – such as Kent Bach, Harry Frankfurt,[9] and Rosalyn Hursthouse[10] – who want to extend the concept of action to include impulsive moves and activities performed routinely and unthinkingly. Such actions, although intentional, do not seem to be willed in the same sense that one willingly writes a letter or utters a sentence.[11] Examples of these "minimal" actions (as Bach calls them) are all kinds of postural and preattentive movements, such as scratching an itch, doodling, brushing a fly, avoiding an object,[12] shifting a gear, and pacing about the room,[13] as well as impulsive and expressive actions such as tearing a photo into pieces out of rage, jumping for joy,[14] and so forth.

Kent Bach[15] offers two main reasons for admitting those unintended-but-intentional bodily behaviors among actions. First, they may well be the only kind of actions that infants, patients with certain executive disorders, and "animals on the middle rungs of the phylogenetic ladder" are able to perform. Second, there is more to an action than its initiation. The way in which an action is carried out does not seem to be determined at the level of a prior intention, when such an intention exists. Although the specific way in which an action is performed may be taken to require a form of awareness, this awareness seems to reside "below the level of intentions and reasons."

John Searle's own revision of the definition of an action integrates the first of Bach's worries. By acknowledging the existence of actions performed *without* prior intentions, Searle's concept of an intention-in-action captures the sense in which infants and nonhuman animals perform actions. Certainly there are situations in which an agent forms a priori the intention to do A – an intention reportable by the linguistic form "I will do A." But actions may be performed even without such prior intentions, but rather with an occurrent thought of the form "I do A." When I scratch my back, I do not form a prior intention to the effect that I will scratch my back; *I just do it* (*Intentionality*, p. 84). But there is no reason, according to Searle, to conclude that I do it unintentionally. This kind of mental state belongs to intentions, because it is constituted – and this is a central point for Searle – *by the conscious experience of acting*. According to Searle, this experience is "inseparable from action," and it is for that very reason that he calls it "an intention-in-action" (ibid.).

Let us note here that an intention-in-action causes not an action but rather a bodily movement. The causal sequence [ia-bm] constitutes the action. There is therefore an important difference between prior intention and intention-in-action: the prior intention *causes* the action that it represents, while the intention-in-action serves in part to *constitute* the action, by presenting and thereby causing the relevant bodily movement. As a consequence, an intention-in-action fails to represent any sort of further goal, such as "switching on the light," "breaking a vase," and so on. What it determines is, rather, a bodily movement. This feature is consistent with the role of intentions-in-action in subsidiary actions: an agent walks as part of realizing her intention to go to work. Things do not fare so well, however, with the dimension of impulsive actions. For such an action is not simply a result of an intention to move in such and such a way; it is a result of the intention *to break the vase, to tear the picture*, and so on.

It is unclear whether prior intentions and intentions-in-action have, in Searle's picture, the function of dynamically controlling the action, a function deemed essential by Bach, Mele, and other theorists of action. As this question is dependent on the notion of reflexive causation, we shall need to turn now to this second feature of Searle's analysis.

2. CAUSAL REFLEXIVITY IN THE CONDITIONS OF SATISFACTION OF AN ACTION

How can a conceptual intentional content be realized in and by a piece of concrete behavior? This central question has two components: first, how are conditions of satisfaction, as represented in a prior intention (when there is one), realized in some possible bodily movement? And second, how can an intention (as an Intentional state) be causally efficacious in producing a change in the world? According to Searle,[16] the answer to these questions consists in recognizing that there are *two* causal links embedded in the intentional chain. The reason why a single causal link cannot do the job resides in the various puzzles raised by deviant causation. As we saw earlier, you can intend to do A and thereby be so affected by entertaining this mental state that you do A unintentionally. Or you can intend to do A, which triggers a corresponding action, but some misfiring occurs that makes your movement fail, which coincidentally produces indirectly an A-result. In both cases, the intention caused you to act in a way that produced the desired event, but you do not recognize the sequence as the one intended. A second causal link must be present to make it a condition of satisfaction of the action that it should be produced by that very intention. The crucial addition consists in making prior intentions as well as intentions-in-action *causally self-referential*. This is apparent in the form of an intention-in-action that we have already seen:

(3)   **ia** (this **ia** causes that bm) CAUSES BM

Similarly for prior intentions:[17]

(4)   **pi** (this **pi** causes action) CAUSES ACTION

In other words, a prior intention's having a specific causal effect as its condition of satisfaction (the mental component of the action) causes a performance of that action. [The difference between (3) and (4) expresses the specific structure of each kind of intention. The prior intention expressed in (4) represents the whole action, which necessarily includes (3) as its part, and thereby causes the whole action. In (3), however, an intention-in-action represents just a bodily movement, and thereby causes this bodily movement. As we saw earlier, a simple action involves only an intention-in-action and its associated bodily movement.]

The claim that intentions are causally self-referential means that it is part of the content of a prior intention that it causes the corresponding action by producing a representation of its own conditions of satisfaction. Similarly, it is part of the content of an intention-in-action that it causes a bodily movement by producing a presentation of its own conditions of satisfaction.

Both kinds of intentions include their own causal roles in their contents; but they differ, as we saw, as to the kinds of representation they are. A prior intention represents the outcome that it will cause in a general way; an intention-in-action presents its conditions of satisfaction in a very specific way – that is, as an experience of acting (*Intentionality*, p. 88). For example, if I form the prior intention to take a train to Brest, I need not represent all the details that carrying out such a project will eventually involve. I need only conceptually represent that I will go to Brest next week, under a certain psychological mode – namely intending. But if I form the intention-in-action of buying my train ticket to Brest, I need to perform a concrete sequence of actions: point with my right finger to the name 'Brest' on a screen, point to a selected time (etc.), insert my credit card in the machine, and so on. In order to perform each one of these subsidiary actions, I need to present to myself the kind of movement that needs to be executed.

If one conceives the experience of acting as normally resulting *from* bodily activity, one might have trouble understanding that it can also *cause* the movement in question. Part of the difficulty is lifted, however, when one observes that Searle defines "experience of acting" in a restrictive way, as a specific combination of a phenomenological and a "logical" component. The phenomenological component, on the one hand, has to do with the specific kind of trying in which the subject engages. Each agent normally knows what she is trying to do. For example, trying to raise one's arm is a different kind of experience from trying to open one's mouth. The experience of trying is normally followed by the corresponding bodily movement. What Searle calls the experience of acting precedes, and may correctly be described as causing, the bodily event, in the sense that the mental experience is realized by a cerebral event that triggers the firings in the relevant motor neurons. What Searle calls the "logical" component of the experience of acting, on the other hand, consists in the presentation of the conditions of satisfaction of that experience. They are, as we saw, [that my arm raises] and [that it raises in virtue of this intention-in-action]. The relation between an experience of trying and the action is analogous to that between an experience of perceiving and the object perceived. A visual experience is normally caused by the object seen, and is also "about" it; an experience of acting normally causes a corresponding bodily movement, and is also "about" it.

At the beginning of this section, the first question we raised was about the connection between a prior intention and a bodily movement. What connects a prior intention to a bodily movement is the Intentional connection between a prior intention and an intention-in-action. The latter is made explicit in the following formula:

(5)   **pi** (this **pi** causes [**ia**(this **ia** causes bm)])

In other words, the intentional content of a prior intention is that this intention itself causes an intention-in-action, whose own content, in turn, is that it itself (this intention in action) causes a corresponding bodily movement.[18]

But this gives only a partial solution to the Intentional causation level of the problem. For one might want to know further how such a connection [pi-ia] is first set up and maintained over time. How is an agent able to relate a prior intention to some specific way of carrying it out? Certainly, it is not a philosopher's task to indicate which specific brain structures will be involved. But the philosopher might still have a theory about how such a connection can be made possible in such a way that it (i) does not require from the agent an implausible search through all the available possibilities and (ii) ensures that the prior intention is not lost sight of during the execution of the required set of subsidiary actions. There is no clear evocation of these two issues in *Intentionality*. Later, in section 6, we will suggest a way of addressing them using Searle's conceptual apparatus.

The second problem raised earlier was how an intention can be causally efficacious in producing a change in the world. This question refers to the right-hand part of formulas (3) and (4) above (CAUSAL in capital letters). The use of capital letters is meant to refer not to causality as represented, but to causality as physically realized in body movements or brain activity. How can Intentional states such as prior intentions and intentions-in-action actually CAUSE a change in the world through some bodily movement or internal operation?

Searle addresses this question in the last chapter of *Intentionality*, by developing a theory of the relations between mental and brain states (*Intentionality*, p. 265ff.). In Searle's view, mental states may be both CAUSED by the operations of the brain and realized in the brain. Searle's metaphysics is nonreductionist: although higher-level mental phenomena are realized in brain states, they still have a distinctive, level-specific kind of causal efficacy. A visual experience, say, is caused by external stimuli triggering activity in the optic nerve and in the visual cortex. But the experience itself is realized in brain structures, too, and can in turn cause other kinds of experiences (memories, desires, etc.) through the corresponding neural firings. The same holds for the experience of acting. A specific instance of trying is an experience realized in firings in the premotor cortex. In turn, this premotor activity normally causes activity in the correlative motor neurons, leading to muscle contraction. The important idea here is that mental phenomena (intending, perceiving, believing) should not be "explained away and redefined or branded as illusory" (p. 267). They do play a causal role at the macro level, although it is also true that they are realized by microphenomena with their own causal efficacy at the micro level.

On the basis of this analysis, one can understand the nature of CAUSATION; what makes an intention produce CAUSALLY a bodily movement is a property of the brain structure that realizes that intention. As a brain event of the executive variety, it has a disposition to trigger internal operations or bodily movements that in turn produce the expected changes in the world. Now, of course, this kind of analysis also applies to the Intentional causation part of formulas (3) and (4). Self-reflexivity and conditions of satisfaction can be appreciated only by an agent who has cerebral states realizing these various epistemic and motivational states, and brain processes CAUSING the required modifications in her beliefs and motivations. But the states and processes involved in Intentional causation are not executive in themselves. They concern self-referential causality, but they are not made CAUSAL in virtue of what they concern. What makes an Intentional state CAUSAL is, again, that it is realized by a brain state whose function is to trigger motor activation.

It is very easy to conflate the two levels. Let us examine one example. It may happen, when an agent is blindfolded, that she believes that she has successfully raised her arm when her arm actually has not moved (for example, because it had been anesthetized) (*Intentionality*, p. 89). In such a case, the phenomenology of trying is dissociated from its normal causal effect on a bodily movement. As Searle also remarks, "What counts as the conditions of satisfaction of my Intentional event is indeed determined by the Intentional event, but that the Intentional event is in fact satisfied is not itself part of the content" (*Intentionality*, p. 130). Now here is one way an objector might go. We can certainly understand in general how a representation can fail to represent, because it is in the essence of a representation to misrepresent in certain circumstances. But it is more difficult to understand how an experience that is essentially causal (being an experience of acting) can fail to cause, for a causal factor, all things being equal, tends to bring about its effect. If a causal capacity fails to produce what it normally produces, it cannot be in virtue of its representational features. Reciprocally, if the experience of acting causes something, it is not, or not only, in virtue of its being an experience with such and such a content.

This objection can easily be accommodated within Searle's metaphysics. The objector contrasts the intentional content of a mental state with the executive properties of the brain state realizing it; but such a contrast is a consequence of Searle's view. An agent may intend to act, in the sense that she enjoys the corresponding experience of trying, while her brain (or her body) fails to have the correlative functional capacity of performing the intended movement. The agent may well be wrong about her own motor capacity (she may be paralyzed); she may also be wrong about her ability to control her behavior intentionally (she may have an attention disorder). The two causal links involved in an intention help to clarify why this may be the case. The first one is represented by the agent in a causal-reflexive way; the second one depends on the physical realization of the mental experience. An experience of acting may thus be essentially causal while failing to cause what it is supposed to.

3. CAUSAL REFLEXIVITY AND PHENOMENOLOGY

An issue hotly debated by Searle's commentators is whether the causal-reflexive relation is an aspect of the *phenomenology* of the experience of intending (or of perceiving, remembering, etc.) or of its *intentional content*. Does causal reflexivity – that is, one of the conditions of satisfaction of the Intentional content of perception, memory, and intention – belong to what is presented in the experience, or to the way in which it is presented? Is it an independent Intentional object, or a specification of the kind of experience in which it is presented? Searle's response is that causal reflexivity belongs both to phenomenology and to the conditions of satisfaction of an action (or of a perception or memory). But its mode of intervention is in each case different.

Let us first consider what happens when a perceiver sees a red object. The experience is of a red object, but the experience itself is not red. Redness is the property that is presented in the experience. In contrast with properties such as redness, causality is part of the experience of perceiving, not of what is perceived (*Intentionality*, p. 131). The perceiver indeed experiences that she is subjected to a visual experience. But she does not see the causal link; the latter is not part of the perceptual content of her visual experience (p. 49). It is, rather, part of the way in which the perceptual object is presented. In other words, a visual experience can be caused by a state of affairs, and include causality in its phenomenology, without *being about* causality.

The same holds for the experience of acting. When an agent acts, she experiences what it is to be an efficient agent in the world. But this experience is not about causality. It is rather about the property that her action brings about (switching on the light, cooking the steak, opening the door). She can, but need not, form a second-order thought about the causal aspect of her experience (reflect, for example, on her strength, her ability or lack thereof); this kind of thought is not part of her ordinary experience as an agent.[19] The agent is, in other words, only implicitly aware of how the conditions of satisfaction of her action are presented to her. Such awareness is a metacognitive feature that does not need to be explicitly represented in order to work effectively as a constraint on what counts as an experience of acting. Even small children and animals might have access to that kind of causal self-referentiality.[20] As Harman also observes,[21] the agent does not need to form a "metaintention" to the effect that the first intention should lead one to do A in a certain way. The first-order intention already contains a reference to itself.

Causation is thus not an object of the (perceiver's or agent's) experiences, but rather part of their mental contents (*Intentionality*, p. 124). As Searle insists, philosophers of mind often confuse experience as a mental event with what the experience is about. As we saw earlier, a perceptual experience has properties that are entirely distinct from the properties specified by its Intentional content. Generally speaking, claims about Intentional content are conceptual (p. 47), whereas claims about experience have ontological import: a visual experience is the way in which the Intentional content of a perception "is realized in our conscious life" (p. 46).

Still, when a judge, say, or some expert has to decide whether a subject did or did not perceive a given event, he needs to use the concept of causal self-referentiality in its full-blown conceptual dimension. For his job is to explore the actual causal relationship between the state of affairs that caused the experience and the content of the experience, and he must make sure that the correct direct and reflexive links are preserved. (He checks whether the required conditions are actually fulfilled.) Did the eyewitness actually see a gun pointing toward the president from a second floor window, or did he just imagine it? Was there such a state of affairs? And assuming that there was one, was the eyewitness in a position to see it? Similarly for acting: an expert will have to examine whether an experience of doing A caused an A-ing, and whether the agent's experience included an adequate mode of presentation of the Intentional content. If I took the money under hypnotic influence, my behavior cannot be described in causal self-referential terms.

To complete our exposition of Searle's theory of action, we need to see how it allows us to overcome the two obstacles mentioned earlier: (i) the asymmetry of beliefs and desires, on the one hand, and intentions, on the other (there are states of affairs not believed and not desired, but no actions not intended), and (ii) deviant causation.

4. SOLVING THE PUZZLES

The puzzle concerning the asymmetry between action and other Intentional states, such as belief and desire, dissolves when one realizes that the reason why there are no actions without some intention is because every action necessarily involves an intention-in-action. Now it might appear that the puzzle is hereby solved in a purely nominal way: Searle is just offering us a definition in which intention is a constituent of action. But the question remains: what makes it *a fact* (rather than a linguistic convention) that an action is Intentional in the sense suggested, namely, that it is caused by a specific experience of acting?

Let us suppose that we are in some future society in which robots and human beings live side by side, and that it is impossible to discriminate by sight whether an entity is a robot or a member of the species *Homo sapiens*. Intuitively, there will be many cases where we want to say that the robots act. There will be cases of cooperation, where a robot helps a human being in some task, executes parts of a common plan. But in such cases, no intentions will have been formed prior to the quasi-action, or while it is being performed, because the robots have no prior or current *experience* of acting.

Clearly, Searle's answer would consist in claiming that the robots do not act. (They simply move, like a feedback missile). But it seems that we need some additional argument in favor of this view. For there is a plausible alternative, namely, acknowledging that they act as we do: their activities have conditions of satisfaction, just like ours; the robots may furthermore have access to some functional equivalent of our metacognitive capacities. Finally, they are able to initiate and control their movements in a fully adaptive way. This kind of capacity may indeed be more central for action than having a certain causal experience in acting. An objector might want to block the assimilation of robot behavior to action by using the classical opposition between following a rule and acting in accordance with a rule. Robots do not have rules in the sense that they can neither understand symbols (as Searle's Chinese Room Argument showed) nor, a fortiori, distinguish a normative from a descriptive statement.

Another line of response to the problem of action would be the following. Robots have only a derived form of intentionality. Although the robots do not have any kind of conscious access to rules, and have no phenomenology for contrasting states of affairs (pleasant/unpleasant, good/bad), rules did inspire the researchers who set up the programs that allow the robots to move adequately. These programmers obviously have no present or past experience of acting when their robots move, but there is a sense in which they control (or fail to control) the robots' behaviors nonetheless. Is not a specific murder executed by a robot imputable to the man who wrote that robot's program?[22] Does the programmer not act, in spite of having no intention-in-action during the killing, not even a prior intention that the robot would do such and such a deed? This case suggests that intention-in-action may be more closely connected to guidance or control of action than to an agent's experience.

Our second difficulty was to show how Searle could deal with all the examples of actions that are caused by prior intentions but that fail to be intentional, because of some deviance in the associated causal sequences. Searle's solution consists in pointing out that all the deviant cases share a common feature: the intention-in-action fails to cause the bodily movement in the way intended in the prior intention. When the full structure of the intention is spelled out, it becomes clear that a clause concerning the way in which the outcome is caused fails to be satisfied (*Intentionality*, p. 109). A full specification of the prior intention (including the causal role of a subsequent appropriate intention-in-action) should dispose of the difficulty.

As Searle observes, however, causal deviance might still affect the link between intention-in-action and bodily movement:

> Suppose that unknown to me my arm is rigged up so that whenever I try to raise it, somebody else causes it to go up, then the action is not mine, even though I had the intention-in-action of raising my arm and in some sense that intention caused my arm to go up. (*Intentionality*, p. 110)

This example, as Searle notes, recalls Malebranche's view of the mind-body problem: God helps us transform our intentions into physical movements. A way of coping with this new deviant causal link, suggested by Searle, is simply to preclude it by convention:

> This class of potential counterexamples is eliminated by simply construing the relation of intention-in-action to its conditions of satisfaction as precluding intervention by other agents or other Intentional states. (*Intentionality*, p. 110)

It would appear illegitimate, however, to preclude such an intervention by fiat if it turned out that intentions-in-action are regularly exposed to it as a result of their very structure. It actually seems quite frequently to be the case that subjects acquire an intention-in-action in a more or less passive way. In this kind of case, the subject has no specific prior intention; furthermore, her intention-in-action triggers a bodily movement in a way that is difficult to rationalize: a deviant causal link triggers an intention-in-action in the absence of any individual reason to act.

A neurological illustration would be echopraxia, a disposition found mainly in schizophrenic patients, but also in children and in normal adult subjects in certain contexts. People with this disposition acquire intentions-in-action in the absence of any congruent prior intention by simply watching or remembering someone else's action. In such a case, an intention-in-action did cause a bodily movement, but the action was not intentional in a straightforward way: the patient reports that in some sense she was made to act. What is interesting in such a case is that no other agent "intervened" or tried to take advantage of the patient's disposition.[23] The perception of someone else's movement seems in such cases to be sufficient to propagate the corresponding intention-in-action. Searle might want to respond that, in this class of situations, his second causally reflexive condition of satisfaction – that the agent performs this bodily movement by way of carrying out this intention – precisely fails to be fulfilled: something crucial is missing from the patient's *experience*, namely, the sense in which she is acting "of her own accord."

It might be argued, however, that the echopraxic patient does not lack the experience of trying to move (she is not in the situation of Penfield's patient whose neurons are externally activated during surgery).[24] Rather, she lacks the experience of *moving in agreement with some prior intention*. She has a good sense of the kind of bodily movement that she has performed, and she also knows that she has been performing it; what she denies is having a reason to do it. Her action can only be explained, from her perspective, as being a consequence of someone else's prior intention.

5. VARIOUS NEW PUZZLES

A. Experience of Acting and Unconscious Acting

We have distinguished the two components, phenomenological and logical (i.e., the component devoted to conditions of satisfaction), of the experience of acting, and we have defended Searle's claim that causation is effected through the very experience that the corresponding intention-in-action provides (see section 2). Now, however, a difficulty arises when an action is performed in the absence of any conscious experience of acting – for example, when driving absent-mindedly. Searle admits that

> [in] such a case the intention-in-action exists without any experience of acting. The only difference then between them [i.e., between this case and the case in which the action is conscious] is that the experience may have certain phenomenal properties that are not essential to the intention. (*Intentionality*, p. 92)[25]

In arguing in this way, Searle aims explicitly at finding a theoretical status for nonconscious intention-in-action *symmetrical to* the case of nonconscious perception in blindsight. A patient with blindsight has no phenomenal experience of seeing that P, but she can still extract spatial properties from vision and use them in action. Similarly, a distracted person may have no phenomenal experience that she is driving. Rather, she has a noncongruent experience of listening to her car radio, or thinking about the election (etc.). Yet she may still accomplish the bodily movements that are part of the intentional conditions of satisfaction for driving.

This symmetry between perception and action is more apparent than real, however. For while a visual content can survive the absence of a visual experience, as a result of the fact that there exists an external object making the extraction of a specific Intentional content possible (*Intentionality*, p. 47), it does not seem open to us to say that the experience of acting can go on causing the corresponding action even when it has no distinctive phenomenological property. In normal perception as well as in blindsight cases, one can be informationally connected with an object without recognizing it consciously. An intention-in-action however, in Searle's analysis, is essentially conscious, and it is supposed to operate through the experience of trying in which it consists. The notion of an unconscious intention-in-action thus remains rather obscure. It is difficult to understand how it might cause adequate bodily movements.[26]

B. The Representational Format of Intentions-in-Action

A question raised by the definitely strategic concept of intention-in-action has to do with the representational format in which a bodily movement is presented. As we saw in section 2, Searle emphasizes that "the contents of the prior intention and the intention-in-action look quite different" (*Intentionality*, p. 93). The first has a whole action as its object, the second a bodily movement. The second is furthermore "much more determinate" than the first, including "not only that my arm goes up but that it goes up in a certain way and at a certain speed, etc." (ibid.). The former may, especially in the case of complex actions, be quite indeterminate (ibid., note 10).

Searle nowhere suggests, however, that the content of a presentation (in an experience of acting) differs essentially from the content of a representation (of a prior intention).[27] On the contrary, the content of a visual perception is taken to be "equivalent to a whole proposition." "Visual experience," Searle writes further, "is never simply *of* an object but rather it must always be *that* such and such is the case," which for Searle reflects the fact that visual experiences have conditions of satisfaction (Searle 1983, pp. 40–1).[28] Perception and action have the same kind of content as belief and desire. What is specific about them consists in their distinctive psychological mode and in the way they appear to us ("in our conscious life") (*Intentionality*, p. 46).

It is arguable, however, that presentations and representations do differ in content. Let us grant that the statement of the conditions of satisfaction of a visual experience or of an action includes implicitly a reference to the corresponding visual experience or experience of acting. It is arguable that some substantial cognitive role must be given to *the way* the experience is realized – that is, to some particular perspectival, continuous, phenomenologically distinctive mode of presentation. Such an experience seems to be lacking in conceptual representation. Imagine that you are asked to distinguish "this hand movement" (twisting it to the right) from "that hand movement" (twisting it to the left). It seems clear that the kind of information on which such a discrimination depends has a specific, nonconceptual format.

Gareth Evans and Christopher Peacocke have offered strong reasons for defending the existence of perceptual nonconceptual content. This term refers to perceptual experiences involving a continuous, qualitatively multidimensional flow that cannot be reported adequately in discrete concepts. Nondemonstrative words do seem to be inappropriate to capture fine-grained perceptual variations in intensity, frequency, and so forth. A first reason is that it seems questionable to so restrict the notion of the content of an experience that a subject deprived of the relevant concepts for characterizing the conditions of satisfaction of her experience should be said to have had no experience at all. It seems, furthermore, that the very capacity to refer to parts of the perceived world through demonstratives presupposes that irreducibly perceptual facts are available to the perceiver. To apply a demonstrative term (such as "this") to a given portion of her visual field, a subject needs to *extract* the relevant nonconceptual content that grounds a corresponding perceptual judgement such as "this is blue." What psychologists call "saliences" reflect the existence of perceptual *preconditions* to demonstrative use. These preconditions are nonconceptual and contentful. Whether a square is seen as a square or as a diamond is not primarily a matter of concept use, but a matter of nonconceptual content.[29]

The same kind of reasoning applies, mutatis mutandis, to action. The way an agent discriminates *this* bodily movement from *that* one depends on nonconceptual preconditions for identifying various types of bodily movements based on how they feel/look when executed, in a specific experiential-perspectival format. These preconditions, furthermore, belong to content, because they contribute rationalizing action and offer genuine reasons for acting in this particular way.[30] For example, a specific way of grasping a hammer, say, is the only efficient way to use it. The right way of handling the tool can be conveyed by displaying it visually much more effectively than in words.

Searle would probably reject the present suggestion. He maintains, as we have seen, that intentions-in-action have propositional conditions of satisfaction of the usual kind. When pushed to offer final reasons for executing this rather than that movement as part of some action, Searle would invoke what he calls the Background, that is, nonrepresentational skills and know-how that make Intentional states specific and determinate (over and above their explicit conditions of satisfaction). The Background, according to Searle, is constantly fed with new habits, freshly acquired skills and routines. Choosing harmonious, flowing movements, adjusting the weight that one places on each foot, picking one specific way of performing a particular action rather than another – all of these result from bodily skills that precisely emerge when representations are made superfluous (for example, through prolonged practice) (*Intentionality*, p. 151). The Background has an intermediate status: not itself Intentional, it is rather a precondition of Intentionality (p. 143).

In response to Wakefield and Dreyfus's paper, which aims at "derepresentationalizing" action, Searle again invokes the Background capacities that permeate our Intentional skills. Moreover, he develops the concept of "flow," which refers to the continuity of experience in Intentional behavior. He seems, interestingly, to resist the view that bodily skills are completely external to Intentionality: "Intentionality reaches down to the bottom level of the voluntary actions,"[31] he says, which might mean that even the simpler movements already have conditions of satisfaction. This claim, also expressed in the view that the Background functions only when activated by "genuine Intentional contents," brings Searle very close to accepting a viewpoint advocated by some defenders of nonconceptual content,[32] according to which a creature cannot be in states with nonconceptual content if it possesses no concepts at all. Another striking similarity consists in the fact that the Background allows us to establish linkages within a practical context: a subject may thus apply her concepts in a quasi-indexical way, without needing an additional rule. Defenders of nonconceptual content argue, similarly, that perceptual concepts presuppose demonstrative linkages with the nonconceptual content of a subject's experience. At this point, it might seem to be a matter of terminological preference to speak of Background skills rather than of nonconceptual content. We will see in the next section,

however, that the point is not just a matter of terminology. To mention one
important difference: Background skills are precisely outside content.

C. Intention-in-Action and Control of Action

There are two main types of process causation. In the simpler cases, a
sequence of changes is initiated without any further intervention of the
initiating causal factor. In more complex cases, once initiation has taken
place, there is a more or less continuous intervention of the causal element
in the whole unfolding dynamic. In feedback mechanisms, for example,
some signal from the goal controls the trajectory of a system. In Searle's
initial presentation, intentions work as a trigger, not as a control device.
A prior intention causes the action, in the sense that it forms a plan and
sets the intention-in-action in operation in an appropriate way. But does its
intervention stop precisely when the intention-in-action comes into play,
or rather only when the goal is reached? There are two reasons why a prior
intention should be seen as playing a role until completion.

First, a prior intention is the only *semantic* representation that can be
used to evaluate and when necessary correct an action when it is already
in progress. For example, is the current step taken toward the goal performed in a way compatible with the desired target event? Is it done in
accordance with what was expected prior to the action? This is the function
of semantic control of action, a function that is crucial to monitoring the
action in a rational, well-planned way. This function was pointed out by
O'Shaughnessy,[33] who saw it as something that a prior intention is typically supposed to provide. Searle happily granted that a swimmer who
intends to cross the Channel needs to evaluate his current progress on the
basis of his prior intention. The latter thus needs to be maintained in active force until the action is finally completed. This extensive monitoring
role of prior intentions is in fact implicit in Searle's comparison of prior
intention/intention-in-action to memory/perceptual experience. The first
pair is a mirror image of the second;[34] just as a memory is based on a
prior experience, but does not wait until the experience is completed to be
formed, so a prior intention may trigger an intention-in-action, but does
not stop when the latter is formed.

A second kind of function of a prior intention consists in evaluating
the result of the action. This is the level at which the action is judged
as completed, as not yet complete, or as failed, with the subsequent realization that a new attempt is or is not necessary. Here again, the prior
intention is the only kind of representation with the appropriate content

for such an evaluation. An intention-in-action is not equipped for *this* kind of control because, although it presents the conditions of satisfaction of a specific trying, it lacks the conceptual means of matching a bodily movement against a final goal, understood as a new state of affairs in the world.

An interesting question is whether intentions-in-action themselves, although they are *not* meant to represent goals conceptually (see section 2), do anything more than simply launch movements or operations. Here, too, there is more to moving than to trying to move; movement has to be guided, adapted to context in an action-relevant way. It is part of the conditions of satisfaction of intentions-in-action that they cause a specific movement or a subsidiary action (and that they cause it as part of their being this particular intention). Therefore, they have to control occurrent behavior in such a way as to guarantee that the intended movement is in fact performed, and performed in the correct way, until completion. If prior intention enables monitoring of the semantic side of behavior, intention-in-action has a parallel function with what we might call the *pragmatic* side of behavior: it is called upon to control behavior in its motor (or mental) aspect until the physical (or mental) operation is successfully executed.

Clearly, the question of the kind of content that belongs to intentions-in-action (see section 5B) is linked to the question of how an intention-in-action monitors behavior. A way of understanding how an intention-in-action can be part of a prior intention, and how it will guide the movement that it causes, consists in suggesting that it has a nonconceptual content that falls under the concepts specified by prior intentions. Such pragmatic nonconceptual content expresses, for example, the kind of physical/mental effort, dynamics, limb segments, and parts of the visual context involved in a given sequence. Several advantages might lead one to favor such a pragmatic account of what is presented in "this bodily movement" over an implication of nonrepresentational levels, such as the Background and the Flow.

First, it is natural, as Searle seems to acknowledge, to consider pragmatic memories of our actions (in their dynamic, qualitative, perspectival properties) to be as much a part of our thoughts as memories of facts and events. We need to plan movements as much as we need to plan actions; we need to reflect over the best way to reduce speed on an icy road, how to serve against a left-handed tennis opponent, and so on. While this important part of our cognition is permeated with conceptual knowledge, it is also independently grounded in our prior experience of agency and in our observation of other agents.

A second advantage of having intentions-in-action nonconceptually control behavior is that the view we have of causal reflexivity thereby acquires a completely new status. For it is a central feature of any theory of nonconceptual content that it allows a subject to establish demonstrative relations to a world both perceived and acted upon. An experiential mode of presentation allows a subject to capture the causal reflexivity of the corresponding experience, but in an implicit way, because nonconceptual contents of action precisely relate a subject to a world presented as being such and such. The content that she perceives, remembers, and acts on is represented through demonstratives, but need not be conceptually registered in a nondemonstrative manner.

The third interesting feature of this view is the close correspondence of the respective parts of nonconceptual and conceptual contents in visual (and auditory) experience and in the experience of acting. Just as the experience of seeing differs from the perceptual judgment that may eventually be delivered by the perceiver, so the experience of acting is different from the prior intention that the agent forms in relation to her action. In both cases, judgment and prior intention apply concepts to experience; while intention-in-action and current acting have a different kind of content, with a more determinate and finer grain that can be captured not by concepts but by vision, proprioception, and perceptual imagery. For example, an agent may have a prior intention to help himself to a glass of water, but choosing the hand to hold the bottle or glass, and the specific grip and timing for the pouring movement, depend on spatial and mechanical properties that are presented in nonconceptual content.

Let us remark, finally, that if Searlian intentions-in-action are allowed to control action and not simply to initiate bodily movement, the possibility of deviant causation seems to vanish completely. For the nonconceptual content of an intention-in-action can now be tightly articulated both with the conceptual content of a prior intention, on the one hand, and with the perceptual feedback from the present context, on the other, without sacrificing the flowing nature of agency.[35]

6. EXPANDING SEARLE'S THEORY

It should be clear by now that the theory of action Searle offers in his 1983 book is extremely rich and interesting. Even if one dissents from some of his claims, it is undeniable that the author has contributed to opening up an entire new field of philosophical questioning. He has shown how processes that may not prima facie look Intentional, because they resist regimentation in clean, verbally expressible propositional contents, may indeed, given some philosophical flair, be found to have exactly the kinds of conditions of satisfaction that define representations.

In our exposition of this theory, we found that there is a fundamentally important idea. It is that action is never just a matter of armchair planning; indeed, in some cases it is not planned at all. Even the respectable part of action – namely, prior intending – has to include reference to nonverbal physical capacities that are subjectively presented to an agent in her active intervention in the world. This kind of inclusion was certainly difficult to accept at first, because the bodily sequence in physical action has tradition- ally been taken to lie outside the realm of the mental, where the body simply "takes over" whatever decisions the mind has come up with. Concerning the role of mental operations in *mental* action, the same kind of prejudice still prevails, in spite of John Searle's effort to show that mental action indeed has a structure similar to physical action.

His book shows, furthermore, that the structure of action is the mirror-image of that of perception and memory. In perception, a specific kind of access allows a subject to grasp content in an implicit causal-reflexive way. In memory, an agent grasps the content that was initially perceived in a different psychological mode, one which presupposes that some perceptual event happened, and which is causally connected to the present memory event (again, in a causal-reflexive way).

We will now take the liberty of suggesting ways in which Searle's pro- posed theory might be modified to accommodate some of the difficulties noted here, while at the same time trying to avoid tinkering and tampering as far as possible. One of the most important tensions that make the theory as unstable as it is consists in the role of an experience of acting as an Inten- tional causal factor. This tension was most palpable when the question was raised of how absent-minded actions are possible in a theory in which the experience of acting is a central causal element (see section 5A). If such a view is taken seriously, then where there is no experience of acting, there is no action. Where there is no grasp of what it is to have an intention to act in such a way that the act is a consequence of this intention, there is no action.

A main source of doubt comes from the fact that there are cases that intuitively count as actions that are not caused by any experience of act- ing, and there are intentions-in-action that are triggered neither by a prior intention nor by an independent sudden impulse of the agent. Searle him- self raised the possibility of disclaiming the role of prior intention as a regular cause of acting. This skepticism may be extended to intentions-in- action. Why should every action have an individual experience of trying as a causal constituent? Alfred Mele[36] has suggested that some intentions-in-action might be passively acquired, just as our beliefs and desires are. This possibility should be left open by our theory of action: some action plans or intentions-in-action may occasionally be driven by some external circumstance, rather than internally generated. It is very likely that much of our instrumental behavior is "stimulus-driven" rather than specifically intended. Consider, for example, how mechanically we use toothbrushes, doorknobs, light switches, and so on. In fact, much of our environment has been built by us in order to control our actions in an adaptive way.

Further, it seems plausible that some actions develop in the absence of any consciousness of acting, in the sense both of trying to act and of exerting an effort toward a goal. This possibility is already realized in absent-minded driving, or in the quick, adaptive bodily movements that may in some circumstances save our lives. This suggests that the conscious way in which an intention-in-action causally produces a bodily movement should not be taken to be relevant to the definition of action. An alternative suggestion was sketched earlier (section 4). On the view suggested, the essential feature of actions does not lie in the conscious experience of acting, but in the monitoring role of a prior or concomitant intention. Having specific representational control over the development and dynamics of a motor (or mental) sequence is what singles out action from mere reflex, passively executed movements, and mental operations.

This proposal aims both at overcoming the problem of unconscious acting and at giving nonconceptual content its own specific role in action. A suggestion responding to both concerns consists in shifting the ontological status of intentions-in-action. The latter might be taken to be executive schemes or pragmatic representations, rather than experiences of acting. In Searle's theory, intentions qualify as representations because they are conscious states of the Intentional variety (they have conditions of satisfaction, a world-to-mind direction of fit, and a specific psychological mode). We suggest retaining all but one of these features. Let us assume that intentions guide behavior even when the agent has *no current experience of acting*. In this alternative picture, the conscious experience of acting reflects, rather than constitutes, the mental process causing the action: conscious awareness may, but need not, accompany representational activity.[37]

In this revised theory, intentions-in-action drive behavior by initiating and monitoring it contextually. Acting physically essentially presupposes the ability to compare the (conceptual or nonconceptual) representation of what is to be done with the various feedback (mainly nonconceptual) representations conveyed by perception. Thus intentions-in-action include nonpropositional content (they represent bodily movements in physical actions or mental operations in mental actions in a way that is subject-relative, imagistic, dynamic and qualitative). Some features of the former theory remain central to the revised one. Intentions are representational, in the sense that they are constituted by conditions of satisfaction. These conditions are causal-reflexive. In the case of prior intentions, Searle's analysis is retained. In the case of intentions-in-action, causal-reflexivity is deferred to those feedback mechanisms that register the conformity or discrepancy of the present state with the goal state.

More formally, we might define *a minimal action as a piece of behavior which is such that a given pragmatic representation controls it and adequately monitors occurrent feedback until its target event is reached.* The conditions of satisfaction of a minimal action would be [that the target event is reached through this controlled bodily movement (or mental operation)]. Such a definition would remain in the spirit of Searle's intention-in-action, and would also preserve causal token-reflexivity. "This bodily movement" and "this mental operation" are now demonstrative expressions whose nonconceptual content involves the context in which they are used.[38]

Being both executive in its function and specific in its content, a pragmatic representation, when applied to a given context, explains how an agent can execute in a concrete and flexible way a general plan. It accounts for the adjustments that the agent has to make in order to reach the target state (by dynamically comparing the observed result to the anticipated goal). This solution further allows that a representation can be activated without being conscious or susceptible of becoming conscious. And it has this final important merit: the activation of a pragmatic representation does not presuppose that the source of the representational activation is constituted by some particular intention to act.

There is a second direction in which it would be interesting to expand Searle's theory of Intentionality. As Searle himself showed, a successful action transforms the world in a way that is internally related to the intention driving the action. The agent should thus be able to directly perceive her own intention, or that of other agents, while the concomitant actions develop, at least in the case of simple physical actions. What kind of account could be offered of how people perceive (rather than infer) intentions in the external behavior of other agents (or, in some cases, in their own)? Is the kind of perception that an agent has of other agents essentially different from the kind of knowledge without observation that an agent has of her own intentions-in-action? There are arguments, which cannot be summarized here, that suggest that knowledge without observation is a philosopher's myth.[39] Be that as it may, if one grants that some of one's intentions can be perceived, the corresponding Intentional state of perceiving an intention poses an intriguing puzzle for the proponent of directions of fit. Although an intention has a world-to-mind direction of fit, it must, when perceived, be the content of a mind-to-world thought. How might the same thought be simultaneously world-to-mind (in its executive dimension) and mind-to-world (in its perceptual dimension)?[40] If there are two thoughts, how are they Intentionally related? I leave this puzzle to the motivated reader.

Notes

1. The unfortunate fact that philosophers use "intentional" – and "intentionality" – to refer both to object-directedness and to goal-directed intending becomes here a serious source of equivocity. In *Intentionality* (Cambridge: Cambridge University Press, 1983), p. 3, Searle suggests that we use *intentional* to refer to mental states causing an action and *Intentional* to refer to the representational capacity in general, a usage that we shall preserve here.
2. See John Searle, *Speech Acts* (Cambridge: Cambridge University Press, 1969).
3. Although some complex intentional states, such as S regretting that P, seem to lack any particular direction of fit, they do include intentional components with conditions of fit; for example, regretting presupposes that S believes that P occurred (mind-to-world direction of fit), and that S would now be disposed to prevent P or P-type events from happening (world-to-mind direction of fit). As we shall see, the same kind of complex embedding of directions of fit may also be present in the realm of action.
4. *Intentionality*, p. 81.
5. *Intentionality*, p. 82.
6. In Donald Davidson, "Freedom to Act," in T. Honderich (ed.), *Essays on Freedom of Action* (London: Routledge and Kegan Paul, 1973), pp. 137–56; see pp. 153–4. Reprinted in *Essays on Actions and Events* (Oxford: Oxford University Press, 1980), pp. 63–81.
7. *Intentionality*, p. 97.
8. John Searle, "The Background of Intentionality and Action," in E. Lepore and R. Van Gulick (eds.), *John Searle and His Critics* (Cambridge: Blackwell, 1991), pp. 289–299, at p. 296.
9. See Harry G. Frankfurt, "The Problem of Action," *American Philosophical Quarterly* 15 (1978): 157–62.
10. See Rosalyn Hursthouse, "Arational Actions," *Journal of Philosophy* 88: 2(1991): 57–68.
11. Searle's effort to construe back-scratchings and the like as actions would therefore be misrepresented if one interpreted an intention-in-action as an additional piece of conscious willing effort (specialized in emergency situations, so to speak), i.e., as a specific *mental act* whose function is to produce on-line active

bodily movements. O'Shaughnessy suggests such an interpretation, while admitting that it might be nothing but surmise. See Brian O'Shaughnessy, "Searle's Theory of Action," in Lepore and Van Gulick (eds.), *John Searle and His Critics*, pp. 271–87, at p. 281; and Searle's response, "The Background of Intentionality and Action," p. 297. See also *Intentionality*, p. 88.

12. See Kent Bach, "A Representational Theory of Action," *Philosophical Studies* 34 (1978): 361–79.

13. Example from Searle's *Intentionality*.

14. Example from Hursthouse in "Arational Actions."

15. In "A Representational Theory of Action."

16. Searle follows Gilbert Harman on this point; see Gilbert Harman, "Practical Reasoning," *Review of Metaphysics* 29 (1976): 431–63.

17. Cf. "The Background of Intentionality and Action," p. 296.

18. Comparing (4) and (5), it is clear that [**ia**(this **ia** causes bm)] spells out the Intentional content of an intention-in-action, which normally allows performing a minimal action.

19. Cf. John Searle, "Reference and Intentionality," in Lepore and Van Gulick (eds.), *John Searle and his Critics*, pp. 227–41, at p. 231.

20. See "Reference and Intentionality," p. 236.

21. See Harman, "Practical Reasoning," p. 86.

22. Note that the programmer need not have wanted the murder to occur in order for him to be liable for it. Even if he failed to prevent the murder from happening, the action remains his. It is a case of an intentional action – setting up the program to do this and that – with unintended consequences.

23. Unfortunately, severe echopraxia of the sort found in the imitation syndrome makes such an intervention possible. See F. Lhermitte, B. Pillon, and M. Serdaru, "Human Autonomy and the Frontal Lobes. Part I: Imitation and Utilization Behavior," *Annals of Neurology* 19: 4 (1986): 326–34.

24. See *Intentionality*, p. 89.

25. See also "The Background of Intentionality and Action," p. 298.

26. In "The Background of Intentionality and Action," Searle claims that a distinction between "experience of acting" and "intention-in-action" is needed because "there are many actions that are performed intentionally, where the agent is quite unconscious of the intention" (p. 298). This claim does not seem compatible with the causal role given to experience in *Intentionality*, or with the phenomenological conditions of satisfaction linked to causal self-referentiality.

27. On this distinction, see section 1.

28. See also "Reference and Intentionality," p. 235.

29. See Christopher Peacocke, *A Study of Concepts* (Cambridge, Mass.: MIT Press, 1992), p. 75.

30. The standard objections that may be directed at these attempts to enlarge the notion of content to include such primitive layers of perception and action are (1) that the latter do not belong to Intentional content, because they are

not expressible in propositions; (2) furthermore, that demonstrative concepts are sufficient to cover all these cases of individual, fine-grained experiences. A full discussion of both objections cannot be developed here. See Joëlle Proust, "Perceiving Intentions," in Johannes Roessler and Naomi Eilan (eds.), *Agency and Self-Awareness: Issues in Philosophy and Psychology* (Oxford: Oxford University Press, 2003).

31. "The background of Intentionality and Action," p. 293.

32. See Gareth Evans, *The Varieties of Reference* (Oxford: Clarendon Press, 1982).

33. In Lepore and Van Gulick (eds.), *John Searle and His Critics*, pp. 271–87. See, in particular, p. 273.

34. See *Intentionality*, p. 97; and "The Background of Intentionality and Action," p. 299 n. 2.

35. See Joëlle Proust, "Indexes for Action," *Revue Internationale de Philosophie*, Neurosciences (1999), 3, 321–45; and Elisabeth Pacherie, "The Content of Intentions," *Mind and Language* 15: 4 (2000): 400–32, for two attempts to solve the puzzle using this framework.

36. Alfred R. Mele, *Springs of Action* (Oxford: Oxford University Press, 1982), p. 184.

37. This view is rather close to a theory defended by Kent Bach under the name Representational Causalism in Kent Bach, "A Representational Theory of Action," *Philosophical Studies* 34 (1978): 361–79, esp. p. 367. It is compatible with later findings and theorizing in the neuroscientific approach to action. See Marc Jeannerod, "The Representing Brain, Neural Correlates of Motor Intention and Imagery," *Behavioral and Brain Sciences* 17 (1994): 187–245.

38. For a more detailed presentation, see Joëlle Proust, "Indexes for Action"; "Awareness of Agency: Three Levels of Analysis," in T. Metzinger (ed.), *The Neural Correlates of Consciousness* (Cambridge, Mass.: MIT Press, 2000), pp. 307–324; and "Perceiving Intentions."

39. See Proust, "Perceiving Intentions."

40. See Proust, "Perceiving Intentions," for an attempt at solving this puzzle.

6 | Consciousness

NEIL C. MANSON

1. THE IMPORTANCE OF BEING CONSCIOUS

Consciousness is central to John Searle's philosophy of mind. He holds that 'the primary and most essential feature of minds is consciousness', and that 'we really have no notion of the mental apart from our notion of consciousness'.[1] Not only is consciousness central to our conception of mind, but Searle insists that 'there is a sense in which it is *the* most important feature of reality, because all other things have value, importance, merit or worth only in relation to consciousness'.[2] He maintains that 'consciousness is the condition that makes it possible for anything at all to matter to anybody'.[3] Searle argues that mind, meaning, and social reality depend upon consciousness. He has sought to develop a rich systematic account of how these various phenomena, all dependent upon consciousness, fit together.[4] There is an order of dependence here. Social facts and linguistic meaning depend upon mind. Mind presupposes consciousness. Our concern here will be limited to mind and consciousness.

Searle takes consciousness to be a natural phenomenon, a feature of the natural world described and explained by the natural sciences. The two assumptions – that consciousness is central to mind and meaning, and that consciousness is a natural phenomenon – give rise to the traditional philosophical problem of consciousness: the problem of how we reconcile the subjective nature of consciousness with the objective nature of the world studied by the natural sciences. The problem of consciousness features in two distinctive ways in Searle's thought. First, he argues that most contemporary thought about the mind is misguided precisely because it views consciousness as something problematic. Second, Searle argues that the problem of consciousness rests upon a number of misguided assumptions and misleading metaphors. He argues that we have been thinking about consciousness, and its relation to the brain, in the wrong way. He has an alternative positive proposal that, Searle insists, implies that 'there is no metaphysical mind-body problem left'.[5]

Searle views consciousness as essential to the mind. Most contemporary thinkers do not. Searle can explain why people fail to give consciousness its proper role by alluding to the problems that people commonly have with consciousness. By getting rid of those problems he paves the way for his own positive philosophy, with consciousness, identified as a natural phenomenon, at its core.

The aim here is to introduce and examine some of the key features of Searle's critical and positive thinking about consciousness by sketching 'the bigger picture' of how various elements of Searle's thought revolve around the central notion of consciousness, and by exploring how Searle's conception of consciousness and mind relates to, and is opposed to, a great deal of contemporary thought. The first part of the chapter examines why consciousness is taken to be something problematic and how the problematic nature of consciousness has led to a 'divide and conquer' strategy, where philosophers have tried to give an account of mind as something independent of consciousness. The second part fixes upon Searle's positive views about consciousness and his 'dissolution' of the mind-body problem. The final section raises a couple of general issues that arise when theorists place consciousness at the heart of their philosophy.

2. CONSCIOUSNESS, INTENTIONALITY, PERCEPTION AND ACTION

Given the complexity of our first topic – the relationship between consciousness and mind – and given that contemporary philosophical discourse is often very technical, it will help if we begin by reminding ourselves of some fairly obvious commonplace facts.

We are conscious. As conscious subjects, we have a first-person point of view. It is like something to be awake, to dream, to feel pain, to see, to hear, to think. Our first-person point of view gives each of us a subjective perspective upon a world that we take to be, by and large, independent of that point of view. We have conscious experiences, sensations, pains and feelings, thoughts, wishes, desires, beliefs. Most of our conscious mental states are *about* things. You see this book before you; I can hear a car passing by; we believe that snow is white; I want to have some coffee. Philosophers have a technical term for this 'aboutness' feature that many mental states have: *intentionality*.[6] Our conscious thoughts and beliefs need not be about our perceptible environment. We can think about and have beliefs about the future or the past, about fictional characters, imaginary objects, hypothetical situations, and unreal numbers. The 'intentional objects' of thought and experience need not exist. If Little Nell thinks that Santa Claus is coming tonight, Santa is the intentional *object* of her thought, but Santa Claus (sorry to say) does not exist. Mental states are about things – have intentional objects – insofar as they have intentional *content*. The intentional content of a mental state is not the same thing as the intentional object of a mental state. If Nell's sister Daisy thinks that Santa isn't coming, the intentional object of Daisy's thought is the same as that of Nell's thought, but the intentional contents of their thoughts differ. There are lots of different kinds of mental states: perceptions, beliefs, pains, hopes, desires, and so on. Different types of mental states can have the same intentional object and intentional content. If Nell hopes that Santa will come, and Daisy doubts that Santa will come, they have different types of mental states with the same (type of) intentional content.

We conscious beings, beings with conscious intentional states, are objects in the natural world. As such, we are part of the causal order of things. Many of our mental states seem to stand in a distinctive kind of causal relation to the world. Mental states and their contents are often caused by events in the world. Think of perception. If light bounces off the surfaces of objects in front of us when our eyes are open and operative, then we see those objects. What we see, the intentional content of our visual experience, is normally causally dependent upon the nature and arrangement of the light entering our eyes. Or consider pain. The none-too-extreme worldly event of pushing a pin under your own fingernail has quite extreme effects in the way things feel to you. The damage to the tender skin under the nail is felt by you in your conscious experience, is felt as being located at a certain place in your body. The intentional content of conscious perception and sensation is causally dependent upon events in the nonmental world.

We are not passive objects. We can act. We can move our bodies in a controlled way in order to bring about certain effects in the nonmental world. What we do depends upon what we believe, what we want, and what we take to be the best way of achieving our ends. Our actions bring about certain effects. If our actions are successful, then we bring about something that we sought to bring about. In such cases, what happens in the nonmental world seems to be causally dependent upon the intentional content of our mental states. It is hard to conceive of action and perception *without* using the idea of intentionality. When we rationally act, we seek to bring about changes in the world as we take it to be (or as we 'represent' it to be, as philosophers sometimes say). We desire certain things, want the world to be *this* way and not that.

From this sketch, we can identify three general features of our conception of mind: first, consciousness; second, intentionality; and third, the
distinctive kind of causal relatedness that we have with the world via our
mental states. It is true that our causal relatedness to the world involves
much more than just perception and action (e.g., emotional reactions, bodily
sensations, feelings of pain). It is also true that there are many other
features of mind that we have not mentioned. But for our purposes,
these three features are sufficient for us to understand the issues and
views that shape Searle's critical and positive positions in philosophy of
mind.

3. WHY ARE CONSCIOUSNESS AND MIND SO PUZZLING?

Philosophers have found the mind puzzling. Why? We human beings occupy a world of objects arranged in space and time: trees, dogs, mountains,
rivers, tables. These everyday objects seem, on further investigation, to be
made out of components, constituents, simpler kinds of stuff. Over the
past two thousand years or so, we have come to hold that the different
types of objects we encounter are all composed of the same fundamental
constituents, albeit arranged and structured in different ways. Supernovae,
dwarf stars, and film stars are all made of the same kind of stuff, the stuff
that the natural sciences measure, describe, explain. This simple line of reflection is an *ontological* one, to do with the nature of being or existence.
In its simplest form, it suggests that everything that exists is part of one
objective world. But what about our conscious minds? When we weigh a
person, cut up a corpse, look at slices of brain, lay out all the chemical constituents of a person, where do we find *consciousness*? Not only do we not
encounter the consciousness of others in the objective world studied by the
natural sciences, it is arguably difficult to even conceive of how something
subjective can emerge out of a combination or arrangement of objective
bits of stuff. When you look at this page before you, how can it be that
your experience is made up of nothing more than activity in the brain?
Such a view seems to be obviously nonsensical. We can readily understand
how different kinds of objective things might all be made out of the same
simple objective components; but when we turn to consciousness, we seem
to require a shift from the objectivity of the constituent parts to the subjectivity of the whole. But how can there be features of the natural world
that aren't part of the objective scheme of things? Consciousness seems to
be impossible to fit into the objective natural world, but there seems to be

no other place to put it. The tension between subjectivity and objectivity is the heart of the philosophical problem of consciousness.[7]

The subjective nature of consciousness poses a puzzle for anyone who holds that conscious subjects are part of the natural world. But what about intentionality? Is it as puzzling as consciousness? At first sight, it seems so. How on earth can a 70 kilo mass of electrochemically agitated meat have states that are about other bits of the world? Worse, how on earth can a bit of the natural world, some hunk of material stuff, have thoughts about things that don't exist, or things that have long since ceased to be? The relation we have to the intentional objects of our thoughts cannot be a simple causal one, because nonexistent things cannot cause anything.

How can consciousness and intentionality be part of the objective, non-intentional world? There are two lines of philosophical response to this puzzle that do not have much support these days. The first is 'substance' dualism. The substance dualist holds not only that there are 'material' things, such as trees, electrons, brains, bodies, but also that there are 'immaterial' or 'spiritual' things, such as souls, spirits, egos, and minds. The spiritual things do not have the properties that material things have. Souls have no mass, no size, no shape; they are not solid, liquid, gaseous; they have no temperature; they have no parts. This 'solution' is a bit like the strategy of converting all your small debts into one really big loan. Consciousness and intentionality are puzzling if we try to view them as features of the brain, but they are not so puzzling if they are features of a very special kind of thing, one that not only can have conscious intentional states, but whose very nature it is to have such states. Unfortunately, this move just makes our problems worse. If souls are nonspatial entities that don't have any of the properties of 'material' objects, how do they get to play a role in the cut and thrust of animal and human life? Philosophical ingenuity is boundless. Over the centuries, various proposals have been put forward as an answer to the problem of 'interaction' faced by substance dualism, but none of them are convincing or unproblematic.

A second line of response is *idealism*. We noted earlier that thoughts and experiences can be about things that don't exist. Idealists hold that the objective world studied by science doesn't really exist, that only thoughts and experiences do. Idealists do not face the problem of interaction, because for them there aren't two ontologically distinct kinds of things (souls and physical objects); there are just souls and their ideas. The price to pay is that we have to deny that the world was there anyway, prior to the existence of minded creatures. Searle and the majority of the people whom he opposes are united in their opposition to idealism, so we need say no more about it here.

The fact that both substance dualism and idealism have such counterintuitive consequences has motivated many thinkers to see if they can account for consciousness and intentionality while fully acknowledging the natural, physical constitution of we human animals. These antidualist, nonidealistic conceptions of mind are species of *materialism*.[8] One materialist proposal is the *logical behaviorism* set forth by Gilbert Ryle and Carl Hempel.[9] Logical behaviorism is the doctrine that our mental concepts are really just concepts of behavioral dispositions. What is it to believe that it is raining? It is to be disposed to behave in certain ways in certain circumstances (e.g., to be disposed to take one's umbrella, to answer 'Yes' to the question 'Is it raining?', and so on). What is it to have toothache? It is to be disposed to behave in a certain way: emitting moans, pointing at one's teeth. This view of the mind seems thoroughly odd. If you are unlucky enough to end up with a pin embedded under your fingernail, there is something about your pain over and above the disposition to scream, swear, run to the phone: the pain feels like something, something very bad indeed. While the pain may dispose the person who has it to do certain things in order to get rid of it, the pain and the disposition are distinct. Behaviorism, Searle points out, 'sounds obviously false because, for example, everyone knows that a feeling of pain is one thing and the behavior associated with pain is another'.[10]

In the middle of the twentieth century, a different 'materialist' approach to the mind emerged. It was argued by a number of thinkers that mental states (or mental 'types') might just be identical to brain states (or brain 'types'). Pains are just a certain type of brain event; beliefs are just a kind of brain state. This is the 'type-identity' theory.[11] One great virtue of this view is that the problem of interaction disappears. There is no special philosophical problem about how events in the brain cause other events in the body. If pains are just a certain type of brain event, then pains (and other conscious states) are part of the natural world insofar as the brain is part of the natural world. Searle points out a very simple objection to the type-identity theory.[12] We seem to be able to identify pains and brain states independently. We can know about pains without knowing anything about the brain, and vice versa. This poses the identity theorist with a challenge. How can they explain the fact that my pains seem to 'present' themselves to me in one way, and to third-person observers in another way? One answer is that there are in fact two distinct properties (pain properties, brain properties) involved. But this response amounts to a denial of the type-identity theory, which holds that pain properties are just properties of the brain. The other response is to insist that pains are brain states; but then the theorist has to deny our intuition that there is at least an apparent difference between pains and brain states.[13]

There is a further problem with type-identity materialism. You and I, and a clever Martian, may all believe that Earth is the third planet from the Sun. But you and I and the Martian may differ in subtle, or not-so-subtle, ways with regard to the features of our brain that underpin that belief. If mental states are just brain states, how can this be so? Sameness of belief would imply sameness of brain state; but sameness of belief does not seem to require sameness of brain state at all. For example, if the Martian learns our language, can *say* that Earth is the third planet from the Sun, and can point to it on a map, our everyday concept of belief seems to demand that we ascribe the belief (that Earth is third from the Sun) to the Martian, whether or not her brain is anything like ours.

4. FUNCTIONALISM TO THE RESCUE?

Logical behaviourism and the type-identity theory spawned a material-ist conception of mind that seemed to have the virtues of both theories, while avoiding some of the problems: *functionalism*.[14] Functionalism can be viewed as a descendant of logical behaviourism. But rather than identifying mental states with dispositions to behave in certain ways in certain contexts, the functionalist, like the type-identity theorist, allows that mental states can be causes of behaviour. But unlike the type-identity theorist, the func-tionalist argues that we do not identify or classify mental states in terms of their physical or neurophysiological properties; rather, we identify and classify them in terms of the *causal roles* that such states play. There is noth-ing very odd about this kind of practice. We identify lots of things in this way. Take pumps. What is it for something to be a pump? We don't iden-tify or classify things as pumps in terms of what they are made of. Pumps can be made of wood, metal, glass, muscle; what makes an object a pump is its causal role. Pumps are devices or organs that play the causal role of raising or moving liquids, compressing or rarefying gases. The function-alist views mental states in a similar way. Consider the philosopher David Lewis's functionalist definition of pain and other mental states.

> The concept of pain, or indeed of any other experience or mental state, is the concept of a state that occupies a certain causal role, a state with certain typical causes and effects. It is the concept of a state apt for being caused by

certain stimuli and apt for causing certain behavior. Or, better, of a state apt for being caused in certain ways by stimuli plus other mental states and apt for combining with certain other mental states to jointly cause behavior.[15]

One reason why functionalism is appealing is that it meets one of the worries that faced the type-identity theorist. Just as pumps can be made of all sorts of different material, the functionalist view of mental states allows it to be the case that you and I and the Martian can all believe that it is raining even though we have no type of underlying physical state in common. What matters is that we all have some state or other that plays the 'belief' role (the issue of the content of beliefs will be discussed in a moment).

One reason for believing in functionalism is that, as we saw earlier, we are already committed to the view that our mental states play a distinctive causal role in our lives. Our beliefs and desires move us to act in certain ways. Our perceptual states are caused by events in the environment and allow us to think about, and act within, that environment in the pursuit of our ends. On this line of thought, functionalism is a philosophical doctrine abstracted from our ordinary thinking about the mind. David Lewis, for example, holds that commonsense psychology provides us with a range of 'platitudes . . . regarding the causal relations of mental states, sensory stimuli, and motor responses'.[16]

In addition to the fact that our everyday psychological concept of mind is – at least in part – a causal one, there is a further reason why function-alism came to be so widely favoured. In the 1950s, empirical psychology underwent a revolution, sometimes referred to as the *cognitive revolution*.[17] Computational theory allowed people to conceive of, design, and build systems that operate upon 'symbols'. When you press the keys '2' '+' '2' on your pocket calculator, your pressing of the '+' key is interpretable as bringing about an operation of *addition* precisely because of the functional relation between the inputs (pressing the '2' key before and after the '+') and the output (a display, a printout, a noise) that is interpretable as 'repre-senting' the number four. Just as pumps can be made of many different types of material, computational programs (ordered sets of simple 'symbolic' operations that serve some purpose of the programmer and user) can be 'implemented' in all sorts of different physical systems. The 'addition' oper-ation can be implemented in something made of silicon chips, and in some-thing made of bits of punched card with knitting needles that slot through holes.

Computational systems are functional systems, defined in terms of what they do. Cognitive scientists, like functionalist philosophers of mind, view psychological and behavioural abilities in functional terms. The difference between cognitive science and philosophical functionalism is that cognitive science seeks to explain, rather than just to define, the nature of our mental life. Cognitive scientific explanations are a species of *functional explanation*.[18] Functional explanations explain the abilities and dispositions of complex creatures or systems by breaking them down ('decomposing' them) into simpler types of causal processes and structures. In cognitive science, the key idea is that the abilities and dispositions that we seek to explain – human thought, memory, perception, action, and speech – all involve symbolic processes, causal processes that are sensitive to the intentional content of representational states. The reason for thinking this is that when we try to describe perception, action, memory and so on, we cannot help but use representational terms. Cognitive scientific explanations give computational models of the symbolic (or intentional) processes that constitute human psychology. Such explanations proceed by specifying (e.g., in a flow diagram) various types of components, causal relations, and symbolic processes in three broad, interrelated, areas: (i) the input of information to a system; (ii) the processing, storage, generation, and use of information within a system; and (iii) the use of information in governing, controlling, and effecting outputs from the system.

If we blend together the functionalist conception of mental states (in terms of causal role) and the cognitive scientific method of explanation (a species of functional analysis), we have the version of functionalism that is sometimes referred to as the *representational theory of mind*.[19] In the representational theory of mind, we seem to have the foundations for a way of thinking about mind, language, inference, thought, perception, action, and so on in causal terms without facing the problems of substance dualism, idealism, behaviourism, or the type-identity theory. Three cheers for functionalism, then?

Not quite, for there is a slight problem. Barbra Von Eckardt notes, in her monograph on the nature of cognitive science, that 'theories in cognitive science seek to explain the human cognitive capacities by, among other things, positing mental representations (that is, entities or states with semantic properties)'.[20] So far, so good. But, Von Eckardt goes on, 'little attention has been devoted to the question of where the posited semantic properties come from. The notion of mental representation has, in other words, been treated as a primitive'.[21] Von Eckardt cites one of the most vocal advocates of computational functionalism, Jerry Fodor, as stating that 'we are in the position of having a representational theory of mind without having a theory of mental representation. This is not a stable position, something has to be done'.[22]

It is one thing to treat computers and robots and even people *as if* they had this or that intentional state, but it is another to actually give an account of how creatures really do get to have intentional states. How does a robot, a person, or a computer get to have a state that is about something? Over the past twenty years or so, many philosophers have spent a great deal of time trying to solve this problem, the problem of how 'representational' or 'intentional' content might be characterized and explained in naturalistic terms. There are many different proposals as to how intentionality might be viewed in naturalistic terms, but all of these proposals are alike in the sense that they all aim to spell out 'in nonsemantic and nonintentional terms, sufficient conditions for one bit of the world to *be about* (to express, represent, or be true of) another bit'.[23] At the heart of all these proposals is the idea that causality is the key.[24] Such accounts are often referred to as 'naturalized' theories of intentional or representational content. Functionalist theorists are not put off by the fact that no one has yet produced an adequate theory of just how states of a natural object (a human being, for example) might get to be about things in the world. They assume that someday, somehow, such an account will be forthcoming. In the interim, the theorist can go ahead and theorise about mind and language, confident that the edifice that is functionalism will, one day, be provided with a firm foundation.

5. DIVIDE AND CONQUER: FIRST CONTENT, THEN 'MENTAL STATE CONSCIOUSNESS'

What about *consciousness*? Hasn't that been left out of the functionalist theory altogether? Suppose for a moment that functionalism has left out consciousness. Is this automatically a bad thing? We saw earlier that puzzles arise when we try to conceive of how intentionality and consciousness could be part of the natural world. Wouldn't it be a good thing if we could prise apart the problem of consciousness and the problem of intentionality? Functionalism allows a theorist to frame her account of mentality independent of consciousness. Functionalism makes room for an appealing methodological strategy.

> It used to be universally taken for granted that the problem about consciousness and the problem about intentionality are intrinsically linked: that thought is ipso facto conscious. . . . Freud changed all that. He made it seem plausible that explaining behavior might require the postulation of intentional but unconscious states. Over the last century, and most especially in Cartesian linguistics and in cognitive psychology, Freud's idea appears to

have been amply vindicated. . . . Dividing and conquering – concentrating on intentionality and ignoring consciousness – has proved a remarkably successful research strategy so far.[25]

Fodor's remark draws upon the assumption that we can conceive of intentionality as something independent of consciousness. If this is right, we can keep the problem of consciousness apart from the problem of intentionality. Functionalism allows us to leave aside issues about subjectivity, allows us to focus on explaining intentionality without worrying about consciousness. It is this motivated neglect of consciousness that Searle bemoans when he remarks that in contemporary philosophy and psychology, it is assumed that 'it is quite possible, indeed desirable, to give an account of language, cognition, and mental states in general without taking into account consciousness and subjectivity'.[26] Searle, like Fodor, identifies the 'motivation for this urge to separate consciousness and intentionality' as stemming from the desire to 'get a theory of mind that won't be discredited by the fact that it lacks a theory of consciousness'.[27]

Viewed in this way, Searle's objection to functionalism might seem to be just that the functionalist hasn't bothered to keep consciousness in her theory of mind, perhaps because functionalism 'can't "handle" consciousness'.[28] But this cannot be the core of Searle's criticism of functionalism, for, as Searle knows, functionalist theorists have also sought to give theories of consciousness. Here, the fact that functionalism is a 'consciousness-independent' conception of mind and intentionality shapes the way in which such theorists seek to explain consciousness. The philosopher Daniel Dennett, in his book *Consciousness Explained*, describes his 'fundamental strategy' in the following way.

> . . . first, to develop an account of content that is *independent of* and *more fundamental than* consciousness – an account of content that treats equally of all unconscious content-fixation (in brains, in computers, in evolution's "recognition" of properties of selected designs) – and second, to build an account of consciousness on that foundation. First content, then consciousness.[29]

Functionalism and cognitive science involve a consciousness-independent conception of mind. The consciousness-independent conception of mind can provide a basis for theorising about consciousness. The first step is to establish a theory of mental states and their content, and the second step is to use that conception of mind in explaining consciousness. Because functionalism allows one to conceive of mental states without their conscious status being an issue, consciousness may seem to be some extra feature that some, but not all, mental states have. Mentality is one thing, consciousness is another. Functionalist philosophers have introduced the special term 'mental state consciousness' for the extra property that they take some mental states to have. The various functionalist and cognitive theories of consciousness are answers to the question of 'what it is for a mental state to be conscious'.[30] The idea is that if we are to explain consciousness, then 'we need to explain the difference between conscious mental states and nonconscious mental states or unconscious mental states or processes'.[31]

Within the broad camp of functionalism and cognitive science there is considerable dispute about just how 'mental state consciousness' is best characterized and explained. One popular theoretical approach to mental state consciousness is the view that conscious mental states are the objects of higher-order thoughts.[32] A mental state is conscious if one is conscious of having it, or being in it.[33] Other functionalists oppose the higher-order thought accounts and offer 'first-order' representational accounts of consciousness. On this latter type of theory, higher-order representation is neither necessary nor sufficient for consciousness: conscious mental states are those representational states *via* which a subject is conscious of some object, or some fact.[34] These higher-order and first-order representational theories both draw upon the idea that intentionality is independent of consciousness.

We cannot discuss the details of these theories, or the many other cognitive scientific theories of consciousness that have been offered in the past few years. There are two reasons for drawing attention to the 'first content, then consciousness' strategy. First, we avoid misunderstanding Searle's objection to functionalism. We have already noted that Searle's objection cannot be just that functionalism happens to have ignored consciousness. His objection is that functionalism, the representational theory of mind, the 'divide and conquer' strategy, cannot ever provide an account of consciousness. Why? The reason is that these theories are all based upon a number of false assumptions about the nature of mind and intentionality. The functionalists can continue to proliferate theories of consciousness, but if Searle is right, such theories are doomed from the start.

The second reason for making explicit the distinctive explanatory approach to consciousness found in functionalist theories of mind is that it allows us to see how Searle's view of consciousness cannot be the notion of 'mental state consciousness' that abounds in contemporary thought. Let us now turn to Searle's view of the connection between mind and consciousness, and his view of consciousness itself.

6. SEARLE'S 'CONSCIOUSNESS-DEPENDENT' CONCEPTION OF MIND

The theories of consciousness found in cognitive science, and in most contemporary philosophy, start with the assumption that mental states and intentional content can be characterised and defined without reference to, or acknowledgement of, conscious subjectivity. It is this foundational assumption that provides the basis for the many different lines of argument that Searle has levied against the dominant conception of mind: his critique of functionalism and cognitive science; his attack on the idea of 'Strong Artificial Intelligence' (the view that if a system runs the right kind of computational program, then that fact alone might be sufficient for mentality); his objection to the 'deep unconscious' of psychoanalysis and cognitive science (that is, the view that there might be mental states that cannot, even in principle, become conscious).[35]

Searle argues that intentionality can be properly understood *only* in terms of consciousness. Why? In order to understand Searle's argument here, we need to take note of some of his technical jargon. We are already familiar with the notion of *intentionality*. Some things – such as the inscriptions on this page, the sounds we make when we speak, traffic signs, and hieroglyphics – have a *derived* intentionality. These phenomena get to be *about* things (to represent things) only because they are produced by and interpretable by creatures like us, who have *intrinsic*, or *nonderived*, intentional states. Many of our conscious mental states have intrinsic intentionality: it is part of their nature to be about things. The fact that your thoughts and pains have the intentional contents that they do is a fact about your consciousness, not a fact about the way other people are willing to interpret you. (It should be stressed that some philosophers deny this, arguing that all intentionality is derived intentionality, that 'aboutness' is just a feature of certain practices of 'interpretation'.)[36] Searle also stresses the fact that we can *use* intentional terms in a metaphorical way: 'The daffodils want a drink'; 'The central heating has finally decided to come on'; 'My computer wants me to delete files to save space'. Searle refers to this as *as-if* intentionality. We act *as if* certain things had intentional states, had desires, made decisions, and so on, even though we know full well that they do not.

Searle insists that only conscious mental states have intrinsic intentionality. First, he claims that at least some of our conscious mental states have intrinsic intentionality; the second step is to show that nothing else does. In order to establish the first claim, Searle points out certain facts that should be obvious to anyone who is not in the grip of a materialist theory of mind. It is through our conscious mental states that we find ourselves in a world of objects, people, events, tables, dogs, and so on. It is like something to be a waking human being, looking at things, hearing things, thinking about things. We can just tell, by reflecting upon what it is to be a waking human being, that we have conscious intentional states. We can, Searle assumes, also tell that the intentional content of our mental states doesn't depend upon the attitudes and interests of other people. The intentionality of conscious states is intrinsic.

So what? Suppose we don't doubt that we have conscious intentional states – surely that doesn't tell us very much? In particular, it doesn't tell us *how* we get to have intentional states, and if our naïve first-person reflection upon our conscious life doesn't tell us *how* we get to have intentional states, how can we be sure that *other* things, other nonconscious things, don't have intentional states, too? How can I tell, just by reflecting on my own experience, that intentionality is *not* made possible by just the kind of causal relations that the 'naturalized content' theorist uses as the basis of her theory of intentionality? It is no good trying to imagine what this unconscious intentionality would be like from the first-person point of view, because if it is unconscious, then it won't feature in one's first-person point of view in the way that one's conscious intentional states do.

It is at this point that Searle offers two further arguments in support of his claim that consciousness is essential to intentionality. First, he points out that everything can be interpreted *as if* it were intentional.[37] Ancient people seemed to be quite happy to ascribe desires to objects in order to explain why they fell downward. ('They want to be closer to their home, the earth'.) If we don't keep the distinction between intrinsic and *as-if* intentionality, then the price to pay would be that 'everything would become mental, because relative to some purpose or other anything can be treated *as if* it were mental'.[38] Of course, this point might be one where the functionalist agrees with Searle. One of the challenges facing naturalistic theories of representation is to secure a distinction between cases where something does represent another and cases where we might, for all sorts of reasons, talk *as if* it did so. Searle needs something more than just the distinction between intrinsic and as-if intentionality if he is to give us grounds to accept that consciousness is essential to the mind.

The second line of argument is meant to do just this. Searle argues that it is only consciousness that provides a plausible basis for the perspectival nature of intentional content. When we think about things, we think about them in a certain way. For example, suppose Lois Lane thinks that she would like to give Superman a kiss. Superman is the same person as Clark Kent, but Lois Lane doesn't think that she would like to kiss dull Clark. Even though

Clark and Superman are one and the same person, Lois Lane thinks about that single person in different ways. Searle uses the term 'aspectual shape' to denote the perspectival nature of thought: 'All representations represent their objects . . . under aspects. Every intentional state has what I call an *aspectual shape*'.[39]

> Whenever we perceive anything or think about anything, we always do so under some aspects and not others. These aspectual features are essential to the intentional state; they are part of what makes it the mental state that it is. When you see a car . . . you actually have a conscious experience from a certain point of view and with certain features . . . , and what is true of conscious perceptions is true of intentional states generally.[40]

The fact that 'our intentional states often have determinate intentional contents with determinate aspectual shapes . . . presupposes consciousness'.[41] So, without consciousness there is no aspectual shape; without aspectual shape there is no intentional content.

This is all very contentious. Philosophers have been exercising themselves over this problem (of how we can think about one thing 'under different aspects') for the past hundred years or so, and many of the proposed solutions do not rely upon consciousness. So why is Searle so sure that consciousness is the only answer? The best explanation I can give is that there are three further lines of support that, when taken together, provide the warrant for Searle's view that consciousness is essential to mind. First, Searle seeks to show that we can have a plausible and coherent account of intentionality and linguistic meaning by taking consciousness as the core notion. Second, he draws attention to the problems that ensue when one's theory of mind and language fails to take consciousness as the core notion. Third, he offers an explanation of why contemporary thinkers prefer the consciousness-independent account, even with all its problems, over the consciousness-dependent account elaborated by Searle.

We cannot go into the details of the first two lines of support here. A proper evaluation of them would require us to compare and contrast Searle's broad account of mind and language with other, similarly systematic, proposals. We would also have to evaluate Searle's many lines of criticism of his opponents. Because our concern is with consciousness, the central notion of Searle's philosophy of mind and meaning, we do need to examine the third line of support, the idea that people favour the consciousness-independent conception of mind found in functionalism precisely because they think about consciousness and subjectivity in the wrong way. One reason why people find functionalism (and other forms of materialism) so appealing is precisely because they have a *problem with consciousness*. Or, as Searle puts it, 'if one had to describe the deepest motivation for materialism, one might say that it is simply a terror of consciousness'.[42] Why fear consciousness? Because 'consciousness has the essentially terrifying feature of subjectivity'.[43]

Searle's thought is that if functionalists were to view consciousness in the right way, then they would no longer be pressured into conceiving of mind and intentionality in causal terms. If there were no problem of consciousness, then there would be no point to the 'divide and conquer' strategy of avoiding consciousness and focusing on intentionality.

7. OVERCOMING OUR PROBLEM WITH CONSCIOUSNESS: SEARLE'S 'HIGHER-LEVEL PROPERTY' ACCOUNT OF CONSCIOUSNESS

What is the right way, then, to conceive of consciousness and subjectivity? We saw earlier that the consciousness-independent view of mind found in functionalism gave rise to a particular conception of consciousness: some mental states have an extra feature – 'mental state consciousness' – and the task of the theorist is to identify this feature and to explain how it is that mental states have it. But this way of framing the problem of consciousness makes no sense upon Searle's consciousness-dependent view of mind. You cannot ask what it is for a mental state to be conscious (as opposed to un-conscious) when intentionality and mentality are essentially aspects of consciousness. Searle's conception of consciousness cannot be that of 'mental state consciousness', that is, some property that certain mental states have over and above their mental nature. Searle takes consciousness to be, first and foremost, a feature that *people* and other animals have. 'What I mean by "consciousness" can best be illustrated by examples. When I wake up from a dreamless sleep I enter a state of consciousness, a state that continues as long as I am awake'.[44]

At any one time we seem to have conscious mental states that are something other than, or at least more specific than, our overall state of being conscious. Any theory of consciousness has to accommodate the distinction between the overall state of waking consciousness and the particular conscious mental states that we have.[45] At this point, we might be tempted to draw the distinction between our overall conscious subjective state and the specific conscious states of perception, belief, and the like, by using a *theater* or *spotlight* metaphor.[46] Our total state of consciousness is the theater, or the lit-up area cast by the spotlight, and our various mental states are the objects and players illuminated (temporarily) on the stage. But this metaphor is of no use to Searle, for it suggests that mental states have an existence independent consciousness – as if our mental states could have an existence as mental states independent of their being 'illuminated' by the spotlight of consciousness. Searle offers an alternative metaphor, one that fits with his consciousness-dependent conception of mentality and with the spatial metaphor central to his doctrine of 'aspectual shape'.

> If we think of my consciousness as like an open prairie, then the changes in my conscious states will be more like bumps and mounds appearing on the prairie. Shifts and changes in the structure of the field, I think, are the correct metaphors for understanding the flux of our conscious experiences. . . . If we think of consciousness in terms of a *field* then we can think of the particular percepts, thoughts, experiences and so on, as variations and modifications in the structure of the field.[47]

This 'field' of consciousness has, in Searle's view, a particular 'mode of existence' or 'ontology'. 'Consciousness has a first-person ontology and so cannot be reduced to, or eliminated in favour of, phenomena with a third-person ontology'.[48] Phenomena with a first-person ontology 'exist only from the point of view of some agent or organism or animal or self that has them'.[49]

In Searle's conception of consciousness, when we wake up after a dreamless sleep we become conscious. We have a 'field' of consciousness, a subjective point of view. There are different aspects or modifications of this point of view at any one time; and over time, changes occur (e.g., think of the changes in your states of consciousness as you cast your eye across a crowded room). It is only within this conscious field that we find intrinsically intentional states. Because intentionality is central to the mind, and because intentionality is a feature of the subjective 'field' of consciousness, Searle claims that 'the ontology of the mind is an irreducibly first-person ontology'.[50]

But doesn't this take us back to square one, to just the kind of claim that has led people to embrace functionalism? If the ontology of mind is 'irreducibly first-personal', how on earth are we to fit it into our conception of the objective world? If something is irreducibly subjective, it just follows, as a matter of definition, that it cannot be objective. Searle, therefore, must be endorsing some kind of dualism, mustn't he?

At this point, Searle asks us to reflect upon what we know about consciousness. We know that consciousness is subjective. But, in addition, we know as a result of empirical psychological investigations that 'brain processes *cause* consciousness'.[51] Searle notes that '[i]t is a fact of neurobiology that certain brain processes cause conscious states and processes'.[52] The brain is a biological organ with a particular constitution, structure, and mode of operation; it plays a vital role in shaping the perceptions, behaviour, thought, and language of certain complex biological organisms. But how can the biological brain give rise to something subjective? Searle's solution is this: conscious subjectivity is a *higher-level feature* of the brain. By way of comparison, liquidity is a higher-level property of certain sets of molecules (at a certain pressure and temperature). The water in a glass may be liquid even if none of the individual molecules is liquid. The property of liquidity is a feature only of the complex set of molecules. In a similar way, consciousness is a feature of the brain even if it is not a feature of its constituents.

But surely consciousness is unlike liquidity? Consciousness is *subjective*. Searle illustrates his conception of consciousness by citing *objective* higher-level properties: liquidity is one example, digestion another. With regard to digestion, he notes that 'once you have told the entire story about the enzymes, the renin, the breakdown of the carbohydrates and so on, there is nothing more to say. There isn't any further property of digestion in addition to that'.[53] Digestion is *reducible* to the complex process involving enzymes and the like. When philosophers and scientists talk of reducing one thing to another they mean, by and large, that we can view the first thing as nothing other than the set of simpler things or processes. But Searle holds that consciousness is not reducible to brain processes. Now he seems to be in a bit of a fix. Surely he has to either (a) give up his claim about the irreducibility of consciousness (and this would allow the analogy with liquidity and digestion to hold) or (b) accept a dualist conception of mind, where consciousness is an ontologically distinct feature of the world.

Searle's response is to ask us to reflect upon what is involved in the idea of reduction. He draws our attention to the fact that there are five distinct senses of 'reduction'.[54] The key notions for our purposes are those of 'causal' reduction and 'ontological' reduction. What is causal reduction? It is the idea that the causal powers of an object (or a type of stuff) are entirely explicable in terms of the causal powers of the simpler ('reducing') phenomena. The causal powers of baseball bats are entirely explicable in terms of the causal powers of their constituent molecules (and their mode of arrangement). 'Ontological' reduction is a stronger notion. It is the idea that things (chairs, baseball bats), types of stuff (water, gold), and properties (heat, solidity) can be shown to be nothing other than something else: a set of simpler things, or the properties of simpler things. Chairs are nothing other than their constituent molecules arranged in a particular way. Heat is nothing other than the mean kinetic energy of molecular motion.

Ontological reduction trades upon the distinction between how things appear and how things are. If we start with our experience of a chair (e.g., the way that it supports us), it may be surprising to learn that it is largely empty space peppered with molecules. Ontological reduction doesn't just involve an explanation of causal powers in terms of the causal powers of simpler components; it requires the theorist to explain why the object or property in question appears to be a certain way. We explain the original appearances as effects of the real phenomena.[55] The chair appears to be solid because solidity is something we encounter when one thing resists passage or penetration by another. This resistance can be explained in terms of the properties of (and relations among) molecules.

The key to understanding Searle's claims about the irreducibility of consciousness is to register the distinction between causal and ontological reduction. The normal practice in science is to take causal reducibility as the first step in ontological reduction. When we can explain the causal powers of something in terms of the causal powers of sets of ontologically more basic things, we can then view the original thing as being *nothing but* a complex arrangement of the simpler things (even if, for practical reasons, we still talk about chairs and baseball bats). Consciousness is odd because it is causally reducible to features of the brain without being ontologically reducible. It is not ontologically reducible because, in the case of consciousness, there is no gap between appearance and reality for the reductionist to trade upon. We cannot explain away the appearances. We cannot do this 'because where consciousness is concerned the reality is the appearance'.[56] So, whereas both solidity and objectivity can be ontologically reduced, consciousness cannot be.

We can see, from this simplified sketch of Searle's 'higher-level property' view of consciousness, that Searle is likely to be misunderstood. The analogy with solidity and digestion seems to imply reducibility, a 'nothing but' claim. Searle's biological naturalism seems to place him in the materialist tradition that he opposes. On the other hand, Searle's claims about 'ontological subjectivity' seem to place him in the dualist tradition, which he also opposes. Materialists can accuse Searle of being too dualist, insofar as he claims that consciousness is irreducibly subjective; while dualists may object that he is too materialist, insofar as he claims that the causal powers of consciousness are determined by the causal powers of the brain. But Searle's view is that the irreducibility of consciousness 'is a trivial consequence of our definitional practices'.[57] Because consciousness is subjective, we cannot 'carve off' the subjective appearances of consciousness and view them as effects of the underlying reality of consciousness. The irreducibility of consciousness has, he suggests, 'no untoward scientific consequences whatsoever'.[58]

Part of the problem with our thinking about consciousness is that it rests upon the false assumption that 'if consciousness is really a subjective, qualitative phenomenon, then it cannot be part of the material, physical world'.[59] We might infer from the fact that we cannot reduce consciousness that it is, therefore, something non-natural, not part of the material world. This assumption, that if consciousness is subjective it must be non-natural, shapes the mind-body debate in philosophy, and it is precisely this assumption that, in Searle's view, we need to drop from our thinking about the mind. If we are properly to understand consciousness and the mind, then we need to abandon 'the traditional categories of "mind," "consciousness," "matter," "mental," "physical," and all the rest as they are traditionally construed in our philosophical debates'.[60] What we need to do is to 'redraw the conceptual map' that shapes our thinking about consciousness and mind.[61]

Our problem with consciousness – that is, our tendency to view it as something that should be kept out of our naturalistic theories of mind – arises because our thinking about consciousness is distorted by certain deeply entrenched assumptions and metaphors. If we think of consciousness as a higher-level feature of the biological brain, and if we register the fact that our model for ontological reduction has to leave consciousness irreducible, then we can accept that consciousness is both ontologically irreducible and a feature of the objective brain. We should accept that consciousness is caused by processes in the brain, and that consciousness itself is a higher-level feature of the brain. Searle concludes, 'once you have granted these two propositions, there is no metaphysical mind-body problem left'.[62]

Searle, unlike certain other philosophers, does not claim to have explained consciousness. Searle's claim that consciousness is a higher-level feature of the brain does not tell us how the brain gives rise to that higher-level feature. But it does point in a certain direction. If Searle is right, then the right way to explain consciousness is to try to find out just how the biological brain gives rise to a specific, but very unusual, higher-level property. According to Searle, the philosophical problem of consciousness – that is, the problem of how to reconcile subjectivity and objectivity – is a by-product of misguided ways of thinking. If we follow Searle, we will accept that '"[t]he problem of consciousness" is the problem of explaining exactly how neurobiological processes in the brain *cause* our subjective states of awareness or sentience'.[63]

Searle's 'higher-level property' account of consciousness plays two roles. First, it undermines the traditional problem of consciousness by suggesting that the problem of consciousness is no more than a by-product of certain misguided ways of thinking. This move is of key dialectical importance for Searle. Recall the remarks by Fodor and Dennett. The orthodox assumption is that consciousness is puzzling. Functionalism and naturalized theories of content seem to offer something of great value: an account of mind and intentionality independent of consciousness. Given that nobody has worked out an acceptable theory of content and mind in causal terms, it may seem odd that theorists continue to work on the assumption that intentionality ought to be characterised in causal terms, independent of consciousness. The reason why people continue to do so is that they believe that it would be a backward step to bring consciousness into the theory of mind and content. But if Searle is right, the naturalistically minded philosopher need not have a 'terror of consciousness', need not try to account for mind independent of consciousness. Consciousness is a natural higher-level feature of the brain, but one that must remain irreducible, given that ontological reduction works by explaining away appearances.

The second role of the account of consciousness is to provide a coherent naturalistic foundation for Searle's positive philosophy. If he had no account of how consciousness could be part of the natural world, then his theory of intentionality, linguistic meaning, and social reality would seem to be grounded in some ultimately mysterious non-natural phenomenon. Now, there are philosophers who might be quite happy with this, but Searle is not. He wants to show how consciousness, mentality, language, and society are, ultimately, part of the natural world. By arguing that we can leave behind the traditional philosophical problem of consciousness, and replace it with the much more tractable problem of giving an account of how the brain causes consciousness, Searle clears the way for his consciousness-based naturalistic philosophy to be, in time, underpinned by new developments and discoveries in neurobiology.

8. THE CENTRALITY OF CONSCIOUSNESS: PROS AND CONS

The aim here has been to outline how various elements of Searle's philosophy of mind, both positive and critical, arise from and relate to his distinctive views of consciousness and its relation to mind. On the way, we have seen that Searle's views place him at odds with the dominant view of mind in contemporary philosophy and psychology, especially with regard to the issue of how consciousness and mind relate to one another. The disagreement that we have been focusing upon is between various kinds of naturalistic theories of mind. Searle and those whom he critically opposes all claim to be naturalists. All are trying to give an account of how intentionality and the mind can be part of the natural world. But Searle and the functionalists fit mind, brain, and consciousness together in very different ways. In Searle's view, it is the brain that generates consciousness, and it is in consciousness that we find intentionality. In the functionalist view, certain causal relations are sufficient for intentionality, and there is then a further question as to how intentional states get to be conscious.

How are we to decide which approach is right? Searle puts forward a wide range of interconnected arguments and claims. In philosophy, everything is disputable. A great deal of philosophical debate is very precise, detailed, and technical, often because entire philosophical systems may rest upon a precise interpretation of a particular term. We cannot begin to explore these many disputes and issues here. I want to leave this introductory sketch with two general remarks about the advantages and disadvantages of Searle's consciousness-dependent view of mind relative to the consciousness-independent conception of mind favoured by the functionalists.

First, any theory of mind that starts with our own first-person reflection on consciousness has an automatic head start on opponents who start their theorizing with questions such as 'How is it possible for a biological creature to have states which are *about* other things'. When we reflect upon our own conscious, intentional mental states, we encounter intentionality without any idea of how it is possible. Searle's account of mind and language has a 'free move' at the beginning, insofar as it draws upon the fact that we find intentionality in our own conscious point of view. We can use our knowledge of the fact that we have intentional states as the basis for further theorising (both about conscious intentionality, and about the role that it plays as the basis for linguistic meaning), without addressing the question of how creatures like us get to have such states. In contrast, the consciousness-independent theorist cannot help herself to naïve first-person descriptions of our own conscious point of view in establishing her account of intentionality. She has to start from scratch. For example, she may start with primitive or simple systems: thermostats, or creatures such as wasps, bees, and frogs. She tries to give an account of how such simple creatures could get to have states that represent objects in the local environment. She then builds up her theory, slowly bringing in an account of misrepresentation and an account of representation of things that don't exist. She may also bring in different types of representation (images, linguistic representation in sentences, and so on). We can't tell just by reflection on our own experience whether such theories are right.

The functionalist can object that Searle's advantage is only apparent, a by-product of placing consciousness at the fore. The functionalist may view Searle's consciousness-dependent conception of mind as one that involves the same kind of debt-management that we saw in the case of traditional substance dualism. All of the problems of linguistic and mental representation are eventually passed over to neurobiology (without any good conception of just how neurobiology is going to provide an account of how intentionality is possible). The functionalist may stress the advantages of the strategy of first trying to work out how simple representational systems are possible and *then* working slowly up to conscious human beings like ourselves. Such an approach may seem to be more plausible, and more likely to succeed in practice, because it allows a kind of step-by-step approach to the theory of mind and consciousness. Of course, Searle will respond that such an approach to intentionality rests upon a mistake. Just because we are willing to *ascribe* intentional states to thermostats and bees on the basis of their causal or functional features does not imply that intentionality just *is* a causal relation between the thermostat or the bee and the objects in their respective environments.

There is a second kind of advantage that Searle's approach to the mind has over the functionalists'. It registers the importance of consciousness for *us*, for we human beings and our lives. Searle might seem to be guilty of overstatement when he claims that 'there is a sense in which it is *the* most important feature of reality, because all other things have value, importance, merit or worth only in relation to consciousness'.[64] But Searle's remark has the merit of reminding us forcefully of the fact that when we engage in theorising about human beings, the objects of our concern are not just masses of meat, or complex causal systems. Our whole sense of what it is to be alive, to care about the world, to feel pain and pleasure, is inextricably bound up with our experience as conscious beings. We have seen that a great deal of contemporary philosophy and psychology has a problem with consciousness. Even if many of Searle's positive philosophical doctrines turn out to be incorrect or indefensible, his work in philosophy of mind serves an invaluable dialectical purpose. It forces us to reflect upon the consequences of leaving consciousness out of our thinking about the mind. A neglect of consciousness is not just a neglect of some strange problematic feature that certain mental states have; it is a failure to register the perspective of our experience, thought, hopes and fears, feelings and failings. Our problems with consciousness, problems that Searle has sought to identify and resolve, are nothing less than problems with our human point of view.

Notes

1. The first quotation is from John Searle, *Mind, Language and Society: Doing Philosophy in the Real World* (London: Weidenfeld and Nicolson, 1999), p. 40; the second is from his *The Rediscovery of the Mind* (Cambridge, Mass.: MIT Press, 1992), p. 18.
2. *Mind, Language and Society*, p. 83.
3. John Searle, *The Mystery of Consciousness* (London: Granta, 1997), p. xiv.
4. *Mind, Language and Society*, p. 161.
5. Ibid., p. 52.
6. See, for example, Franz Brentano, *Psychology from an Empirical Standpoint*, ed. L. L. McAlister, trans. A. C. Rancurello, D. B. Terrell, and L. L. McAlister (London: Routledge, 1995), p. 88; and John Searle, *Intentionality: An Essay in the Philosophy of Mind* (Cambridge: Cambridge University Press, 1983).
7. Colin McGinn, *The Problem of Consciousness* (Oxford: Blackwell, 1991)
8. See *The Rediscovery of the Mind*, Chapter 2.
9. Carl G. Hempel, "The Logical Analysis of Psychology," in Herbert Feigl and Wilfrid Sellars (eds.), *Readings in Philosophical Analysis* (New York: Appleton Century Crofts, 1949); Gilbert Ryle, *The Concept of Mind* (London: Hutchinson, 1949).
10. *The Mystery of Consciousness*, p. 137.
11. Ullin T. Place, "Is Consciousness a Brain Process?," *British Journal of Psychology* 47 (1956): 44–50; J. J. C. Smart, "Sensations and Brain Processes," *Philosophical Review* 68 (1959): 141–56.
12. *The Rediscovery of the Mind*, pp. 35–40.
13. Ibid., pp. 36–7.
14. See David Braddon-Mitchell and Frank Jackson, *The Philosophy of Mind and Cognition* (Oxford: Blackwell, 1996), for an excellent overview of the arguments for and against functionalism.
15. David Lewis, "Mad Pain and Martian Pain," in Ned Block (ed.), *Readings in the Philosophy of Psychology*, 2 vols. (Cambridge, Mass.: Harvard University Press, 1980), vol. 1, pp. 216–22, at p. 218.
16. David Lewis, "Psychophysical and Theoretical Identifications," *Australasian Journal of Philosophy* 50 (1972): 249–58. Reprinted in Block (ed.), *Readings in the Philosophy of Psychology*, vol 1, pp. 207–15, at p. 212.
17. Martin Gardner, *The Mind's New Science: A History of the Cognitive Revolution* (New York: Basic Books, 1985).

18. Robert Cummins, *The Nature of Psychological Explanation* (Cambridge, Mass.: MIT Press, 1983).

19. Kim Sterelny, *The Representational Theory of Mind: An Introduction* (Oxford: Blackwell, 1990).

20. Barbara Von Eckardt, *What Is Cognitive Science?* (Cambridge, Mass.: MIT Press, 1993), p. 197.

21. Eckardt, *What Is Cognitive Science?*, p. 197.

22. Fodor, quoted in ibid., p. 197.

23. Jerry Fodor, *Psychosemantics* (Cambridge, Mass.: MIT Press, 1987), p. 98.

24. See Stephen Stich and Ted Warfield (eds.), *Mental Representation: A Reader* (Oxford: Blackwell, 1990), for samples of the main contemporary approaches to intentionality.

25. Jerry Fodor, "Too Hard for Our Kind of Mind?," *London Review of Books*, June 27, 1991, p. 12.

26. *The Rediscovery of the Mind*, p. 10.

27. Ibid., p. 153.

28. Ibid.

29. Daniel Dennett, *Consciousness Explained* (London: Penguin Books, 1992), p. 457.

30. David M. Rosenthal, "A Theory of Consciousness?," in Ned Block, Owen Flanagan, and Guven Güzeldere (eds.), *The Nature of Consciousness: Philosophical Debates* (Cambridge, Mass.: MIT Press, 1997), pp. 729–53.

31. Robert Van Gulick, "What Would Count as Explaining Consciousness?," in Thomas Metzinger (ed.), *Conscious Experience* (Exeter: Imprint Academic, 1996), pp. 61–80.

32. See, e.g., Rosenthal, "A Theory of Consciousness"; William Lycan, *Consciousness and Experience* (Cambridge, Mass.: MIT Press, 1996); and his "A Simple Argument for a Higher order Representation Theory of Consciousness," *Analysis* 61 (2001): 3–4; Peter Carruthers, *Language, Thought and Consciousness* (Cambridge: Cambridge University Press, 1996); and his *Phenomenal Consciousness* (Cambridge: Cambridge University Press, 2000).

33. See Neil C. Manson, "The Limitations and Costs of Lycan's 'Simple' argument," *Analysis* 61 (2001): 319–23, for a simple critique of the higher-order representation view.

34. Fred Dretske, "Conscious Experience," *Mind* 102 (1993): 263–83; Michael Tye, "A Representational Theory of Pains and Their Phenomenal Character," *Philosophical Perspectives* 9 (1995): 223–39.

35. See, e.g., *The Rediscovery of the Mind* for the critique of cognitive science and materialism more generally; for Searle's attack on 'Strong AI' see "Minds, Brains and Programs," *Behavioral and Brain Sciences* 3 (1980): 417–24; for his critique of the notion of unconscious mentality, see "Consciousness, Explanatory Inversion and Cognitive Science," *Behavioral and Brain Sciences* 13 (1990): 585–642.

36. See, e.g., Donald Davidson, "Belief and the Basis of Meaning," *Synthese* 27 (1974): 309–23; Daniel Dennett, *The Intentional Stance* (Cambridge, Mass.: MIT Press, 1987).

37. *The Rediscovery of the Mind*, p. 81, p. 156.

38. Ibid., p. 156.

39. Ibid., p. 131.

40. Ibid., p. 157.

41. Ibid., p. 164.

42. Ibid., p. 55.

43. Ibid.

44. Ibid., p. 83.

45. Neil C. Manson, "State Consciousness and Creature Consciousness: A Real Distinction," *Philosophical Psychology* 13 (2000): 405–10.

46. See Bernard Baars, *In the Theater of Consciousness* (New York: Oxford University Press, 1997), for a cognitive scientific theory that takes the theater metaphor seriously.

47. *Mind, Language and Society*, p. 82.

48. Ibid., p. 52.

49. Ibid., p. 42.

50. Ibid., p. 95.

51. Ibid., p. 191.

52. Ibid., p. 52.

53. Ibid., p. 55.

54. *The Rediscovery of the Mind*, Chapter 5.

55. Ibid., p. 120.

56. *The Mystery of Consciousness*, p. 213.

57. *The Rediscovery of the Mind*, p. 124.

58. Ibid.

59. *Mind, Language and Society*, p. 50.

60. Ibid., p. 51.

61. *The Mystery of Consciousness*, p. 195.

62. *Mind, Language and Society*, p. 52.

63. *The Mystery of Consciousness*, p. 192.

64. *Mind, Language and Society*, p. 83.

7 The Intentionality of Perception

FRED DRETSKE

What must be true for you to see a yellow station wagon? To begin with, there must actually *be* a yellow station wagon. If there isn't, you may think – you may even say, quite sincerely – that you see a yellow station wagon, but you are simply wrong. It only looks like a yellow station wagon. Maybe you are hallucinating – or just terribly confused.

Since there obviously are (or were) yellow station wagons I have never seen, what else must be true for me to see one? Once again, most folks will agree that there must be some causal relation between the station wagon and me. It must, somehow, affect me. If the car is in your garage, then I can't see it, because the garage walls prevent a causal interaction. Light reflected from the car never reaches my eyes. If you run the engine, I might *hear* it (in this case, the causal relation between the car, or the car's engine, and me is via my ears), but I won't see it.

Just affecting me, though, is surely not enough. Many things affect me that I never perceive. I don't have to see or feel poison ivy (the plant) for it to affect me. I know it was there, in the field I walked through yesterday, but not because I saw it. I know it was there because today I perceive the effects – an ugly rash – that it had on me.

Opinions start to diverge at this stage, but, pushing on, it seems safe enough to say (I'll say why in a moment) that for normal human beings, at least, perception of an object requires that the effect be a conscious experience of some sort. The object we perceive must cause, in us, an experience of it. That's what the poison ivy failed to do with me. If the experience it causes is a visual experience, we see the object. If it is an auditory experience, we hear it. If it is gustatory, we taste it. And so on.

Though this last claim will be contested by some philosophers, it is, I think, safe enough to assert it here because John Searle agrees with it – and this is, after all, an essay on Searle's views about perception. Searle, wisely enough, expresses some hesitation about whether the event or state that x causes in S must be a conscious experience in order for S to see x (p. 47).[1] He mentions "blindsight." Brain-damaged patients are able to "see," in some

154

sense, objects without having conscious experiences of them. This leads Searle to qualify a bit. It is an empirical fact – not, as it were, a conceptual truth – that perception of x requires a conscious experience. For beings like us (i.e., normal human perceivers) it may be required, but who knows about brain-damaged people, animals, or extraterrestials.

So John Searle and I (and, I hope, the reader) agree about this much. If we are normal human perceivers, we perceive x only if x causes in us a conscious experience of some sort. This still isn't *enough*, but we agree that it is necessary. One reason it isn't enough is that *the way* x causes an experience in us may be so unusual or deviant that we refuse to count it as a perception of x. Suppose temporary damage to S's nervous system results in optical stimuli from yellow station wagons arousing in S, not a normal visual experience, but olfactory sensations. Does S thereby see (smell?) a yellow station wagon? Are the olfactory sensations experiences *of* a yellow station wagon? If not, then x's causing in S a conscious experience is not enough for S to perceive x. Something more is required. We could say, I suppose, that it would suffice if x caused in S not just *a* conscious experience (of whatever sort) but, more specifically, a conscious experience *of x*. Yes, that might do, but that leaves the question of what, besides (or in addition to) causation *by* x, is needed to make a conscious experience an experience *of x*?

Searle is aware of these problems, and he has illuminating things to say about the problem of "deviant causality" – the problem of just how x must cause an experience in order for that experience to qualify as an experience of x. I pass by this issue here, since it is not one that divides us. I don't have anything much better to say about deviant causality than what Searle has already said (particularly about plannable consistency – pp. 135–43), so I'm happy to assume that he is right about all this, and to express points of agreement thus far by saying that we agree that a necessary condition of S's seeing x is that x cause, in some appropriate (nondeviant) way, a conscious experience in S. The question is whether, as thus amended, this condition is not also sufficient. With some fine-tuning, I (and a lot of other philosophers) think it is. Searle doesn't. I think that if a yellow station wagon causes, in the right way, a visual experience in S, then S's visual experience is an experience of the yellow station wagon. S sees it. He is visually aware of a yellow station wagon – in fact, *that* yellow station wagon, the one causing him to have the experience. John Searle doesn't believe this. He thinks that in order for S to see the car, for S's experience to be *of* the car, S's experience must, in addition, have an intentional content of a special kind. Only when the experience has this intentional content, only when it represents (or *presents*) the yellow station wagon in a certain way (as the cause of the experience), will it be an experience *of* the station wagon. Only then will S *see* the station wagon.

By way of understanding Searle's philosophy of mind and language, a lot hangs on this point. His claims about perceptual experience do not form an isolated doctrine. They are not mere corollaries of an independently motivated theory of mind and intentionality. In fact, they form the crucial "first step" (p. 49) in a series of arguments that purport to overthrow widely accepted theories by Hilary Putnam (on whether meanings are in the head), Tyler Burge (on *de re* statements and beliefs), and Perry and Kaplan (on singular propositions and indexicals), and much else besides. Many of these arguments depend, in a critical way, on perceptual experiences' having the kind of self-referential content that Searle says they do. If experiences do not have a content, or a content of this kind, then nothing much works in the way Searle says it works. It is important, then, to evaluate his theory of experience. It is the cornerstone of his theory of intentionality, mind, and language.

Why does Searle think that visual experiences have Intentionality? (He capitalizes the word to indicate a philosophical term of art.) It might be thought that such experiences *must* have Intentionality, because Intentionality is stipulated (on the very first page of the very first chapter of *Intentionality*), at least in a preliminary way, to be "that property of many mental states and events by which they are directed at or about or of objects and states of affairs in the world." If that is all Intentionality amounts to, then, of course, experiences of yellow station wagons – being experiences *of* yellow station wagons – have Intentionality. So what's the problem?

The problem is that after this preliminary characterization, Searle goes on to say (pp. 4–5) that Intentionality (note the capitalization) is a species of representation, that Intentional states represent objects *in the same sense of "represent" that speech acts represent objects.*[2] Given this further claim about Intentionality, it may be more or less obvious that Intentional states are *of* or *about* things (whatever objects and states of affairs they represent), but the converse is by no means obvious. It is by no means obvious that if an experience is an experience *of* a yellow station wagon, then it must represent the yellow station wagon *in the way a statement (order, question, etc.) about the car represents it.* This is not obvious because, on the surface at least, one object can be *of* or *about* another object without representing it in this way. Think about photographs. What makes a photograph[3] of a yellow station wagon a photograph *of* a yellow station wagon – indeed, a photograph of *my* (not your) yellow station wagon – are facts about the causal origin of the image on the paper. If the film from which this image was produced was exposed by light reflected from my yellow station wagon (in some nondeviant way), then it is a picture of my yellow station wagon. If the light came from your car, then it is a picture of your car, and it would be a picture of your car even if it were indistinguishable from a picture of mine – a perfect forgery, as it were. What makes a photograph of x a photograph of x is not that it looks like x. It may not. It is not that we regard it as, or take it to be, a picture of x. We may not. Nor is it that it represents x as x. It needn't. A photograph of a yellow station wagon taken in funny light, at an unusual angle, and at a great distance may not look like a yellow station wagon at all.[4] What makes it a picture of a yellow station wagon – in fact, a picture of *my* (not your) yellow station wagon – is simply the fact that it is my (not your) car that is at the other end of an appropriate causal chain. It is my car that (via camera, film, developing, etc.) affected the paper. If this is true of photographs, why isn't it true of perceptual experiences? Why aren't they *of* whatever objects or events are at the other end of an appropriate (i.e., nondeviant) causal chain?

Searle insists (p. 61) that material objects can be the objects of visual perception (and, thus, that direct realism can be vindicated) only if perceptual experience has Intentional content. Why is Intentional content necessary? Why can't one be a direct realist on a causal theory of experience in the same way that one can, according to the causal story, be a "direct realist" about the objects of photographs? One doesn't need Intentional content to make the photograph a photograph of my Aunt Minnie. A causal theory will do quite nicely. Besides, a causal theory neatly solves (Searle describes it as the "currently fashionable solution" – p. 63) what he calls the "particularity problem," the problem of what makes experiences of a yellow station wagon experiences of a *particular* yellow station wagon. A causal theory solves this problem in the same way that it solves the same "problem" for photographs: photographs of yellow station wagons are always photographs of *particular* cars, because it is always a particular car that causes (in a nondeviant way) the image on the paper.

Searle rejects this nifty solution because the problem, he says, is not how to get a particular yellow station wagon as the object of a perceptual experience, but how to get the "particularity" into the Intentional content. The question, he says (p. 64) is not "Under what conditions does one see Sally whether one knows it or not?," but rather "Under what conditions does one *take oneself to be seeing that* Sally is in front of one?" But this, clearly, is *Searle's* problem, not a problem for a causal theory of perception. The original question, remember, was a question about what it takes to see Sally (or a yellow station wagon). What are the truth conditions for "S sees x." As far as I can see, a causal theory of perception provides an elegant answer to *this* question. It does not, by itself, provide truth conditions for seeing *that* Sally is in front of one. It is not a theory about what it takes to *know*, *believe*, *regard*, or *take* oneself to be seeing Sally. But that, clearly, is an altogether different question. The question has been changed – from what it takes to *see* Sally, to what it takes to *think one sees* Sally – so that Intentionality has some work to do. In changing the question, Searle creates a problem where none exists. Or, if there is a problem, it is one to which a causal theory of perception provides a satisfactory answer.

It isn't just photographs. Recordings, reflections, impressions (in wax, say), and even signatures are *of* the people, voices, faces, or objects that cause them. A reflection of my face doesn't say or mean – surely not in the way that a speech act might say or mean it – that it is a reflection of me. It doesn't represent the object that it is a reflection of in some propositional way, and, even if it did, *this* is not what would make it a reflection *of* that object. The of-ness or about-ness of reflections and photographs is completely fixed by the causal arrangement. Why isn't the same true of experiences? Why do experiences need the kind of representational content that speech acts possess?

In comparing experiences to photographs, reflections, and recordings, I do not mean to suggest that experiences of yellow stations wagons are, literally, pictures, recordings, or reflections in the head. That would be silly. Though visual experiences (of yellow stations wagons) are in the head, no one (anymore?) thinks that these experiences (like photographs) actually *have* the properties (color, shape, size, etc.) that the object being represented is represented as having. No, the point in comparing visual experiences to photographs and reflections is, rather, to suggest that the relation between an experience and its object, the relation described by saying the experience is *of* a yellow station wagon, is a causal relation, pure and simple. It is with photographs and reflections. Why not with experience? We don't *need* Intentionality. Searle may need it, but experiences don't.

I am not here defending a causal theory of perception so much as asking what reasons Searle gives for going beyond it. Why should anyone want to drag in Intentionality and muddy the perfectly clear (and, I think, perfectly adequate) waters provided by a causal theory? Why insist that perceptual experiences, in addition to being caused (in an appropriately nondeviant way) by the objects that they are experiences of, must also have the kind of representational content that speech acts possess?

In Chapter 1 of *Intentionality*, Searle draws an interesting and illuminating analogy between certain mental states – those that are sometimes called "propositional attitudes"[5] – and speech acts. He takes these points of similarity to be reasons for thinking that the directedness of mental states is best understood in the same representational terms in which we understand the directedness of speech acts. The points of similarity are:

1. The distinction between the propositional content (it is snowing) and the illocutionary force (e.g., asserting that, questioning whether) of speech acts carries over to mental states such as belief, desire, intention, and so on. We can have different "attitudes" (belief, desire, hope, fear, etc.) with the same propositional content.

2. Some mental states have a direction of fit (mind to world vs. world to mind) corresponding to the direction of fit (word to world vs. world to word) of speech acts.

3. When performed, Speech acts with propositional content *express* mental states with the same propositional content: in making the statement that p I express the belief that p, in giving an order to do p I express a wish or desire that you do p, and so on.

4. The conditions of satisfaction of a speech act (a statement is satisfied if and only if it is true, an order is satisfied if and only if it is obeyed, etc.) are identical to the conditions of satisfaction of the expressed mental state.

These points of similarity lead Searle to conclude (p. 13) that certain mental states – those with a direction of fit – represent their conditions of satisfaction in the same way that speech acts do.[6]

All this is very interesting, but what does it have to do with perception? What does it have to do with *seeing* a yellow station wagon, with *experiences of* a yellow station wagon? At best, it seems, we have learned something about a certain class of mental states – for instance,

*   believing that there is a yellow station wagon in the driveway
*   wanting to own a yellow station wagon
*   fearing that yellow station wagons are going out of fashion
*   regretting that I sold my yellow station wagon
*   intending to buy a yellow station wagon
*   hoping to ride in your yellow station wagon

And so on. But these, it should be noticed, are all mental states that one cannot be in without understanding what yellow station wagons are. This, indeed, is symptomatic of propositional attitudes – those mental states whose descriptions take, or can easily be rendered as taking, a factive nominal (a that-clause) as complement of the verb. I cannot believe, fear, regret, be sorry, or desire that P without understanding what situation "P" describes. But seeing a yellow station wagon is not at all like this. One can see, hear, or feel a yellow station wagon without knowing what a yellow station wagon is. Seeing a yellow station wagon is like being run over by a yellow station wagon. You don't have to know what hit you in order to get hit. You don't have to know what you see in order to see it. Small children and animals, those who do not know what yellow station wagons are, see them as well – often better – than more astute adults. The first time I saw an armadillo (it was on a Texas road), I thought it was a tumbleweed. This mistake about what I was seeing didn't prevent me from seeing the armadillo. I did, after all, swerve to avoid it. "What is that before me?" is a question one can sensibly ask about things that one sees in total ignorance of what they are.

This fact about perceptual experiences – the fact that they are not, nor do they embody,[7] a propositional attitude – is often obscured by assimilating (or just plain confusing) seeing an x that is F (an object that *is* a yellow station wagon) with seeing x *as* F (which, at least on one reading, is a propositional attitude – viz., taking x to be F) or seeing *that* x is F (which, on any reading, is a propositional attitude – viz., knowing, hence believing, that x is F). It is quite clear, though, that seeing (having a visual experience of) a yellow station wagon has nothing to do with one's cognitive, conceptual, or representational powers, the kind of powers involved in seeing that there is (or seeing something as) a yellow station wagon in front of one. It has nothing to do with recognition or identification. It is not, in fact, an epistemic or cognitive relation at all. Sentience, the ability to see yellow station wagons, is one thing; sapience, the ability to represent them as yellow, as station wagons, or merely as vehicles of some sort, is quite another.

So we come back to the question: why does John Searle think that experiences have Intentionality?[8] Maybe beliefs (and the other propositional attitudes) have Intentionality, but why does he think that experiences must represent their object (the object they are experiences of) in the same way that statements do? The key argument occurs at the beginning of Chapter 2 of *Intentionality*, "The Intentionality of Perception." The argument (p. 39) is that experiences are as inseparable from their conditions of satisfaction as are beliefs and desires. One can no more separate a visual experience from the fact that it is, say, an experience *of* a yellow station wagon than one can separate a belief that it is raining from its (representational) content, its condition of satisfaction – viz., that it is raining. This isn't to say we can't separate the belief from *the fact* that it is raining (from, as it were, the rain).

For there need not be a fact (that it is raining) in order for us to believe that it is raining. The belief can be false. But the fact that would make the belief true if it were true – the (putative) fact, namely, that it is raining – is a (putative) fact that is part and parcel of what makes the belief the belief it is. That it is raining is the representational content of the belief, and the representational content of a belief makes the belief the belief it is. In this way, we can "read" the conditions of satisfaction (the conditions that would make the belief true) off the belief itself. Once we know what belief we are talking about, we know what fact would make the belief true. And exactly the same is true, Searle insists, of an experience of a yellow station wagon. We can "read off" the experience its conditions of satisfaction, what worldly condition would make it a true (veridical) experience. This gives it a representational content, makes it Intentional, in the same way that the statement (or belief) that there is a yellow station wagon in front of one is representational.

As an argument for a patently false conclusion, this isn't bad. I would be happy to have done as well for some of my own false conclusions. But the mistake becomes apparent if one thinks of seeing a yellow station wagon *not* in good light at a close distance (when it actually looks like a yellow station wagon), but in bad light at a great distance. Suppose the yellow station wagon is so far away that it looks like a tiny speck. One may, in fact, think that it actually *is* a speck (of dirt, say) on the windshield. Curious, though, one keeps one's eye on it as it comes closer. As the car approaches, one recognizes it as a vehicle of some sort – color indeterminate. Then, as it gets even closer, one is finally able to recognize it as – see that it is – a yellow station wagon. Question: when one *first* saw the yellow station wagon, at the time when it looked like (and you thought that it might actually be) a speck on the windshield, did one's experience of it represent it as a yellow station wagon? Could one, as it were, "read off" the experience its conditions of satisfaction in the same way that one could "read off" a belief or a statement about a speck (that it is a yellow station wagon) its conditions of satisfaction? Does the experience represent the speck as a yellow station wagon in the way that a statement or belief represents it that way? How could it? The experience, after all, is exactly the same as the experience one would be having (at this distance and in this light) of a purple station wagon, a red convertible, or a Martian spaceship. If it were, in fact, a red convertible, one would be seeing a red convertible, it is true, but we are now talking not about *seeing* a yellow station wagon (which, I agree, requires the experience to be an experience of a yellow station wagon) but about the *kind* of experience one has when one sees a yellow station wagon – something one can have (in this light and at this distance) when seeing a red convertible. The experience of a yellow station wagon, Searle is careful to tell us, is just like a belief: something one can have without its conditions of satisfaction being satisfied. So that kind of experience can be had when one is seeing a red convertible. This being so, what makes the speckish experience (of a yellow station wagon) say or mean that there is a yellow station wagon in the distance? What makes it represent (whether truly or falsely) its conditions of satisfaction in the way that a belief or a statement (that there is a yellow station wagon in the distance) represents its conditions of satisfaction?

The fact is – or so it seems to me – that there need be nothing in or about an experience of x that reveals what it is an experience of (i.e., x), any more than a photograph of x must reveal what it is a photograph of. One might think there must be only if one thinks of experiences (or pictures) of a very special sort – those that are produced in optimal conditions in which the experience (or photograph) contains enough information to enable a knowledgeable person to identify the object that it is an experience (picture) of. But experiences (and photographs) are not always like that. Experiences (photographs) of identical twins, thumbtacks, and paper clips are *never* like that. Given just the experience (photograph), you can't tell one thumbtack (paper clip) from another. They all look the same. Nonetheless, the experience (picture) is always of a particular thumbtack. There is sometimes enough information in an experience (photograph) to identify what it is an experience (photograph) of – for example, an animal of some sort, a person, a woman, an old woman, an old woman smiling, and so on. But sometimes there isn't. One can, after all, see (and take pictures of) smiling old women from behind, at dusk, and at a great distance.

One way of trying to rescue the representational character of experience is by thinking, confusedly, of experiences in propositional terms. If an experience *of* a yellow station wagon is, despite all grammatical appearances to the contrary, really seeing *that* it is a yellow station wagon, then, since *seeing-that* is a form of *knowing-that* (by using your eyes), and *knowing-that* is (among other things) *believing-that*, then all seeing is believing. And if believing is representational – a plausible view – so is seeing. "From the point of view of Intentionality," Searle says, "all seeing is seeing *that*" (p. 40). He goes so far (p. 61) as to claim that from the point of view of a theory of Intentionality, questions about the truth conditions for "S sees a yellow station wagon" should really be expressed as questions about the truth conditions for "S sees that there is a yellow station wagon in front of S." I wonder whether, from the point of view of a theory of Intentionality, questions about the truth conditions for "S stepped on an ant" should really be questions about the truth conditions for "S realized (knew, believed) that he stepped on an ant" in order to highlight the Intentionality of *stepping on*.

Lots of philosophers (Searle is by no means the only one) are attracted by this move. I have never (at least, not since 1969)[9] been able to understand why. It seems to me as plain as the nose on your face that seeing a yellow station wagon in front of you is not, nor does it require, seeing that it is (or that there is) a yellow station wagon in front of you. Searle, though, is forced into this strange view by his earlier mistake. Once he accepts the false notion that experiences have conditions of satisfaction, he is driven to accept that experiences have a propositional content, since conditions of satisfaction are always that such-and-such is the case (p. 41). The logic is inexorable: to see a yellow station wagon is to have an experience of it; an experience of it (just like a belief about it) is a mental event or state that has conditions of satisfaction. A condition of satisfaction is a condition that must obtain in order for the mental state to be true, veridical, or (in general) satisfied. So experiences of yellow station wagons, having conditions of satisfaction, are most perspicuously described by making this propositional content explicit – that is, by describing experiences of a yellow station wagon as experiences *that* there is a yellow station wagon. Seeing x is thereby transformed into seeing that there is an x. It is amazing what impeccable logic and a false premise can make you say.

Searle tries to sweeten the pill by suggesting that there are "syntactical" arguments that lead to the same conclusion (p. 41). The "syntactical" arguments are, in fact, Gricean implicatures masquerading as (syntactic) implications. It is quite true, as he points out, that one would not normally *say* one saw a station wagon in front of one unless one saw *that* there was a station wagon in front of one. But, for exactly the same reasons, neither would one normally say one stepped on an ant unless one believed (knew, saw that) it was an ant that one stepped on. Does this show that stepping on ants has propositional content? That it is, implicitly, representational in the way speech acts are representational?

The most striking part of this discussion (pp. 41–5) is that Searle correctly identifies a fundamental logical difference between *seeing-x* reports and *seeing-that-p* reports – the fact that the first is extensional the second intensional – but then uses this difference in support (!!) of treating seeing-x as a form of seeing-that-there-is-an-x-there. I would have thought that if

> S sees the bank president.
> The bank president is my cousin.
> ─────────────────────────────
> S sees my cousin.

is a valid argument (as Searle agrees that it is), and if

> S sees that the bank president is there.
> The bank president is my cousin.
> _____
> S sees that my cousin is there.

is not a valid argument (as Searle agrees that it is not), this would be the strongest possible reason for concluding that "seeing the bank president in front of me" describes a completely different perceptual achievement from "seeing that the bank president is in front of me." For reasons that I do not fathom, Searle takes it to support the opposite conclusion.

The fact that "seeing x" (where "x" is some concrete noun phrase like "a yellow station wagon") is extensional is, I think, a reason to think that "seeing" does not describe an intentional or representational relation at all. Compare the first of the two arguments just presented, the one involving "seeing x," with:

> S stepped on (kicked, touched, pushed, broke) x.
> $x = y$
> _____
> S stepped on (kicked, touched, pushed, broke) y.

These are also valid arguments. They describe a causal (or perhaps causal/spatial) interaction or relation between S and x, and since descriptions of causal (spatial) relations are extensional, descriptions of these actions are extensional. Even more suggestively (since the causal action goes the other way):

> S's visual experience (death, injury) was caused by x.
> $x = y$
> _____
> S's visual experience (death, injury) was caused by y.

is valid. Doesn't this suggest – it doesn't prove, of course, but doesn't it suggest – that maybe "S sees x" (like "x killed S") is extensional because it describes a causal relation between S and x? S sees x because x *affects* S in the right way, and if x affects S in that way, y affects S in that way if, indeed, x is y. That is why, whether you know it or not, you see my cousin whenever you see the bank president. You do so because my cousin *is* the bank president. It certainly suggests this to me.

It is certainly true that we speak of experiences as being *veridical, misleading*, and *illusory*. This might be taken to mean that experiences have a direction of fit, and therefore conditions of satisfaction, and therefore, representational content. Searle (p. 43) takes it to mean this. I don't think it does mean this. There are other, more plausible, explanations. Consider the fact that we also speak of photographs, reflections, and recordings as misleading, distorted, and illusory. Why aren't experiences misleading or distorted in exactly the way that photographs are misleading or distorted? They tend to produce false beliefs about what they are of. This, incidentally, is why we don't speak of an illusion merely because something doesn't look the way it is. An x might not look like an x (thus making identification difficult), but the look-of-x may nonetheless not be illusory or misleading, because no one would be misled by the look-of-x. It is just (say) too far away to tell. The speckish look of a yellow station wagon seen at 600 yards is not illusory or misleading. Why? Because, at this distance, few people are misled. Lots of things look like a speck at that distance. So normal perceivers are not misled. For the same reason, a photograph of a yellow station wagon at 600 yards is not misleading or illusory. No one is likely to be misled about what it is a picture of.[10] But an experience of my Uncle Bert when seen in good light from a few yards away *is* misleading, it is illusory, if the photograph makes him look like my Aunt Minnie. A photograph of Bert, taken close up in good light, that made him look like Aunt Minnie would, for the same reason, be misleading. Experiences of Bert (at the same distance and in the same light) would be misleading or illusory for the same reason.

What this suggests is that the representational (and, hence, misrepresentational) potential of experience may, like the representational (and consequent misrepresentational) power of photographs, be a *derived* intentionality. It derives from the beliefs and purposes of those who depend on experience (or photographs) as a source of information about the world. Taken by themselves – intrinsically – experiences are no more veridical (or illusory) than an accurate (or broken) thermometer is veridical (or illusory). The only sense in which experiences are false or misleading is the sense in which thermometer readings can be false or misleading: they can produce false beliefs in those who depend on them for information.[11]

I say all this *may* be so. It strikes me as a plausible story – much more plausible, indeed, than Searle's Intentionalistic account of experience – but since I haven't the time to argue for it, I leave it merely as an option. Why not think of experience in this way? If you do, you can have your simple, uncluttered, causal theory of perceptual experience and, at the same time, account for the veridicality of experience. This option has an added advantage: it gives you something plausible to say about experiences of yellow station wagons seen at a distance. If, as Searle claims, such experiences really represent a yellow station wagon (as their cause), what do they represent it as? As a speck on the windshield? Then the experience is illusory. As a yellow station wagon? If so, then the experience must be different in some way from the speckish experience of a red convertible. What is this difference in the experience itself?

Searle insists (p. 50) that type-identical experiences, those that are phenomenally identical, can nonetheless have different contents, different conditions of satisfaction. This is so because their content is self-referential. One experience of a yellow station wagon says that *I* am caused by a yellow station wagon; another, different, experience of a yellow station wagon says that *I* (a numerically different experience) am caused by a yellow station wagon. They will, as a result of this difference in reference, have different content, different conditions of satisfaction. Fair enough – but can phenomenally identical experiences differ not only in this (self-referential) way, but also in what they say about what is causing them? Can one (an experience of a yellow station wagon) say that it is caused by a yellow station wagon, while another (an experience of a red convertible) says that it is being caused by a red convertible? How do experiences manage to "say" (represent) their causes so differently when what they say about their cause is so totally inaccessible to the person having the experience? The experiences, after all, could be the same in every intrinsic respect, every respect detectable by the person having them, and still be experiences of completely different objects. I find this mysterious. Searle's talk of *Background* and *Network* (pp. 65ff.) – his answer to how they manage to say what they say – does nothing to clarify it for me.

By way of concluding, I should mention Searle's discussion of the way language and expectation affect perception (pp. 53–7). Having been forced by the requirements of his own theory to mistakenly identify perception of an x with perception that it is an x, Searle attempts to buttress this conflation with some psychological "facts." Perception, we are told (p. 53), is a function of expectation. Language itself affects the perceptual encounter. It is hard to evaluate these claims, because it isn't clear what Searle is talking about when he talks about "perception" and "perceptual encounter." He started the chapter of *Intentionality* by talking about the perception of objects such as yellow station wagons, but, as we have seen, he slides back and forth between seeing a yellow station wagon and seeing that it is (or that there is) a yellow station wagon (in front of one). If the claim about perception and perceptual encounters is a claim about the latter, about seeing (identifying, recognizing) *what* is in front of one, or seeing the object in front of one *as* a yellow station wagon, then his claims about the influence of language and expectation seem plausible enough. Animals and human infants that lack a language for describing and thinking about yellow station wagons are not likely to identify what they see *as* a yellow station wagon. They are not likely to see an approaching vehicle as a yellow station wagon. How could they? That would be like my seeing an approaching vehicle as a rigabartom when I have absolutely no idea of what a rigabartom is or what it looks like. But this isn't the point. We are supposed to be talking about perceiving material objects – that is, yellow station wagons (or rigabartoms) – and it is not at all clear that perception of objects is influenced by language and expectations. Maybe it is, maybe it isn't. This is an empirical question. But it merely muddies these waters to claim (as Searle does, – p. 54) that perceptions of x are different (the experiences are different) because one person sees x as an F while another sees x as a G. What a person *sees* is one thing. What she *sees it* (what she sees) *as* is quite another. Arguing that differences in the latter make for differences in the former is like arguing that if I see a car as a yellow station wagon and Fido does not, then Fido's experience of the car is different from my experience of the car. Maybe Fido's experience is different from mine. It probably is. But the fact that Fido doesn't know (believe, expect, etc.) what I know (believe, expect, etc.) about the car that we both see is certainly no argument that it is.

Notes

1. Unless otherwise noted, page references are to Searle's *Intentionality: An Essay in the Philosophy of Mind* (Cambridge: Cambridge University Press, 1983).
2. Representing them "in the same way" is consistent with there being differences in the way speech acts and mental states represent. For instance, speech acts have a derived form of Intentionality; mental states have their Intentionality intrinsically (p. 5).
3. I speak here of *photographs*, not of pictures in general. It may be (I do not say it *is*) that what makes a drawing or a statue a drawing or statue of Charles DeGaul is that that is the person the artist intended it to be a drawing or statue of. Even if it turns out to be a bad drawing (S is so inept), even if the statue looks more like Winston Churchill than Charles DeGaul, it is still a picture (statue) of DeGaul because (it might be argued) the object of an artistic representation is whoever or whatever the creator intends it to be. Even if this is true of paintings, drawings, and other forms of artistic expression, it is not true of photographs.
4. Nelson Goodman taught us long ago, in his *Languages of Art* (Indianapolis, Ind.: Hackett, 1976), to distinguish between pictures of black horses (which needn't look like black horses) and (what he called) black-horse pictures (which do). Not all pictures of black horses are black-horse pictures (i.e., represent the object they are of *as* black horses). And not all black-horse pictures are pictures of black horses.

5. I am aware of Searle's cautionary footnote (p. 19) that the Russellian terminology of "propositional attitudes" is confusing. It suggests that beliefs (desires, etc.) are attitudes toward or about a proposition. I agree that this is possibly misleading. I will be careful *not* to be misled. I will be careful *not* to suppose that a propositional attitude is an attitude toward or about a proposition. I use the terminology nonetheless, because it picks out the class of mental states that I am interested in: viz., those whose description takes (or can easily be rendered as taking) a factive nominal, a that-clause (expressing a proposition), as complement of the verb.

6. Searle cautions the reader not to misinterpret his use of the concept *representation*. He uses it loosely and vaguely. The sense of "representation," he says, is meant to be entirely exhausted by the analogy to speech acts. The sense in which a belief represents its conditions of satisfaction is the same sense (whatever that is) in which a statement represents its conditions of satisfaction.

7. In the way that, say, a desire embodies (or is a shorthand way of describing) a propositional attitude, an unspecified desiring-that. If you desire a yellow station wagon, you must want to *own* (*lease? buy? steal?*) one, and wanting to own (lease, buy, steal) one can be expressed by saying that one desires *that* one own (lease, etc.) one – something you cannot desire without understanding what a yellow station wagon (not to mention *owning, leasing, buying, stealing*) is.

8. He thinks they have an Intentionality that, in certain respects, is quite unlike the Intentionality of beliefs and desires. Experiences, for instance, have a content that is self-referential, and the experience, giving (as he says) the experiencer direct "access" to the object it is an experience of, is best thought of as a special kind of representation – what he calls a *presentation*. None of these details will matter to my discussion. If experiences are not Intentional *at all*, then they certainly are not Intentional in the special presentational, self-referential way that Searle describes.

9. Fred Dretske, *Seeing and Knowing* (Chicago: University of Chicago Press, 1969).

10. They could be misled if, for instance, they misinterpreted the distance between the camera and the object that the photograph was a photograph of. They might then think that the picture was a picture of, say, a speck of dust. But an experience of a station wagon (at this distance and in this light) might equally mislead. One might think that one was seeing a speck of dust.

11. Readers familiar with *Naturalizing the Mind* (Cambridge, Mass.: MIT Press, 1995), a book in which I defend a representational theory of experience, should not suppose that I am being inconsistent here. Experiences represent, yes, but not in the way that statements and beliefs represent. They are not Intentional in the way that Searle uses this word.

8 | Sense Data

BRIAN O'SHAUGHNESSY

1. INTRODUCTION

(1) John Searle describes himself as a "naive realist" or a "direct realist," so far as visual perception is concerned.[1] The theory that he endorses begins with the following claim. Whenever we visually perceive some physical item in the environment, a visual experience occurs that possesses the property of intentionality, and the intentional content or internal object of that experience generally matches whatever outer object is perceived. Thus, I seem to see a table, and a table is indeed present and seen by me. While this need not always be the case, for one can perceive an object as what it is not, it is the usual and normal situation.

However, this is not yet a statement of Searle's "direct realist" position, since most theories of visual perception can agree with such an account of the visual situation. What more is needed? I think the following suffices to give the gist of his theory. If we add a further claim, namely that the visual perception of physical objects is an experience that is of the physical object and is not also at the same time an experience of a mediating psychological object, then that seems to state a "direct realist" position of the kind that Searle endorses. Such an account rates as "direct" in virtue of the fact that nothing of a psychological nature interposes as attentive object between the mind and the physical object that is perceived: the mind strikes through to its object in one blow. So much for a brief rendering of John Searle's "direct realist" position on visual perception. While his account of visual perception ranges farther afield than this, it incorporates these "direct realist" elements. I now turn to those theories that are in opposition to this theory.

(2) It is probable that several theories of visual perception travel under the name "sense-datum theory." Nevertheless, it may well be that we so use the expression that a necessary condition of being a "sense-datum theory" is, that it posit some psychological phenomenal individual as the immediate

object of the visual experience, a psychological individual that stands attentively between the mind and the physical object of perception. Where the several "sense-datum theories" differ, lies in the supposed character of this object. Thus, one might suppose that one sees "lights and colours" "out there" in physical space, and believe that these entities are nonetheless in some sense mental in character. Alternatively, one might think that one actually sees the visual experience in having that one and the same experience (though, as it stands, this doctrine is barely intelligible). Or third, one might think that the seeing of physical objects consists in a visual experience whose internal object is a distinct psychological individual of which one is at that moment immediately and confrontationally aware: as we say, one might *hypostatise* the intentional content, supposing that seeing involves the immediate awareness of such an hypostatic entity. Thus, if one has the visual experience of seeming to see Mr. X, this experience might be *analysed* into the occurrence of (i) a mental phenomenon whose description is (something like) "Mr. X-representation" or "Mr. X-appearance," together with (ii) a separate mental phenomenon that is the immediate awareness of that supposed distinct mental entity. This doctrine seems certain to lead to regress, since the intentional content of the latter direct awareness must in turn suffer hypostatisation.

Here we have three theories of visual perception. Then there seems to be little doubt that the latter two theories are false and very weak theories. As for the first theory, it is as it stands too vague to be seriously considered, and needs to be made more specific before one can properly assess it. Now theories of the latter two kinds are explicitly mentioned by John Searle, and he – rightly, as I see it – rejects them outright. Thus he writes:

> Colour and shape are properties accessible to vision, but though my visual experience is a component of any visual perception, the visual experience is not itself a visual object, it is not itself seen. (p. 38)

and

> ... the traditional sense-data theorists ... mislocated the Intentionality of perception in supposing that experiences were the objects of perception. (p. 60)[2]

and:

> The mistake of the sense-data theorists seems to me analogous to the mistake of treating the propositional content of the belief as the object of the belief.... (p. 60)[3]

However, it would be false to suppose that Searle's "direct realist" position on visual perception consists merely in a rejection of these two doctrines. It is surely proper to construe him as saying that in the phenomenon of seeing, nothing of a psychological nature is seen or noticed or given to awareness as its immediate extensional object. The theory that he proposes clearly affirms that in seeing the mind is immediately aware of the physical object.

(3) In my opinion there exists a theory, which I shall hereinafter call Theory A, which has a right to be called a "sense-datum theory," which is in opposition to Searle's "direct realism," and which seems immune to Searle's criticisms.

It is a theory that overlaps in part with the accounts proposed by some of the best-known adherents of sense-datum theory, notably by G. E. Moore in his reply to O. K. Bouwsma in *The Philosophy of G.E. Moore*.[4] Such a theory as I shall spell out does not suffer from the various blemishes just mentioned, yet it opposes Searle's "direct realism" in positing a mental entity as the immediate, distinct, nonintentional object of visual perception. While I myself believe in this theory, I will not here offer any arguments in its favour. I shall merely explicate it, and try to demonstrate that it can handle objections of the kind John Searle makes to sense-datum theories generally.

The theory takes the following form. The first element in the theory posits the existence of a type of phenomenon that merits the title "visual sensation." Examples of this phenomenon are readily discovered in after-imagery, but also elsewhere in the mind – say, in those "lights" that are caused by a brain probe and designated as "phosphenes," or in the "moons" that one sees when, with eyes closed, one presses one's eyeballs in a certain manner. The second part of the theory states that, if one restricts oneself to monocular seeing (merely for simplicity), then when one has a visual experience of the environment, one's visual field is wholly occupied by mental phenomena of this kind, distributed in two-dimensional space and susceptible of description in terms of right-left/up-down and color-bright terminology. The third part of the theory states that to become attentively aware of, or to notice or to see, any part of this sensory array, is one and the same event as noticing or becoming aware of or seeing some physical item in the environment – provided that the sensations in question owe their existence, as well as their character and layout, in regular reliable causal manner to the object in the environment. For example, if the setting sun causes a round red patch of visual sensation in the middle of one's visual field, and does so in nondeviant manner, then the theory claims that the very existence of this round red sensation is one and the same state of affairs as the sun's being present in the visual field. All that is then required for the sun to be seen or perceived is, that the round red sensory patch come to awareness or be noticed. This theory of visual perception may in some ways run counter to common sense, but it seems to me to be free of the obvious weaknesses of the theories mentioned earlier.

I could sum up this contentious doctrine in the following way. With one's eyes closed one tilts one's head backwards, and then opens one's eyes. At that very moment the blue of the sky fills the visual field from one end to the other. Then what Theory A is claiming is, that at that same instant something *blue*, and *psychological*, and *one's own*, enters existence. The becoming visible to one of the blue of the sky *is* the coming into existence of a sensation of blue that stands in suitable nondeviant regular causal relation to the light impacting upon one's retina at that time. And the noticing or seeing the blue of the sensation is *one and the same event* as the noticing or seeing the blue of the sky.

2. CLARIFICATION

(1) Before I attempt to defend this theory against the criticisms that John Searle has leveled against sense-datum theory generally, a few words of clarification are in order concerning the exact claims of Theory A.

Perhaps the first thing to be accomplished is an explanation of my use of the expression "visual sensation." Here we encounter a somewhat wayward application of the word "sensation." Normally, the term is applied to bodily sensations such as itches and pains and tickles, even though people sometimes do speak of "visual sensations," although generally without clarifying what sense they are giving to the expression. Now it probably does not really much matter whether or not the word "sensation" is correctly applied to after-imagery: that particular issue may be little more than verbal. However, underlying the verbal question lie nonverbal considerations of importance. Thus, it seems to me that the following are properties of such phenomena as after-images, phosphenes, and so forth.

A. They are psychological individuals.

B. They are endowed with *quale* (idiosyncratic distinctive quality).

C. They have regular extra-psychological bodily causes.

D. They are individuated in body-relative physical space (more exactly, through their body-relative directional properties).

E. They stand to the attention in the same relations as do itches, (etc.), relating to the attention as a possible direct object rather than as an occupant.

F. They can be noticed: that is, they can be the distinct and direct object of an awareness experience.

G. And they can exist unnoticed, as well as marginally noticed.

Now these properties are probably the main characteristics of phenomena such as after-images and "phosphenes" and the "moons" that we see on pressing our eyes. And they are properties also of bodily sensations. To my mind, this constitutes sufficient justification for applying the expression "visual sensation" to them. In particular, the principle of individuation is the same in either case. Thus, a red after-image can coexist with an internally indistinguishable second after-image at the very same moment in time, being individuated by its position in the visual field (and ultimately by its position in body-relative physical space), just as one can simultaneously have two internally indistinguishable bodily sensations at different places in the body (and as one cannot simultaneously have two internally indistinguishable thoughts). In addition, there exist regular causally sufficient conditions of (say) a red after-image (to wit, sudden stimulus by bright green light to the retina); and after-images can be noticed or unnoticed or poorly noticed etc.; and here also comparable properties are encountered in the case of bodily sensations. In a word, these phenomena must be something more than a "manner of speaking": they are genuine psychological individuals, with much in common with bodily sensations.

(2) Where in space are these items? Perhaps the first thing to say is, that these sensations are not to be located at a depth out from us. An after-image continues to occupy the same place – let us say, as one swings one's head – whether or not it is now set against a wall, now against the sky, now on a tree, and so on; for we would not judge these changes in its projective site – caused merely by bodily movements – as alterations in its position. This is because the after-image has the following two individuating spatial characteristics: position in the visual field, and direction in relation to the body – and that is all. These sensory items are given as lying in a direction out from the body of their owner, and simultaneously as positioned in a visual field that likewise is usually experienced as set before one directionally (these two properties not being in competition).

Then Theory A supposes that when we see physical objects in the surrounding environment, phenomena of the type of visual sensations are present in the visual field, are given to one directionally in relation to the body, and are seen or noticed. It is not, of course, supposed that these phenomena actually *are* after-images, since their causal ancestry is unsuitable for such a characterisation; but the claim is that in themselves they are the very same kind of phenomenon.

It has to be emphasised that this theory supposes there to be only one event in the attention when, at one and the same moment in time, we perceive physical objects in the environment and visual sensations. The claim is that one and the same event falls under the several descriptions: "noticing the visual sensation," "noticing the physical item that occupies the same point in the visual field as that sensation." To be sure, the internal or intentional object of the one visual experience will generally make no mention of sensations, and usually is given exclusively in terms of material objects and events lying at a distance in physical space (as well as in a direction). But it is the same event, and it has (at least) two external or extensional objects, even though it has only one intentional object. Indeed, since I am persuaded that we see the light coming from the object at that same moment in time, and opt for a light-representationalist theory of the perception of physical objects[5] in three-dimensional space, I endorse the view that the attention usually has three quite distinct external objects when we visually perceive items in the environment: sensation, light, publicly perceptible material object (etc). These objects stand to one another in regular causal relation, and it is this fact that makes possible this multiplication of extensional objects of the one visual experience. I propose now to see if this theory can stand up to the criticisms that Searle levels against "sense-datum theories" in general.

3. JOHN SEARLE'S OBJECTIONS TO SENSE-DATUM THEORY

(a) Sense Data and the Visibility of Objects in Three-Dimensional Space

(1) John Searle does not consider this particular theory of sense-data. Indeed, he does little more than lay out the bare outlines of sense-datum theory generally; and, strictly speaking, I cannot assume that he would reject this particular version of sense-datum theory. Nonetheless, he makes certain objections to sense-datum theory in general,[6] and it seems reasonable to suppose that he would think they applied to this account of visual perception.

I begin with the question of whether or not this doctrine is consistent with the perception of (say) material objects. Thus, at several places Searle says that, according to sense-datum theory, the sense datum is said to be perceived, and the material object is "apparently not." For example:

> According to them [representationalism and phenomenalism] what is seen is always, strictly speaking, a visual experience (. . . a "sensum" or a "sense datum," or an "impression"). They are thus confronted with a question which does not arise for the naive realist: What is the relationship between the sense data which we do see and the material object which apparently we do not see?[7]

It is the latter assumption – that representationalism is obliged to endorse the proposition that in the normal visual situation one does not manage to see the material object – that I wish at this point to question. Theory A, which is surely "representationalist" in type, sidesteps such a claim in a very simple manner. It does so merely by supposing that the perception of the sense datum is *one and the same event* as the perception of the material object. To my mind, this constitutes a completely adequate answer to the problem mentioned by Searle.

(2) Nevertheless, the latter doctrine has to defend itself against certain natural objections, objections which are in a sense a development of the criticism made by Searle. The first of these objections takes as its starting point the fact that visual perception is a directional phenomenon. Thus, when we see an object we see it down a line in space called "the line of sight": objects are given as lying in certain directions out from us in three-dimensional space. Then the phenomenon of seeing is such that any one object in the field of view visually gets between the viewer and any other object lying at a greater distance down the same line, and usually hides it from view. If two objects are located at the same moment in time on the same spatial line coming from the eye, the only way visibility of both could be realised would be if the nearer of the two objects was what we call *"transparent"*: if the near object is not transparent and occupies some given sector of the visual field, then it must *obscure* the remoter object. Then what is the situation in this respect in the case of sense data? Theory A claims that sense-data are given directionally to their owner in his experience, and thus on a particular line of sight, and the theory does not posit transparency in the sense datum. How, then, could a sense-datum endowed with these properties help obscuring from view whatever physical objects happen to

lie along the same line of sight? It is all very well to say that this theory manages to sidestep the problem through identifying the sensation and the visibility to one of the corresponding physical objects, but how can this identification be possible if – as seems, on the face of it, to be the case – the phenomena of transparency and obscuration hold universally for all visible objects? To answer this objection, we need to look a little more closely at the phenomenon of transparency.

(b) Transparency

Now the concept of transparency has a limited applicability or utility. Thus, while a measure of transparency in an object permits the simultaneous visibility of two objects down the one line of sight, it inevitably accomplishes this at the cost of losing a measure of visibility in both visibilia. For example, looking through coloured glasses at a distant object, we see something of the colour of the glass but fail to see that of the object; looking through a dirty window, we can manage to see both landscape and window at the same time, but wherever part of the window is visible something of the scene is not. Accordingly, a summary account of the situation must go like this: in the absence of the property of transparency, any one visible object must hide whatever object lies down the same line of sight; and even when a measure of transparency obtains in the near object, the visibility of both the near and remoter object are inevitably qualified in various respects.

Let me develop the latter point, since it has an interesting ramification that poses a difficulty for Theory A. Thus, one can see one's surroundings through a transparent monochrome coloured piece of glass, but the property of transparency is such that a coloured object of this kind could not continue to show the monochrome character of its own colour if one happened to be perceiving a scene through it. For example, normally a transparent red glass makes everything lying beyond look red; but the outlines of the objects lying beyond are visible, not through being of the same red as the glass, but through being darker or lighter versions of that colour. If they all looked exactly the same in hue, nothing would be visible but the redness of the glass – which could not, in consequence, be transparent after all. Imagine what one would do if one were a painter, attempting to portray a monochrome red window as transparent, and showing something of the scene lying beyond. Would one reach for the one hue of red? But if so, one would show merely an expanse of colour and nothing of the scene behind! The conclusion we must draw is, that the property of transparency is such that it is not possible for a transparent object to display all of its own visible properties *and* those of whatever objects it is permitting to show through it.

For this reason alone, Theory A is not in a position to claim that the sense datum is transparent. After all, Theory A states that there is a *total match* of colour and contour between the sense datum and the objects it represents, and we have just seen that the property of transparency is such that there cannot of necessity be a total match between the visible properties of a transparent object and those of whatever is showing through it. Indeed, if *per impossibile* there could exist such a match, to which of the two objects would the visible qualities be ascribed? To the near transparent or to the remoter object? Suppose one were to look through monochrome blue glass at a sky of exactly the same hue. Which object is the owner of the blue that we see? It may be that this question simply has no answer: if we say the blue belongs to the glass, then the glass ceases to be transparent; while if we say it is of the sky, then we are obliged to assume that the blue of the glass has been rendered invisible at that moment! Whatever the exact truth on this particular problem, it has become clear that sense-datum theory cannot answer the argument that the sense datum must get in between the object and viewer and so obscure it, by claiming that it instead allows for the visibility of the object in the mode of transparency. And this looks like a difficulty for Theory A.

And the same reply has to be given concerning the light that is, in my opinion, a visible mediator between the viewer and the objects that the light brings to view. For it is not transparent light – whatever that might be! – that is postulated by such a theory. It is merely light that is endowed for sight with the very same two-dimensional directional visible properties as the objects that it makes visible, viz., colour and the two-dimensional spatial layout of that colour. If the round red setting Sun is made visible representationally through the light coming to us from the Sun, this is because the light that is seen comes to us as at once red, lying in the same direction out from head/eyes/trunk as the Sun, and in the form of a round red occupant of the visual field. This light is in fact situated at the retina, even though it is not seen *as* or *to be* at the retina, but its colour and two-dimensional shape are nonetheless visible (along with the light itself). Do we not sometimes see the two-dimensional shape of a beam of light? After all, the light coming from a window at night might be seen as a luminous rectangle set at right angles to the line of sight. Then here, too, the identity of the properties ascribed to the light and to the material objects, in such a light-representational theory of the perception of material objects as I have suggested, ensures that by implication the theory cannot intelligibly attribute the property of transparency to the light.

(c) Answering the Objection

(1) In the absence of the property of transparency, any one visible object must hide whatever object lies down the same line of sight. So let us return to the original question: what is the situation in this respect in the case of the sense datum? How can sense-datum theory avoid the force of this consideration? Theory A claims that sense data are given to us directionally in body-relative physical space, and thus on a particular line of sight, and we have just seen that the theory cannot intelligibly posit transparency in the sense datum. Then how can the sense datum help obscuring from view whatever physical object happens to lie along the same line of sight?

This latter complaint is a natural reading of Searle's claim that, if we see a sense datum, "apparently we do not see the material object." This is an objection to the effect that the sense datum must, on Theory A, block the field of view. And it is an objection of some weight, for it is based on a principle that has application throughout the mind. The principle in question is the familiar truism spelled out several times already, to the effect that if a physical item occupies a point in the visual field, is in line with a second distinct object, and is not transparent, then it must hide the second object. Such a principle holds even in the case of phenomena such as "floaters," which are publicly visible physical entities (despite being merely directionally seen by their owner); indeed, it applies even to after-images (which can surely "block the view"). Then if it holds even for visual sensations such as after-images, why should it not hold for the subclass of visual sensations called "visual sense-data"? It is possible that considerations of this kind might have led John Searle to assume that one of the implications of sense-datum theory is that the supposed presence of a visible sense datum necessitates the invisibility of the physical object it is said to represent.

(2) In answer to this problem, Theory A continues to take refuge in the simplicity of its position. Thus, Theory A posits *neither* transparency *nor* opacity in the sense datum; and in view of what emerged in the earlier discussion, it is difficult to see how it could intelligibly do so. Instead, the theory asserts that the sense datum is merely directionally given, out from oneself in body-relative physical space – say, directly in front of one's face/forehead/trunk – and proceeds to identify the visibility to one of the sense datum with that of its represented objects. Then how could the visibility of such a sensory

object – let us say, of a dark red circle in the middle of one's visual field – constitute a visual obstacle (an *opacity*) to seeing whatever lies in that direction in space? And how could its failing to be a visual obstacle be due to its possessing the property of *transparency*? How could either of these possibilities be realised, if the dark red circular visual sensation is simply one and the same thing as the visibility to its owner of the (dark, red, circular) physical occupant of that sector of the visual field?

Nevertheless, bearing in mind that visual sensations such as after-images and phosphenes (etc.) obscure from view whatever lies along the same line of sight in the physical environment, this reply might not convince everyone. After all, why should not those visual sensations that we deem veridical sense data likewise obscure remoter objects on that line? Or, to express the same point in different terms, how can a doctrine that identifies the sensation and the visibility to one of objects on the line of sight be theoretically viable, if sensations equally as much as other visibles can obscure the view of the environment? Well, it seems to me that in the veridical perceptual situation, a qualitative change occurs: a novel state of affairs is born. Thus, whereas something of *different appearance* lay behind (say) the obscuring after-image, in the case of a veridical sense datum nothing of different appearance lies behind the sensory patch: rather, (two) physical items of precisely identical appearance do so, each of which is suitably causally related to that sensation, viz., light and object. For Theory A is above all else a theory of the *visibility* of physical objects, a theory that purports to *explain* that visibility; for whereas the visibility of visual sensations is not problematic, that of physical objects at least presents a problem. And so Theory A replies to the charge that the sense datum hides from view the object that occupies the identical sector of the visual field, in the following way. Far from hiding or obscuring, the sense datum actually *makes visible* what otherwise would be invisible. Indeed, it *confers* visibility both upon the light coming from the object and upon the object itself, for it is owing to its own visibility that they come to possess this property: it nondistributively shares this property out with them. In a word, it *shows* both light and object. I want now to clarify how it is that it manages to do so.

(d) Modes of Showing

(1) Now there is "showing" and "showing." Consider one familiar variety of showing: a television image showing a spectacle. This is a different "showing" from that of *making visible*, and in fact could never manage to be a making visible. For example, there is no way in which (say) a complete

identity of content, together with simultaneity of occurrence, could succeed in making up the "shortfall" from seeing, since the source of that "shortfall" lies elsewhere than in content and timing – as we shall discover. Thus, one might in principle manage to see on TV an image that is spatially adjacent to, visually indistinguishable from, and simultaneous with that which is visible and being televised, yet without making up the "shortfall" in question. Here we correlate two internally indistinguishable appearances, and relate one to the other causally. Then even though this (TV) variety of showing is representational in kind, it is not such that in seeing the image we see the object it represents. The reason is, that in this case we really do encounter a second visible item that is distinct from, and that might in certain situations obscure or hide, whatever visible item is the cause of this image. While attentive representationalism from two to three dimensions is viable (as in the case of the light-representationalism of physical objects), attentive representationalism at a distance within three spatial dimensions seems to be an impossibility. Accordingly, we could look at the scene, and then at the TV image, and whereas in one case we really would be looking at the scene, in the other case we would be looking at an array of coloured patches before us *as* presenting to view a particular simultaneous spectacle; and the one simply is not the other. Despite the identity of content and appearance and time, and despite the significant overlap of cognitive utility in the case of these two phenomena, only one of these visual experiences is an example of "seeing the scene in the flesh," of actually "setting one's eyes upon" that scene.

(2) Contrast looking at a mirror image of a scene, a sight that in another sense of the term *shows* us the scene in question. Here one is initially inclined to say that the mirror shows the scene in the very same sense of the term as the TV image. That is, one might offer an account structurally comparable to the one just presented, and say that in one case we see "the real thing" and in the other case "merely an image of the real thing." But if we do not see "the real thing" when we see the mirror image, what that is *not* "the real thing" do we see when we stare at whatever it is that we see when we look into a mirror? It is empty verbiage to say that we see "an image," bearing in mind that in this situation we are unable to produce an analogue of the colored areas on the TV screen. And yet why should we not claim that when (as we say) we "see the objects in the mirror," what we really see is the light reflected by the mirrored objects? Well, why not, indeed – but the same can be said in the case of "the real thing." For here likewise the light that is reflected by the object of sight enters our visual field when we see that "real

thing." In short, citing the light merely sidesteps the problem: it fails to tell us whether or not we really do see the object when we see it in a mirror.

Now it is true that, when a mirror is showing a reflection of an object, one might first of all look at the mirror image and then turn away and look at "the real thing." Indeed, these two visibilia might even be objects of one and the same visual experience, the two visibles sitting side by side before one in a single experience, so that one might (say) see a tree in the right half of one's visual field and a mirror image of the same tree in the left half! Then if one experience is seeing "the real thing," of what can the other be but *something other*? In a word, not "the real thing"! So, at least, one is inclined to say – in my view erroneously. Yet this much of this latter interpretation is certainly true: that the *beams of light* are two and different: after all, one beam travels along one straight line from object to eye, while the other beam comes along another line; and there is no way that the seeing of the one beam can *be* the seeing of the other. However, the analogous conclusion does not follow when it comes to the seeing of the material object reflector of these two beams of light. One could point in the direction of the light showing in the mirror and say, "That light is not the light I see coming from the direction of the visible object," and here the intentional object is a particular beam of light. But a different situation is realised when the intentional object is the material object coming to view from a given direction. Thus, while one will execute two different physical gestures when one points to whatever material object is on view, first of all "in the flesh" and then "in the mirror," these two modes of reference to material objects are comparable to using "the morning star" and "the evening star" as different ways of picking out the planet Venus. In either case, one may not *know* that one has singled out one and the same object, but if the intentional object of the intentional acts of pointing is "the material object that I now see" (rather than "the light beam entering my visual field from that direction"), then in each case the act of pointing will have singled out one and the same material object.

(3) Then the way in which the sense datum and the beam of light *show* the material object that they make visible is different from each of the above two modes: that is, both from the mode of the TV image and from that of the mirror image. In the case of the sense datum and light, we are concerned with causal mediators and (above all) with *attentive mediators* intervening between us and the visible material object, and in the other two cases we are not. It is true that the mirror image is one presentation of the object, and the normal sight of the object is another, and in either case we manage to see the material object; but in no sense is the mirror image a *visible*

mediator – that is, a something that is *that via which* the material object is seen, a visible X such that seeing that X *is* seeing the material object and is at the same time *that via which* the material object is seen.

In sum, while in the case of the mirror the visible image shows the object itself, it does so in a special way: it shows it in such a manner that the object's spatial position is distorted in regular manner: we see the object – where it is not. Meanwhile in the case of the television the visible image shows the object in the sense that it shows to us the appearance of the object, and therefore relates to the original in such a way as to count as a representation of that original object, but not in such a way as to show to us the object itself. Then by contrast with this latter case, the sense-datum and the light show the object in both of these senses. Thus, they do so in the sense that even though neither entity is the same as the material object, they nonetheless in the first place present to view the appearance of the object (and via such a causal avenue as to count as a representation of the object), but do so secondly in such a causal context that the seeing of any one of these two visibilia is identical to the seeing of the object. In short, they bring both the object *and* its appearance to view.

Here we have three different ways in which a material object can be shown to us: in a TV image, in a mirror image, and via a sense datum (or a beam of light). In each case we look at something; in each case a different situation is realised; nonetheless, on each occasion we make the acquaintance of the appearance of the material object. This justifies the application of the term "show" across these diverse cases.

4. THE NATURE OF ATTENTIVE CONTACT WITH AN OBJECT

(1) It seems to me that misunderstanding the nature of attentive or perceptual contact with an object may play a determining role in some of the objections that tend to be raised to sense-datum theory. Thus, John Searle speaks as if the existence and perceptibility of the sense datum must be in direct opposition to the perceptibility of the object it represents. What lies behind this conviction? Well, it may be that "attentive contact" is here being understood in terms that are inappropriate. Whether or not this is true in Searle's case I cannot pretend to know, but I believe there exists a natural tendency to think along the following lines.

I think there is a tendency to conceive of attentive contact, which is to say of perceptual awareness, as a kind of palpable or concrete contact of the mind with its object. And in one sense of these terms, this belief is surely correct. For perceptual awareness is in a good sense "concrete," the establishing of a relation not by the application of concepts or by the use of the thought, but by the concrete instantiation in Nature of a regular causal tie linking object and awareness, a relation that is largely independent of one's conceptual system. However, there is a tendency – or perhaps an imagery of a kind that may be at work in one's mind – to overinterpret this "concreteness," to think of it as in some way akin to, as a mental analogue of, something drawn from the realm of *things* – a palpable connection of some kind, rather as if the gaze literally reached out and touched its object. Then to the extent that such imagery or such a way of thinking is at work in one's mind, to that extent one may come to consider the relation between mind and object to be such that perception of a material object could not conceivably be identical to perception of a distinct and second item, to wit a sense datum. After all, the sense datum is distinct from the physical object it is said to represent; and just as touching one object cannot *be* touching a second distinct other, so here in the case of such supposed mental contactings. These "speculative diagnostics" on my part (as one might call them) are merely an attempt to explain the counterintuitiveness of doctrines such as Theory A: specifically, to explain why one might be resistant to the idea that sense-datum theory of this kind manages to sidestep the problem of visual opacity.

(2) When an event that is a perception occurs, an experience of a distinctive kind occurs in the "stream of consciousness," viz., a noticing. Some perceptible item will have come to perceptual awareness, and this is an event of such a nature and in such a causal context that one finds oneself in a position to offer a description of that perceived object – say, as "a round red circle," "a whistle," "a ringing sound," and so on. Now it is a necessary property of attentive contact, not that one knows through this experience of the present existence of the perceived object, but that a regular causal relation links the experience and its object cause. What this implies is, that a *cognitive link* has been established in the world, whether or not one knows that it has. Then if one is in fact aware of the existence of this cognitive link, one is in a position to put this latter piece of knowledge, together with knowledge of the character of the experience, to use in arriving at knowledge of the environment. Attentive contact is like money in the bank – even if one does not know of the existence of the account: it is there to be tapped.

There has to be a *match of content* between "inner" and "outer," as well as the aforementioned causal bridge or channel, if one is to have such "cognitive credit." After all, what use would it be to know that an experience related regularly to some outer phenomenal item, if there were nothing in common between the content of the experience and its "outer" object? For example, upon seeing a red circle in one's visual field that one knew to be a visual sensation related via a causally reliable channel to an "outer" source, one would not be in a position to deduce that anything red and round caused this experience, unless the situation reliably realised such a match of content. But if it does, so that the elements of the content of the cause stand in regular causal relation to the very same elements of the content of the caused, and if one knows that the conditions determining one's present visual experience are reliable, then one will find oneself in a position to infer from a visual experience with some given content to the existence of a causative phenomenon with exactly the same properties. Here we have stated in brief the real variety of "contact" that is realised in "attentive contact": it is not the creation of a kind of psychic *thing*; and it precisely is not the acquisition of *knowledge*; but it is instead the occurrence of an event in one's awareness which *puts one in a position* to acquire knowledge. Misunderstanding this fact in the more primitive mode of a kind of literal mental contact, can stand in the way of understanding the special mode of representation that is realised in visual perception.

5. REPRESENTATIONALISM AND RESEMBLANCE

(1) John Searle endorses a claim of Berkeley's concerning the resemblance said by representationalists to hold between the sense datum and the physical object it supposedly represents. It is a claim that he and Berkeley believe constitutes an insuperable difficulty for representationalism. He expresses the point in the following way:

> As Berkeley pointed out, it makes no sense to say that the shape and colour we see resemble the shape and colour of an object which is absolutely invisible or otherwise inaccessible to any of our senses.[8]

And Searle proceeds to sum up the situation as follows:

> In short, the representational theory is unable to make sense of the notion of resemblance, and therefore it cannot make any sense of the notion of representation, since the form of representation in question requires resemblance.[9]

(2) In the remaining part of this chapter I want to show how Theory A is equal to the challenge posed by these assertions of Searle. Now Theory A

posits a representational mediator that takes the form of a visual sensation, an entity that (at least in the case of monocular vision) is said to be given to one in at least (and perhaps merely) two-dimensional terms. Consider an example of such a phenomenon: I see a round red setting Sun, and according to Theory A do so through noticing a round red visual sensation. I wish now to bring out the existence of a resemblance, holding in at least two respects, between this internal sensory object and the outer physical object that it is said to represent. However, in order to simplify the discussion, I choose to discuss a different example. Thus, even though after-images are not sense data, I shall discuss the case of what in normal parlance we would call "a round red after-image." I choose this phenomenon merely because it is a relatively unproblematic example of the kind, one that should enable me to spell out how resemblance can hold between physical objects and internal items that are examples of the same general type as sense data. If resemblance of the right kind can hold between after-imagery and physical objects, there is no reason why it could not hold between sense data and the objects that they are said to represent.

Let us suppose that at some point in time in a visual field there occurs in the right-hand portion the round red setting Sun, and in the left-hand portion a round red after-image that is unnaturally persistent and at that moment visually indistinguishable from the Sun. Does not the sensory item in the left-hand portion of the visual field share certain properties with the public physical object that is making its appearance in the other half of the visual field? Is there not a resemblance in several visible respects between the after-image and the actual physical Sun? For one thing, they are both red. Furthermore, they possess an identical contour: the after-image is round, while the contour of the Sun, which is the two-dimensional shape it presents to the angle at which it is being viewed, is also round. In short, these two entities, the one "inner" and the other "outer," have these two visible properties in common.

Objection is liable to be made to the claim that the after-image has a round contour. And yet there can be no objection to the claim that bodily sensations have shapes – even though we do not *experience* them as shaped. For example, we locate a sensation of contact precisely at the point of contact; and just as a set of those various points constitute a shape in physical space, so too does a single extensive sensation of contact. Then what can be the objection to the idea that a red after-image, which lies in a particular direction in body-relative physical space, also possesses a shape? The after-image is real; it can scarcely be said to lie *behind* one; and one would point down a line in physical space *in front of* one in indicating the direction in which it is visible. Indeed, if it were extensive enough we would indicate a set of directions that would together trace out in physical space a two-dimensional shape like a circle upon a transverse plane: it is this shape in physical space that we attribute to the image, and do so by the description "a round after-image."

A minor difficulty for this thesis is presented by the following fact. It may be the case that both the sensation of contact and the after-image are brain processes. If so, it would follow that they must literally be situated in the brain. So how can they be presumed to have the shapes that they experientially seem to have? Well, in ordinary speech the site of what we call a "toothache" is given as the tooth, despite the possible truth of Physicalism, and this ascription is precisely correct – the reason being, that what we normally *call* "the place of a sensation" is not the place at which it actually *is*, but rather *the real place in physical space* in which it *really is given experientially to us*. This latter sense takes some explicating, but we are all familiar with it and by implication constantly endorse its validity in our common speech. Then it is such a sense that is invoked in the case of the after-image. And it should be emphasised that it refers to real places in physical space. Thus, just as it is a real physical place on the body surface that we attribute to the sensation of contact, so it is real physical directions that are cited in mapping the two-dimensional shape of the after-image, and that is to say that it is a real physical shape that we give to it. In fact, it would be true to say that a "round after-image" satisfies the equation for circularity, viz., $x^2 + y^2 = a^2$, where the variables stand for the visible extensities of visual sensation (to be measured either in body-relative angular or *minima visibilia* terms). In short, circularity is in common between the round after-image and the visible contour of the setting Sun, and so also between the round sense datum that Theory A claims represents the Sun and the Sun itself. Such a sense-datum theory is in no way committed to the idea that after-images and visual sensations generally occupy some private psychological "visual space." Why should it be? No one believes that bodily sensations are something apart from the physical body and physical space. Why should it be any different in the case of the visual variety?

(3) What of colour? Objection might also be made to the claim that the after-image has the same colour as the colour the Sun is presenting to view at that moment. How can an after-image have a colour? And yet surely it has an *appearance*. And surely in the case of a "red after-image," that appearance is *red* in character. True, this example of red is visible only to one being, and in principle so. True, the red of the Sun is *for* humans (at least) *in* normal

viewing conditions, and this cannot be said of the after-image (which is, instead, intrinsically and essentially red). But do these differences matter? We are pinning one and the same property on the sensation and the Sun, and attaching different conditions for its application: no more!

This reply may not satisfy everyone. Thus, when we describe the Sun as "red," are we attributing the property "red" to the Sun, or the property "red to humans in daylight"? If the latter, then how can we be attributing the same property to the after-image and to the Sun? After all, while the Sun looks red to humans generally, the after-image looks red uniquely to one individual. However, while this latter claim is surely true, it does not I believe imply that we are attributing something different to the after-image and to the Sun when describing them as red. I adduce the following consideration in support of this view. Let us suppose, fantastically, that grass looks red to turtles in an environment irradiated by electrons (just as blood looks red to humans in daylight). Then I suggest that if turtles could talk, and were discussing the look of the grass, then they would be speculating about the very property that we visually detect in blood – despite the different conditions and assumptions lying behind their speech activities. Although a little thought should make it apparent that when we say that blood is red, we imply that it is red to humans in daylight, and implicitly acknowledge that it might conceivably be (say) blue to cats when steadily irradiated by (say) linear beams of electrons, yet in all of these cases it is the one and same "red" that is under consideration. And this is all that we need for the resemblance to hold between the after-image (and sense datum) and the Sun. The same *colour* is instantiated in both, even though the conditions underlying its attribution vary from case to case (rather as "twin Earth" reds really are *red* – to "twin Earthlings," and the word "red$_{(TE)}$" would translate as the word "red$_{(E)}$").

As claimed earlier, this seems to suffice for the relation of resemblance in respect of colour to hold between the sense datum and the physical object that it brings to view, and thus also for the relation of representation in this regard. And yet what need in the final analysis of these words "resemble" and "representation"? After all, the real substance of the "representational" Theory A is: that the appearance in the visual field of a visual sensation of red *is*, given certain regular causal projective relations with the Sun, the appearance in the visual field of the Sun, and the literal instantiation therein of its colour and contour. The words "representation" and "resemble" can look after themselves. While the theory would unquestionably be classed as "representationalist," so far as Theory A is concerned this is a deduction from the theory – a second-order property, as one might say.

(4) Note that I have not in this chapter argued for the truth of Theory A, and it would not be appropriate to the nature of this volume for me to do so. My aim has been merely to demonstrate that a viable account of visual perception can be advanced, which is undoubtedly a theory of sense-data, that is at odds with the claims of John Searle concerning sense-data theories generally, and that is able to withstand the criticisms levelled by him at such theories.

Notes

1. John Searle, *Intentionality* (Cambridge: Cambridge University Press, 1983), p. 57.
2. Ibid.
3. Ibid.
4. P. A. Schilpp (ed.), *The Philosophy of G. E. Moore* (Evanston, Ill.: Northwestern University Press, 1942), pp. 627–49.
5. See Brian O'Shaughnessy, *Consciousness and the World* (Oxford: Oxford University Press, 2000), Chapter 16, "Seeing the Light."
6. *Intentionality*, pp. 38, 58–61.
7. Ibid.
8. *Intentionality*, p. 59.
9. Ibid., p. 60.

9 The Limits of Expressibility

FRANÇOIS RECANATI

I. THE DETERMINATION VIEW

A basic tenet of contemporary semantics is that *the meaning of a sentence determines its truth conditions.* This determination of truth conditions by linguistic meaning can be more or less direct. In nonindexical cases, the meaning of the sentence directly determines (and can even be equated to) its truth conditions. The sentence 'Snow is white' means that, and is true if and only if, snow is white. To give the meaning of such a sentence is to give its truth conditions. When the sentence is indexical, the situation is more complex. The sentence has truth conditions only 'with respect to context'. The sentence 'I am English' uttered by John is true if and only if John is English; uttered by Paul, it is true if and only if Paul is English, and so forth. Still, the truth conditions, in each context, are determined by the meaning of the sentence (with respect to the context). The meaning of 'I am English' determines that, if that sentence is uttered by *a*, then it is true if and only if *a* is English.

The thesis that meaning determines truth conditions can be dubbed the Determination View. It goes largely unquestioned in contemporary analytic philosophy (as it did in early analytic philosophy). Fifty years ago, the situation was different. So-called ordinary language philosophers rejected the Determination View.[1] But ordinary language philosophy has suffered a spectacular loss of influence over the last thirty years and is nowadays little more than an object of scorn and caricature. The interest aroused by Wittgenstein and his work has not, paradoxically, ceased to grow, even though the current of ideas from which his thought is inseparable has undergone the aforesaid decline. But Wittgenstein's more or less intentional obscurity, even if contributing to his impact and popularity, limits the effective dissemination of his ideas.

Among contemporary theorists, only a few resist the Determination View. John Searle is one of them. He holds that linguistic meaning *radically underdetermines* truth conditions. According to Searle, even after the reference or semantic value of all the indexical expressions contained in a sentence, including tenses, has been contextually fixed, we still *cannot* specify a state of affairs *s* such that the sentence (with respect to those contextual assignments) is true if and only if *s* obtains. For every candidate – that is, for every such state of affairs – Searle shows that we can imagine a context with respect to which the sentence would not, or not necessarily, be considered as true, even though the relevant state of affairs obtained. That is so because in specifying the state of affairs in question we take many things for granted. If we get rid of those tacit assumptions (by imagining some weird context in which they do not hold), the state of affairs we have specified no longer corresponds to the intuitive truth conditions of the utterance.

II. BACKGROUND ASSUMPTIONS

There are many things that we take for granted, both in speaking and in interpreting the utterances of others. Among those things that we take for granted, some are articulated in the sentence itself: they are the 'presuppositions' of the sentence. Thus if I say that John has stopped smoking, I presuppose that John smoked before, in virtue of the appropriateness conditions of the verb 'to stop'. But there are also things that we take for granted that are in no way articulated in the sentence itself. Searle calls them 'background assumptions'. For example,

> Suppose I go into the restaurant and order a meal. Suppose I say, speaking literally, 'Bring me a steak with fried potatoes.' . . . I take it for granted that they will not deliver the meal to my house, or to my place of work. I take it for granted that the steak will not be encased in concrete, or petrified. It will not be stuffed into my pockets or spread over my head. But none of these assumptions was made explicit in the literal utterance.[2]

Though unarticulated, those assumptions contribute to determining the intuitive conditions of satisfaction (obedience conditions, truth conditions, etc.) of the utterance. The order 'Bring me a steak with fried potatoes' does not count as satisfied if the steak is delivered, encased in concrete, to the customer's house. It is mutually manifest to both the hearer and the speaker that the speaker intends the ordered meal to be placed in front of him on the restaurant table he is sitting at (etc.). Though not explicitly said, that is clearly part of what is meant. Yet one does not want to say that that aspect of utterance meaning is conveyed indirectly or nonliterally (as when one says something and means something else). The utterance 'Bring me a steak with fried potatoes' is fully literal. It is a property of literal and serious utterances that their conditions of satisfaction systematically depend upon unstated background assumptions.

Another example given by Searle involves the word 'cut' in (literal utterances of) sentences such as 'Bill cut the grass' and 'Sally cut the cake'. The word 'cut' is not ambiguous, Searle says, yet it makes quite different contributions to the truth conditions of the utterance in the two cases. That is so because background assumptions play a role in fixing satisfaction conditions, and different background assumptions underlie the use of 'cut' in connection with grass and cakes, respectively. We assume that grass is cut in a certain way, and cakes in another way. The assumed way of cutting finds its way into the utterance's truth conditions:

> Though the occurrence of the word "cut" is literal in [both] utterances . . . , and though the word is not ambiguous, it determines different sets of truth conditions for the different sentences. The sort of thing that constitutes cutting the grass is quite different from, e.g., the sort of thing that constitutes cutting a cake. One way to see this is to imagine what constitutes obeying the order to cut something. If someone tells me to cut the grass and I rush out and stab it with a knife, or if I am ordered to cut the cake and I run over it with a lawnmower, in each case I will have failed to obey the order. That is not what the speaker meant by his literal and serious utterance of the sentence.[3]

Examples can be multiplied at will. Searle convincingly shows that such background assumptions have the following properties: (i) for every utterance, there is an indefinite number of them; (ii) if we manipulate them by imagining weird situations in which they do not hold (e.g., a situation in which steaks are standardly encased in concrete, or a situation in which grass is sliced into strips and sold to customers who want a lawn in a hurry), the intuitive truth conditions of the utterance are affected; and (iii) we cannot make them explicit in the sentence itself without bringing in further background assumptions involved in the interpretation of the new descriptive material. These properties entail that the Determination View must be given up. Truth conditions depend not only upon the meaning of the sentence and the contextual parameters relevant to the interpretation of indexicals, but also upon what Searle calls 'the Background'. Change the background, and you change (or possibly destroy) the truth conditional content of the utterance.

III. CONTEXTUALISM

As mentioned earlier, ordinary language philosophers, from Wittgenstein to Strawson, also rejected the Determination View. Their emphasis was on speech rather than language. As Searle writes,

> [Early analytic philosophers] treat the elements of language – words, sentences, propositions – as things that represent or things that are true or false, etc., apart from any actions or intentions of speakers and hearers. The elements of the language, not the actions and intentions of the speakers are what count. In the late thirties and especially after the Second World War these assumptions came to be vigourously challenged, especially by Wittgenstein.[4]

According to the alternative view put forward by Wittgenstein, Austin, and their followers, it is not natural language *sentences* – and not even sentences 'with respect to context' – that have truth conditions, but full-blooded speech acts – meaningful actions performed by rational agents. That view I call 'contextualism'.

Two purported refutations of contextualism were offered in the sixties, by Grice and Geach, respectively. One of the reasons why contextualism has lost ground is that those refutations have been generally considered to be successful. Another reason for the demise of contextualism is the striking success of the intellectual entreprise known as formal semantics. Formal semantics is based on the Determination View, and its success seems to give the lie to contextualism.

In this chapter I will not deal with Grice's and Geach's arguments against contextualism,[5] nor will I consider whether or not it is possible to reconcile contextualism with the project of giving a systematic semantics for natural language. I will be concerned only with Searle's critique of the Determination View, and its relation (both historical and theoretical) to contextualism.

Even though he was trained in Oxford under Austin and Strawson, Searle himself was not a contextualist when he wrote *Speech Acts*. To be sure, he held that "the unit of communication is not, as has generally been supposed, the symbol, word or sentence, or even the token of the symbol, word or sentence, but rather the *production* or issuance of the symbol or word or sentence in the performance of the speech act."[6] At the same time, however, he issued warnings such as the following:

> A commonplace of recent philosophizing about language has been the distinction between sentences and the speech acts performed in the utterances

of those sentences. Valuable as this distinction is, there has also been a tendency to overemphasize it.[7]

It is possible to distinguish at least two strands in contemporary work in the philosophy of language – one which concentrates on the uses of expressions in speech situations and one which concentrates on the meaning of sentences. Practitioners of these two approaches sometimes talk as if they were inconsistent, and at least some encouragement is given to the view that they are inconsistent by the fact that historically they have been associated with inconsistent views about meaning. . . . But although historically there have been sharp disagreements between practitioners of these two approaches, it is important to realize that the two approaches . . . are complementary and not competing.[8]

The main reason why Searle kept his distance from the contextualism of his teachers was his acceptance of a basic principle that he put forward called the 'Principle of Expressibility'.

IV. THE PRINCIPLE OF EXPRESSIBILITY

In general, the content of a speech act – what the speaker communicates and the hearer understands – cannot be equated with the content of the sentence uttered in performing that speech act. That is due to many factors. (i) The uttered sentence is often elliptical, indeterminate, or ambiguous, even though what the speaker communicates by uttering the sentence in context is perfectly determinate and univocal. (ii) The referring expressions used by the speaker do not, in general, uniquely determine what the speaker is referring to: appeal to the speaker's intentions is necessary to fix the reference of, say, demonstrative pronouns. (iii) Besides what she says, there are many things that the speaker conveys implicitly or nonliterally by her utterance – for example, in indirect speech acts, irony, and metaphor. These three factors result in a gap between literal sentence meaning and speaker's meaning or utterance meaning. But that gap can always be closed: that is the gist of the Principle of Expressibility, according to which *whatever can be meant can be said*. In principle, if not in fact, it is always possible to utter a *fully explicit sentence*, that is, a sentence whose linguistic meaning exactly corresponds to, and uniquely determines, the force and content of the speech act one is performing. It follows that "a study of the meaning of sentences is not in principle distinct from a study of speech acts. Properly construed, they are the same study."[9]

Interpreted at face value, the Principle of Expressibility is incompatible with contextualism. According to contextualism, the sort of content that utterances have (in virtue of the speech acts that they serve to perform) can never be fully encoded into a sentence; hence it will never be the case that the sentence itself expresses that content solely in virtue of the conventions of the language. Sentences, by themselves, do not have determinate contents. What gives them the determinate contents that they have (in context) is the fact that they are used in performing meaningful actions. In brief, contextualism says that the gap between sentence meaning and speaker's meaning can never be closed, while the Principle of Expressibility says that it can always be closed. A consequence of the Principle of Expressibility, Searle says, is that "cases where the speaker does not say exactly what he means – the principal kinds of cases of which are nonliteralness, vagueness, ambiguity, and incompleteness – are not theoretically essential to linguistic communication."[10] According to contextualism, however, the underdetermination of communicated content by linguistic meaning is an essential feature of linguistic communication.

Just as it is incompatible with contextualism, the Principle of Expressibility seems to be incompatible with Searle's findings about background dependence. For the later Searle, as much as for Austin and Wittgenstein, linguistic meaning essentially underdetermines communicated content. As we have seen, it is impossible to make explicit the background assumptions against which an utterance is interpreted – first, because there is an indefinite number of such assumptions, and second, because one cannot make them explicit without bringing in further background assumptions against which the new descriptive material is interpreted. It follows that the content communicated by an utterance cannot be fully encoded into the sentence.

Yet Searle has explicitly *denied* that background phenomena threaten the Principle of Expressibility. In "Literal Meaning", he writes: "There is nothing in the thesis of the relativity of literal meaning which is inconsistent with the Principle of Expressibility, the principle that whatever can be meant can be said."[11] How are we to make sense of that denial?

V. EXPRESSIBILITY AND EFFABILITY

Searle's principle is incompatible with contextualism and the thesis of background dependence when interpreted at face value. But Searle's formulations are vague, and it is possible, if somewhat strained, to distinguish several possible interpretations of the principle.

On the strongest, and most natural, interpretation – that which I have taken for granted so far – Searle's Principle of Expressibility is equivalent to Katz's Principle of Effability.[12] Katz defines the (grammatical) meaning of a sentence as the meaning it has in the 'null context'; and he says that what the speaker means by uttering a sentence S in a context C (the 'utterance meaning' of S) can always be made explicit as the 'grammatical meaning' of an alternative sentence S′ that the speaker might have uttered. Katz says this Principle of Effability "was propounded in somewhat different form by ... Searle"[13] in passages such as the following:

> If you ask me "Are you going to the movies?" I may respond by saying "Yes" but, as is clear from the context, what I mean is "Yes, I am going to the movies," not "Yes, it is a fine day" or "Yes, we have no bananas." Similarly, I might say "I'll come" and mean it as a promise to come, i.e., mean it as I would mean "I promise that I will come," if I were uttering that sentence and meaning literally what I say. In such cases, even though I do not say exactly what I mean, it is always possible for me to do so – if there is any possibility that the hearer might not understand me, I may do so.[14]

One possible difference between Searle's and Katz's respective principles lies in Katz's appeal to the notion of 'null context' in characterizing grammatical meaning (a notion that Searle later criticized). Where Katz invokes the distinction between grammatical meaning, thus characterized, and utterance meaning, Searle appeals to a vaguer distinction between 'sentence meaning' and 'intended speaker meaning'. Not only is that distinction in Searle's writings vague, it is also ambiguous, as I have pointed out elsewhere.[15] In "Austin on Locutionary and Illocutionary Acts," Searle says that sense and reference are two "of the aspects ... in which intended speaker-meaning may go beyond literal sentence-meaning."[16] Here Searle presumably identifies literal sentence meaning with the linguistic, 'determinable' meaning of the sentence-type, and intended speaker meaning with what the speaker says in uttering this sentence.[17] That is more or less the same distinction as Katz's distinction between grammatical meaning and utterance meaning, or Austin's distinction between 'phatic' meaning and 'rhetic' meaning. But in "Indirect Speech Acts" (and again in "Metaphor"), what Searle calls 'sentence meaning' is what the speaker literally says (by uttering the sentence in context), and what he calls 'speaker's utterance meaning' is what the speaker actually conveys or communicates (which may, and typically does, go beyond or otherwise diverge from what is said). The following table (borrowed from an earlier paper of mine)[18] summarizes Searle's ambiguous use of the sentence meaning / speaker's meaning distinction.

	Linguistic meaning of the sentence type	What is literally said by uttering the sentence in context	What is thereby communicated
Searle 1968	sentence meaning(1)	speaker's meaning(1)	
Searle 1975		sentence meaning(2)	speaker's meaning(2)

Given that ambiguity, it is tempting to substantiate Searle's claim that the Principle of Expressibility is consistent with his later findings by interpreting the Principle as follows:

> The gap between sentence meaning(2) and speaker's meaning(2) can always be closed. In other words, what is implied or indirectly conveyed can always be said literally or directly conveyed. But what the sentence says – its literal content [sentence meaning(2)] – can still be treated as context-relative and background-dependent.

On that interpretation of the Principle of Expressibility, it is no longer entailed that the content of every speech act can be fully encoded into the linguistic meaning of a sentence type.

That interpretation of the Principle of Expressibility is clearly *not* what Searle intended when he wrote the relevant passages in his early works, however. It is not just nonliteralness, but *all* cases of divergence between sentence meaning and speaker utterance meaning, including (*inter alia*) 'vagueness, ambiguity, and incompleteness', that he says are not theoretically essential to linguistic communication, in virtue of the Principle of Expressibility. There does not seem to be any significant difference between Searle's Principle of Expressibility and Katz's Principle of Effability in that respect. In particular, there is no reason to think that Searle would have disapproved of anything in the following passage, in which Katz talks about the divergence between grammatical meaning and utterance meaning:

> Given that the utterance meaning of a sentence S can be expressed as the grammatical meaning of another sentence S', why isn't our performance mechanism designed to use S' in the first

place? What purpose is served by having it produce S and depend on information about the context to supply the hearers with part of the utterance meaning of S? One function performed by such a mechanism is to increase our repertoire of verbal behavior by permitting us to speak nonliterally. Its principal function, however, is that it allows speakers to make use of contextual features to speak far more concisely than otherwise. Imagine how lengthy utterances would be if everything we wanted to express had to be spelled out explicitly in the grammar of our sentences. Pragmatics saves us from this wasteful verbosity. Thus instead of using sentences like (1), we can, on occasion, use sentences like (2).

(1) The man who just asked the stupid question about the relation betwen the mental and the physical has, thank God, left the room.

(2) Thank God, he's gone.[19]

VI.   EXPRESSIBILITY AND INDEXICALITY

It is ironic that Katz used the 'Thank God' example, for many years before (in 1959) Arthur Prior had published an article entitled "Thank Goodness That's Over," in support of the opposite conclusion: that there are sentences whose content *cannot*, even 'in principle', be made fully explicit in a context-independent manner:

> One says, e.g. 'Thank goodness that's over', and not only is this, when said, quite clear without any date appended, but *it says something which it is impossible that any use of a tenseless copula with a date should convey.*[20]

In contrast to Prior, Katz insists that reliance on contextual clues *can* be dispensed with, in principle, if not in fact. That follows from the Principle of Effability, and it seems to follow from the Principle of Expressibility as well. Yet Searle, contrary to Katz, does not say so explicitly. He expresses no firm views on these matters but seems to oscillate between two positions.

On the one hand, Searle allows that one way of making explicit who one means by, for example, the pronoun 'he' is to *demonstrate* the referent – to point to him. The ability to provide a demonstrative identification of the referent in context counts as satisfying the Principle of Expressibility, he says, just as much as the ability to provide a description such as 'The man who just asked the stupid question about the relation betwen the mental and the physical'.

> Applied to the present case of definite reference, [the Principle of Expressibility] amounts to saying that whenever it is true that a speaker *means* a particular object..., it must also be true that he can say exactly which object it is that he means. ...A limiting case of *saying* is *saying* which involves *showing*; that is, a limiting case of satisfying... the principle of expressibility is indexical presentation of the object referred to.[21]

On the other hand, Searle also speaks as if the contextual demonstration itself were a way of 'communicating', without making fully explicit, a sense that *could* be made fully explicit by replacing the demonstration by linguistic symbols. Since the pointing gesture is not part of the linguistic 'expression' but part of the 'context', the ability to articulate the sense of the pointing gesture *in words* is part and parcel of what the Principle of Expressibility requires. Thus, a sentence such as 'The man [or: that man] is a foreigner' (accompanied by a glance or a pointing gesture) could be rephrased more explicitly as 'There is one and only one man on the speaker's left by the window in the field of vision of the speaker and the hearer, and he is a foreigner'.[22]

Be that as it may, the Principle of Expressibility can and should be weakened so as not to entail that indexicality is eliminable. One way of doing that would be to broaden the notion of 'sentence meaning' so as to admit among determinants of sentence meaning contextual assignments of semantic values to indexical expressions. Thus interpreted, the Principle of Expressibility is no longer equivalent to the Principle of Effability; it does not say that the content of the speech act can always be fully encoded into the linguistic meaning of a sentence type, but rather that it can be literally expressed by a sentence type 'with respect to context', where context consists of a time of utterance, a place of utterance, a speaker, a hearer, a sequence of demonstrated objects, and so on. (That is the 'context' in the narrow sense in which some formal semanticists use the notion.)

Thus weakened, the Principle of Expressibility is still incompatible with Searle's later findings about the background. What those findings show is that, however explicit the sentence, its linguistic meaning does not determine a set of truth conditions even 'with respect to context'. In order to account for the phenomena adduced by Searle in his later writings, we would have not only to relativize sentence meaning to context but *also* to broaden the notion of context so as to include the total 'background'. If we broaden the notion of context in that way, however, we fall back on the interpretation of the Principle of Expressibility of which I said earlier that it is obviously not what Searle intended. An utterance is not explicit, by Searle's early standards, if it is an utterance of a vague or ambiguous sentence. But if the 'context', in the richest possible sense, is allowed to compensate for the lack of determinacy of the sentence, then even the utterance of a vague or ambiguous sentence will count as explicit. That is clearly not what Searle originally meant when he talked of an utterance being explicit (or not).

VII. LOCAL EXPRESSIBILITY, GLOBAL INEXPRESSIBILITY

Let us go back to the passage in which Searle says that the Principle of Expressibility is compatible with background phenomena:

> There is nothing in the thesis of the relativity of literal meaning which is inconsistent with the Principle of Expressibility, the principle that whatever can be meant can be said. It is not part of, nor a consequence of, my argument for the relativity of literal meaning that there are meanings that are inherently inexpressible.[23]

The last sentence suggests another possible weakening of the Principle of Expressibility. The principle could be understood as saying *simply* that whatever is meant can be made explicit. That entails that every background assumption relied upon in interpreting an utterance can be made explicit, but this is compatible with the fact (i) that they cannot *all* be made explicit at the same time, and (ii) that whenever we make one assumption explicit by adding more descriptive material, further background assumptions are implicitly called upon for the interpretation of that new material. Thus weakened, the Principle of Expressibility becomes a Principle of *Local* Expressibility. In one passage in *Speech Acts*, Searle seems to have had such a weak version in mind:

> Another application of this law [the Principle of Expressibility] is that whatever can be implied can be said, *though if my account of preparatory conditions is correct, it cannot be said without implying other things.*[24]

Even that weakening is not satisfactory, however. The Principle of Expressibility, thus weakened, no longer supports the claim that "the study of sentence meanings and the study of speech acts are one and the same study." If expressibility can only be local, then a principle of global *in*expressibility also holds, according to which what is said explicitly is always said against a background of unarticulated assumptions. That is sufficient to justify the contextualist claim that there is more to the content of a speech act than can be encoded into the meaning of a sentence. But Searle uses the Principle of Expressibility precisely to argue against such a view.

Before concluding that Searle was mistaken when he said that the phenomenon of background dependence does not refute the Principle of Expressibility, there is a last option that should be considered. I think it may well be what Searle had in mind.

VIII.   THE GENERALIZATION OF BACKGROUND DEPENDENCE TO ALL INTENTIONAL STATES

Searle says that what is true of linguistic meaning is true of all Intentional states: thoughts, perceptions, intentions, and so on. In all cases, the Intentional content of the state determines satisfaction conditions only relative to background assumptions that cannot be realized as further aspects of that content. If this is right, then there is a sense in which there may well be a perfect fit between the meaning of the sentence (which determines conditions of satisfaction only against a background of assumptions) and what the speaker means by uttering the sentence (since the speaker's meaning intentions *themselves* are background-relative in just the same way). In other words, a sentence can be explicit, in the sense that it corresponds exactly to what the speaker means, without ceasing to underdetermine the conditions of satisfaction of the speech act. On that view, the content of the speech act *is* the content of the sentence; *both* underdetermine the conditions of satisfaction. The Principle of Expressibility is therefore satisfied despite the phenomenon of background dependence. Absolute explicitness is impossible, since background dependence is ineliminable; but relative explicitness can be achieved, consistent with the Principle of Expressibility. By 'relative' explicitness, I mean a perfect fit between (i) the semantic content of the sentence, (ii) the content of the speech act performed by uttering the sentence, and (iii) the content of the Intentional states expressed by the utterance.[25] Thus when I say 'The cat is on the mat', the literal meaning of the sentence (with respect to a contextual assignment of values to the incomplete descriptions 'the cat' and 'the mat') is the same thing as the content of the assertion that the cat is on the mat, and that is identical to the content of the expressed belief that the cat is on the mat. Background dependence applies in all three cases; and it applies as well to the perception that the cat is on the mat:

> In my present experience I assume that I am perceiving the cat and the mat from a certain point of view where my body is located; I assume that these visual experiences are causally dependent on the state of affairs that I perceive; I assume that I am not standing on my head and seing cat and mat upside down, etc.; and all these assumptions are in addition to such general assumptions as that I am in a gravitional field, there are no wires attaching to cat and mat, etc. Now, the Intentionality of the visual experience will determine a set of conditions of satisfaction. But the purely visual aspects of the experience will produce a set of conditions of satisfaction only against a set of background assumptions which are not themselves part of the visual experience. . . . In this case as in the literal meaning case, the Intentionality of the visual perception only has an application, only determines a set of conditions of satisfaction, against some system of background assumptions.[26]

To sum up: what one literally says depends upon the Background, but what one believes and what one perceives also depend upon the Background. In all cases, the content of the representation – be it linguistic or mental – determines conditions of satisfaction only against a background of unarticulated assumptions. The question of whether the beliefs that one communicates can be exactly expressed by the sentences that one utters can therefore be answered affirmatively, in accord with the Principle of Expressibility, even though the uttered sentence can't be fully explicit in the *absolute* sense.

That view, which it is reasonable to ascribe to Searle, stands in sharp contrast to an alternative position, deriving from Wittgenstein. The alternative position sets linguistic meaning *apart from* Intentional states: it says that words are special, because they are inert and (as Searle himself insists) devoid of 'intrinsic Intentionality'. What gives them 'life' is the use that is made of them. There is no such thing for Intentional contents. In contrast to words and sentences, thoughts and concepts are not 'tools', and they are not 'used'. Accordingly, they lack the semantic indeterminacy that characterizes sentences and linguistic material generally. While sentences are semantically indeterminate except in the context of a speech act,[27] thoughts are semantically determinate. Hence it is a category mistake to generalize, as Searle does, the sort of contextual dependency exhibited by linguistic meaning to Intentional states in general.

In the remainder of this chapter, I will, first, scrutinize the view that I have (tentatively) ascribed to Searle: the view that generalizes the phenomenon of background dependence to all Intentional states and is thereby able to protect the Principle of Expressibility. I will show that the attempted generalization fails. I will then elaborate the Wittgensteinian position and show that it can accommodate the phenomena adduced by Searle in his critique of the Determination View.

IX. LITERAL MEANING VS. INTENTIONAL CONTENT

Searle's view rests on the following equation:

$$\frac{\text{Sentence meaning}}{\text{Conditions of satisfactions of utterance}} = \frac{\text{Content of speech act}}{\text{Conditions of satisfactions of speech act}} = \frac{\text{Content of Intentional state}}{\text{Conditions of satisfactions of Intentional state}}$$

If that equation could be maintained, it would indeed be possible to conciliate the Principle of Expressibility and the phenomenon of background dependence. But I do not think the equation can be maintained, for the following reason.

Even if 'sentence meaning' is understood as the meaning of the sentence with respect to contextual assignments of values to indexicals, it is still much *more* indeterminate, much *more* susceptible to background phenomena, than the content of the speech act or the content of the expressed psychological state. There is this basic difference between the two sorts of case. If we change the background while keeping the meaning of the sentence constant, we change the truth conditions – that is what Searle's examples show. But we simply cannot, by manipulating the background, change the conditions of satisfaction of the speech act or of the Intentional state while leaving its content unchanged. The content of the speech act (or of the Intentional state) lacks the form of 'indeterminacy' that the meaning of the sentence possesses, and that makes it possible to keep it constant while varying the conditions of satisfaction.

Searle's formulations are misleading in that respect. For he repeatedly says that the content of a speech act, or the content of an Intentional state, determines conditions of satisfaction only against a background of unarticulated assumptions, just as the meaning of the sentence determines conditions of satisfaction only against the Background. But in the case of speech acts and Intentional states, the relevant 'contents' are *not* separable from the conditions of satisfaction that they determine. The order to cut the grass is not the same order when 'cut' is understood as 'slice' and when it is understood as 'mow'. This is so because you can't change the conditions of satisfaction (by manipulating the background) without, *eo ipso*, changing the content and therefore (since the act/state is individuated in part by its content) without changing the state or the act itself.

The inseparability of content from conditions of satisfaction shows up everywhere in Searle's writings. Here are a few quotations from *Intentionality*:

> An Intentional state only determines its conditions of satisfaction – and thus only is the state that it is – given its position in a Network of other Intentional states and against a Background of practices and preintentional assumptions that are neither themselves Intentional states nor are they parts of the conditions of satisfaction of Intentional states.[28]

> The Intentional content which determines the conditions of satisfaction is internal to the Intentional state: there is no way the agent can have a belief or a desire without it having its conditions of satisfaction.[29]

> Intentional contents in general and experiences in particular are internally related in a holistic way to other Intentional contents (the Network) and to nonrepresentational capacities (the Background). They are internally related in the sense that they could not have the conditions of satisfaction that they do except in relation to the rest of the Network and the Background.[30]

> Intentional states only have the conditions of satisfaction that they do, and thus only are the states that they are, against a Background of abilities that are not themselves Intentional states.[31]

The following passage is particularly interesting:

> It would ... be incorrect to think of the Background as forming a bridge between Intentional content and the determination of conditions of satisfaction, as if the Intentional content itself could not reach up to the conditions of satisfaction.[32]

What is interesting here is the *contrast* with literal meaning. For in the case of literal meaning, there *is* a clear sense in which the meaning of the sentence itself 'does not reach up to the conditions of satisfaction'. Searle says so in many places. For example: "If somebody instructs me to cut the sand, I do not know what I am supposed to do. For each [such] case ['cut the sand', 'cut the mountain', etc.] I can imagine a context in which I would be able to determine a set of truth conditions; but *by themselves, without the addition of a context, the sentences do not do that.*"[33] The sentence, with its meaning, can easily be separated from the conditions of satisfaction that, in context, it determines. Not so with Intentional states (or speech acts) and their contents.

In general, to convince ourselves that the equation on page 202 can't be maintained, there is a very simple procedure: one has only to consider what happens if we replace 'sentence' by 'Intentional state' (or 'speech act') and 'literal meaning' by 'content' in one of the numerous passages in which Searle describes the underdetermination of truth conditions by literal meaning. The results are instructive. Here is one example:

Original passage:
The literal meaning of a sentence or expression only determines a set of truth conditions given a set of background assumptions and practices. Given one set of these a sentence or expression may determine one set of truth conditions and given another set of assumptions and practices the same sentence or expression with the same meaning can determine a different set of truth conditions.[34]

Same passage after substitution:
The content of a speech act or Intentional state only determines a set of truth conditions given a set of background assumptions and practices. Given one set of these a speech act or Intentional state may determine one set of truth conditions and given another set of assumptions and practices the same speech act or Intentional state with the same content can determine a different set of truth conditions.

In view of the inseparability thesis, the claim that 'the same speech act or Intentional state with the same content can determine different sets of truth conditions' is nonsense. Again, if you change the conditions of satisfaction, the content does not stay constant. So the content of the speech act or Intentional state does not play the same role, and does not have the same properties, as the meaning of the sentence; for it is crucial to Searle's argument in "Literal Meaning" and elsewhere that the meaning of the sentence stay constant when the truth conditions are made to vary by manipulating the background.

X. LITERAL MEANING, SENSORY CONTENT, AND THE BRAIN

When he stresses the analogy between literal meaning and Intentional content, Searle often appeals to the example of perception. The following passage is characteristic:

> All of the arguments for the context dependency of the sentences "Bill cut the grass", "4 + 5 = 9" and "Snow is white" are also arguments for the context dependency of the *beliefs* that Bill cut the grass, that 4 + 5 = 9 and that snow is white. The content of those beliefs determines the conditions of satisfaction that they do determine only against a background. "Well," we might imagine our objector saying, "if so that is because those beliefs would naturally come to us in words. But how about wordless Intentional states, and how about the primary form of Intentionality, perception?" If anything the contextual dependency of perceptual contents is even or more striking [sic] than the contextual dependency of semantic contents. Suppose I am standing in front of a house looking at it; in so doing I will have a certain visual experience with a certain Intentional content, i.e. certain conditions of satisfaction; but suppose now as part of the background assumptions I assume I am on a Hollywood movie set and all of the buildings are just papier maché façades. This assumption would not only give us different conditions of satisfaction; it would even alter the way the façade of the house looks to us, in the same way that the sentence "Cut the grass!" would be interpreted differently if we thought that the background was such that we were supposed to slice the grass rather than mow it.[35]

Perception indeed supports the analogy to some extent. Even in that case, however, Searle acknowledges that *the content of the visual experience* changes when the background is altered:

> It is part of the content of my visual experience when I look at a whole house that I *expect* the rest of the house to be there if, for example, I enter the house or go around to the back. In these sorts of cases the character of the visual experience and its conditions of satisfaction will be affected by the content of the beliefs that one has about the perceptual situation. I am not going beyond the content of my visual experience when I say, "I see a house" instead of "I see the façade of a house," for, though the optical stimuli may be the same, the conditions of satisfaction in the former case are that there should be a whole house there.[36]

If the content of the visual experience changes when the conditions of satisfaction are manipulated by altering the background, is there something that stays constant and can be compared to the constant meaning of the sentence? Searle mentions two candidates: 'the purely visual aspects of the experience' and 'the optical stimuli'. Now, the optical stimuli are not a good candidate. To use a contrast made famous by John McDowell,[37] they may be a *bearer* of content, but they are not an *aspect* of content. What we need, in order for the analogy with literal meaning to hold, is an aspect of semantic content that stays invariant when background assumptions are manipulated. The 'purely visual aspects of the experience' seem to fit the bill. It is common to distinguish two forms of, or two levels in, perception. *Cognitive* perception is higher-level perception, and it presupposes a lower level of *sensory* perception. Sensory perception is modular and unaffected by background knowledge; cognitive perception is nonmodular and background-dependent.[38] If the distinction is sound, the content of sensory perception corresponds to what Searle calls the 'purely visual aspects of the experience', and that is indeed analogous to the linguistic meaning of the sentence.

The problem is that the distinction between the aspects of visual content that are modular and those that are cognitive and background-dependent cannot be generalized to all Intentional states. There is no such contrast for beliefs, desires, or intentions. Nor is there such a contrast for thought in general. The distinction seems to be limited to perceptual states and processes. It is indeed similar to the distinction we find in the language case, but that similarity itself does not provide an explanation of the phenomenon of background dependence in the language case; rather, it constitutes a further fact in need of explanation (a fact that I will leave aside here).

Searle mentions a third candidate for the analogy with literal meaning, a candidate that has the relevant degree of generality. The neural configuration in the brain that realizes a given Intentional state can stay constant even though we radically alter the Background. For example, take Jimmy Carter's desire to run for the presidency of the United States and the corresponding neural configuration in Carter's brain. We can suppose that "exactly these same type-identical realizations of the mental state occurred in the mind and brain of a Pleistocene man living in a hunter-gatherer society of thousands of years ago."[39] Because of the dependence of Intentional contents on Network and Background, "however type-identical the two realizations might be, the Pleistocene man's mental state could not have been the desire to run for the Presidency of the United States."[40]

Granted. It is well known that content, in general, is not an intrinsic but a relational property of the content-bearing state. That is the lesson of Externalism. Were the environment sufficiently different, the same neural state that realizes a given Intentional content would realize a different content (or no content at all). But this is not the same phenomenon as background-dependence. The neural state that realizes a given Intentional content is not an aspect or level of content; it is, again, a vehicle, a bearer of content. As such, it is analogous to the sentence qua syntactic object, rather than to the linguistic meaning of the sentence. What corresponds to Externalism in the linguistic case is therefore the fact that the sentence (type) could have meant something different from what it actually means: it would do so if the conventions of the language were different than they are. This has nothing to do with the underdetermination of semantic content (*given* a fixed linguistic meaning). Similarly, the fact that a neural state realizes a given Intentional content only in a certain context does not show that in thought, as in language, there is a level of content that underdetermines conditions of satisfaction.

I conclude that the analogy between the Background dependence of Intentional content and the background dependence of semantic content breaks down at crucial points and does not, as it stands, provide an explanation for the facts adduced by Searle in his critique of the Determination View. I therefore suggest that we turn away from the Principle of Expressibility, turn instead to the contextualist approach, and see what can be done within that framework.

XI. A CONTEXTUALIST PERSPECTIVE

The account of the phenomenon of background dependence that I am about to provide takes its inspiration from Austin's theory of truth (cf. the paper "Truth" in his *Philosophical Papers*) and, especially, from the remarks of Waismann on the open texture of empirical predicates,[41] remarks that themselves presumably echo Wittgenstein's views (see, in particular, sections 66ff. of *Philosophical Investigations*). The central idea is that words are not primitively associated with abstract 'conditions of application', constituting their conventional meaning (as on the Fregean picture). Rather, they are associated with *particular applications*.

Consider what it is to learn a predicate P. The learner, whom I shall call Tom, observes the application of P in a particular situation S; he associates P and S. At this stage, the 'meaning' – or, as I prefer to say, the semantic potential – of P for Tom is the fact that P is applicable to S. In a new situation S', Tom will judge that P applies only if he finds that S' sufficiently resembles S. To be sure, it is possible that S' resembles S in a way that is not pertinent for the application of P. The application of P to S' will then be judged faulty by the community, who will correct Tom. The learning phase for Tom consists in his noting a sufficient number of situations that, like S, legitimate the application of P, as opposed to those, like S′, that do not legitimate it. The semantic potential of P for Tom at the end of his learning phase can thus be thought of as *a collection of legitimate situations of application* – that is, a collection of situations such that the members of the community agree that P applies to those situations. Let us call the situations in question the *source situations*. The future applications of P will be underpinned, in Tom's usage, by the judgement that the situation of application (or *target situation*) is similar to the source situations.

In this theory, the semantic potential of P is *a collection of source situations*, and the conditions of application of P in a given use, involving a given target situation S″, are *a set of features that S″ must possess in order to be similar to the source situations*. The set of features in question, and so the conditions of application for P, will not be the same for all uses; it is going to depend, among other things, on the target situation. One target situation can be similar to the source situations in certain respects, and another target situation can be similar to them in different respects. But the contextual variability of the conditions of application does not end there. Even when the target situation is fixed, the relevant dimensions for evaluating the similarity between that situation and the source situations remain underdetermined: those dimensions will vary as a function of the subject of conversation, the concerns of the speech participants, and so on.

One particularly important factor in the contextual variation is the relevant 'contrast set'. As Tversky has pointed out, judgements of similarity are very much affected by variations along that dimension.[42] If we ask which country, Sweden or Hungary, most resembles Austria (without specifying the relevant dimension of similarity), the answer will depend on the set of countries considered. If that set includes not only Sweden, Hungary, and Austria but also Poland, then Sweden will be judged more like Austria than Hungary; but if the last of the four countries considered is Norway and not Poland, then it is Hungary that will be judged more like Austria than Sweden. The explanation for that fact is simple. Poland and Hungary have certain salient geopolitical features in common that can serve as basis for the classification: Hungary and Poland are then put together and opposed to Austria and Sweden. If we replace Poland with Norway in the contrast set, a new principle of classification emerges, based on the salient features shared by Norway and Sweden: in this new classification, Hungary and Austria are back together. Tversky concludes that judgements of similarity appeal to features having a high 'diagnostic value' (or classificatory significance), and that the diagnostic value of features itself depends on the available contrast set.

XII. ACCOUNTING FOR BACKGROUND DEPENDENCE

Within that simple contextualist framework, let us reconsider the phenomenon of background dependence. It goes along with the *global* character of the similarity between target situation and source situations. The source situations are concrete situations with an indefinite number of features. Some of these features are ubiquitous, and their diagnostic value in a normal situation is vanishing.[43] They belong to the most general and immutable aspects of our experience of the world: gravity, the fact that food is ingested via the mouth, and so on. When we specify the truth conditions of a sentence (for example, the sentence 'The cat is on the mat'), or the conditions of application of a predicate (for example, the predicate 'on' in that sentence), we mention only a small number of features – the 'foreground' features – because we take most of the others for granted; so we do not mention gravity, we presuppose it. Nevertheless, gravity is one of the features possessed by the situations that are at the source of the predicate 'on'; and there is an indefinite number of such features. These background features of the source situations can be ignored inasmuch as they are shared by all of the situations of which we may wish to speak when we utter the sentence; but if we imagine a target situation where the normal conditions of experience are suspended, and where certain background features of the source situations are not present, then we shatter the global similarity between the target situation and the source situations. *Even if the target situation has all of the foreground features that seem to enter into the 'definition' of a predicate P, it suffices to suspend a certain number of background features in order to jeopardize the application of P to the target situation.* That shows that the semantic potential of P is not, as in Fregean semantics, a set of conditions of application determined once and for all, but a collection of source situations such that P applies to a target situation if and only if it is relevantly similar to the source situations.

A caveat: as Searle himself emphasizes, the fact that the target situation does *not* possess certain background features of the source situations does not automatically entail the nonapplicability of the predicate P. It can be that the background features that the target situation does not possess (for example, gravity) are contextually irrelevant and do not affect the application conditions of the predicate. For the same sort of reason, the possession by the target situation of what I have called the foreground features of the source situations is no more a necessary condition for the application of the predicate than it is a sufficient condition. In order for a predicate (or a sentence) to apply to a target situation, that situation must resemble the source situations under the contextually relevant aspects. So a predicate can apply even if the target situation differs markedly from the source situations, as long as, in the context, and taking into account the contrast set, the similarities are more significant than the differences. Thus, in certain contexts, the predicate 'lemon' will apply to plastic lemons, or the word 'water' to XYZ. Putnam himself, in "The Meaning of Meaning," recognizes the legitimacy of such uses, made possible by the contextual variability of the relevant dimensions of similarity.[44]

XIII. CONCLUSION

I take the phenomenon of background dependence to reveal quite fundamental features of natural language. Searle must be given credit for having drawn attention to that phenomenon and for having appreciated its importance. I have criticized Searle's *explanation* of the phenomenon, however. According to Searle, the underdetermination of semantic content is a special case of a more general phenomenon that affects all representations, whether linguistic or mental. In order to determine whether or not a representation is 'satisfied', that representation must be *interpreted*. Searle cites the Wittgensteinian example of an image showing a man climbing a slope: the man could just as well be seen as going backward down the slope – the image itself does not tell us which interpretation is correct.[45] For Searle, the underdetermination of satisfaction conditions derives from the fact that representations, whether linguistic or mental, are not 'self-interpretive' or 'self-applicative'. From that follows the nonrepresentational character of the Background, which bridges the gap between the representation and its application. To add a second representation to the first one in order to interpret it does no more than postpone the problem, for the second representation would also need interpreting. Ultimately, a representation can be applied only if it is inserted into a nonrepresentational milieu – if it plays a role in a *practice*. Whence Searle's insistence on the fact that the Background consists largely in behavioural dispositions and know-how. "Intentionality occurs in a coordinated flow of action and perception, and the Background is the condition of possibility of the forms taken by the flow."[46] What we assume, we assume in virtue of the way we act and navigate through the world. We assume gravity, the solidity of objects, and the existence of other minds, in virtue of the way we act; we do not, or need not, entertain thoughts about these things.

I take Searle to be right concerning both the need for interpretation and the importance of the 'practical' dimension of cognition. But I doubt that the two things are related in the way that Searle makes them appear to be. Moreover, I do not think that we can simply *invoke* the nonself-interpretive (or nonself-applicative) character of representations; we must explain it. *Why* do the representations conveyed by words apply to the world only via a process of interpretation? Why aren't they self-applicative? If linguistic meaning conforms to the Fregean image, that is, if it consists in conditions of application, then they ought to be. If, in virtue of the conventions of the language, a predicate P possesses definite conditions of application, as the Fregean thinks it does, then either the reality of which we speak satisfies those conditions and the predicate applies, or it does not satisfy them and the predicate does not apply. I grant the nonself-applicative character of linguistic representations as an empirical datum, attested by Searle's examples; but in order to give an account of that feature, an alternative to the traditional view of meaning inherited from Frege must be proposed. In section XI, I sketched such an alternative.

Searle's generalization of background dependence to all Intentional states enables him to save the Principle of Expressibility, which is the heart of his earlier theory of speech acts. That move I do not find very convincing, for I have always been struck by the tension between the earlier philosophy, based on the Principle of Expressibility, and the later views, which pull in the opposite direction. Be that as it may, I have shown that the attempted generalization fails. It follows that the Principle of Expressibility cannot be saved. More important, we are left without an explanation of the phenomenon of background dependence. Where does it come from?

Impressed by the similarity between Searle's background dependence and Waismann's 'open texture', I have offered a contextualist account of background dependence. On this view, the content or sense of words – their contributions to the truth conditions of utterances – must be contextually constructed in an active process of interpretation; it is not ready-made. What is given as part of the language is not the sense of words, which must be constructed, but only what I have called their semantic potential. To construct the (context-dependent) sense of a word out of its (context-independent) semantic potential, nothing short of the full situation of utterance will do. An impoverished 'context' consisting only of values for a given set of parameters does not provide the sort of input that is needed for the process of sense construction to get off the ground; for that process relies on a global assessment of similarity between situations possessing, in principle, an indefinite number of features.

Notes

1. Among 'ordinary language philosophers' I include Wittgenstein and Waismann as well as the Oxford philosophers (Austin, Strawson, etc.).

2. John Searle, *The Rediscovery of the Mind* (Cambridge, Mass.: MIT Press, 1992), p. 180.

3. John Searle, "The Background of Meaning," in J. Searle, F. Kiefer, and M. Bierwisch (eds.), *Speech Act Theory and Pragmatics* (Dordrecht: Reidel, 1980), pp. 222–3.

4. John Searle, "Introduction" to Searle (ed.), *The Philosophy of Language* (Oxford: Oxford University Press, 1971), p. 6.

5. For a critique of Grice's argument against contextualism, see my "Contextualism and Anti-contextualism in the Philosophy of Language," in S. Tsohatzidis (ed.), *Foundations of Speech Act Theory* (London: Routledge, 1994), pp. 156–66.

6. John Searle, "What Is a Speech Act?," in M. Black (ed.), *Philosophy in America* (Ithaca, N.Y.: Cornell University Press, 1965), pp. 221–2; reprinted in John Searle, *Speech Acts* (Cambridge: Cambridge University Press, 1969), p. 16.

7. John Searle, "Austin on Locutionary and Illocutionary Acts," in G. Warnock (ed.), *Essays on J. L. Austin* (Oxford: Clarendon Press, 1973), p. 153.

8. *Speech Acts*, p. 18.

9. Ibid.

10. Ibid., p. 20.

11. John Searle, *Expression and Meaning* (Cambridge: Cambridge University Press, 1979), p. 134.

12. Jerrold J. Katz, *Semantic Theory* (New York: Harper and Row, 1972), pp. 18–24.

13. J. J. Katz, "Effability and Translation," in F. Guenthner and M. Guenthner-Reutter (eds.), *Meaning and Translation* (New York: New York University Press, 1978), p. 209.

14. *Speech Acts*, p. 19.

15. See my *Meaning and Force* (Cambridge: Cambridge University Press, 1987), pp. 255–6, and the paper referred to in note 18.

16. "Austin on Locutionary and Illocutionary Acts," p. 149.

17. See L. Forguson, "Locutionary and Illocutionary Acts," in Warnock (ed.), *Essays on J. L. Austin*, p. 179.

18. F. Recanati, "Qu'est-ce qu'un acte locutionnaire?," *Communications* 32 (1980): 206.

19. J. J. Katz, *Propositional Structure and Illocutionary Force* (New York: Crowell, 1977), pp. 19–20.

20. Arthur Prior, "Thank Goodness That's Over," in his *Papers in Logic and Ethics* (London: Duckworth, 1976), p. 84. The emphasis in the quotation is mine.

21. *Speech Acts*, p. 88.

22. Ibid., p. 92.

23. *Expression and Meaning*, p. 134.

24. *Speech Acts*, pp. 68–9; emphasis mine.

25. As far as (ii) and (iii) are concerned, Searle points out that, in virtue of the theory of speech acts, the content of the speech act always corresponds to the content of the Intentional state that it expresses.

26. *Expression and Meaning*, p. 136.

27. According to James Conant, this Wittgensteinian principle is a generalization of Frege's celebrated Context principle: "[Wittgenstein] seeks to generalize Frege's context-principle so that it applies not only to words (and their role within the context of a significant proposition) but to sentences (and their role within the context of circumstances of significant use)." James Conant, "Wittgenstein on Meaning and Use," *Philosophical Investigations* 21 (1998): 233.

28. John Searle, *Intentionality* (Cambridge: Cambridge University Press, 1983), p. 19.

29. Ibid., p. 22.

30. Ibid., p. 66.

31. Ibid., p. 143.

32. Ibid., p. 158.

33. "The Background of Meaning," pp. 225–6.

34. Ibid., p. 227.

35. Ibid., p. 231.

36. *Intentionality*, pp. 54–5.

37. John McDowell, "*De Re* Senses," in C. Wright (ed.), *Frege: Tradition and Influence* (Oxford: Basil Blackwell, 1984), p. 103n.

38. See, e.g., Fred Dretske, "Seeing, Believing, and Knowing," in D. Osherson et al. (eds.), *An Invitation to Cognitive Science*, vol. 3 (Cambridge, Mass.: MIT Press, 1990), pp. 138–46.

39. *Intentionality*, p. 20.

40. Ibid.

41. See Friedrich Waismann, "Verifiability," in A. Flew (ed.), *Logic and Language,* first series (Oxford: Basil Blackwell, 1951), pp. 117–44.

42. See Amos Tversky, "Features of Similarity," *Psychological Review* 84 (1977): 327–52.

43. See ibid., p. 342: "The feature 'real' has no diagnostic value in the set of actual animals since it is shared by all actual animals and hence cannot be used to classify them. This feature, however, aquires considerable diagnostic value if the object set is extended to include legendary animals, such as a centaur, a mermaid or a phoenix."

44. See Hilary Putnam, "The Meaning of Meaning," in his *Mind, Language and Reality: Philosophical Papers*, vol. 2 (Cambridge: Cambridge University Press, 1975), pp. 238–9.

45. *The Rediscovery of the Mind*, p. 177.

46. Ibid., p. 195.

10 | The Chinese Room Argument

JOSEF MOURAL

The Chinese Room Argument is one of the widest and best-known single-issue debates in recent philosophy. Its name originates from a thought experiment proposed by Searle in 1980 in the paper "Minds, Brains, and Programs." The debate has far exceeded the disciplinary boundaries of philosophy, and has had an impact especially in the fields of artificial intelligence and cognitive science.[1] In 1990, Searle proposed a new, closely related argument that did not catch as much attention but that is, according to Searle, deeper and more powerful than the original Chinese Room Argument.[2]

One of the striking features of the Chinese Room debate is the lack of consensus as to what exactly is the matter of controversy. One is easily reminded of the worry – charmingly expressed by Hume – that "questions which have been canvassed and disputed with great eagerness" often rest on some misunderstanding that tends to "keep the antagonists still at a distance, and hinder them from grappling with each other."[3] Since it is contentious even *what the Chinese Room Argument is*, it is one of my main aims to get clear about that. As we shall see, this will also help us in dealing with some hitherto unsettled controversies about its validity.

To anticipate, I am going to claim that there is a core of Searle's argument that is highly plausible (perhaps closely approaching the point of being "trivially true") and in fact seldom contested by Searle's opponents. It is possible to formulate a minimal position that withstands any criticism known so far, except perhaps the criticism that it is minimal to the point of being universally acceptable and hence not very interesting.[4] However, surrounding this core, which is more or less beyond controversy, there are areas where Searle's opponents do have a point, areas where Searle's position is in need of clarification, and areas with loose ends, some of which perhaps cannot be tightened up, given the nature of the problem and the current stand of scientific knowledge.

1. THE CHINESE ROOM ARGUMENT AS STATED IN SEARLE'S TEXTS

In this part of the chapter, I summarize the main tenets of the original Chinese Room Argument, aiming to keep rather close to Searle's own presentation. I shall, however, organize the material somewhat differently than Searle does, distinguishing throughout between (1) the Chinese Room *thought experiment*, (2) the related theoretical *argument*, and (3) a couple of more peripheral issues. From now on, I shall use the phrases "the thought experiment" and "the argument" to refer to components (1) and (2) of Searle's original position. (Notice that *the argument* in this sense is only a part of what is normally called the Chinese Room Argument, that is, of the whole cluster involving the thought experiment, the argument, and several other topics).

Searle lectured about the Chinese Room in a number of places during the late 1970s,[5] and he first published on the matter in 1980 in an article entitled "Minds, Brains, and Programs" (henceforth MBP) in *The Behavioral and Brain Sciences*.[6] In accordance with the general policy of the latter journal, Searle's paper was followed immediately by numerous short papers commenting on it and by Searle's answers thereto (three more instalments of peer commentary plus author's responses appeared in 1982, 1985, and 1990). The next main presentation of the Chinese Room was in one of Searle's Reith Lectures for the BBC, published as *Minds, Brains, and Science* (henceforth *MBS*)[7] in 1984, and in his 1984 Oxford lecture "Minds and Brains without Programs."[8] Among Searle's later presentations of the Chinese Room, the best-known is probably the 1990 paper "Is the Brain's Mind a Computer Program?" from *Scientific American* (henceforth IBM),[9] on which he received numerous (and mostly antagonistic) replies. The most recent major presentation is contained in *The Mystery of Consciousness* from 1997 (henceforth *MC*).

The initial paper has become a classic. It can conveniently be divided into three parts. In the first, Searle aims to show why he does not accept certain claims that can be made about Schank and Abelson's stories-understanding software, and makes his point by introducing a thought experiment involving a room and texts in Chinese and English (MBP, pp. 417–18). In the second part, he discusses six types of objections to the thought experiment that he had received so far (MBP, pp. 418–22). In the third, he explains his own position by answering a number of questions put by a fictional interlocutor (MBP, pp. 422–24). Searle's discussion of typical objections, occupying already about half of the relatively short paper, will be our topic later (section 2.1.); we now focus on the presentation of his own position in the first and the third parts of the paper.

As already indicated, it is useful to distinguish among several relatively separate threads in Searle's presentations of the Chinese Room. Now we shall look more closely at what Searle has to say about them, both in his initial paper and in his later work. First, we shall deal with the Chinese Room thought experiment; second, we shall turn to the corresponding theoretical argument, which attempts to render in an abstract form the strength of the thought experiment; and third, we shall look briefly at some more peripheral issues: Searle's remarks about what the Chinese Room Argument does and does not show, his views regarding certain related questions, and his characterization of the position of his opponents.

1.1. The Chinese Room Thought Experiment

Searle's point of departure in producing the original version of the Chinese Room thought experiment was Schank and Abelson's software that specialized in answering questions (put in plain English) concerning various features of events depicted in short stories (written in English) given to the software in advance, including features not stated explicitly in the text. It could do so because the programmers had supplied it with a knowledge base storing information about the environment and the typical characters of the stories. Consequently, the stories had to be set in the particular environment and peopled by characters corresponding to the knowledge base representation in order for the software to work successfully. Roughly, the software identified the features of the events that were stated explicitly in the English text and used the knowledge base to deduce other features that would typically go along with them.[10]

For the sake of argument, Searle takes it for granted that the software is successful in producing appropriate answers to such questions. What he focuses on are two claims that could be made about a machine running such software, claims that he disagrees with:

> 1. that the machine can literally be said to *understand* the story and to provide the answers to questions, and
> 2. that what the machine and its programs do *explains* the human ability to understand a story and answer questions about it. (MBP, p. 417)

Searle adds that his disagreement does not have to do with anything about Schank and Abelson's software in particular; he says that "the same argument would apply to ... any Turing machine simulation of human mental phenomena" (MBP, p. 417).

In order to show why he disagrees with these two claims, Searle proposes the following thought experiment. Suppose that Searle himself does not understand any Chinese, and imagine that he is locked in a room and given a large batch of Chinese writing. Then he is given a second batch of Chinese writing together with a set of rules for correlating the second batch with the first. The rules are written in English; Searle understands them well; and he can follow them, since they refer only to formal properties of the Chinese texts (and, he says, "all that 'formal' means here is that I can identify the symbols entirely by their shapes" – MBP, p. 418). Then he is given a third batch of Chinese symbols together with instructions in English that, when duly obeyed by Searle, lead him to identify (again using only formal properties) certain Chinese symbols and give them back as a response. The three batches of Chinese correspond to the knowledge base, the story, and the question in Schank's model; the instructions in English correspond to the computer program; and the symbols given back by Searle correspond to the answerlike output of the software. Thus, in following the instructions, Searle supposedly behaves exactly like a computer executing a program: he performs "computational operations on formally specified elements" and produces the answers "by manipulating uninterpreted formal symbols" (MBP, p. 418). The point of the thought experiment is that, under such conditions, Searle could provide correct answers to questions in Chinese about stories in Chinese *without understanding any Chinese* (and, a fortiori, without understanding the stories written in Chinese).

Thus, Searle believes that he can refute the claims in question. With regard to the first, he says that the computer running Schank's software understands nothing of any story, since "the computer has nothing more than I have in the case I understand nothing" (MBP, p. 418). With regard to the second, granted that the computer provides correct answers and yet there is no understanding, it seems to Searle that comprehending its functioning does not contribute in any significant way to the explanation of human understanding of stories. In particular, Searle disagrees with the position claiming that

> when I understand a story in English, what I am doing is exactly the same – or perhaps more of the same – as what I was doing in manipulating the Chinese symbols. It is simply more formal manipulation that distinguishes the case in English, where I do understand, from the case in Chinese, where I don't. (MBP, p. 418)

Searle admits that he has not demonstrated that the second claim is false; but he hopes to have made it incredible.

The form of the thought experiment scenario in the initial paper owes much to Searle's intention to match closely the functioning of Schank's software. It is possible to simplify the scenario in various ways without losing what is important for Searle's argument. For example, nothing relevant gets lost if the three steps of the original scenario are contracted into just one step, with one batch of Chinese writing (including the content of all three batches in the original scenario, i.e., the knowledge base, the story, and the question, separated in a convenient way) and one set of rules. In a more radical simplification, one can drop the whole story-understanding portion of the original scenario; what remains are simply questions in Chinese plus rules in English leading to the production of appropriate answers in Chinese. (And, of course, there should be plenty of Chinese writing stored in the room, so that the operator has enough to give back.) Obviously, the possibility of asking questions about stories (presented as a part of a question) is retained as a special case in this more general scenario, which corresponds to the so-called Turing test.[11] In later writings, Searle tends to use this simplified version of the thought experiment: in *MBS*, he still combines the permanent rule book in English, as a part of the room equipment, with additional rules in English presumably coming with each question (*MBS*, p. 32); in IBM, he drops the additional rules and has all of the symbol manipulation determined solely by the permanent rule book (IBM, p. 20).

Searle's point remains intact in these simplified versions: that by shuffling Chinese symbols according to a given set of rules, one does not learn any Chinese (*MBS*, p. 32). While behaving exactly as if one understands Chinese, one does not really understand a word thereof (*MBS*, p. 33).

> But if going through the appropriate computer program for understanding Chinese is not enough to give *you* an understanding of Chinese, then it is not enough to give *any other digital computer* an understanding of Chinese. And again, the reason for this can be stated quite simply. If you don't understand Chinese, then no other computer could understand Chinese because no digital computer, just by virtue of running a program, has anything that you don't have. All the computer has, as you have, is a formal program for manipulating uninterpreted Chinese symbols. (*MBS*, p. 33)

In order to further illustrate his point, Searle proposes as part of the scenario that, occasionally, the man in the room (who speaks English very well) be given questions in English and be asked to answer them in English.

According to Searle, there is a sharp difference between what he does in this case and what he does in the case of questions in Chinese. The man understands the questions in English, because they are expressed in symbols whose meanings are known to him, and he knows what he is saying when he gives the answers (*MBS*, pp. 33–4).

1.2. The Argument

Besides the thought experiment and the argumentation connected directly to the thought experiment scenario, Searle seeks to provide a further theoretical argument to the same effect. In the original article, the argument starts from a question:

> Could something think, understand, and so on *solely* in virtue of being a computer with the right sort of program? Could instantiating of a program, the right program of course, by itself be a sufficient condition of understanding? (MBP, p. 422)

Searle's answer is *no*, and his main reason is the following:

> [T]he formal symbol manipulations by themselves don't have any intentionality; they are quite meaningless, they aren't even *symbol* manipulation, since the symbols don't symbolize anything. In the linguistic jargon, they have only syntax but no semantics. (MBP, p. 422)

Later (in *MBS*, pp. 39–41) Searle provides a version of his main argument stated in the form of numbered premises and conclusions. Searle lists the premises (together with the status he ascribes to each of them) as follows:

> P1. Brains cause minds (a fact about the world, admittedly stated too crudely).
> P2. Syntax is not sufficient for semantics (a conceptual truth).
> P3. Computer programs are defined entirely by their formal, or syntactical, structure (true by definition).
> P4. Minds have mental contents; specifically, they have semantic contents (an obvious fact).

From these four premises, Searle draws the following four conclusions:

> C1. No computer program is by itself sufficient to give a system a mind. Programs, in short, are not minds, and they are not by themselves sufficient for having minds (follows from P2, P3, and P4).
> C2. The way that brain functions cause minds cannot be solely in virtue of running a computer program (from P1 and C1).

C3. Anything else that caused minds would have to have causal powers at least equivalent to those of the brain (directly from P1).

C4. For any artefact that we might build which had mental states equivalent to human mental states, the implementation of a computer program by itself would not be sufficient. Rather, the artifact would have to have powers equivalent to the powers of the human brain (from C1 and C3).[12]

Basically the same premises and conclusions figure prominently also in "Minds and Brains without Programs" (1987), pp. 231–2, and in IBM, pp. 21–3. In more recent presentations of the Chinese Room, Searle tends to confine himself to presenting only the core argument, consisting of premises P2–P4 and conclusion C1, typically in somewhat modified, concise reformulations. The state-of-the-art version from 1997 runs as follows:

1. Programs are entirely syntactical.
2. Minds have semantics.
3. Syntax is not the same as, nor by itself sufficient for, semantics.
Therefore, programs are not minds. (*MC*, pp. 11–12)

In his "Reply to Jacquette" (*Philosophy and Phenomenological Research* 49 [1989]), Searle is more explicit than usual about the modality of his claim. He depicts his opponents as saying:

Necessarily (program implies mind),

where "program" stands for the right program – that is, one that, according to Searle's opponents, is sufficient to give the system a mind. The form of Searle's counterargument is then:

It is not the case that (necessarily (program implies mind))
because
It is possible that (program and not mind) (pp. 701–2),

where it is this latter point that Searle is aiming to illustrate in his thought experiment. (Later we shall discuss whether Searle does not in fact sometimes make stronger claims than this.)

Searle does not spend much time discussing logical relationships between the thought experiment and the argument. In the initial paper, the not-yet-fully-developed argument component is introduced as amounting to "general philosophical points implicit in" the thought experiment (MBP, p. 422), and the main claim (C1) is established by "the main argument of this paper" (MBP, p. 417), by which he most probably means the thought experiment or the then not-yet-separated union of the thought experiment and the argument.[13] In the subsequent early presentations, Searle would basically let them stand side by side and leave their mutual relationship unspecified (*MBS*), or say that the argument is *a summary* of what he attempts to show by the thought experiment ("Minds and Brains without Programs," p. 231). More recently, he typically suggests that the role of the thought experiment is to support (IBM, p. 21) or to illustrate premise P2 of the argument,[14] which nonetheless (as a conceptual truth)[15] can do as well without it.

Summing up crudely the main point of his argument, Searle says that "symbol shuffling by itself does not give any access to the meaning of the symbols" (IBM, p. 24). By his Chinese Room Argument, Searle aims to

> remind us of a fact that we knew all along. Understanding a language, or indeed, having mental states at all, involves more than just having a bunch of formal symbols. It involves having an interpretation, or a meaning attached to those symbols. And a digital computer, as defined, cannot have more than just formal symbols because the operation of the computer . . . is defined in terms of its ability to implement programs. And these programs are purely formally specifiable – that is, they have no semantic content. (*MBS*, p. 33)

The strength of computer programs – the fact that strictly identical abstract programs can run on profoundly different hardware – is also their weakness: their pure formality entails the absence of any situatedness in the here and now, and consequently an entire lack of that sort of content that would be bound with this or that bearer of the operations or with this or that environment.

1.3. Peripheral Issues

The Chinese Room is intended by Searle primarily as a polemic device against the research program that he calls *strong Artificial Intelligence*. He distinguishes between weak and strong AI, and says that he is in favor of weak AI, that is, of research using computer models and simulations as a tool for the study of mind. What he opposes is strong AI, characterized by the claim that an appropriately programmed computer necessarily *is* a mind: that it is able to understand and to have other cognitive states (MBP, p. 417). The key idea of strong AI is that it should be possible to describe all that is essential about mental activity in terms of formal programs doing some sort of "information processing." If that were the case, an implementation of such a program on any kind of hardware would preserve all of the features characteristic of the mind. The Chinese Room Argument is an attempt to show that, in principle, the research program of strong AI cannot succeed. "In principle" here means regardless of any future improvements in technology, as long as we speak about programs understood as performing a sequence of formally defined operations on formally defined data (in Turing-machine style).

According to Searle, the slogan of strong AI is: "mind is to brain as program is to hardware" (MBP, p. 423; *MBS*, p. 28). In the initial paper, he points out three weaknesses of such a position (MBP, p. 423). First, a program is an abstract entity and can be realized on all sorts of hardware, including bizarre ones such as a sequence of water pipes. Now these, according to Searle's intuitions, clearly do not have the causal power of the biological brain; they are "the wrong stuff to have intentionality." Second, Searle insists that while programs are purely formal, intentional states are not. Intentional states are defined in terms of their content, not of their form; and their content is characterized primarily by their conditions of satisfaction.[16] Third, while the mind literally is the product of the brain, a computer program is not the product of the computer hardware.[17]

Searle also provides three tentative general characteristics of the position of his typical opponent, the partisan of strong AI.[18] First, the opponent is likely to be a behaviorist, someone who believes that we should ascribe mental properties to entities solely on the basis of their performance experienced from the third-person point of view. For an adherent of such a position, granted that the system consisting of the room plus the operator behaves as if it understood Chinese, there is no question of whether the system understands or not: if it behaves that way, it also has the property of understanding, because that is what the word means. Second, the opponent is likely to be a dualist, someone who wants to dissociate the mind and mental properties from their material, biological causes. The opponent believes that the mind is an abstract structure of "information processing" independent of the hardware on which it is implemented. This focusing on an abstract structure instead of on the causal power of the brain is the fatal mistake of such an approach, according to Searle. Third, the opponent is likely to confuse simulation with duplication. While we normally do not expect that a computer simulation of a rainstorm would leave us wet, Searle's opponents tend to believe that in the case of mental activity, the computer simulation *is* the real thing.

In order to avoid misunderstanding as to the thesis that he purports to demonstrate in the Chinese Room Argument, Searle clarifies his standpoint on three issues with which this thesis is sometimes confused. Searle accepts that: (1) Machines can think, since we are machines (given the rather broad definition of a machine as a physical system capable of performing certain types of operations), and we think. (2) Artificial, human-created machines could think if they could be endowed with causal powers equal to those of the human brain. (3) Digital computers can think, if by a "digital computer" is meant anything that at some level of description can be correctly described as an instantiation of a computer program, since even we can be so described, and we think.[19] What is at stake in the Chinese Room Argument is different from those three issues, and can be formulated as: could something think *solely* in virtue of being an instantiation of a right sort of program? Here, the answer suggested by Chinese Room Argument is: no, it could not.

What is it, then, that according to Searle enables one to understand English or Chinese, if it is not one's being an instantiation of a computer program? "As far as we know," he says, it is one's being "a certain sort of organism with a certain biological (i.e. chemical and physical) structure, and this structure, under certain conditions, is causally capable of producing perception, action, understanding, learning, and other intentional phenomena. And part of the point of the present argument is that only something that had those causal powers could have that intentionality." (MBP, p. 422)

2. CRITICISM AND REPLIES

I now turn to various responses to the Chinese Room Argument. The literature on the Chinese Room is a vast and rampant jungle, where everyone but a truly wild reader in mental philosophy can easily get lost. Regrettably, in the limited space of this chapter I can hardly even attempt to do justice to all of the commentators and critics.

Chronologically, we can distinguish three layers of commentary. The earliest consists of the six objections to the Chinese Room thought experiment collected by Searle in his early, pre-publication lectures and already put forward – anonymously, but specifying where they came from – in the initial paper. Then comes the second layer: the initial paper is immediately followed by a large number[20] of short replies by various authors (under the umbrella heading "Open Peer Commentary," MBP, pp. 424–50) and by the author's response to them (pp. 450–6).[21] The third layer, by far the thickest, consists of all the commentary that follows the publication of the initial paper. Understandably, apart from the first two layers, not all of the subsequent comments have been responded to by Searle.

Studying the Chinese Room Argument debate, we notice certain peculiarities. Not only is there no agreement as to whether or not Searle is right (which is pretty common in such major debates), there is remarkable lack of agreement as to what his argument consists in and what its target is. Especially those who agree that there is something wrong with Searle's argument seldom agree what it is and how to show it. According to Georges Rey, one can even explain the impact of the Chinese Room Argument by the fact that it contains "a surprising number of simultaneous confusions," which causes its opponents to fight one another about which blunder is more crucial and leaves Searle in the comfortable position of someone against whose position no criticism has been raised that would be widely accepted.[22] Also, we should keep in mind that for quite a time the general pattern of the debate was that of Searle's opponents focusing more or less exclusively on the thought experiment, and Searle insisting that the real issue was his theoretical argument (eventually fortified by the related argument from 1990).[23]

2.1. The Thought Experiment Debate: First Layer

In his initial paper, Searle discusses six types of reply to the Chinese Room thought experiment that he has received, attaching a nickname to each of them. Two of them he brushes away quickly as missing his point: the *many mansions* and the *other minds* replies. *Many mansions* is not really an objection, says Searle; rather, it expresses a view that he is happy to share, namely, that it may be possible to modify the AI project in such a way that it would take into account the causal powers required for producing mental states. Yes, it may, agrees Searle; but that would make it a different project from the one he attacks (MBP, p. 422). *Other minds* is an old argument in favour of behaviorism: when ascribing mental states (such as understanding Chinese) to other people, one cannot but proceed solely on the basis of their behavior. By analogy, one should be ready to ascribe mental states to computers on the basis of their behavior. Searle says that this reply is based on an epistemic issue irrelevant to his concern in the Chinese Room Argument (MBP, pp. 421–2).

Of the four remaining replies, two are especially important: the *systems* and the *robot* replies. In a way, these are the two paradigmatic objections to the thought experiment, setting the ground for a number of subordinate queries. They represent the two rather natural directions in which reacting to the thought experiment might proceed: first, that there has to be some sort of understanding of Chinese going on, if the system gives appropriate answers; and second, that the system might learn to attach meanings to the syntactic units, especially if we tear down the walls of the Chinese room and allow the system to see, hear, and act in the real world. We need to have a closer look at both of these.

The *systems* reply claims that it is wrong to look for understanding only in the mind of the room operator; rather, if there is some understanding going on in the thought experiment situation, then it should be ascribed to the whole system of which the operator is only a part. Searle's main answer to that is an important modification of the scenario, the *Internalized Version* of the thought experiment: this time, the operator has memorized all of the rules and learned to recognize and to write Chinese scripts, so that he can proceed in the same way as before, without using the room (or, one can say, using the internalized copy instead of the real room) or even while working outdoors. Still, Searle insists, manipulation with uninterpreted symbols in the mind does not bring him any closer to understanding Chinese. Besides, Searle is happy to scorn the idea that, according to his opponents, it is not the operator but the room that is supposed to understand (MBP, p. 419). We shall need to consider how far Searle's answer is satisfactory and, insofar as it is not, what consequences this has for Searle's position.

The *robot* reply proposes that Searle consider a different kind of AI program than that of Schank and Abelson: instead of taking formal symbols as input and returning others as output, the computer is now placed inside a robot, takes as its input the data supplied by cameras, microphones, touch sensors, and so on, and produces as output commands that actually dictate the robot's physical motion, speech generation, and so on. According to Searle, there are two points of view from which he can respond to this reply. First, he can say that, as with *many mansions*, this reply supports rather than undermines his claim, since "it tacitly concedes that cognition is not solely a matter of formal symbol manipulation" and since by proposing to add "a set of causal relations with the outside world," it in effect makes the same point as Searle himself – namely, that what needs to be focused on are the causally efficient factors and not just abstract structures, which are causally inert. Thus, this sort of addition, insofar as it is indeed a substantial change, is a step away from the position of strong AI criticised by Searle. Second, Searle can also say that, to the degree that one can isolate the residual strong AI position within this reply (and, in so doing, do justice to the intention of those who raise it as an objection to Searle's view), the original argument applies all the same. For regardless of where the data come from, they are in themselves nothing but syntactical units for the program, and the output commands for the robot remain meaningless syntactical units also. The source of the input data and the effects of the output data make no difference as long as we restrict our view only to the data processing performed by the program.[24]

The two remaining replies are the *brain simulator* and the *combination* replies. The *brain simulator* reply has the computer simulate the processes going on in the brain of someone who understands Chinese; this would (allegedly) transform Chinese input into Chinese output in exactly the same way as the human brain. Searle's answer is, first, that this reply again moves beyond the boundaries of his original target, strong AI, by reverting the order of dependence: according to strong AI, the brain understands because it instantiates the right program, while here, the program is right because it does exactly what the brain does. But second, such a simulation captures the wrong things about the brain: as long as it just pushes the computing process through stages corresponding to the stages of the brain process, "it won't have simulated what matters about the brain, namely its causal properties" (MBP, pp. 420–1). The causal properties of the brain, causing both (vertically) intentional states and (horizontally) the next stage of the process, are replaced by causal features of the program implementation. One can see the difference between the two by, for instance, observing that while you can interrupt the run of a computer simulation at any moment and then resume it again, or run it *n* times faster or slower (etc.), you can hardly do this sort of things with the living brain.

Finally, the *combination* reply merely puts together features of the three preceding replies (by placing a brain-simulating computer inside a robot and considering the result as a system). Because both the *robot* and *brain simulator* replies have been shown to be irrelevant (at least as regards Searle's polemics against strong AI in the strict sense), Searle does not address this reply in any detail,[25] and neither shall I.

I am convinced that Searle's answers to all of the earliest replies except *systems* are quite satisfactory, at least in their main points. I shall, however, argue against one line of Searle's strategy in answering the *systems* reply, namely, his insistence that if there is some understanding going on in the thought experiment situation, it must be in the mind of the operator. I shall also show that conceding this point to the *systems* reply does not undermine the Chinese Room Argument in its core version.

2.2. The Thought Experiment Debate: Second and Third Layers

Given that the second and the third layers of commentary on the thought experiment are rather thick, I can hardly do more here than to summarize a few contributions that strike me as particularly important or remarkable.

The *neglected scales* objection focuses on Searle's playing down the complexity and speed of the symbol shuffling required by his scenario, and suggests that our intuitions can easily mislead us if we start with a picture of a clerk moving a piece of script from one basket into another. This objection is typically intended to work in support of some other reply, most often the *systems* reply (or the *connectionism* reply to be discussed later). The point can be illustrated by a thought experiment analogous to the Chinese Room but supporting the opposite claim. One particularly witty case of such an experiment has been proposed by Paul and Patricia Churchland in their "Could a Machine Think?"[26] They invite us to imagine that, shortly after Maxwell has suggested (in 1864) that light and electromagnetic waves are the same, his opponents propose the following experiment: consider a man holding a bar magnet in a dark room. If he starts to pump it up and down, it should, if Maxwell is right, produce light. Of course, to Maxwell's opponents it is quite clear that the room would remain as dark as it was. Now imagine poor Maxwell replying to them that (1) in order to produce a visible amount of light in this way, the man would have to pump about 10^{15} faster, and that (2) nonetheless there is some light produced by the man's exercise, only it is of too long a wavelength and too low an intensity to be perceptible. Maxwell's reply, conclude the Churchlands, would have been "likely to elicit laughter and hoots of derision," since it presumably seemed quite obvious that light is not the sort of thing that could be produced by moving rods in space. Searle's answer to the Churchlands is that the analogy does not hold: while light and electromagnetism are both natural phenomena and the eventually discovered connection between them "a causal story down to the ground," syntactical units are abstract objects, and there is no way to discover their previously unknown causal properties, since they can't have any.[27]

The *connectionism* reply, proposed by the Churchlands in the same paper, claims that brains indeed are computers, but of a radically different style than the classical, von Neumann–architecture computers. They are not digital; they are not programmed; and rule-governed symbol manipulation is not their basic mode of operation. It seems that Searle's answer should have been primarily positive, that he should have embraced this proposal in a manner similar to his answer to *many mansions*: for the *connectionism* reply, too, proposes that we leave strong AI behind and do something else (potentially paying attention to the causally relevant features of the structures under study), and thus it escapes Searle's original criticism. However,

Searle does not take this option. Rather, he argues that, to the degree that there is a residuum of strong AI in the Churchlands' reply, the same argument applies as was used in the second step of his answer to the *robot* reply, an argument that can be illustrated with the help of a slight modification of the original thought experiment. Instead of one operator, we now have a number of them, all working according to their rule books in one room, now called the Chinese Gym. While they conceivably could produce appropriate Chinese output, none of them understands any Chinese, and there is no way for the system as a whole to learn the meaning of any Chinese word (IBM, p. 22).

Searle was perhaps misled as to what sort of computer architecture the Churchlands had in mind. While they seem to mean a connectionist network, they refer to it as "parallel processing" (p. 30), which is taken by Searle to mean simply a modification of the von Neumann architecture – involving parallel execution of more than one instruction at a time (which can indeed be understood as the execution of a single, if far more complex, meta-instruction) – and not its abandonment.[28] Searle is right that the move towards this slight modification does not change anything with regard to his argument; and it is even misleading to introduce the Chinese Gym scenario, for it would be enough to say that all of the physical symbol manipulation done simultaneously by many men in the gym could be done subsequently by one man and lead to production of the required Chinese output just as well (which better corresponds to the theoretical part of Searle's answer at IBM, p. 22). One could call this the *Chinese Flu* scenario: all of the gym operators except one stay at home with the flu, and the remaining one has to do all the work until they recover. On the other hand, with regard to genuine connectionist networks it would not do to argue, as Searle did in IBM, that the original argument applies to them as well simply because they can be simulated on conventional computers. It would not do because in case of such a simulation the connectionist network is nothing but the data that are being processed. And it surely is not a part of Searle's argument that if something can be processed by a computer program as data, it must lack semantics (think, for example, of digitally processed telephone calls).

The *instantiation* reply given by Jerry Fodor[29] is accompanied by a useful classification of possible replies to the Chinese Room thought experiment. As the thesis that Searle wants to establish with its help is that one can conceive an instantiation of the right program without the required mental state, there are exactly three ways to counter it: (1) to deny the absence of the required mental state, (2) to deny that the program that Searle envisages is the right one, and (3) to deny that the Chinese Room setup instantiates the program.[30] The previous objections, continues Fodor, tried options (1) (the *systems* reply) and (2) (*robot, brain simulator*, and *many mansions*); now it's time to try (3) and to say that "Searle's setup is not, in the intended sense, a Turing machine." According to Fodor, Searle managed to escape criticism because he was using a weak concept of instantiation, based only on a correlation of the sequence of states between the program and its instance. What is needed is a concept of instantiation that would require relevant efficient causes bringing the machine each time from one state to another. Fodor's reply points to a real difficulty, but his formulation of what is required from the stronger concept of instantiation is not precise enough, and this offers Searle an easy way out. For Fodor's requirement is consistent with the possibility that the relevant efficient cause is the Chinese Room operator, and thus leaves Searle's position intact.

David Chalmers takes up where Fodor and Searle left the issue in 1991 and proposes a *one more mind* reply, which can be seen as an improved version of the *systems* reply.[31] Chalmers points out that the mental states of the operator (such as his understanding or not understanding Chinese) are irrelevant with regard to the question at stake, that is, whether the required mental states are *produced* by the implemented program. This is so because the operator functions in the scenario merely "as a kind of causal facilitator," an arbitrary replacement of the blind causal forces that do the same work in the more conventional kinds of instantiation (of course, in order to ensure that they do, they have to be assembled in a highly ingenious way by the engineers). What is supposed to be relevant about the system is "the dynamics among the symbols." If there can be any understanding produced by a running program, it is not the understanding in the conscious mind of the Chinese Room operator.[32] One could add that if Searle assumes that the relevant understanding can be located only in the mind of the operator, then the thought experiment is set up unfairly to begin with, for the computer does not have anything corresponding to the conscious Chinese Room operator, and thus it is clear from the start that it could not understand.

Several authors object to Searle's assuming that he is in a position to tell whether he (as an operator in the Chinese Room) understands or not. Ned Block says (MBP, pp. 425–6) that it is just an intuition on the part of Searle, and one that is a matter of controversy. For while normally my conscious experience of understanding or of its lack largely agrees with what others say on the basis of my behavior, in Searle's thought experiment we get a sharp disagreement (especially regarding the Internalized Version). To prefer one side of this contest betrays a bias and threatens to disqualify the procedure in the eyes of those who do not share this preference. Searle's slogan, "Remember, in these discussions, always insist on the first person point of view" (MBP, p. 451) comes as an a priori methodological postulate, not as a result of a discussion starting from uncontroversial premises.[33] Larry Hauser traces the difficulty to Searle's unjustified move from the careful "*it seems to me quite obvious...that* I do not understand" to the blunt "*I understand nothing*" at MBP, p. 418 (italics added).[34] Searle's answer could be, first, that the difficulty is merely epistemic, since in cases such as this there is a fact of the matter whether one understands or not (MBP, p. 451),[35] and second, that his opponents face a parallel problem insofar as they claim that the operator understands, since such a claim is no less controversial: "In short, the systems reply simply begs the question by insisting without argument that the system must understand Chinese" (MBP, p. 419). With that, we have reached an impasse, and it is not clear what kind of philosophical tools could help us to break out of it.[36]

2.3. The Argument Debate

We proceed to comments concerning Searle's theoretical argument, beginning with the following point made by Colin McGinn:[37]

> ...*if* a computer deals only in syntax it cannot confer semantic features such as our conscious intentional states have. However, it does not follow that the symbols manipulated by the computer program cannot have semantic properties – all that is shown is that they cannot have these in virtue of the rules of the program. The clear-headed computational theorist will agree with Searle about the non-semantic character of program rules but point out that symbols manipulated can have other sorts of property too, and these might be what give the symbols semantic features.

While we can say that this only spells out what Searle is saying anyway, what it makes manifest is how crucially the argument depends on the heavy-duty work of qualifying terms such as "by itself" and "solely in virtue of" in the crucial premise "Syntax is *by itself* not sufficient for semantics" (we shall come back to this later).

Proceeding from McGinn's point, we can notice with Rapaport that some mathematics – say, solving linear equations such as $3x + 5 = 17$ – can be done purely syntactically, that is, by manipulation with symbols according to a set of rules specified in a formal way (in the sense employed by Searle), but that we can also do the same thing on the basis of understanding the contents expressed by the signs – for example, by seeing the equation as representing an equilibrium and operating on it in a way that preserves the balance that we are interested in (subtraction on the left side has to be compensated by simultaneous equal subtraction on the right, etc.).[38] We can solve the equation either way, and often we can hardly tell which method we used in a particular case: does that not shatter the matter-of-fact status of understanding, of the presence of Searle's semantic level? Again, this sort of question probably does not worry Searle too much, for he can say that while it can be tremendously difficult (epistemically) to tell which of the two methods we were using, that does not change anything in the (ontological) matter of fact that we must have been using either one of the two methods or some specifiable blend thereof.

Pushing further along this line of thought, we see that these considerations may open the door for an attempt to rehabilitate a certain more moderate version of the explanatory project of strong AI: granted that the mind is semantic on the whole, there could be modules in it that do a purely syntactical job. And since the semantic properties we are interested in can be preserved during the appropriate syntactic manipulation – and indeed not just preserved, but rather reconfigured in such a way as to make manifest what was not manifest before the manipulation started (as in the case of solving an equation) – one can perhaps speculate that at least on some intermediate level between the mind as a whole and the neurophysiology, there can be modules working in a purely syntactic way. We shall discuss Searle's answer to this hypothesis (which he calls "cognitivism") later.

Turning to the second issue concerning the relationship between syntax and semantics, we should begin with a point that may seem obvious but is in fact well worth making, namely, that according to Rapaport only *programs as running* could reasonably be considered candidates for having or producing mental properties such as understanding.[39] Thus, although the "textbook definition of computation" is likely to speak about abstract structures (such as Turing machines and algorithms), if the thesis of strong AI were that it is a program as an abstract structure that understands, it would hardly be worth any complicated refutation. Eventually, Searle accepts this point without hesitation: in 1997, he makes it clear (*MC*, pp. 11–12) that he means (also) running programs when he says, "Programs are entirely syntactical." But this point, seemingly innocent in itself, opens the door to further considerations that, in my opinion, lead to the very central issue of the argument. The abstract syntactic units manipulated by abstract programs are not just defined as being syntactic; rather, we should say that what they are is exhausted by their syntactic function. However, the physical states that represent the syntactic units in the real world are likely to have a lot of other properties besides the distinctive one of being describable and recognizable as representing the relevant syntactic units.[40]

Thus, it should be of crucial importance for the discussion of the argument to focus on the relationship between abstract programs and their physical implementation and to ask what sort of properties have to be added to the syntactic ones in order that the abstract programs can run in the physical world. It certainly seems possible to speculate that there could be a way of reformulating the strong AI strategy along these lines: granted that something *has* to be added, one needs only find out what necessary additional properties come with what sorts of programs, and then on the basis of that knowledge design the Right Program that could not be run without producing mental states.[41] To be sure, we do not have anything like the required knowledge of the necessary additional properties at present, and it is on open question, in case we do indeed gain it at some time in the future, whether it will speak in favor of the possibility of mental properties coming necessarily with any implementation of a certain class of programs. Chalmers, in his *The Conscious Mind*, employs this kind of strategy. However, he seems to overestimate the chances that the hypothetical future knowledge of the necessary additional properties would turn out in favor of strong AI, and his particular argument seems to me to be undermined by Searle's original answer to the *brain simulator* reply (that our current knowledge of the brain does not give us any clue as to what to simulate, and the hypothetical future knowledge might turn out to exclude the possibility of computational simulation). If Chalmers's confidence is based on a general functionalist outlook, it is clear that to take that for granted when arguing with Searle leads to an impasse, at best.

To sum up: the truth of the matter seems to be that Searle does not have any resources for claiming that future research could not show that, for a certain class of programs, the additional causal properties required for implementation have to be powerful enough to produce mental states. However, he can safely claim that his opponents are in just the same situation: they too cannot justify the claim that there exists a nonempty class of programs whose implementation requires such additional causal properties (at least, not along the lines of argument just considered and under the current state of research).[42] And he does not need to say more, as long as his claim is of the sort, "I deny that the opponent has shown so and so to be true."

Among the smaller-scale comments, three types of criticism have repeatedly been made regarding Searle's claim that any system capable of causing minds "would have to have causal powers (at least) equivalent to those of brains."[43] One problem with this claim is that, if we imagine placing causal powers of mind-causers on a linear scale (and, presumably, neglecting differences in causal powers among actual human – not to speak of other biological – brains), there seems to be no reason to assume that the causal power of, say, human brains is exactly the smallest possible amount sufficient to cause mind. A seemingly natural amendment would be to introduce the concept of a threshold, that is, of the minimal causal powers sufficient to cause mind, and to claim that (1) human and (some) other biological brains are above that threshold, and that (2) any potential mind-causer would have to be above it, too.[44] However, this amendment does not help with regard to the second type of criticism, namely, that we have no reason to assume that all things that cause minds work on the same principles. To realize this means that with regard to their relevant causal powers, there could be differences not only in terms of more/less but also in terms of either/or, and this means also that we should drop the idea of the linear scale. In other words, we have no reason to conclude from the premise that the causal powers of the brain are a sufficient condition of mind in the case of humans (and other animals) that causal powers of the same type are a necessary condition of mind in general.[45]

Searle's answer to these two types of criticism is that indeed he does not intend to claim that potential mind-causers need to have causal powers (1) higher than the hypothetical threshold or (2) similar to the powers of the human (biological) brain in any respect other than that they are sufficient to cause mind. In particular, he does not conclude from C's being a sufficient condition of M that it is a necessary condition; rather, he means, "generally and trivially, that it is a *necessary* condition of being able to do it [i.e., to produce mind] causally that any such system must have powers *sufficient* to do it causally."[46] At this moment, however, a third variety of criticism rushes to add that this explanation makes Searle's point quite vacuous: "what causes mind must have the causal power sufficient for doing it" is a conceptual truth, and there is no need to draw it as a conclusion in the way that Searle does in the early versions of the argument.[47]

2.4. Peripheral Issues Debate

Among the peripheral issues, one that has given rise to interesting debates is the problem of the *universal realizability* of programs, of the possibility of "crazy realizations" (MBP, p. 423). Notoriously, Searle claimed that, on the standard definition of computation,

> the wall behind my back is right now implementing the WordStar program, because there is some pattern of molecule movement that is isomorphic with the formal structure of WordStar. But if the wall is implementing WordStar, then if it is a big enough wall it is implementing any program.[48]

Claims like this (together with similar claims made by Hilary Putnam)[49] have been criticized by David Chalmers as wildly implausible and based on too permissive a concept of implementation.[50] These criticisms contributed to the subsequent emergence of a clearer and more nuanced picture of what program realization is, a development that was clearly welcome to Searle, who already in 1990 had envisaged the possibility of blocking universal realizability "by tightening up our definition of computation" in such a way as to emphasize "such features as the causal relations among program states, programmability and controllability of the mechanism, and situatedness in the real world," as well as the need for "a causal structure sufficient to warrant counterfactuals."[51]

We can distinguish between a finite sequence of abstract formal operations (a "run" of an abstract program) and an abstract pattern by which such a finite sequence may be determined (or codetermined, when taken together with an abstract input). Examples of such abstract patterns are computer programs and Turing machines.[52] Let us call a finite sequence of abstract operations a *computation*. The notion of the physical realization of a computation is logically more basic than that of the realization of a program: for in the case of computations, realization can be defined, roughly, as a suitable correspondence between the abstract computational state transitions and the state transitions within a physical system. The permissiveness of this definition will depend on the kind of correspondence we choose to require. There are at least the following three dimensions along which we can make the definition narrower or wider at will: (1) the *selectivity* of the definition of physical states, (2) the *complexity* of the computational state representation, and (3) *counterfactual* robustness.

First, because the space of computational states is discrete, and the space of measurable physical properties is (for our purpose) continuous, we need to "digitalize" or "granularize" the physics, that is, to define states of the physical system (or components of a complex state) always as *intervals* or *bands* of values of a certain physical quantity. One way of making the definition of realization stronger or weaker would be to play with the *selectivity* in the definition of physical states, that is, with the required relative magnitude of neutral zones separating the intervals that define the relevant physical states. We can, say, have the voltage $4V \pm 10\%$ define one state, the voltage $7 V \pm 10\%$ the other, and say that other voltages define no relevant state at all; but we can also have any voltage up to and including 5 V define one state, and any voltage above 5 V the other. Second, we can think of computational states as decomposed into a *complex* state-vector (consisting, say, of the full content of the relevant abstract memory and of the stage of computation, i.e., the position within the sequence of abstract operations), and require a fixed mapping between the components of the abstract computational state and the components of the physical system state. Third, it is also possible to require some *counterfactual* guarantees – for example, that the physical system will perform the same sequence of state transitions each time it happens to get into the relevant initial state.

For programs without variable input, there is a one-to-one correspondence between programs and computations. For programs with variable input, what corresponds to the program is the class of all computations determined by the program together with a permissible input configuration. A physical system S *instantiates* a computation C if there is a mapping between components of the computational states of C (of a chosen complexity) and physical states defined (with a chosen selectivity) as intervals on measurable properties of S such that the sequence of the computational state transitions of C corresponds to the sequence of state transitions of S (observable in some chosen time intervals). A physical system S *implements* a program P if it is capable of instantiating all computations corresponding to P (with a chosen amount of counterfactual robustness).[53] Within this framework,[54] one can surely choose a definition loose enough that a wall would instantiate a particular WordStar computation, but one can also choose a definition strict enough to make it very difficult for a the wall to instantiate a WordStar computation, let alone to implement the WordStar program.

Another interesting point is Hauser's distinction[55] among three threads involved in Searle's concept of strong AI. First, there is a metaphysical thesis, identifying mental processes with "information processing" in the computational manner.[56] This may be called the *essentialist* thread within strong AI: the consequence of the essentialist claim is that not only is it the case that "where there is a right computation, there must be a mind," but also that "where there is mind, there must be a right computation." Second, there is the thread (let us call it *empiricist*) that cares simply for ascribing mental predicates to computers running the right software, understands such ascriptions as nontrivial and based on observation,[57] and does not necessarily hold the converse (i.e., "mind entails computation"). Third, there is the claim that the functioning of the right programs explains what is going on in human cognition; this we can call the *explanatory* thread. We might here add also a *functionalist* thread, emphasized, for example, in Searle's remark that "the basic premise of strong AI is that the physical features of the implementing medium are totally irrelevant. What matters are programs, and programs are purely formal" (IBM, p. 25). Also, within the essentialist thread, we can distinguish between the *behaviorist* and the *mentalist* variety: the former redefines mental states in terms of behavior, the latter claims that running the right software is actually the same thing as what we ordinarily call mental states.[58] It is worth considering that different threads may be susceptible to somewhat different kinds of refutation (we come back to this in section 4).

Hauser's point needs some clarification, especially regarding the second, empiricist thread. One could get confused about Searle's attitude toward it: on the one hand, he should not care about the second thread at all, for he claims to be agnostic and indifferent about ascribing mental predicates to computers (see, e.g., MBP, p. 422); on the other hand, one can also find in Searle's writings passages hostile to such ascription (e.g., the denial that the computer running Schank and Abelson's software understands – MBP, p. 417). I propose that we can understand the situation in the following way: Searle does not have a quarrel with possible correct ascriptions of mental predicates to real world computers (i.e., with the second thread as formulated by Hauser); he says repeatedly that it is for him an open question whether that will happen or not. What he has a quarrel with is the claim that there are computers that have such and such mental properties *solely by virtue of the software they are running*. This is a far stronger version of the empiricist claim, and it is exactly what we get if we add a certain amount of essentialism to the basic empiricist claim (for it is a part of the essentialist assumption that whatever has mental properties has them solely by virtue of its running the right software).[59] Thus, we simply need to distinguish here between Searle's own agnostic attitude toward the question of ascribing mental predicates to computers, on the one hand, and his refutation of a particular attempt to answer it, on the other.[60] The refutation is a reductio ad absurdum of a certain position, making use of the assumptions held by that position, and, as such, it does not commit Searle to any hostility toward the second thread claim in its basic, weak version as stated by Hauser.

With regard to the mutual relationships of the four threads, it seems clear that the essentialistic position entails the third and the fourth, for the identity of the mind with computational information processing would guarantee the explanatory power of information processing structures as well as the irrelevance of the hardware. It does not entail the empiricist thread, for it is possible to combine essentialism with scepticism as to whether man-made computers will ever be advanced enough to implement the right software, that our brains are implementing. Thus, it seems that we end up with two relatively independent threads constituting the position that Searle is out to refute: the essentialist and the empiricist (in the stronger version). It is, however, not entirely clear that Searle would like to characterize strong AI directly as committed to the essentialistic claim. He does quite often speak in this way,[61] but sometimes it seems that he would prefer to view the essentialistic thread as just one option within strong AI and to stick to the initial, two-component definition of strong AI as consisting of the two claims, "The machine can literally be said to *understand*" and "What the machine and its program do *explains* the human ability to understand." Of course, it may be difficult to imagine what the latter claim could be based on, if not on some version of the essentialistic thesis. But the relationship perhaps can be seen as that of mutual support: essentialism would not be plainly assumed, but rather viewed as following from the (alleged) success of the – at first only hypothetical – explanation.

Daniel Dennett, asking what is the logical relationship between Searle's denial that the computer (i) has semantics, (ii) is a mind, and (iii) is conscious, advances the opinion that it is (iii) that is crucial for Searle.[62] He does not offer much support for this claim – in fact, he jumps to it immediately after quoting a passage that, at best, makes consciousness one candidate along with the others (p. 335) – and Searle brusquely dismisses it as a misstatement of his position:

> He thinks that I am only concerned to show that the man in the Chinese room does not consciously understand Chinese, but I am in fact showing that he does not understand Chinese at all, because the syntax of the program is not sufficient for the understanding of the semantics of a language, whether conscious or unconscious. (*MC*, p. 128).

But there may be a grain of truth in Dennett's claim. First, it is not just any abstract semantics independent of the mind that Searle is talking about, but semantics as a correlate of the mind's understanding, as is clear not only from the sentence just quoted ("syntax . . . is not sufficient for the *understanding of the semantics*"), but also, primarily, from Searle's general theory of meaning as based on the mind's intentionality.[63] And second, given Searle's Connection Principle[64] and his more recently advanced hypothesis stressing the basal role of the unified field of consciousness, it may be reasonable to consider a version of the Chinese Room argument that focuses on consciousness instead of on semantics. In fact, Searle himself published such a version in 1993.[65]

3. THE NEW ARGUMENT: COMPUTATION IS OBSERVER-RELATIVE

The point that computation is observer-relative was made by Searle in March 1990 in "Is the Brain a Digital Computer?," his Presidential Address to the American Philosophical Association,[66] which became (slightly modified and extended) Chapter 9 of his book *The Rediscovery of the Mind* (*RM*). Roughly simultaneously, he also presented it – more concisely but rather clearly – in "Who Is Computing with the Brain?" (henceforth WCB).[67] It has reappeared several times in Searle's more recent output – for example, in his self-descriptive entry in *A Companion to the Philosophy of Mind* (1994) and, together with the most up-to-date brief restatement of the original Chinese Room argument, in *The Mystery of Consciousness* (1997). Unlike the original argument, the new argument does not have any well-established nickname as yet; it may conveniently be called *the observer-relativity of computation* claim, or – for our purposes here – simply "the new argument."

3.1. The New Argument as Presented in Searle's Texts

The new argument is, basically, that *computation is observer-relative*, since (1) syntax is observer-relative and (2) all that is characteristic of computation as computation is exclusively syntactic. And syntax is observer-relative because there is nothing in the physical make-up of the tokens of syntactic units that makes them such tokens independent of anyone's intentionality. Let us look somewhat more closely at how Searle presents his point and why he thinks it is important.

Searle starts by asking: is it possible to discover that the brain is a digital computer (or, equivalently, that brain processes are computational)?[68] He answers: no, because syntax or symbolic manipulation, in terms of which computation is defined, is not itself defined in terms of physics.

> Any physical object can be used as a symbol, but for the same reason, no object is a symbol just by virtue of its physics. Syntax and symbols are matters of the *interpretations* that we assign to the physics: we do not discover, for example, 0's and 1's in nature the way we might discover circles and lines, because syntax is not intrinsic to physics. (WCB, p. 636)

Any attempt to find out "whether or not some object in nature is intrinsically a symbol manipulating device is, therefore, misconceived." Searle then emphasizes that his point is not that there are a priori limits on the patterns that we could discover in nature, but rather that any pattern we discover would not be a computation without somebody's assigning it a computational interpretation. "In short," concludes Searle, "syntax and symbol manipulation are in the eyes of the beholder" (WCB, p. 636).

He also provides a summary of his argument in a sequence of numbered points:

> 1. On the standard textbook definition, computation is defined syntactically in terms of symbol manipulation.
> 2. But syntax and symbols are not defined in terms of physics. Though symbol tokens are always physical tokens, "symbol" and "same symbol" are not defined in terms of physical features. Syntax, in short, is not intrinsic to physics.[69]
> 3. So computation is not discovered in the physics, it is assigned to it. Certain physical phenomena are . . . interpreted syntactically. Syntax and symbols are observer-relative.
> 4. It follows that you could not *discover* that the brain or anything else was intrinsically a digital computer, although you can assign a computational interpretation to it as you could to anything else. (WCB, p. 637; *RM*, p. 225)

In WCB, Searle says that he presents these points "with some hesitation, because they depend on taking the standard definition of computation as symbol manipulation literally," and that perhaps a better definition of computation will make it possible to avoid these conclusions (p. 637). In later writings, this cautionary remark does not appear. Instead, in *RM*, Searle suggests that the detour through syntax is not necessary and that the same point can be made directly about computation: "A physical state of a system is a computational state only relative to the assignment to that state of some computational role, function, or interpretation" (*RM*, p. 210).[70]

The meaning of Searle's point obviously depends heavily on his distinction between *observer-independent* (or, in earlier terminology, intrinsic)[71] and *observer-relative* features of the world.[72] This distinction has played a central role in his recent philosophy, and in *The Construction of Social Reality*[73] Searle claimed that it is "more fundamental" than the distinction between mental and physical (p. 9). Searle does not define or explain the distinction in other, more basic terms (which is a legitimate policy where we are dealing with basic notions); he just introduces it with the help of examples and occasionally discusses possible misunderstandings (WCB, p. 639). His examples of what exists intrinsically are molecules and gravitational attraction; his examples of what exists relative to the intentionality of observers or users are bathtubs and chairs (RM, p. 211).[74] Searle certainly is aware that many of his opponents do not accept the distinction; he says, for example, that functionalism "is an entire system erected on the failure to see this distinction" (MBP, p. 452).

Searle thinks that his point is important because it refutes another mistaken doctrine: while the Chinese Room Argument refuted strong AI, the new argument refutes cognitivism, the view that the brain is a digital computer. It shows it not to be false, but rather not to have any good sense. It does not have any good sense because the question "Is the brain a digitial computer?" – taken by many as a plain empirical question – can be understood in two ways, and in either case there is a trivial answer. To the question "Can we assign a computational interpretation to the brain?," the answer is trivially yes, because we can assign a computational interpretation to anything. To the question "Are brain processes intrinsically computational?," the answer is trivially no, because nothing is intrinsically computational (except conscious agents intentionally going through computation – RM, p. 225). The new argument is more powerful than the original Chinese Room because it refutes more: it refutes what strong AI holds about the human mind (because if the brain is not a digital computer, it cannot produce mind by running the right program), but it also refutes a milder position than Strong AI, the position of those who admit that the right program is not sufficient for the mind, but who nonetheless believe that the brain or some of its modules are likely to be organized computationally and that there can be a level at which the behavior of the brain can be explained by finding out what computations it somehow instantiates (RM, p. 201).

3.2. From the Debate Related to the New Argument

Dale Jacquette made an interesting point, which is closely related to Searle's new argument but which was meant as a criticism of the old one.[75] He thinks that there is no such thing as "syntax entirely divorced from semantics."

> Without at least some semantic content, what is sometimes loosely referred to as pure syntax is nothing but marks on paper or magnetic patterns on plastic disks. (p. 294)

But if there is no pure syntax, then programs cannot be purely syntactical, and premises P2 and P3 of Searle's argument need to be reformulated.

Jacquette then proposes to modify these premises by replacing "syntactical" with "syntactical and at most only derivatively semantical" (and he holds that, when modified in such a way, the argument is circular – p. 295). It seems that Searle agrees with Jacquette that there is no such thing as syntactic units in a world entirely devoid of understanding and meaning.[76] But he is careful enough not to jump to the conclusion that those very syntactic units have to be endowed with some semantic content. What he says in the new argument is rather that there has to be someone who *understands* them as syntactic units, for whom they *count as* such, who *assigns* to the physical objects in question the function of being syntactic units. Thus there has to be some intentionality added to the dried-up "physical world" in order for there to be syntax, but this is not the derivative intentionality ascribed to the syntactic units (as in Jacquette), but the intrinsic intentionality of the observer or user of the syntactic system. Thus, Searle is not bound to reformulate his old argument because of the new one; by being observer-relative, programs do not cease to be purely syntactic (on the contrary, they could not be syntactic without being observer-relative).

Chalmers's *The Conscious Mind* (1996) contains the following passage criticizing Searle:

> Some have argued that no useful account of implementation can be given. In particular, Searle (1990) has argued that implementation is not an objective matter, but instead is 'observer-relative': any system can be seen to implement any computation if interpreted appropriately. (p. 316)

The reference is to Searle's "Is the Brain a Digital Computer?," but this cannot be quite right even as a summary of the position Searle states in this paper (though without embracing it), for Searle's concern for the size of the wall – "if the wall is implementing WordStar then *if it is a big enough wall* it is implementing any program" (p. 27) – clearly suggests that the situation described is not one in which anything can implement any computation.

But we have already seen that this is not Searle's position: the passage about WordStar is introduced by the phrase, "On the standard definition of computation," and seven lines later Searle begins a paragraph with: "I think it is probably possible to block the result of universal realizability by tightening up the definition of computation." Thus, Searle and Chalmers seem to stand close to one another on this point (it is just that Chalmers advances further than Searle by actually providing crucial parts of such a tightened definition rather than just proposing how it might be done). Finally, Chalmers is wrong in suggesting that observer-relative status precludes an objective account of implementation for Searle; for Chalmers here neglects Searle's distinction between ontological and epistemic objectivity (*CSR*, pp. 8–9), which allows implementation to be at the same time ontologically subjective and epistemically objective.[77] In fact, Chalmers' position corresponds to Searle's pretty closely in this respect, too: even after providing his tightened definition, Chalmers admits that any system that implements a complex computation will, *eo ipso*, be implementing many simpler computations and that the notion of implementation is to this extent "interest relative" (ontologically) – but that, at the same time, "the question of whether a given system implements a given computation is still entirely objective" (epistemically).[78]

4. CONCLUSIONS

My goal here is to provide a clear and systematic reconstruction of Searle's position, and to discuss some issues not yet settled. Such reconstruction is complicated by the fact that the original Chinese Room Argument – unlike the new argument – is conceived primarily as a refutation of a specific position, which means that Searle is operating, so to speak, on the enemy's territory, and makes use of what he finds there. What he tries to establish is thus often of the form "It is not true that the opponent has succeeded in establishing *p*" rather than of the form "It is true that *q*" – often, but not always; and it is important to keep track of how Searle borrows (for the purposes of reductio) and returns various components of the opponent's position. The opponent's name is strong AI, and it is named and defined by Searle for the purpose of refutation. I am not going to inquire how many real life adherents the varieties of strong AI as defined by Searle ever had, but I would find the long-lasting reaction to Searle's paper most peculiar if it were true that he attacks a position that no one ever held.[79]

There are two core structures in Searle's argument, one having to do with *causal powers*, the other with *semantics*. Basically, their point is, first, that what is abstract and formal is, as such, causally inert; and, second, that what is syntactic is, as such, semantically empty. We shall see that both points are, at least in their minimal versions, very plausible and perhaps even trivially true. But we shall also see that within the complex framework of the Chinese Room Argument they sometimes figure in contexts that include assumptions not subscribed to by Searle (assumptions that were borrowed from the opponent precisely for the purpose of refutation).

When looking at Searle's arguments, we shall also discuss whether the refutation addresses the opponent directly or an impartial judge. Arguments refuting the opponent directly are rare: in presenting them, one needs to stick to the opponent's terminology and to use only premises with which the opponent agrees. More often, the winning argument takes the form of addressing an impartial spectator: in such cases, one is not bound to use only the opponent's terminology and premises, and it is normally crucial to making one's point that one use plausible premises or observations that the opponent neglects or denies. Of course, real-life philosophers can look at would-be rejections of their own views as if they were impartial spectators, and in some happy instances they actually do so.

4.1. The Transition from the Thought Experiment to the Core Arguments

Although I claim that the most important elements of what is going on in the Chinese Room are the two core arguments mentioned earlier, it is useful to start with some observations concerning the thought experiment, in order to see how the argument topics naturally grow out of different branches of the thought experiment dispute. We may remember that Searle used the thought experiment to make two slightly different points:

(1) "a system, me for example, could implement a program for understanding Chinese . . . without understanding any Chinese at all,"[80]

and

(2) "if I do not understand Chinese solely on the basis of implementing a computer program for understanding Chinese, then neither does any other digital computer solely on that basis, because no digital computer has anything I do not have" (*MC*, p. 11).

We can see these two points as addressing two distinct (though almost certainly overlapping) target groups: the first, the essentialist thread within strong AI ("implementing the right program and having the appropriate mental states is the same"); the second, the empiricist thread in the version that Searle has a quarrel with ("there are computers that have mental states solely on the basis of the software they are running"). Let us look in some detail at each of these points.

We have noticed that (1) is intended to refute the essentialist claim of strong AI by showing that

> instantiating a program could not be constitutive for intentionality, because it would be possible for an agent to instantiate the program and still not have the right kind of intentionality. (MBP, pp. 450–1)

Now, within the essentialist thread of strong AI we may distinguish between its behaviorist and its mentalist varieties. For a behaviorist, the identification of (the right sort of) computation with mental life involves a redefinition of the latter in terms of behavior; for the mentalist, it is mental life in the ordinary, nontechnical sense that is being identified with computation. In either case, Searle's refutation does not directly address the opponent, since a stubborn essentialist of either variety would not have to accept Searle's thought experiment as a refutation. Let's look at the behaviorist first: he listens to Searle's story about the man in the room and simply does not see any refutation in it: "If you accept," says he, "that understanding was redefined in terms of specific input/output behavior, the man understands all right, doesn't he?" It is the impartial spectator who is impressed by Searle's story, which shows how unbearably impoverishing the acceptance of such a redefinition would be.

The case of a stubborn mentalist essentialist is more complicated. At first, he would not be much worried, either. "Most likely," he would say, "the software the operator was running in your story was not *the right software*, if there really was no understanding, and thus the story refutes nothing more than the particular assumption that this was the right software; but no story of this sort can refute our general claim, the identification of the right software with mental life." To that, Searle might answer: "But wait a minute, there was nothing in my story related to the particular piece of software that the operator was running. I would give you the same story for any piece of Turing-machine-like software." The mentalist replies: "Perhaps, but this does not save you from an inconsistency in your thought experiment scenario. Remember, your thought experiment proves something only if the operator runs the right software. But how do you know it was the right software? From the fact that it produces perfect Chinese output? This may impress the behaviorist essentialist, but not me. From my point of view, if understanding does not occur, the software could not have been the right one." This impasse leads to a reformulation of the issue, a shift from the thought experiment ("You give me the right software, I instantiate it and show that it was not really right") to a more general level of discourse: "My point is really," Searle could say, "that there could not be the right software you envisage, since if there were, I could provide an instantiation that would disqualify it." And, in response to the "How do you know?" reply, he naturally moves to the level of the argument – specifically, to the *semantic* core argument showing that meaning is in principle inaccessible to computational operations performed on uninterpreted data.

Now we turn to (2), the second of the points made by Searle on the basis of the thought experiment: if the operator did not understand, neither would a computer, since the latter *does not have anything the operator does not have*. This point targets the empiricist thread within strong AI, the claim that computers have mental states solely by virtue of the software they are running. Stated along the lines of (2), this point is not exactly watertight: we have seen that the computer must compensate for the absence of a human operator by a highly sophisticated assembly of causal powers that do the symbol shuffling (under a description!) instead of the operator. Now, this particular kind of assembly is something that any human operator most likely *does not have*.[81] Thus, in this case too, it is quite natural to move the dispute from the thought experiment level to the argument level, this time focusing on the *causal powers* core argument.

4.2. The First Core Argument: Causal Powers

We have noticed how crucial was the role of the qualifying phrase "solely by virtue of" (or some such phrase) in the standard formulations of Searle's argument. Now we proceed toward clarifying the role of that qualification, first in the context of the *causal powers* argument. Again, it should help us first to get clear about what the strong AI thesis is that Searle is out to refute. As far as I see, the *causal powers* argument is meant to refute the claim ascribed to strong AI that

> mental properties correctly ascribed to the computer are produced *by the software without any causal contribution from the hardware*.[82]

In this section, we shall look at what supports the view that Searle is refuting this claim, and whether the refutation is successful.

From the beginning, Searle is entirely clear that he *is not* refuting the claim that there can be mental states causally produced by the running of computers.[83] What he is out to refute is the claim that it is the "program, by itself" (MBP, p. 424), that produces mental states. For any such strategy, it is crucial to make sure that one can think of the would-be productive power of the software as perfectly isolated from the causal powers of the hardware. And since Searle is not doing any heavy lifting on that very point, it is natural to conclude that he takes this component of the logical structure to be provided by his opponent, the hypothetical strong AI supporter. If strong AI holds to the irrelevance of the causal powers of the hardware, it is not Searle's business to show how such irrelevance is to be understood, and he certainly need not be committed to the view that such irrelevance is plausible. It is just fine for him to show why the entire view in question cannot be upheld.

Now, Searle is reasonably clear that strong AI, as conceived by him, is committed to the *irrelevance of the causal powers of the hardware* view as just stated. Let me quote two relevant passages:

> [T]he basic premise of strong AI is that the physical features of the implementing medium are totally irrelevant. What matters are programs, and programs are purely formal. (IBM, p. 25)

> Is the program by itself constitutive of thinking? This is a completely different question because it is not about the physical, causal properties of actual or possible physical systems but rather about the abstract, computational properties of formal computer programs. (IBM, p. 20).

Here, the abstract and formal characteristics of programs are claimed to be the sole relevant factor in their producing mental states, and it is explicitly excluded that any causal properties of the physical implementation could be allowed to play any role (according to strong AI).

But now look at the slightly different point made in the following passage:

> [A]ny system capable of causing consciousness and other mental phenomena must have causal capacities to do it equivalent to the biological capacities of animal brains . . . If that sounds trivial, it should. It is, however, *routinely denied* by any amount of confused contemporary philosophy of mind that tries to treat consciousness as some *purely formal abstract phenomenon independent of any . . . physical reality* at all. Contemporary versions of this view are sometimes called 'Strong Artificial Intelligence'.[84]

Here, Searle not only ascribes to strong AI the *separation of powers* view, but already takes one step along the path of refutation and claims that (given that abstract, formal systems alone can have no causal powers) strong AI is in effect committed to the view that the right configurations of shufflings of abstract formal units somehow produce (or are?) mental phenomena in other than a causal way.

Now that we know what view is being refuted, let's look at the refutation. It is, once again, addressed to an impartial spectator, because Searle relies on it in his premise P1, which claims that all existing minds are produced causally by brains or by other physical systems with the needed causal capacities. (The term "physical" is here compatible with any amount of chemical, biological, etc., observer-independent properties.) If P1 is granted, the refutation is simple and very plausible. Unimplemented programs are abstract, formal systems that have no causal powers at all, and, as such, cannot (granted P1) produce minds. When formal programs are implemented in the physical world, all causal properties of the implementation are irrelevant for the production of mental properties, according to the separation of powers thesis (supposedly held by Strong AI); thus the situation is in no relevant way different from that of unimplemented software.

Now the impartial observer may be inclined to say: "All right, this is valid, but it is not a very deep point." I believe that Searle would happily agree: in fact, he keeps saying that the point of the Chinese Room Argument is very simple, that it is more or less trivially true, and that he is somewhat embarrassed that, because it has not been widely recognized as such owing to some misunderstandings, he has been called upon to repeat and explain it over and over again. Nonetheless, having settled the question of the validity of the core point of the Chinese Room Argument relating to causal powers, we may still be interested in what happens in the implementation case if we remove the arbitrary assumption of the irrelevance of the causal powers of the hardware.

There seem to be two separate issues that we are facing in such a situation. One of them has been discussed already in section 2.3, where we saw that if we can allow that there are ways to produce mind causally and that we can gain knowledge about what physical features a system must have in order to be capable of implementing a class of programs, then it is conceivable that there is a class of programs, requiring such hardware for their implementation, that has causal powers to produce mind. I said that it is an open question (given the current state of scientific knowledge) if there is such a class of programs, and that in this respect, Searle can safely make a negative point: "It is not the case that the opponent has established that there is a class of programs such that their running would necessarily produce mind."

The other issue concerns the causal power of the physical representations of formal units. This leads to the fascinating but difficult issue of *being a cause under a description*, specifically, to the area where the would-be cause-under-a-description is observer-relative. We don't have space to address this issue here. Instead, I shall just quote what Searle says about it in *RM*, where he suggests thought that recognizing the observer-relative ontological status of the program is enough to settle the issue:[85]

[T]he 0's and 1's as such have no causal powers because they do not even exist except in the eyes of the beholder. The implemented program has no causal powers other than those of the implementing medium because the program has no real existence, no ontology, beyond that of the implementing medium. (p. 215)

Of course, Searle admits, knowing that a system is implementing such and such software and being familiar with that software provides one with a powerful predictive and explanatory tool regarding how the system behaves. But none of this helps at all in explaining "how the system actually works *as a physical system*" (p. 219).

4.3. The Second Core Point: Semantics

In discussing the dispute between Searle and the essentialist of the mentalist kind (in section 4.1.), we saw that it is impossible for Searle to claim that "it is not the case that (necessarily (the Right Program implies mind))," because the Right Program is simply defined as one that is of such a kind that it produces mind.[86] Rather, the proper matter of controversy should be: is it possible at all that a Right Program of this sort exists? While engaged in the dispute with the behavioristic essentialist, it was enough to imagine that the system produces understanding-like *behavior* without understanding, but here we need to show more: that the system as conceived has no computational resources that could help it to gain understanding, regardless of what program it runs.[87] Searle's way of showing this is via his point about syntax and semantics.

The view that Searle refutes can be stated as follows: purely by running a formal program, a system can gain access to the meaning of at least some of the symbols that it operates on.[88] Refutation of this claim is what is required in Searle's dispute with essentialist strong AI, but it is also his last resort in the dispute with the *systems* reply:

> [T]he decisive objection to the Systems Reply is one I made in 1980: If I in the Chinese Room don't have any way to get from the syntax to the semantics then neither does the whole room.[89]

There is an alternative version of the refuted view, one that claims the system's access to intentionality, not just to meaning. Searle seems to treat the two versions as interchangeable, and surely a refutation of the intentionality claim entails refutation of the meaning claim, given Searle's theory of meaning as grounded in intentionality. In what follows, I shall focus first on the version involving meaning. The refutation addresses an impartial observer once again, since Searle's opponents do not necessarily agree with his conception of intrinsic intentionality and of meaning as grounded therein.

In the initial paper, the words "syntax" and "semantics" are introduced somewhat reluctantly as belonging to "the linguistic jargon." After Searle made the claim that instantiating the Right Program could not by itself be a sufficient condition of understanding, the interlocutor asked, "Why not?," and Searle answered:

> Because the formal symbol manipulations by themselves don't have any intentionality; they are quite meaningless; they aren't even *symbol* manipulations, since the symbols don't symbolize anything. In the linguistic jargon, they have only syntax but no semantics. (MBP, p. 422)

But Searle has found it convenient to formulate his point in terms of syntax and semantics, and we have no reason not to follow him in that. What is meant by "syntax" here are relationships between uninterpreted formal units, especially with regard to how they can and how they cannot be concatenated into linear aggregates. What is especially important for our purposes is the concept of a purely syntactically defined operation, which is an operation on such linear aggregates (sometimes called strings) that is defined solely on the basis of syntactic properties, that is, referring solely to the identities of the uninterpreted units as defined within an abstract formal system. By "semantics" is meant here the property of an object to mean or to symbolize something beyond itself in a way that is understood by (at least some) users of the object.

Searle does not devote much energy to spelling out any details of the refutation.[90] Most often, he just says that it is a conceptual truth that syntax is not sufficient for semantics (which, admittedly, is a well established view in both logic and linguistics), and that this (premise P2) together with the fact that programs, as such, operate solely on the syntactic level (premise P3) leads to the conclusion that no implementation of a program can grasp meaning solely by virtue of running that program.[91] Let us look more closely at what is going on here.

First, it is not important at all for the argument that the syntactic objects that the program operates on do not themselves bear meanings ("are quite meaningless"). This is also true about a mind-endowed reader dealing with an alphabetic text: the letters themselves are pretty meaningless for the most part. (The fact that "i" sometimes bears a meaning in English does not do away with the fact that, in most occurrences, "i" is as meaningless as, say "m" or "z.") What is important is the character of the operations that are performed on the meaningless units. Remember, when the operator in the Chinese Room sees an English word, he understands what it means, and when he sees a string of Chinese signs, he does not. And the crucial point for Searle is that no operation performed on a string of meaningless syntactic units according to computational rules involves assignment of a meaning. Why? Because the operations are so defined: they include identification of a unit in the string regarding its identity as a token of a certain predefined type, replacement of a unit in the string by another, a move to another position in the string, a change of internal state, and that's it. No meaning assignment is involved; only recognition of predefined identities of syntactic units. This is, again, a fairly limited point, having to do just with what computation can do, all by itself. Nothing in the argument is incompatible with the fact that the data that become syntactic units for the software can be seen as meaning-loaded by its mind-endowed users, and I am pretty much convinced that Searle is not blind to this fact (*pace* Block and Rey).[92]

4.4. Some Remaining Issues

It may seem that Searle has a third independent core argument, which serves to establish that running software, as such, is not sufficient for the emergence of intentionality. We have noticed that the claim about intentionality may be stronger than that about meaning, and it is not clear how the argument based on the definition of computational operations supports the claim about intentionality. Let us consider an argument running as follows: what is characteristic of intentionality is its "aboutness," the directedness of something (primarily a mental state) toward something else. What is characteristic of formal syntactic units is their being what they are, having an identity defined as and exhausted by being a token of a predefined type. Now, it surely is possible to assign meaning to any such unit, but the only power that can do this is an intentionality-endowed mind. There is no way in which anything without intentionality could do it, because the very act of doing it is testimony to the fact that the doer has intentionality.

This kind of argument would be close to the semantics core argument in establishing the same point – the sharp difference between the self-containment of syntactic units and the aboutness of meaning and intentionality. But while the semantics argument does this in a bottom-up fashion – that is, by focusing on the limits of what can be achieved solely by any number of syntactically defined operations on uninterpreted terms – the envisaged intentionality argument does it top-down – that is, by focusing on the closure of the realm of aboutness. It is possible to find in Searle passages suggesting an argument of this kind.

Now, there is a difficulty connected with such an argument, namely, that it may be too strong to be true. Specifically, the difficulty consists in the suspicion that, if valid, it would show not only that you cannot get intentionality from syntax, but also that you cannot get intentionality from anything that does not already have intentionality.[93] This conclusion would be incompatible with Searle's biological naturalism – more specifically, with premise P1 (brains cause minds), at least on a natural reading. It is possible that Searle's new argument about the observer-relativity of computation blocks this undesired conclusion, but to be clear about that requires (once again) mastering the difficult area of being a cause under a description. Tentatively, one could sketch out the blocking as follows: brains (etc.) can produce minds, intentionality (etc.) because they have the required causal powers. Syntactic units, programs (etc.) cannot (as such) do this, because they are only observer-relative and, as such, have no causal powers of their own. However, accepting this would make the third argument in a way dependent on the causal powers argument, and perhaps not really necessary in the overall structure of Searle's refutation of strong AI.

What are we to think about the *systems* reply? It has, especially in its *one more mind* version (section 2.2.), considerable force against some ways of drawing a conclusion from the thought experiment. Specifically, I think that it forces Searle to weaken the modality of the basic conclusion: instead of claiming "I implement the program and it is the case that no understanding occurs," he can claim only "I implement the program and it is conceivable that no understanding occurs"[94] – which, nonetheless, is still enough to make his point against behaviorism. But Searle is right that the decisive answer to the *systems* reply is to be found on the level of the argument (the semantics point), rather than on that of the thought experiment (see section 4.3).

In *The Mystery of Consciousness* (p. 11), Searle says about the Chinese Room Argument: "This is such a simple and decisive argument that I am embarrassed to have to repeat it." I hope I have succeeded in showing that Searle's argument is indeed decisive against its main target (namely: strong AI as construed by Searle). I have not succeeded in showing that it is simple: in my opinion, while both of the core arguments themselves are very simple, the overall structure of Searle's argumentation has considerable complexity, which I have attempted to analyse and to clarify.[95]

Notes

1. While it would be difficult to measure exactly the impact of the Chinese Room debate on the artificial intelligence community, both those sympathetic and those not quite sympathetic to Searle's view seem to agree that it has been enormous. According to Stevan Harnad, the Chinese Room Argument "has shaken the foundations of AI." Harnad, "Minds, Machines, and Searle," *Journal of Experimental and Theoretical Artificial Science* 1 (1989): 5. According to P. J. Hayes, the core task of the (then) emerging discipline of cognitive science "consists of a careful and detailed explanation of what's really silly about Searle's Chinese room argument." Hayes, "Introduction," in M. M. Lucas and P. J. Hayes (eds.), *Proceedings of the Cognitive Curricula Conference* (Rochester, N.Y.: University of Rochester Press, 1982), p. 2.

2. See John Searle, *The Mystery of Consciousness* (New York: New York Review of Books, 1997), p. 17; and "Searle, John R.," in Samuel Guttenplan (ed.), *A Companion to the Philosophy of Mind* (Oxford: Blackwell, 1994), p. 547.

3. David Hume, *An Enquiry Concerning Human Understanding*, ed. L. A. Selby-Bigge, 3d. ed. (Oxford: Oxford University Press, 1975), pp. 80–1.

4. And, of course, with the exception of criticism that consists simply in confronting Searle with a position based on assumptions foreign to him (such as, say, a straight denial of intrinsic intentionality) and blaming him for not holding this position rather than the one he does hold.

5. The prehistory of the Chinese Room begins in 1977, when Roger Schank read a paper about his and Abelson's story-understanding software in Berkeley, and Searle criticized Schank in the discussion. Hubert L. Dreyfus, *What Computers Can't Do*, 2nd ed. (New York: Harper and Row, 1979), p. 311, n. 102. However, the Chinese Room was not a part of that criticism, and Searle invented it only later, reportedly on the way to a lecture at Schank's artificial intelligence research group at Yale. Gustavo Faigenbaum, *Conversations with John Searle* (Montevideo: Libros en Red, 2001), p. 78.

6. *Behavioral and Brain Sciences* 3 (1980): 417–57 (of which the original paper is pp. 417–24, the open peer commentary pp. 424–50, and the author's response pp. 450–6).

7. John Searle, *Minds, Brains, and Science* (Harmondsworth: Penguin, 1984).

8. John Searle, "Minds and Brains without Programs," in Colin Blakemore and Susan Greenfield (eds.), *Mindwaves: Thoughts on Intelligence, Identity and Consciousness* (Oxford: Blackwell, 1987); see esp. pp. 210–15 and 231–2.

9. John Searle, "Is the Brain's Mind a Computer Program?," *Scientific American* 262:1 (1990): 20–5 (in some mutations, 26–31).

10. R. C. Schank and R. P. Abelson, *Scripts, Plans, Goals, and Understanding* (Hillsdale, N.J.: Erlbaum, 1977); cf. Searle, "Minds and Brains without Programs," pp. 211–13.

11. Alan Turing, the inventor (in 1936) of an abstract model of a universal computing machine – i.e., of a machine programmable to perform any kind of syntactically defined symbol manipulation – claimed in 1950 that questions such as "Can

machines think?" are hopelessly ambiguous and that they should be abandoned in favor of questions such as "Can machines imitate intelligent behavior successfully?" Answers to questions of the latter type can be tested, and Turing proposed one such test: the "imitation game" (later known as the Turing test), in which a human player, on the basis of written answers to his or her questions, aims to distinguish whether a conversational partner (invisible to him or her) is a machine or a human being. Searle's thought experiment (in the simplified scenario) shows that Turing's proposal, when taken as a restatement rather than a replacement of the initial problem, is not entirely successful, for it is conceivable that one could have an observationally perfect imitation of understanding *without understanding*. See Alan Turing, "Computing Machinery and Intelligence," *Mind* 59 (1950): 433–60.

12. A similar but less complete structure appears already in the "Abstract" of the initial paper. There, Searle introduces what corresponds to P1 and C1–C4, and announces that what corresponds to C1 is to be established by the main argument of the paper (MBP, p. 317).

13. Consider, however, what happens if the word "this" in "The aim of the Chinese room example was to try to show this by showing . . ." (MBP, p. 422) refers not to the main claim (C1) stated three paragraphs earlier (i.e., that nothing thinks, understands, etc., *solely* in virtue of being an instantiation of the right computer program), but rather to the content of the immediately preceding paragraph (roughly, P3, with hints at something like P2). Then Searle would already in the original article see the role of the thought experiment as lying in the support it gives for the point about syntax and semantics.

14. "[T]he story about The Chinese Room illustrates the truth of [P2]." Searle, in "Searle, John R.," p. 546; the same view is found at *MC*, p. 12.

15. *MBS*, p. 39; IBM, p. 21.

16. See John Searle, *Intentionality: An Essay in the Philosophy of Mind* (Cambridge: Cambridge University Press, 1983), Chapter 1.

17. There can be software-writing software, but the program executed by a computer when it is switched on has to be inserted from the outside.

18. They appear in MBP, pp. 423–4; *MBS*, pp. 37–8; IBM, p. 25.

19. MBP, pp. 422–3; *MBS*, pp. 35–6; IBM, pp. 20–1. The claim that "anything whatever can be described as implementing a computer program" (*MBS*, p. 36) is sometimes called *universal realizability* (*RM*, p. 207). In IBM, Searle uses a different criterion for what a computer is: "since anything that can be simulated computationally can be described as a computer, and since our brains can at some level be simulated, it follows trivially that our brains are computers" (p. 21).

20. As with nearly everything concerning the Chinese Room Argument, there is little agreement in the literature even as to how many of these contributions there were: Hofstadter (Douglas R. Hofstadter, "Reflections," in Douglas R. Hofstadter and Daniel C. Dennett [eds.], *The Minds I* [New York: Basic Books, 1981], p. 373) says twenty-eight; Searle (IBM, p. 29) has it as twenty-six. In my opinion, twenty-seven comes closest to the truth.

21. Searle's response to the comments is sometimes quoted under its own title, "Intrinsic Intentionality."

22. Georges Rey, *Contemporary Philosophy of Mind* (Oxford: Blackwell, 1997), p. 271 and p. 284 n. 14. It seems, though, that this can hardly be a full explanation.

23. Retrospectively, one can see that it was Searle's way of presenting his position in his initial paper (and especially his laying so much weight on the six replies, which deal exclusively with the thought experiment) that has been largely responsible for directing the debate to the thought experiment rather than to the theoretical argument. I leave to others possible speculation as to how far this could have been a purposeful Machiavellian strategy on the part of Searle (aimed at distracting and dividing the opponents, in the manner envisaged by Rey).

24. MBP, p. 420. The dilemma is further illustrated in Searle's answer to Fodor: either the causal impact is supposed to produce intentionality in the agent (causally), or it is irrelevant where the data happen to come from. MBP, p. 454.

25. Daniel Dennett thinks it is a pity, probably because he also seems to believe that the modified thought experiment scenarios are intended by Searle to supersede the original one (in which case it would be natural to require Searle to combine the internalization with the robotization). MBP, p. 429.

26. Paul M. Churchland and Patricia Smith Churchland, "Could a Machine Think?," *Scientific American* 262: 1 (1990): 29 (in some mutations, 35). The *neglected scales* objection has been made many times, by, among others, William G. Lycan, MBP, p. 435; Hofstadter, "Reflections," pp. 373–5; and David J. Chalmers, *The Conscious Mind* (New York: Oxford University Press, 1996), p. 325.

27. IBM, p. 24. I am modifying slightly Searle's actual answer in the light of Searle's new argument (to be discussed later, in section 3).

28. For Searle's later recognition of the profound difference between the von Neumann architecture and connectionism, see "The Failures of Computationalism," *Think* 2 (1993): 68–73; and CSR, pp. 140–1.

29. Jerry Fodor, "Afterthoughts: Yin and Yang in the Chinese Room," in David M. Rosenthal (ed.), *The Nature of Mind* (New York: Oxford University Press, 1991), pp. 524–5.

30. I have deviated slightly from Fodor's way of formulating alternative (2). He says simply that the second option is to propose a modification of the conditions of the setup (e.g., by allowing for greater causal connection with the world, as in the *robot* reply). The advantage of my formulation (besides making the logical exhaustion of the field of options clearer) is that it evades the objection that a proposal to modify the setup conditions is relevant only if one construes Searle's thesis as stronger than it is. It is enough for Searle, the objection runs, to show the possibility of program instantiation's not producing understanding in one case, and any number of positive cases under modified conditions could not deprive him of victory.

31. David Cole makes a point similar to that of Chalmers, and argues that this kind of objection is different from the *systems* reply in not claiming that it is "the whole

system" (including the operator as its part) that understands, but rather that it is (supposedly) another mind resulting from the operator's symbol manipulation. David Cole, "The Causal Powers of CPUs," in Eric Dietrich (ed.), *Thinking Computers and Virtual Persons: Essays on the Intentionality of Machines* (San Diego: Academic Press, 1994), pp. 140–1.

32. David Chalmers, *The Conscious Mind* (New York: Oxford University Press, 1996), pp. 324–5. (See also p. 326 for Chalmers's objection to Searle's old answer to the *systems* reply, i.e., the internalization of the Room.) Chalmers's positive argument in favor of AI (pp. 320–2, 326) is a version of the *brain simulator* reply.

33. Similarly, when Searle remarks that functionalism "is an entire system erected on the failure to see [the] distinction" between intrinsic intentionality and observer-relative ascription of intentionality (MBP, p. 452), he needs to be aware that an argument built on such a distinction may fail to impress those who do not already share his view. Of course, it may well be that in certain situations one simply cannot build a relevant argument based on uncontroversial premises. If this hypothesis is plausible, its implications for the self-understanding of philosophy, as well as for the question of what kinds of procedures are appropriate in such cases, are problems deserving closer attention.

34. Larry Hauser, "Searle's Chinese Box: The Chinese Room Argument and Artificial Intelligence," Ph.D. dissertation, Michigan State University, 1993, Chapter 3, section 2.

35. Searle also believes that this matter-of-factness of understanding puts his point into a different class from the anti-functionalist points based on *qualia*, such as Thomas Nagel's "What Is It Like to Be a Bat?," *Philosophical Review* 83 (1974): 435–50; and Frank Jackson's "Epiphenomenal Qualia," *Philosophical Quarterly* 32 (1982): 127–36. But, insofar as the point is not about *qualia*, it is not clear what resources Searle relies on in settling so quickly the controversial issue (especially in the interiorized version scenario) of whether he understands Chinese or not.

36. Fortunately, we probably don't need to worry, for (if we accept Chalmers's argument in the preceding paragraph, or my argument to the same effect) the question of whether the operator understands or not is in the end irrelevant. See sections 4.3. and 4.4.

37. Colin McGinn, "Could a Machine Be Conscious?," in Blakemore and Greenfield (eds.), *Mindwaves*, p. 286. Donald O. Walter (*MBS*, p. 449) was possibly marking at the same spot when he spoke about the ambiguity in Searle between "adequately definable through form or shape" and "completely definable through nothing but form or shape" (presumably concerning the syntactic units).

38. William J. Rapaport, "Searle's Experiments with Thought," *Philosophy of Science* 53 (1986), p. 273.

39. William J. Rapaport, "Syntactic Semantics: Foundations of Computational Natural Language Understanding," in James H. Fetzer (ed.), *Aspects of Artificial Intelligence* (Dordrecht: Kluwer, 1988), pp. 81–131. A similar point has been made by Dennett, who departs more radically from Searle by denying that minds have mental contents and that programs are purely formal and by claiming that

syntax is sufficient for semantics. See the chapter "Fast Thinking" in his *Intentional Stance* (Cambridge, Mass.: MIT Press, 1987), pp. 336–7.

40. This point had been suggested by Dennett already in 1980: "nothing could be only the implementation of a formal program." MBP, p. 430.

41. In Searle's view, this amounts to abandoning the strong AI project in the strict sense.

42. I take it that much of what has just been said had already been suggested in the very thoughtful early commentary by John Haugeland in MBP, pp. 432–3.

43. IBM, p. 23, and similarly elsewhere (see also conclusion C3 in section 1.2. here); the formulation "at least equal" is still to be found in "Searle, John R.," p. 547.

44. This kind of modification is discussed in Ted A. Warfield, "Searle's Causal Powers," *Analysis* 59 (1999): 29–32. Warfield claims that Searle has already modified his formulation along the lines suggested, but that when he uses the thesis in argumentation, he sticks to the old and stronger claim.

45. This point was made simultaneously by Philip Cam, "Searle on Strong AI," *Australasian Journal of Philosophy* 68 (1990): 103–8, and Kenneth G. MacQueen, "Not a Trivial Consequence," *Behavioral and Brain Sciences* 13 (1990): 163–4, and hinted at by Richard Rorty in MBP, pp. 445–6.

46. John R. Searle, "The Causal Powers of the Brain: The Necessity of Sufficiency," *Behavioral and Brain Sciences* 13 (1990): 164.

47. This point is discussed in Larry Hauser, "Searle's Chinese Box: Debunking the Chinese Room Argument," *Minds and Machines* 7 (1997), pp. 203–5.

48. John Searle, *The Rediscovery of the Mind* (Cambridge, Mass.: MIT Press, 1992), pp. 208–9. Henceforth *RM*.

49. Hilary Putnam, *Representation and Reality* (Cambridge, Mass.: MIT Press, 1988), pp. 120–5.

50. Chalmers proposed a more restrictive definition in "On Implementing a Computation," *Minds and Machines* 4 (1994): 391–402. See also his "Does a Rock Implement Every Finite State Automaton?," *Synthese* 108 (1996): 309–33; and his *The Conscious Mind* (New York: Oxford University Press, 1996), pp. 315–20.

51. John Searle, "Is the Brain a Digital Computer?," *Proceedings of the American Philosophical Association* 64: 3 (1990), p. 27. Taken in its context, Searle's statement about WordStar is best viewed as seeking a reductio ad absurdum of the then-current definition of implementation. This is made rather clear by the phrase added to the sentence introducing the passage about WordStar in *RM*: "On the standard definition of computation, *it is hard to see how to avoid the following results*" (p. 209, italics added).

52. In what follows, we shall confine ourselves to programs, although Chalmers's formalism is general enough to deal with other kinds of patterns as well.

53. It may be natural to add a few further requirements – for example, to the effect that the mapping of (at least) those state-components that correspond to input and output variables is in some convenient way uniform across all relevant instantiations.

54. This framework is based on Chalmers, "On Implementing a Computation." The most important additions are the distinction between instantiation and implementation and the recognition of the role of selectivity in the definition of physical states.

55. Hauser, "Searle's Chinese Box," p. 200. I modify the order in which Hauser presents the threads, and add some characteristics.

56. "[M]ental processes are computational processes over formally defined elements" (MBP, p. 422).

57. Cf. Hofstadter, "Reflections," p. 382: "the way we will know" if programmed machines already have the causal powers needed to produce mind "is by talking to them and listening carefully to what they have to say."

58. For the mentalist variety of essentialism, see, e.g., "the idea is that an appropriately programmed digital computer would have a mind and consciousness in exactly the same sense that you and I have minds with consciousness. I call this thesis Strong Artificial Intelligence (Strong AI)." John Searle, "Turing the Chinese Room," in T. D. Singh (ed.), *Synthesis of Science and Religion: Critical Essays and Dialogues* (San Francisco: The Bhaktivedanta Institute, 1988), p. 295. Again, "according to strong AI, the mind just is a computer program and consequently any system that was appropriately programmed, regardless of its physical composition, would literally have a mind in the same sense that you and I do." John Searle, "Cognitive Science and the Computer Metaphor," in Bo Göranzon and Magnus Florin (eds.), *Artificial Intelligence, Culture and Language: On Education and Work* (Berlin: Springer Verlag, 1990), p. 24.

59. In other words, Searle has a quarrel with the second thread claim, insofar as it is not considered separately but taken as a part of the whole strong AI package.

60. And anyway, the whole Chinese Room thought experiment is based on taking for granted what the strong AI thesis holds, namely that there exists – now or at some time in the future – the right mentality-producing software; and this is another assumption Searle would not make when thinking on his own.

61. "And the point is not that for all we know it might have thoughts and feelings, but rather that it must have thoughts and feelings, because that is all there is to having thoughts and feelings: implementing the right program" (MBS, p. 29); and "[t]he point of strong AI is...that there isn't anything to intentionality other than instantiating the right program" (MBP, p. 450). See also RM, p. 201; "Searle, John R.," p. 546; and MC, p. 9.

62. Daniel Dennett, "Fast Thinking," in his *The Intentional Stance* (Cambridge, Mass.: MIT Press, 1987), pp. 323–37.

63. See *Intentionality*, pp. 27–8 and Chapter 6.

64. See his "Consciousness, Explanatory Inversion, and Cognitive Science," *Behavioral and Brain Sciences* 13 (1990): 585–96; RM, pp. 155–62.

65. John Searle, "The Problem of Consciousness," *Social Research* 60 (1993): 14–15.

66. Published in *Proceedings of the American Philosophical Association* 64:3 (1990): 21–37.

67. WCB is, as the author's response, the third part of Searle's "Consciousness, Explanatory Inversion, and Cognitive Science," *Behavioral and Brain Sciences* 13 (1990): 585–642, occupying pp. 632–40. In WCB, Searle still refers to the new argument as an "extension" of the Chinese Room Argument (p. 636); in the Presidential Address, he says that it "is a different argument from the Chinese Room Argument" and that he should have seen this ten years earlier (p. 27).

68. One can see this point as stemming from Searle's answer to the Churchlands' story of Maxwell and the Luminous Room. There, Searle claimed that while it is possible to discover that light consists in electromagnetic radiation, for these are both physical phenomena with an observer-independent mode of being (at least, there is a sense in which "light" means a natural, observer-independent phenomenon), there is in principle no chance of any such discovery being made about mind and computation, since computation is not a physical phenomenon (IBM, pp. 24–5).

69. In other words: "The ascription of syntactical properties is always relative to an agent or observer who treats certain physical phenomena as syntactical" (*RM*, p. 208). Perhaps one can think about it like this: in the physical world without any observer, there is no room for two or more *tokens* of the same *type*; what you have are just individuals, and the whole type/token distinction collapses. In order to get two or more individuals to be generically identical by being tokens of the same type, or to get one individual to stand in a specific relationship to another (and not only the relationship of *nonidentity* in which it stands to everything else indifferently), you need an observer with a specific point of view. Notice that by "physical world" we mean here a certain ontological abstraction, not the world of physics – for physics could not do without classifying, measuring, etc., which are activities requiring an interested, selective observer.

70. See also "Searle, John R.," pp. 547–8; *MC*, pp. 14–17.

71. Searle now prefers the term "observer-independent," because "intrinsic" is normally taken as the opposite to "relational," which is not what Searle means. John Searle, "Mental Causation, Conscious and Unconscious: A Reply to Anthonie Meijers," *International Journal of Philosophical Studies* 8 (2000): p. 172.

72. Searle first used the distinction to distinguish *intrinsic intentionality* from all kinds of observer-relative intentionality (which include *as-if* intentionality and *derived* intentionality) – see MBP, pp. 451–2; *Intentionality*, p. 27; WCB, p. 639; *RM*, p. 80.

73. John Searle, *The Construction of Social Reality* (New York: The Free Press; Harmondsworth, Middlesex: Penguin, 1995).

74. Of course, the way we think and speak about molecules is dependent on our intentionality – but that does not change anything about what they are intrinsically (see *CSR*, Chapter 7). And, of course, "chair" is just a description of something that does exist intrinsically, for a chair is created by assigning a function to a physical object, and, obviously, not all objects are equally suitable for performing this function - but the fact that we do not assign the function arbitrarily does not change anything in the fact that a chair's existence is dependent on that assignment (see *CSR*, Chapter 1).

75. Dale Jacquette, "Fear and Loathing (and Other Intentional States) in Searle's Chinese Room," *Philosophical Psychology* 3 (1990): 287–304.

76. Cf. "an entity can only have a syntactical interpretation if it also has a semantical interpretation." John Searle, *Consciousness and Language* (Cambridge: Cambridge University Press, 2002), p. 117.

77. Searle's explanation of how it is possible occupies Chapters 1–6 of *CSR*.

78. Chalmers, "On Implementing a Computation," p. 397.

79. Searle's attitude seems to me entirely legitimate on this point. It might be expressed as follows: "It is not my business to do any damned opinion polls among the strong AI people; I gave them my point, and if they agreed with it they should have said so."

80. This is what Searle occasionally calls the summary of the basic argument in one sentence. John Searle, "Consciousness, Explanatory Inversion, and Cognitive Science," *Behavioral and Brain Sciences* 13 (1990), p. 585.

81. The other side of the same coin is that the man-made electronic computer's behavior does not involve the gap that is involved in human action. See Searle's *Rationality in Action*.

82. Alternatively, one can consider also the claim that

> mental properties correctly ascribed to the computer are produced *by the software with the causal contribution of the hardware limited to the instantiation of the relevant computation.*

It would be rather difficult to cash out what the italicized part means, especially given Searle's new argument about the observer-relativity of computation. But Searle could work with some such claim by treating it as an assumption borrowed from the opponent for the purpose of refutation, without being committed to justifying or clarifying the refuted view.

83. See, e.g., his answer to the *many mansions* reply (MBP, p. 422).

84. John Searle, "Animal Minds," *Midwest Studies in Philosophy* 19 (1994), p. 214.

85. Searle's more recent remarks about the causal efficacy of institutional reality (which, of course, is no less observer-relative than computer programs) – for example, in *Mind, Language and Society: Philosophy in the Real World* (New York: Basic Books, 1998), pp. 132–3 – suggest that he may be reconsidering the problem. It is quite possible that what is needed here first is a further clarification of the vexing concept of causality itself (personal communication with Searle, November 2001).

86. In this respect, the formulation in Searle's "Reply to Jacquette," p. 702, may need to be modified.

87. In other words: against behaviorism it was enough to have one implementation of one supposedly right program that does not understand; now we need to show that *no* right program can ever understand solely by virtue of its programlike features.

88. Which is, roughly, a generalization of the claim that a machine running Schank and Abelson's software "can literally be said to *understand*" (MBP, p. 417).

89. John Searle, "The Failures of Computationalism," *Think* 2 (1993): 68–73.

90. Cf. "The Churchlands complain that I am 'begging the question' when I say that uninterpreted formal symbols are not identical to mental contents. Well, I certainly did not spend much time arguing for it, because I take it as a logical truth" (IBM, p. 25).

91. Which then, together with the premise that minds do grasp meaning (P4), establishes the conclusion that program implementations are not sufficient to produce mind solely by virtue of the running of the program.

92. Ned Block and Georges Rey, "Mind, computational theories of," in Craig (ed.), *Routledge Encyclopedia of Philosophy* (London: Routledge, 1998), Vol. 6, p. 392.

93. The danger has been pointed to, for example, by Dennett, MBP, p. 430; and by Harnad, "Harnad Responds," *Think* 2 (1993): 74.

94. Searle in effect concedes that much by shifting the burden of proof to the *systems* reply side: what are their reasons for believing that understanding emerges? Cf. "In short, the systems reply simply begs the question by insisting without argument that the system must understand Chinese" (MBP, p. 419).

95. My work on this paper was supported by grant 401/01/0968 from Grantová Agentura Česk Republiky. I benefited greatly from the intellectually most stimulating environment in the Department of Philosophy of the University of California at Berkeley, where I was a Fulbright Research Fellow during the academic year 2001–02. My understanding of the difficult matters discussed in the paper gained from many discussions over many years; in particular, I'd like to thank David Chalmers, Hubert Dreyfus, John Haugeland, Ivan Havel, Richard Rorty, Mark Sainsbury, Barry Smith, Ernst Tugendhat, and, above all, John Searle.

Searle, Derrida, and the Ends
of Phenomenology

KEVIN MULLIGAN

1. SEARLE VERSUS THE REST OF THE WORLD

In marked contrast to his Anglophone peers, Searle has written extensively, and invariably critically, about deconstructionism, postmodernism, and other parts of what is sometimes called (although not by Searle) "Continental Philosophy"[1] or CP. Anglophone, analytic philosophers have written very little, for or against, about what has been said within the different traditions of CP. Richard Rorty's enthusiastic embrace of CP and Searle's withering dismissals are perhaps the two best-known results of contact between these traditions and analytic philosophy.[2] This is a striking fact. In many disciplines there has been a critical reaction to the invasion of the humanities by what are, after all, philosophical claims. When Ranke's view that history could and should describe "what was really the case" was turned on its head, a minority of historians were quick to react.[3] Similarly, when literary critics began to theorise away claims such as Arnold's – "the aim of criticism is to see the object as in itself it really is" – some of their fellow critics reacted.[4] But philosophers did not follow suit.

The relations among Searle, Derrida, CP, and phenomenology are complex. The writings of Derrida, the most influential figure within CP, are inseparably bound up with phenomenology and with the transformation of phenomenology effected by Heidegger. Indeed, a large part of CP grew out of phenomenology. It has often been claimed that Searle's own contributions to the philosophy of mind advance claims already put forward by the phenomenologists; and Searle himself has given his own account of phenomenology – in particular, of the role of idealism in phenomenology. In what follows, I argue that the preoccupations of early phenomenology are often those of later analytic philosophers – a point that remains invisible so long as phenomenology is looked at from the point of view of what it later became – but that Searle's philosophy of mind differs on most central points from that of Husserl. On the other hand, Searle's criticisms of Derrida and of the philosophical parts of postmodernism do indeed have

much in common with the criticisms put forward by the early phenomenologists, and by Husserl himself, of what they saw as phenomenology's
gradual transformation and degeneration and of related irrationalisms. A
grasp of these similarities will suggest the beginnings of an answer to the
question of why Searle's anti-Derridas and anti-postmodernisms are such
splendidly isolated examples of the genre.

2. WHAT WAS PHENOMENOLOGY?

Phenomenology in the narrow sense begins in 1900 with the publication
of the first volume of Husserl's *Logical Investigations*[5] and of Pfänder's *Phenomenology of Willing*. The theoretical framework outlined by Husserl was
accepted by a large number of enthusiastic young philosophers in Munich.
Roughly, the framework runs as follows. A properly theoretical philosophy of logic and of objects in general must begin with a general account
of essences or types and of their possible instantiations. It must proceed
from there to give specific accounts of the essences of meanings, propositions, judging, reasoning, and of various types of object – ideal objects,
tropes, substances, parts, and quantities. Formal logic and formal ontology
and the philosophies thereof are to be distinguished from metaphysics (and
thus, for example, from all realist or idealist claims about the existence of a
mind-independent spatiotemporal world, and indeed from all claims about
matters of fact). Claims about what does or does not belong to the essence
of a proposition – or of some other whole – provide the ground for, but are
not identical with, modal claims. (For example, an emotion essentially has a
representational base and so has one necessarily; a truth-bearer essentially
contains a predicate and so necessarily). Clarification of what does or does
not belong to the essence of this or that involves providing "logical analyses," "analyses of meaning," truths both analytic and synthetic a priori. Such
clarification also involves developing central parts of a theory of knowledge
and of a descriptive psychology or philosophy of mind. Husserl was, however, often sceptical about analysis where this means providing definitions,
the necessary and sufficient conditions of an analysandum. His scepticism
about analysis so conceived seems to have been a reaction against the analyses of Brentano and, especially, of Bolzano – perhaps the author of more bi-
conditional decompositions than Frege, Russell, Moore, and Wittgenstein
together. Hence Husserl's frequent warnings to the effect that equivalences
are not propositional identities. In what often seems to be his preferred
sense of the word, to analyse is to describe what provides the ground for a
proposition or other structure.

Many of the philosophers who adopted Husserl's framework applied it in the philosophies of mind, language, and society to problems that belong neither to the philosophy of logic nor to formal ontology – the nature of perception, emotions, sentiments, the will, collective intentionality, and communication.

Husserl makes almost no metaphysical claims in the *Investigations*. But it seemed obvious to his earliest pupils that he was committed to realism about the external world, not least because of his extended defence of a sophisticated, naive-realist account of visual perception. These pupils made up the schools of realist phenomenology of Munich (where Pfänder taught) and of Göttingen (where Husserl taught). Realism and antirealism can, of course, be understood as formal claims, rather than as metaphysical theses in the sense already mentioned. Husserl's position in 1901 was that propositions dealing with ideal objects cannot simply be assumed to obey the law of excluded middle, where this law is understood as an ontological thesis (for every object and for every property, either the object has the property or it does not). This law, he says, holds only for temporal objects.

In a wider sense, phenomenology, or "descriptive psychology," comprehends the philosophies of all of the pupils of the Austrian philosopher Franz Brentano – Meinong, Marty, Ehrenfels, Stumpf, and Twardowski, as well as Husserl.

Husserl inherited from Brentano a very strong version of the view that philosophy can and should be a theoretical science. Philosophy, so conceived, is seen as being perpetually threatened by practical motives and by the doctrine that philosophy is or should be a primarily practical discipline. The ideal of theoretical philosophy is regularly overthrown, and as a consequence, philosophy sinks into an abyss of obscurantism and nonsense.[6]

The early realist phenomenologists and other heirs of Brentano were thus more than a little disturbed by a double shock administered by Husserl in 1913 (at the latest). First, in his *Ideas* of that year, Husserl announced his conversion to a form of idealism – a metaphysical, spiritualist, or dualistic idealism (sometimes described as a form of transcendental idealism). Second, it became apparent that Husserl's ability to practice theoretical philosophy was no longer what it had been. The extended analyses, descriptions, and arguments of the young Austrian philosopher had given way to programmatic pronouncements and rhetoric of the sorts associated with the various neo-Kantian schools.

Critical reaction by admirers of the *Investigations* to Husserl's change of direction marked the beginning of a series of such reactions to the way in which phenomenology as a whole was developing.[7] By 1927 (at the latest), it seemed that something had gone very wrong. What, exactly? First, the turn to idealism in one form or another was closely bound up with the increasing respectability of the philosophies of German Idealism. Second, the irrationalisms of Nietzsche, Dilthey, and Bergson had come to be seen by many as providing a more-than-acceptable alternative to the bloodless philosophies of mind and logic of Brentano and his immediate heirs. The rest is history – or rather, contemporary philosophy: Heidegger, Sartre, Merleau-Ponty, Derrida, Lyotard, and Foucault. The rearguard action by the philosophers who were formed in the traditions of realist phenomenology and still endorsed a full-blooded version of philosophy as a theoretical enterprise (Moritz Geiger, Max Scheler, Nicolai Hartmann, Edith Stein, Ortega y Gasset, and Roman Ingarden, all of whom drew on the work of Adolf Reinach, who died in World War I) – in particular, the still-unsurpassed defences of realism by Hartmann and Ingarden – did not succeed in making themselves heard above the din of two world wars. As Brentano had foreseen, the triumph of Dilthey and the obsession with the meaning of "life as a whole" would lead to a new Dark Age, a prediction Brentanians such as Oskar Kraus and Paul Linke found to have become all-too-horrifyingly true.[8]

3. PHENOMENOLOGY AND OXFORD PHILOSOPHY – A LOST CAUSE?

This sketch of the death of phenomenology proper is an unfamiliar one, at least for those accustomed to seeing the early Husserl merely as a precursor of, or Aunt Sally for, the later Husserl, Heidegger, Sartre, and Derrida, a habit that blinds many commentators to the role of realist, theoretical philosophy in early phenomenology and a *fortiorissimo* to the latter's Austrian, anti-Kantian context. Before we turn to the relation between Searle and phenomenology, it will be useful to reinforce the point of the sketch by considering the immediate context of Searle's work: Oxford philosophy.

Searle is, as he likes to put it, an "Oxford chap." Now, some of the best-known philosophical problems, solutions, and theses associated with Oxford philosophy are to be found in realist phenomenology and in other parts of the legacy of Brentano. And in each case, the problems, solutions, theses, and distinctions have some claim to be considered novel. This claim is easily documented across most areas of philosophy – the philosophy of language and of mind, epistemology, ethics, logic, and metaphysics.

Grice's influential analysis of meaning in terms of what a speaker means or intends by doing something on a particular occasion extends a related analysis given by Brentano's pupil Marty in 1908. Austin's description of performatives and of such linguistic acts as promising is in many ways less thorough than Reinach's 1913 anatomy of what he calls "social acts" and of promising in particular. Ryle (the author of eight pieces on the philosophers he called the "scions of Brentano" and very much at home on the Bolzano–Brentano–Husserl–Meinong railway line) was, like Husserl and Hartmann, a diagnostician of category mistakes and, like Hartmann, an adept of dilemmas. Two of his most influential positive theses concern the imagination and attention. In a number of places, he defends an account of imagination in terms of make-believe and pretence. The forerunners of Ryle's account are the analyses of suppositions, make-believe seeing, and other "non-positing acts" given by Husserl and Meinong at the beginning of the twentieth century. And, although Husserl and Ryle have very different views about the nature of mental phenomena, each defends a version of the "adverbial" theory of attention against theories of attention popular in the nineteenth century. The idea set out by Gareth Evans that visual perception is direct and yet involves nonconceptual content had already been extensively explored by Husserl before the First World War and was then taken up by many of his pupils.

Kneale defended the view that logical consequence is a strongly modal relation, Husserl that it is an essential and so a modal relation (that it is essentially necessary). Kit Fine, more recently, has developed a theory of the relation between essence and modality that is, as he points out, in central respects that of Husserl. More recently still, Williamson has defended the view that knowledge is not built up out of belief. That neither cognition nor knowledge is built up out of belief, conviction, or "mere" judgement was also the view of Husserl, Reinach, and Hartmann.

Bernard Williams's extended rejection of the claims of Kantianism and utilitarianism, like Scheler's critique of these, is rooted in an ethical psychology – for example, of shame, the subject of monographs by both Scheler and Williams. Scheler's *Ethics* is built around a detailed account of the moral sentiments and of the distinction between norms (universal ought-to-do's) and values (universal and individual) and the claim that values provide the ground for norms. "It is absurd," writes Scheler, "to make the medication of obligations and prohibitions our normal moral nourishment." Urmson's account of supererogation is anticipated by what Meinong and his pupils had to say on the subject.

Dummett's revision of Frege's account of thoughts, which ties them to utterances and utterance-types, is anticipated by Husserl's revision of his own earlier account of ideal thoughts during the first decade of the twentieth century. According to the revised view, subsequently developed by many of Husserl's heirs, thoughts are "bound" idealities, unlike such pure idealities as numbers. They are bound to the earth and linguistic and cognitive activity on Earth (or, Husserl adds, on Mars).

I adduce this baker's dozen of examples – a list that it would be easy to extend – merely in order to make plausible the claim that there was considerable overlap between the concerns of Oxford philosophy and those of Brentano's heirs. It is essential to the plausibility of the claim that we do not find in the overlaps mentioned, on the Austro-German side, mere aperçus, but rather extended analyses and arguments – and that, by contrast, the thirteen points mentioned do not loom large in the traditions of either Kantianism or of naturalistic materialism that formed the main rivals to early phenomenology. There is a widespread perception that the Oxonian contributions listed were novel contributions to philosophy; similarly, the phenomenologists often claimed that in their most important contributions to philosophy they had seen what had invariably been overlooked. As far as I can see, there is a lot to be said in favour of the latter view, and in favour of the view that twentieth-century Oxonian and Austro-German philosophy was both original and valuable.

But, of course, if Gilbert Ryle's proclamation – that phenomenology was, from its birth, a bore – were correct, these views would have to be revised. Whether or not the spirit of early, realist phenomenology went to Oxford – to die or to live – it was certainly considered there to be one of the causes for which Oxford is famous. According to the ever-quotable Ryle, the presuppositions of the phenomenologists made phenomenology a lost cause from the start (Oxford's *morgue anglaise*?).[9] But, I suggest, the problems and solutions discovered by the heirs of Brentano and Bolzano in fact enjoyed and deserved a life of their own.[10]

However, none of these thirteen innovations of the early phenomenologists was to be pursued, developed, criticised – if criticism presupposes comprehension – or even understood by the "thinkers" who took on the mantle of phenomenology in the eyes of the world.

4. PHENOMENOLOGY AND SEARLE

It is often suggested that Searle's analysis of intentionality was anticipated by Husserl's *Logical Investigations*. I have lost count of the number of times I have been informed, with a knowing shrug – in German, Italian, and Californian – that what Searle says is "all in Husserl."

This is not the case. As Searle once said, on being introduced to a friend of mine who (modestly under-) described himself as a phenomenologist, "I am an analytic philosopher. I think for myself." And Searle's conclusions are not Husserl's. In fact, just as many analytic philosophers are proud of their ignorance of the history of philosophy – including that of analytic philosophy – so, too, in my experience, phenomenologists are often ignorant of the history of phenomenology. And the former at least have the excuse that they do philosophy.

Searle's project of analysing and describing the structure of mind and intentionality in a way that does not lose sight of the first-person perspective is, of course, also a Husserlian project. Searle's descriptivist élan, which he shares with Wittgenstein and Austin, as well as with Brian O'Shaughnessy, is one of the most important similarities between his philosophy of mind and those of the Brentanian tradition. More particularly, the general project of analysing the contents and satisfaction conditions of different attitudes is common to Searle and Husserl. And, like Husserl, Searle distinguishes between the mode (which Husserl also calls the "quality" of an "act") and the content of psychological states and events.

But on almost every specific issue, Searle's conclusions are very different from those of the early Husserl and his followers. First, and perhaps most importantly, Husserl, unlike Searle in *Intentionality*, allows for intentional, nonpropositional attitudes or acts, as well as for intentional, propositional attitudes or acts. (Searle – rightly, I think – does not use the word 'act' in the way that the phenomenologists use '*Akt*', namely, to refer to mental [psychological or 'spiritual'] states or events.) According to Husserl, the most basic types of seeing – "simple," "direct" seeing – and of memory, as well as pleasure or admiration based on simple seeing, and even the act of referring within the context of a propositional attitude, all have nonpropositional contents. And within the class of nonpropositional contents, Husserl distinguishes further between conceptual and nonconceptual contents.

Husserl was the first philosopher to defend the view that judging and belief, for example, represent states of affairs (*Sachverhalte*), which obtain or do not obtain, and which are wholly distinct from the propositional contents representing them. But he thought that an account of the "relations" of intentionality of such contents – of what is, for example, the case when a judgement corresponds to an obtaining state of affairs – and an account of the degrees of satisfaction, fulfilment, or verification of such contents had to be complemented by – indeed, built on – an account of the way that nonpropositional contents latch on to objects and of the degrees of fulfilment of such contents. (Notice that what Husserl calls "satisfaction" or "fulfilment" (*Erfüllung*) is not what Searle calls "satisfaction." The latter corresponds rather to what Husserl discusses under the heading of "intentionality." Husserl's analysis of what he calls "satisfaction" is, rather, an account of verification and related phenomena.)

Second, in his accounts of seeing, seeing that, and of desire or will Husserl nearly always rejects attempts to put into the content of such an attitude any reference to a causal relation between a worldly item and the attitude. But the main claim in Searle's analyses of perception and of intention in Chapters 2–4 of *Intentionality* is that seeing and intending have causally self-referential conditions of satisfaction. Husserl was undoubtedly familiar with Brentano's frequent resort to the category of such reflexive contents and with Bolzano's resort to such contents in his analysis of perception. But he was not convinced. Thus, in his early philosophy, Brentano specifies the content of intentional states of willing in terms of causal relations involving these states:

> Every volition or striving in the strict sense refers to an action. It is not simply a desire for something to happen but a desire for something to happen as a result of the desire itself.[11]

But this is not how Husserl understands the propositional content of desirings and willings, nor is it how he understands seeing, simple or propositional, in the *Investigations*.[12]

A third major difference concerns the nature of singular reference. On Husserl's view, producers and consumers of proper names typically grasp a sense expressed by the name. But, unlike Searle (and Frege), Husserl thinks that a sense of this sort is, in the most basic cases, simple and involves no attribution or description but is based on nonconceptual contents.[13]

Searle has himself claimed, in discussion, that his view about the nature of mind differs from that given by Husserl because his account is naturalistic.[14] In fact, although Husserl was to accuse the author of the first edition of the *Logical Investigations* of naturalism, the author of that text, in accordance with his metaphysical neutrality there, "leaves it open whether and how physical and psychic things . . . are to be distinguished."[15]

Although, as we have seen, the early Husserl and Searle differ on each of what they doubtless took or take to be three of the most important questions within the descriptive parts of the philosophies of mind and language – "Is intentionality always propositional?," "Do the contents of willing and perception contain a causal specification?," and "Is the sense of a proper name descriptive?" – Husserl's heirs did occasionally arrive at novel positions first set out with the required precision by Searle. This is true of parts of Searle's accounts of social entities in terms of collective intentionality and of the Background.

Thus Scheler, Walther, Hartmann, Ortega, Ingarden, and Bühler argued that social and cultural entities – such as voting, money, tools, institutions, and word meanings – are not merely "bound idealities" but are entities that depend on collective intentionality, on we-attitudes, both in order to come into being and for their continued existence.

Searle notes that one of the main forerunners of his account of the Background is Wittgenstein's *On Certainty*.[16] The analysis of primitive, ungrounded certainty was developed by many phenomenologists, in particular by Ortega in the 1930s. Thus Ortega argues that a theory of critical or founded beliefs must be built on an account of the primitive, unfounded beliefs that we "count on," sometimes collectively and sometimes individually.

5. SEARLE VERSUS DERRIDA: THE END OF PHENOMENOLOGY AND ITS BEGINNING

For many of us, Searle's patient and sometimes impatient criticisms of Derrida's deconstructions of Austin's account of speech acts and other bits and pieces of contemporary philosophy of language invariably hit all the nail on the head. But this impression is not, apparently, shared within the strongholds of postmodernism, "Theory," and CP. In view of the relative absence of attempts to defend Derrida, it is perhaps advisable to try to come to grips with Derrida in a way that does not retrace ground covered by Searle. Clearly, Derrida and Searle have very different conceptions of what arguments in philosophy are and can do. Derrida vaunts his "rigorous arguments." Searle is apparently blind to this aspect of deconstructionism. And even Rorty writes that "Searle is . . . right in saying that a lot of Derrida's arguments . . . are just awful."[17]

Searle thinks that, in interpretative disciplines, understanding requires that we repeat in the "explanation of a phenomenon the very same intentional content that functions causally in producing the phenomenon to be explained."[18] Can we repeat the very same intentional content that produces some of the typical "effects" of a Derridean text? In order to try to do so, in order to try to understand the end of phenomenology in Derrida's writings, we must go back to an idea to be found at the beginning of phenomenology, an idea that seems to have exercised a great attraction for Derrida.

One of Derrida's invariable starting points is the observation that many of the conceptual oppositions central to philosophy are, or are correlated with, axiological differences. Not only are the first terms of, for example, life versus death, expression versus indication, literal versus metaphorical, grammaticality versus agrammaticality, presence versus absence, reality versus appearance, speech versus writing, often held to be conceptually prior to the respective second terms, each opposition is often held further to involve or to be associated with an axiological claim: speech is good, writing is bad, speech is better than writing, and so forth. One common goal of Derrida's writings is to arrive at a different axiological character-isation of these oppositions (not one that is a mere reversal of the initial axiological characterisation). How might one try to get from the starting point – Derrida's observation about conceptual oppositions – to this goal? One strategy is suggested by passages such as the following:

> I repeat, therefore, since it can never be repeated too often: if one admits that writing (and the mark in general) *must be able* to function in the absence of the sender, the receiver, the context of production etc., that implies that this power, this *being able*, this *possibility* is *always* inscribed, hence *necessarily* inscribed *as possibility* in the functioning or the functional structure of the mark. Once the mark *is able* to function, once it is possible for it to function in case of an absence etc., it follows that this possibility is a *necessary* part of its structure, that the latter must *necessarily be such that* this functioning is possible; and hence, that this must be taken into account in any attempt to analyze or to describe, in terms of necessary laws, such a structure. Even if it is sometimes the case that the mark, in fact, functions *in-the-presence-of*, this does not change the structural law in the slightest. . . .[19]

How should we go about understanding this and related passages? As was noted earlier, Derrida's philosophy is inseparable from phenomenology. As we have also seen, the central distinction of the phenomenologists is that between essences and their instances, actual and possible. Essentiality, according to Husserl, involves, but is not the same as, necessity. An essential truth provides the ground for, but is not itself, a necessary truth. It is, therefore, not surprising that the concepts of necessary possibility and of essential possibility are prominent in Husserl's accounts of essence and modality (cf. *Ideas*, §§86, 135, 140). And they are present, too, in all of his applications of these accounts – that is to say, everywhere in his writings – and also in the work of his followers (for example, in the work of one of the first logicians to defend the principles of the modal logic S5, Oskar Becker).

If I am right in thinking that Derrida's very generous use of modal locutions and ideas is a repetition of locutions and ideas of Husserl, then part at least of what Derrida is getting at in the passage quoted and in many related passages[20] is crystal clear: if a written mark can (essentially) function in the absence of its producer, then this possibility is an essential, and so necessary, possibility. So far, so good. But it is still not, I suggest, possible to repeat the very same intentional content that Derrida seems to be expressing in the passage quoted. The obstacle is Derrida's insistence that the necessity of certain possibilities is "inscribed" somewhere, "inscribed" in a "structure" ("this possibility is always inscribed, hence necessarily inscribed as possibility in the functioning or the functional structure of the mark"). Derrida's thesis – that if a written mark can function in the absence of its producer, then this possibility is a necessary possibility – is not strong enough to provide any sort of undermining of the distinction between presence and absence nor of any axiological distinction correlated with this. The apparently stronger thesis – that necessary possibilities are "inscribed" somewhere – remains simply unexplicated.

Perhaps some sense can be made of it. But neither Derrida nor his followers display any interest in this project. This is unfortunate, for Derrida often appeals to necessary possibilities and their "inscription" in order to undermine apparently straightforward distinctions. In an early paper, he discusses Husserl's version of a Principle of Expressibility. As we have already noted, Husserl thinks that the content of simple seeing, remembering, and imagining is not conceptual. As he (rather unfortunately) puts it at §124 of *Ideas*, such contents have a sense (*Sinn*) but no conceptual meaning (*Bedeutung*). But, Husserl claims, every nonconceptual sense can be conceptualised or even expressed, can "stamp" or "impress itself" conceptually. And the "can" here, he thinks, is that of essential possibility. In his discussion of this paragraph, Derrida says that, according to Husserl, "sense in general, the noematic sense of every experience, is something which, by its very nature, must be already able *to be impressed* on a meaning, to leave or receive its formal determination in a meaning." So far, so good – or, at least, so far, so Husserlian. But Derrida continues:

> Sense would therefore [*donc*] already be a kind of blank and mute writing which is reduplicated in meaning.[21]

But can we really conclude from the essential possibility that a nonconceptual sense can be conceptualised, even expressed aloud or written down, that to see is to write? If we had any grasp of what it means to say that a necessary possibility is "inscribed" in the bearer of the possibility or in the bearer's essence, we could perhaps begin to evaluate this "conclusion."[22]

Is Derrida's way with necessary possibilities peculiar to his writings on the philosophy of language (on Husserl, Austin, Searle)? Not at all. Consider the following passage at the heart of Derrida's "*incontournable*" discussion of Lacan's interpretation of Poe's story "The Purloined Letter":

> It is not that a letter never arrives at its destination but it belongs to its structure to be able, always, not to arrive at its destination. And without this threat . . . the circuit [*circuit*] of the letter would not even have begun.[23]

Derrida appears to draw a number of substantive conclusions, couched in the vocabulary of psychoanalysis, from this claim. Similarly, in a discussion of a sentence found, between quotation marks, in Nietzsche's *Nachlass*, the German for "I have forgotten my umbrella," Derrida writes:

> Perhaps one day, with work and luck, it will be possible to reconstitute the context, internal and external, of this "I have forgotten my umbrella." Now this factual possibility will never prevent it being marked in the structure of this fragment . . . that it can simultaneously remain whole and forever without any other context, cut off not only from the place [*milieu*] of its production and from every intention and meaning [*vouloir dire*] of Nietzsche. . . .[24]

Derrida's "conclusions," his claims to have undermined this or that venerable opposition, turn out again and again to have been arrived at by modifying a claim by Husserl – which, whether true or false, is comprehensible – to the effect that certain possibilities are essentially and so necessarily possible. The modification is the claim that possibilities are necessarily "inscribed" in the "structure" of their bearers. Why, we may wonder, have those who find Derrida's conclusions so agreeable made no effort to explain the modification? One plausible explanation is that they lack the relevant theoretical interest.

6. CANT, COGNITIVE VALUES, AND REALISM

In his critical discussions of parts of CP, Searle concentrates his fire on *hypocrisy*, *antirationalisms* and *antirealisms*. Much of what goes on in various humanities departments in the United States, he writes, is "based on a quite specific form of hypocrisy and deception": "institutional structures, and particularly funding, are based on a traditionalist justification, but the actual money and effort are devoted to undermining traditionalist ideals."[25] These ideals, of course, are knowledge and understanding, their extension and transmission. There is, he writes, "an atmosphere of bluff and fakery that pervades much (not all, of course) deconstructive writing."[26] Now a natural, empirical question about such claims is whether the widespread hypocrisy in question is not based on more enduring attitudes and behaviour – for example, cant. Not just the "cant political" and "cant literary" that Byron refers to, but also philosophical cant. But then what is cant? And what is cant philosophical and, more generally, cant theoretical? The original title of the famous book by Sokal and Bricmont was *Impostures Intellectuelles* (translated as *Fashionable Nonsense: Postmodern Intellectuals' Abuse of Science*).[27] Are the impostures or deceptions that they document merely that, or are they rooted in more enduring attitudes, such as cant? The concept is no longer a very familiar one. Writing in 1972 about the "intellectual mode that once went under the name of cant," Lionel Trilling noted that the "disappearance of the word from the modern vocabulary is worth remarking."[28]

Writing about the United States, Searle says: "ideals of truth, rationality, and objectivity, for example – are rejected by many of the challengers, *even as ideals.*"[29] And he goes on to formulate six tenets of what he calls the Western Rationalistic Tradition. Three of these tenets, as they stand, are not axiological tenets: the claims that reality exists independently of our representations, that meaning and communication make reference to language-independent objects and states of affairs, and that knowledge is objective. Two of the tenets might be thought to deal with cognitive values: truth is a matter of accuracy of representations; logic and rationality are formal. These five tenets have "on a natural interpretation . . . the following consequence," the sixth tenet: "Intellectual standards are not up for grabs. There are both objectively and intersubjectively valid criteria of intellectual achievement and excellence."[30] Does this commit one to the view that such achievement and excellence are intrinsically valuable? Or to the view that truth or knowledge is intrinsically valuable? And if knowledge, say, is intrinsically valuable, what is the relation between this claim and the values of consistency, justification, and clarity? There is one uncontroversial way in which value is added to true beliefs, knowledge, and justification. They often acquire extrinsic value relative to the value of the realisations of our practical projects. But such value, for me or for you or for this or that group, is not intrinsic cognitive value. What is the relation between added cognitive value and the intrinsic value of knowledge, if there is such a thing? And what is the relation between cognitive value and the cognitive emotions?

Searle argues that realism is the foundation of his six tenets and that a commitment to realism is a part of scientific activity. On one way of understanding this claim, it is open to familiar objections. Doing empirical science need not involve any philosophical commitment, either to idealism or to realism – as Carnap, for example, argued. But the way in which Searle understands "commitment" undercuts such objections. The system of six tenets does not function as a theory but rather as "part of the taken-for-granted background of our practices."[31] By way of illustrating his claim that a commitment to realism belongs to the background of our practices, Searle considers the case where, ill, I call a doctor who turns out to be a deconstructionist doctor. What is the relation between what Searle calls in such cases "a breakdown in communication" and the extrinsic disvalue for me of the doctor's beliefs? Arguably, the former involves the latter. But even if extrinsic or added cognitive value is very important in ordinary life, might it not be the case that knowledge is intrinsically valuable?

Most of the philosophical questions raised in the last three paragraphs were raised and answered by the early realist phenomenologists. It is above all in his account of the nature of theoretical enterprises – in particular, of philosophy – and in his defence of such enterprises that Searle turns out to be of one mind with his phenomenological precursors. Some of the answers given by the phenomenologists to the questions just raised complement what Searle says; others may be felt to correct what he says. From its beginnings, phenomenology was intrigued by the relation between cognitive sentiments and cognitive value, and, following in their master's footsteps, many of Brentano's heirs devoted many pages to criticising what they saw as threats to scientific philosophy and attempts to discredit cognitive values. This aspect of phenomenology, however, made much less of an impression than the strident and melodramatic postures struck by the logical positivists in Vienna.

7. CANT PHILOSOPHICAL AND CANT THEORETICAL

Hypocrisy and cant, bullshit, imposture, humbug, accommodation, falseness, phoniness, and fakeness, form a family of phenomena that – unlike their simplest relative, the lie direct – have not perhaps been analysed in analytic philosophy[32] as obsessively as in phenomenology. The phenomenologists were very interested in understanding sham (*unechte*) beliefs, sham desires, sham sentiments and emotions, sham behaviour and lives, as well as the sham products – for example, kitsch and pseudo-inquiry – of such attitudes and behaviour. Their main predecessors are the distinguished analysts of cant in the series that runs from Burke through Hazlitt to Shaw and Wilde. In the simplest cases, sham beliefs and sentiments are brought into being and maintained by wishful thinking: in *ressentiment*, as analysed by Scheler, the grapes, which were first judged sweet (good) come to be regarded as sour (bad) simply because of a perceived incapacity to obtain them. Similarly, a change in impersonal evaluations based solely on one's perceived inability to live up to some ideal is an example of *ressentiment*. Shaw distinguishes a related case: the sloes, which are sour, are judged to be sweet (evaluated positively) simply because one already has them. (Hence Shaw's advice: "Take care to get what you like or you will be forced to like what you get.")

One early distinction between cant and hypocrisy is due to Hazlitt:

> He is a hypocrite who professes what he does not believe; not he who does not practice all he wishes or approves. . . . Thus, though I think there is very little downright hypocrisy in the world, I do think there is a great deal of cant. . . . Though few people have the face to set up for the very thing they in their hearts despise, we almost all want to be thought better than we are, and affect a greater admiration or abhorrence for certain things than we really feel. Indeed, some degree of affectation is as necessary to the mind as dress is to the body; we must overact our part in some measure in order to procure any effect at all. . . . In short, there is and must be a cant about everything that excites a considerable degree of attention and interest, and that people would be thought to know and care rather more about them than they actually do. Cant is the voluntary overcharging or prolongation of a real sentiment; hypocrisy is the setting up a pretension to a feeling you never had and have no wish for. ("On Cant and Hypocrisy")

The very idea of a philosophy of cant and of the sham got a bad name when Heidegger, and then Sartre, launched accounts of "authenticity" (*Eigentlichkeit*) and inauthenticity in which sui generis philosophical anthropologies were served up with a decisionist rhetoric. (As a distinguished ex-Oxford philosopher once said: "Only portraits are authentic.") Perhaps this explains why the early phenomenology of fakeness was so quickly forgotten. While the *Weltanschauungen* of authenticity were being worked out and were winning adherents, however, the interest of the phenomenologists in sham attitudes and in cognitive values took a new turn. No less than three heirs of Brentano – Musil, Ortega, and Nicolai Hartmann – turned their attention to understanding foolishness and stupidity.

Hartmann explored the variety of sham beliefs and sentiments and the self-deception they involve – in mass suggestion, majority opinions, public opinion, political parties, the press, art, taste, lifestyles, conventional

morality – in order to ask an important question. What, if anything, coun-
teracts the spread of the sham? His answer is that knowledge of all types and
the pursuit of knowledge – in particular, science – are the only spheres that
are essentially free of sham, because of their essentially critical dimension
and cumulative character. "There is no 'sham knowledge'."[33] The pursuit
of knowledge and an awareness of the intrinsic value of knowledge are,
he argues, what works against all those "tendencies which turn although
nothing turns with them." And, in particular, he notes that much of the
"critique of science" that was so popular in Germany during the 1920s and
1930s – particularly, we might add, in the Heideggerian milieu – involves
the particular sort of sham sentiment introduced earlier, *ressentiment*.[34]

Searle and many other commentators have claimed that one of the driving forces behind much "Theory," postmodernism, and many aspects of
CP is the desire to defend or propagate claims that are axiological and,
for one reason or another, popular. If this is true, then cant philosophical
and cant theoretical might be described as what happens when such claims
are defended with an appearance of some genuine theoretical motivation by
appealing to what look like reasons – by using *donc* and *also* – but in fact have
little or no theoretical content because their authors are at best indifferent
to cognitive values. It is this sort of indifference that Julien Benda had in
mind in talking of the "intellectual dandyism" of Bergson and Bachelard.

A real sentiment – for example, a commitment to the ethical and political value of tolerance – can be artificially prolonged by "arguing" that
without relativism or subjectivism there can be no tolerance. The attrac-
tiveness of tolerance then comes to be seen as bound up with the attractions
of relativism or subjectivism. In many parts of CP, bits and pieces of gar-
bled theoretical philosophy, often from early phenomenology, have been
employed to make plausible a variety of axiological claims, whether religious (as in Heidegger's supernatural naturalism or godless mysticism),
ethical, or political. But "making plausible" here stops well short of any
sort of properly theoretical activity. Whether religious, ethical, or political,
such claims often have an aesthetic dimension. Many of the profundities
of CP have an appeal that stems from their sublime appearance[35] – there
is nothing outside texts, writing is repressed and oppressed, the voice of
Being is struggling to be heard. Such profundities open up endless vistas,
are difficult to manipulate, and are politically, ethically, or religiously attractive. They have the features of the sublime identified by Burke – they
are deep, great, or all-embracing – and attitudes toward them display the
combination identified by Burke as appropriate to the sublime: they attract
and they repel. The sublime appearance can also, of course, turn out to be
a case of the false sublime, of the grotesque.

8. COGNITIVE VALUE AND REALISM

As we have seen, Searle locates his six tenets in the background of our practices. He also thinks that these tenets, since they are the conditions of intelligibility of our practices, "cannot themselves be demonstrated as truths within these practices. To suppose that they could was the endemic mistake of foundationalist metaphysics."[36] This would have surprised the phenomenologists. Ortega, for example, thought that the commitment to cognitive values was an essential part of the primitive certainties, which we rarely try to make explicit because we "count on them." Hartmann argued that the origin of our belief in a mind-independent reality is to be found in a variety of emotional experiences in which we run up against reality – as when our practical projects are frustrated, or when we come to see that finding out whether p is very difficult. (The ways of truth, as the poet puts it, are hard and rough to work.) Hartmann locates the source of all sham beliefs and sentiments in a "lack of contact" with the things themselves.[37] But neither Ortega nor Hartmann thought that such claims ruled out the possibility of a metaphysics, whether realist or indeed antirealist, in which a metaphysics of values, cognitive and noncognitive, would be prominent.

The importance of a theory of cognitive values emerges if we bear in mind the fact that the view (of Sidgwick, for example) that all cognitive value is extrinsic – that is to say, is merely added value – is one of the most popular views within postmodernism and CP. Scheler argued, and more frequently proclaimed, that only the most theoretical parts of science and (his sort of) philosophy had intrinsic cognitive value. For the rest, the value of science was the value of the domination of nature that it made possible. His distinction was soon overlooked. From Heidegger to Foucault, the idea that the value, usually negative, of science is a function of its internal relation to the domination of nature and to domination or power *tout court* swept all before it.

But whatever we think about these questions, there is a relatively modest way of distinguishing between explicit and implicit commitments to cognitive values and realism that throws some light on the attitudes of CP and postmodernism toward cognitive values and realism.

Is the desire *to know whether p* a desire *that one knows whether p*, as the desire *to smoke* is a desire *that one smokes*? Meinong and his pupils argued that there is an important difference between the two cases. To desire to know whether p need not involve thinking of anything under the concept of knowledge, whereas a desire to smoke, as opposed to a mere impulse or craving, must involve a representation of smoking. In a desire to know whether p, the attitude is that of desiring-to-know; in a desire to smoke, the attitude is just desire.[38] Similarly, we may add, neither astonishment nor wonder, the initiators of the disinterested desire to know, need contain any thought of knowledge. Not only do cognitive sentiments not necessarily involve thoughts about knowledge, we often attribute a commitment to cognitive values to people who have never thought of anything as having or not having cognitive value.

Contrast these cases with the Victorian Sage who asks himself every morning before breakfast: "What is my duty to Truth today?" Such a Sage is a figure of fun, and rightly so. But, curiously enough, he has a precise counterpart who is not, in many circles, perceived as grotesque: the contemporary postmodernist who "attacks," "deconstructs," or mocks truth, reason, and science – or, as he likes to put it, "truth," "reason," and "science." The Sage and the postmodernist guru adopt practical attitudes toward truth and reason under those descriptions. The philosopher, of course, also talks at length about truth and reason under those descriptions. But his philosophical attitudes are theoretical. Everyone has practical attitudes toward values and virtues – ethical, aesthetic, political, and cognitive. But such attitudes come in two very different kinds – they are pharisaical or nonpharisaical. The ethical Pharisee, as Scheler points out, is distinguished by the fact that he desires to be good under that description. The non-Pharisee desires, for example, to help his neighbour. Other things being equal, his intention is a good one. But he does not desire that he be good. Similarly, he is curious, and, other things being equal, his intention is a good one. But he does not desire that he know.

The Sage, I suggest, is a cognitive Pharisee, an epistemic Pharisee. The postmodernist is his pharisaical counterpart, not an epistemic Pharisee but an "epistemic" Pharisee. His motto is, "Obscurity be thou my clarity." Just as the Sage may actually be quite indifferent to cognitive questions, so, too, the postmodernist may be unusually sensitive to a variety of such questions, in spite of his rhetoric. Unfortunately, although epistemic Pharisees are relatively harmless figures, the same is not true of "epistemic" Pharisees.

9. S*R*L IN 1911

Although, as we have seen, Husserl himself came to be considered a less than wholly successful example of a scientific philosopher by his earliest followers and admirers, his little monograph *Philosophy as a Rigorous Science*,[39] of 1911 (the year in which Russell baptised analytic philosophy and logical atomism and pleaded for a scientific philosophy – in French), contains many of the motifs that were to be taken up by the heirs of Brentano who took seriously the task of defending philosophy as a serious enterprise before the Second World War.[40] Husserl restates many points made by Brentano and even earlier by Bolzano, in their anti-Kants and anti-Hegels. But he also reacts to the contemporary situation and, for example, grapples with the increasingly influential hermeneutics of Dilthey, the ex–literary critic.

Husserl distinguishes those philosophies, especially his own phenomenology and naturalism, that see philosophy as a science from philosophies that reject scientific philosophy – historicism, relativism, scepticism, and *Weltanschauungsphilosophie*. He has two philosophical targets: first, traditions that do not take seriously philosophy as a theoretical enterprise, and second, traditions that attempt to do philosophy in ways of which he approves but which, he thinks, get everything wrong. Historicisms, relativisms, and *Weltanschauungsphilosophie* are guilty of conceiving of philosophy as, in the first instance, a practical enterprise. What Husserl calls "naturalism," like positivism and pragmatism, is innocent of the first charge but, he thinks, wrong about both the mind and about ideas or essences. All of them – historicisms and *Weltanschauungsphilosophie* and naturalism – are a danger to culture, a practical danger (§13, §93) and a danger to empirical science and philosophy. Historicisms take as their point of departure the fact that all theoretical activity is bound up with its historical and cultural context and advance to more or less ambitious claims to the effect that once such contexts are completely understood, no place is left for the idea that the products of such activity are true or false. Husserl notes, presciently, the possibility of an extreme historicist who would say just this of the results of the natural sciences (§69).

Weltanschauungsphilosophie aims to satisfy "as far as possible our need for definitive, unifying, all-inclusive" knowledge (§73). It is a form of wisdom and so "is an essential component of that human habitus that comes before us in the idea of perfect virtue" (§76). Although there is a "radical vital need" (§89) for the sort of answers provided by *Weltanschauung* philosophies, scientific philosophy and science cannot help us to meet this need. But nor can we wait for their answers.[41] Husserl insists on the importance of separating the two types of philosophy. One is impersonal; the other is personal and involves teacher-pupil relationships.

In the present connexion, perhaps the most important claim that Husserl makes is that, although philosophy is often praised for its profundities, in fact

> profundity [*Tiefsinn*] is a symptom of chaos, which real science wants to turn into a cosmos. . . . Science proper, as far as its real theory reaches, knows no profundity. (§95)

Husserl's philosophical contemporaries in 1911 – the neo-Kantians and a variety of naturalists, positivists, and materialists – were not, by and large, adepts of sublime profundities, as opposed to programmatic vacuities. But Bergson and Dilthey were beginning to have an effect – for example, on Scheler – and very soon the Spenglers, Klages, and Heideggers were to turn philosophy in Germany into a green valley of sublime profundities.

10. SEARLE'S SPLENDID ISOLATION

Searle's critical campaign against parts of CP, as noted earlier, is something of a rarity. Why? One plausible explanation, I believe, is that Searle's conception and practice of philosophy differ from the analytic norm. Two striking features of Searle's way of doing philosophy are his descriptivism and his "scientific," that is, *wissenschaftliche* approach to philosophy. By the latter, I mean simply his conviction that philosophy can advance, has made progress and is doing so, that it can in principle begin to take the form of a definite body of knowledge, and this in cooperation with empirical science. By "descriptivism," I mean Searle's interest in providing detailed and complete descriptions of mental states and social acts. Descriptivism involves taxonomy, and much turns on getting the details right. Real realists have descriptivist leanings.

Neither Searle's "scientific" approach to philosophy nor his descriptivism have been common within analytic philosophy. The "scientific" approach is a very strong form of the idea that philosophy is through and through a theoretical and so a cumulative enterprise. Analytic philosophy, it is true, is invariably done *as though* it were a theoretical enterprise – arguments, distinctions, elucidations, analyses, objections, counterexamples, theory construction – in particular, the construction of formal theories – are the rule or at least recognised as desirable. But this way of doing philosophy is compatible not only with a number of different positions about what sort of theoretical enteprise philosophy is – for example, with the view that philosophy's goals are theoretical but purely negative – but also with views to the effect that philosophy is not a theoretical enterprise, that its goal is practical – for example, therapeutic – or that it is through and through aporetic, or that philosophical progress is as absurd a notion as that of ethical progress.

Descriptive analysis has rarely occupied a central position within analytic philosophy. Perhaps the two most influential exceptions are the writings of Wittgenstein and those of J. L. Austin and of their followers. In the case of Wittgenstein, description is subordinated to therapeutic goals (almost invariably – in his remarks on colour, for example, the goal recedes into the background). Austin's descriptions often have either negative, theoretical goals – that of playing Old Harry with this fetish or that absurdity – or, so it has often been thought, are not descriptions of anything of interest to a philosopher. In many quarters, Wittgenstein and Austin have given description in philosophy a bad name.

Description in philosophy cannot, of course, succeed without arguments – in particular, arguments about counterexamples and about the consequences of descriptions. But the culture of the argument and even of theory construction can flourish in the absence of all except the most exiguous descriptions. Remarkable arguments and sophisticated theories are compatible with the most primitive belief–desire–action psychologies.

Searle's conception of philosophy makes it natural for him to see parts of CP as a theoretical and practical enemy and to do something about it. A philosopher who, however impressively theoretical his way of doing philosophy may be, does not really take philosophy to be a growing branch of knowledge and does not really take cognitive values seriously will perhaps be less inclined to waste his time in quarrelling with CP.

Whatever the value of this hypothesis, it was a very similar combination of descriptivism and a conception of philosophy as a theoretical enterprise in the strongest possible sense that led Husserl – as well his early followers and also, for example, Musil and such heirs of Brentano as Linke and Kraus – to grapple publicly with the beginnings of CP, a type of activity that, some polemical pieces by members of the Vienna Circle apart, was almost moribund until Searle came along.

Three years before his death, Husserl wrote:

> Philosophy as a science, as serious, rigorous, indeed apodictically rigorous science – the dream is over.[42]

Just what he meant has been the subject of conflicting interpretations. I believe that he was still convinced that Brentano was right to claim that periods in which philosophy is taken seriously as a theoretical enterprise regularly give way to scepticism, then to dogmatism, and then to mysticism and obscurantism in which preaching predominates. The point that Husserl wanted to make in 1935 was that everything indicated that such a transition had already taken place. Philosophers who shared his approach to philosophy, Husserl saw, were few and far between.[43] The tragedy is, as Searle suggests,[44] that Husserl's own turn to idealism played an important role in bringing this situation about.

Searle's role as a critic of the tail-ends of the phenomenological movement seems, I have speculated, to have been motivated by the very same
outlook that led Brentano's early heirs to condemn what was happening
to what they called "analytic phenomenology," an outlook by no means
widespread within analytic philosophy. Whether or not this is the case, we
may wonder whether analytic philosophy – Russell's dream – is still flour-
ishing. Where, after all, are the young American Chisholms, Davidsons,
van Fraassens, Hochbergs, Kripkes, Lewises, Putnams, and Searles?

Notes

1. John Searle, "Reiterating the Differences: A Reply to Derrida," *Glyph* 1
   (1977): 198–208. This is a reply to Jacques Derrida, "Signature Event Context," *Glyph* 1 (1977): 172–97; Derrida replies to Searle's reply in "Limited Inc," *Glyph* 2 (1978): 162–254. See also John Searle, "The World
   Turned Upside Down" and "Reply to Mackey," in Gary B. Madison (ed.),
   Working through Derrida (Evanston, Ill.: Northwestern University Press,
   1993), pp. 170–83, 184–8; "Rationality and Realism, what Is at Stake?,"
   Daedalus (Fall 1993): 55–83; "Literary Theory and Its Discontents," *New
   Literary History* 25 (1994): 637–67; and "Postmodernism and Truth," *(TWP BE
   (a journal of ideas))* 13 (1998): 85–7.

2. Susan Haack's *Manifesto of a Passionate Moderate* (Chicago: University of Chicago
   Press, 1998) concentrates more on what I take to be the distant effects of CP
   than on CP itself. Analytic philosophers outside the Anglophone world have of-
   ten criticised parts of CP with great and effective vigour. See, for example, Hans
   Albert, *Transzendentale Träumereien*, (Hamburg: Hoffmann and Campe, 1975);
   Jonathan Barnes, "Heidegger spéléologue," *Revue de Métaphysique et Morale*
   95 (1990): 173–95; Jacques Bouveresse, *Le philosophe chez les autophages* (Paris:
   Minuit, 1984); and his *Rationalité et Cynisme* (Paris: Minuit, 1984); and Pascal
   Engel, *La Dispute. Une Introduction a la philosophie analytique* (Paris: Minuit,
   1997). Needless to say, such criticisms are rarely translated into English.
   An exception: Jacques Bouveresse, "Why I Am So Very unFrench," in Alan
   Montefiore (ed.), *Philosophy in France Today* (Cambridge: Cambridge University
   Press, 1982), pp. 9–33. See also *Continental Philosophy Analysed*, a special number
   of *Topoi*, ed. Kevin Mulligan, 1991; *Philosophy and the Analytic-Continental Divide*,
   a special number of *Stanford French Review*, 17.2-3, ed. Pascal Engel, 1993; and
   European Philosophy and the American Academy, ed. Barry Smith (La Salle, Illinois:
   The Hegeler Institute, 1994).

3. Cf. Keith Windschuttle, *The Killing of History: How Literary Critics and Social
   Scientists Are Murdering Our Past* (New York: The Free Press, 1996).

4. Cf. Brian Vickers, *Appropriating Shakespeare: Contemporary Critical Quarrels* (New
   Haven, Conn.: Yale University Press, 1993).

5. Edmund Husserl, *Logische Untersuchungen* (The Hague: Nijhoff, Husserliana
   XVIII, XIX/1, XIX/2, 1975–1984); trans. by J. Findlay as *Logical Investigations*, 2
   volumes, (London: Routledge and Kegan Paul, 1970).

6. Cf. Balázs Mezei and Barry Smith, *The Four Phases of Philosophy*, (Amsterdam: Rodopi, 1998).

7. Perhaps the best of the many criticisms of Husserl's idealism by early phenomenologists are Theodor Celms' 1928 monograph on Husserl's phenomenological idealism reprinted in *Der phänomenologische Idealismus Husserls und andere Schriften 1928–1943*, ed. J. Rozenvalds (Frankfurt: Peter Lang) and Roman Ingarden, *Schriften zur Phänomenologie Edmund Husserls* (Tübingen: Niemeyer, 1998). The best criticism both of idealist phenomenology and of Husserl's new way of doing phenomenology is by the great psychologist Carl Stumpf: *Erkenntnislehre*, 2 vols. (Leipzig: Barth, 1939), vol. 1, pp. 188–206. Stumpf was one of Brentano's earliest pupils and the man to whom Husserl had dedicated his *Investigations*. "Pure phenomenology," Stumpf says, is a "phantom, a contradiction in itself." Husserl's *Ideas* is "lacking in examples and the few examples provided are simply misleading" – a particularly cruel criticism, since, at the beginning of his career, Husserl had dismissed a book by an influential neo-Kantian, Rickert, in similar terms.

8. In an unpublished work ("Phenomenology and Idealism," forthcoming), Searle has argued that phenomenology is characterised by idealism and a failure to appreciate the role of logical analysis. If I am right, this is not true of early phenomenology, a current that Searle does not mention.

9. The story sketched here of the overlap between Oxford and Austro-German philosophies has a counterpart – the story of the quite different overlap between Cambridge and Austro-German philosophies, a story that Ryle occasionally hints at.

10. Certain qualifications are, as always, in order. Thus Marty's account of utterer's meaning is clearly anticipated by the grandfather of Austrian philosophy, Bolzano; and Reinach's account of social acts is anticipated by Reid. And what I have called "overlapping concerns" between phenomenology and Oxford philosophy coexist with enormous differences – the phenomenologists typically assume that they are describing essences that they have "seen" and, like other heirs of Brentano, that mental states and acts have a structure all their own. The worlds of the phenomenologists and of Oxford philosophers are very different. But philosophical presuppositions are one thing and philosophical discoveries and work quite a different thing.

11. Franz Brentano, *Psychology from an Empirical Standpoint* (London: Routledge, 1995), p. 257.

12. For one concession to theories like that of Brentano, see *Logical Investigations*, V §15 (a), and *Logische Untersuchungen*, II 2, p. 885 (material not included in English translation). In later work, Husserl sometimes accepts the view that at the very primitive level of motivated associations, in both perception and desire, causality is represented in nonpropositional contents.

13. See, for example, *Logical Investigations*, IV §§3–4, VI §5.

14. Cf. "biological naturalism" in John Searle, *Intentionality: An Essay in the Philosophy of Mind* (Cambridge: Cambridge University Press, 1983), p. 264.

15. *Logical Investigations*, V §4 (A).

16. "Literary Theory and its Discontents," p. 666, note 6.

17. Richard Rorty, "Essays on Heidegger and Others," in his *Philosophical Papers II* (Cambridge: Cambridge, University Press, 1991), pp. 94–5.

18. "Postmodernism and Truth," p. 86.

19. Derrida, "Limited Inc," p. 184; cf. also p. 195.

20. Cf. Derrida's references in "Signature Event Context" to Husserl on "the essential possibility of writing" and "the structure of possibility" of an utterance (p. 184); Derrida's claim that "Austin does not ponder the consequences issuing from the fact that a possibility – a possible risk – is *always* possible, and is in some sense a necessary possibility" and his question,"What is a success when the possibility of infelicity continues to constitute its structure?" (p. 189)

21. Jacques Derrida, "Form and Meaning: A Note on the Phenomenology of Language," in his *Speech and Phenomena and Other Essays on Husserl's Theory of Signs* (Evanston, Ill.: Northwestern University Press, 1973), p. 117; originally published as "La forme et le vouloir-dire. Note sur la phénoménologie du langage," *Revue internationale de philosophie* 81 (1967): 277–99, cf. 288. The expression "principle of expressibility" is used by Searle for the principle "that whatever can be meant can be said": *Speech Acts: An Essay in the Philosophy of Language* (Cambridge: Cambridge University Press, 1980), p. 19. Searle's principle is, therefore, not the principle that Husserl sets out in §124 of *Ideas*.

22. The importance in Derrida's writings of essential and necessary possibilities was pointed out, approvingly, by Silvano Petrosino in *Jacques Derrida e la legge del possibile* (Naples: Guida editori, 1983), pp. 158ff. My account of Derrida's merry way with modal concepts ("How Not to Read: Derrida on Husserl," in "Continental Philosophy Analysed," *Topoi*, 1991, pp. 199–208, made points that were already perfectly familiar to my two colleagues and friends, Jacques Bouveresse and Anne Reboul. It forms a part of a criticism of Derrida's grasp of Husserl's thought. For other criticisms, see Joseph Claude Evans, *Strategies of Deconstruction: Derrida and the Myth of the Voice* (Minneapolis: University of Minnesota Press, 1991), Part I; and his "The Rigors of Deconstruction," in Smith (ed.), *European Philosophy and the American Academy*, pp. 81–98, especially pp. 86–8.

23. Jacques Derrida, "Le facteur de la vérité," in *La carte postale de Socrate à Freud et au-delà* (Paris: Flammarion, 1980), pp. 439–524, at p. 472.

24. Jacques Derrida, *Eperons. Les Styles de Nietsche* (Paris: Flammarion, 1978), p. 105. Searle criticises a related passage from *Eperons* in "Literary Theory and Its Discontents," p. 661.

25. "Postmodernism and Truth," p. 87.

26. "Reply to Mackey," p. 188.

27. Published in the United States by Picador, 1999.

28. Lionel Trilling, *Sincerity and Authenticity* (Cambridge, Mass.: Harvard University Press, 1972), p. 169. Trilling makes this remark in the course of discussing David Cooper's introduction to the English translation of Foucault's *Histoire de la Folie*. Of the piece of cant that is the "view that insanity is a state of human existence which is to be esteemed for its commanding authenticity,"

he writes that to "deal with this phenomenon of our intellectual culture in the way of analytical argument would, I think, be supererogatory" (pp. 168–9).

29. "Rationality and Realism, What Is at stake?," p. 55.

30. "Rationalism and Realism, What Is at stake?," pp. 67–8.

31. "Rationalism and Realism, What Is at stake?," p. 80.

32. But cf. Haack, *Manifesto of a Passionate Moderate*, pp. 7–31; Harry Frankfurt, "On Bullshit," in his *The Importance of What We Care About: Philosophical Essays* (Cambridge: Cambridge University Press, 1988), pp. 117–33.

33. Nicolai Hartmann, *Das Problem des geistigen Seins* (Berlin: de Gruyter, 1962), pp. 379, 381.

34. Ibid., p. 400. Hartmann (p. 366f., p. 372) notes that his descriptions of sham forms of life overlap with those given by Heidegger in *Being and Time* and points out, as quietly as the time (1933) makes appropriate, that what Heidegger opposes to such sham forms of life is not the shamless nature of knowledge but rather guilt, *Angst*, and collectedness. It is indeed difficult to imagine Heidegger, for whom "science does not think," endorsing Hartmann's views.

35. On metaphysical pathos, the pathos of the obscure and of the esoteric and sublimity, see Arthur Lovejoy, *The Great Chain of Being: A Study of the History of an Idea* (New York: Harper, 1960), pp. 10–14.

36. "Rationalism and Realism, What Is At Stake?," p. 80.

37. Hartmann, *Das Problem des geistigen Seins*, p. 390.

38. One attractive alternative: If x desires to know whether p, then he desires that (if p, he knows that p and, if not-p, he knows that not-p).

39. Edmund Husserl, *Philosophie als strenge Wissenschaft* (Frankfurt am Main: Klostermann, 1980); this was first published in *Logos* 1 (1910–11).

40. Both Kraus and Musil were particularly active in this respect. Since Bergson not only played an important role in transforming phenomenology but also contributed directly to the present shape of Francophone philosophy, it is perhaps appropriate to mention France's very own remorseless critic of Bergonism and associated irrationalisms, the Julien Benda already mentioned – like Musil, an essayist of the first order – and to mention that philosophy in France was not only laid low but also brought into being by philosophers of Irish origin – which is to say by Bergson and Eriugena, respectively.

41. Husserl and Musil were to arrive at similar solutions to this practical problem, which might be summarised as: "Live exactly!" Musil discusses the problem under a number of headings – for example, "provisional morality," "inductive humility," "the passion for exactness."

42. Edmund Husserl, *The Crisis of European Sciences and Transcendental Philosophy* (Evanston, Ill.: Northwestern University Press, 1970), p. 389.

43. Certainly, the three most influential philosophers of the twentieth century – Heidegger, Wittgenstein, and Derrida – all arrived at the view that what they were doing, although intimately connected with it, was not a part of philosophy. All three proclaim their practical goals; all three aim to destroy and deconstruct ("*Destruktion*," "destroy," "*déconstruire*"). This point is, of course, consistent with

the following difference between Wittgenstein, on the one hand, and Heidegger and Derrida, on the other. In reading the Austrian philosopher, one has good reason to believe, in the midst of the therapy and destruction, that he has a firm grasp of the relevant theoretical questions (if only because he was often the author of at least one distinguished answer to such questions).

44. In "Phenomenology and Idealism."

Further Reading

Selected Books by Searle

Speech Acts: An Essay in the Philosophy of Language. Cambridge: Cambridge University Press, 1969.

The Campus War. New York: World, 1971; Harmondsworth, Middlesex: Penguin, 1972.

Expression and Meaning: Studies in the Theory of Speech Acts. Cambridge: Cambridge University Press, 1979.

Intentionality: An Essay in the Philosophy of Mind. Cambridge: Cambridge University Press, 1983.

Minds, Brains and Science: The 1984 Reith Lectures. London: British Broadcasting Corporation, 1984, 1989; Cambridge, Mass.: Harvard University Press, 1985.

The Rediscovery of the Mind. Cambridge, Mass.: MIT Press, 1992.

The Construction of Social Reality. New York: The Free Press; Harmondsworth, Middlesex: Penguin, 1995.

The Mystery of Consciousness. New York: New York Review of Books, 1997.

Mind, Language and Society: Philosophy in the Real World. New York: Basic Books, 1998.

Rationality in Action. Cambridge, Mass.: MIT Press, 2001.

Consciousness and Language. Cambridge: Cambridge University Press, 2002.

Selected Articles by Searle

"Proper Names." *Mind* 67 (1958): 26–54.

"Meaning and Speech Acts." *Philosophical Review* 71 (October 1962): 423–32.

"How to Derive 'Ought' from 'Is'." *Philosophical Review* 73 (January 1964): 43–58.

"What Is a Speech Act?" In Max Black (ed.), *Philosophy in America*. Ithaca, N.Y.: Cornell University Press, 1965, pp. 221–39.

"Austin on Locutionary and Illocutionary Acts." *Philosophical Review* 77: 4 (October 1968): 405–24.

"A Taxonomy of Illocutionary Acts." In Keith Gunderson (ed.), *Language, Mind and Knowledge* (Minnesota Studies in the Philosophy of Science, Vol. 7). Minneapolis: University of Minnesota Press: 1975: 344–69.

"Literal Meaning." *Erkenntnis* 13 (1978): 207–24.

"What Is an Intentional State?" *Mind* 88: 349 (January 1979): 77–92.

"Minds, Brains, and Programs." *The Behavioral and Brain Sciences* 3 (1980).

"Indeterminacy, Empiricism, and the First Person." *The Journal of Philosophy* 84: 3 (1987): 123–46.

"How Performatives Work." *Linguistics and Philosophy* 12 (1989): 535–58.

"Collective Intentionality and Action." In P. Cohen, J. Morgan, and M. E. Pollack (eds.), *Intentions in Communication*. Cambridge, Mass.: Bradford Books/MIT Press, 1991, pp. 53–70.

Selected Commentary on Searle

Burkhardt, Armin. *Speech Acts, Meaning and Intentions: Critical Approaches to the Philosophy of John R. Searle*. Berlin and New York: W. de Gruyter, 1990.

Dietrich, Eric (ed.). *Thinking Computers and Virtual Persons*. San Diego, Calif.: Academic Press, 1994.

Faigenbaum, Gustavo. *Conversations with John Searle*. Libros En Red, 2001.

Fotion, Nick. *John Searle*. Princeton, N.J.: Princeton University Press, 2000.

Grewendorf, Günther, and Meggle, Georg (eds.). *Speech Acts, Mind, and Social Reality*. Dordrecht: Kluwer, 2002.

Hirstein, William. *On Searle*. Belmont, Calif.: Wadsworth, 2001.

Lepore, Ernest, and Gulick, Robert van (eds.). *John Searle and His Critics*. Oxford: Blackwell, 1991.

Koepsell, David (ed.). *John Searle*. Special issue of the *American Journal of Economics and Sociology*, 62, 2003.

Meggle, Georg (ed.). *Social Facts and Collective Intentionality*. Frankfurt: Dr. Hänsel-Hohenhausen A. G., 2002.

Meijers, Anthonie. *Speech Acts, Communication and Collective Intentionality: Beyond Searle's Individualism*. Leiden: Rijksuniversiteit, 1994.

Parret, Herman, and Vershueren, Jef (eds.). *(On) Searle on Conversation*. Amsterdam and Philadelphia: John Benjamins, 1992.

Preston, John, and Bishop, Mark (eds.). *Views into the Chinese Room: New Essays on Searle and Artificial Intelligence*. Oxford: Oxford University Press, 2002.

Searle. Special issue of the journal *Revue Internationale de Philosophie*, June 2001.

Speech Act Theory: Ten Years Later. Special issue of the journal *Versus*, 26/27, 1980.

Index